*Chinese Bronze Age Weapons*

# CHINESE BRONZE AGE WEAPONS

舊藏三代青銅兵器圖錄　北京故宮博物院楊寧史

The Werner Jannings Collection in the Chinese National Palace Museum, Peking

by MAX LOEHR

*Ann Arbor: The University of Michigan Press*
*London: Geoffrey Cumberlege, Oxford University Press*

# PREFACE

The collection described in this catalogue, more than one hundred specimens of Chinese weapons chiefly of the Shang and Chou dynasties, was formed by Mr. Werner Jannings, of German nationality, during his many years of residence and travel in China. In 1944, while still adding to his superb collection which also comprised a great number of choice examples of ritual vessels, Mr. Jannings entrusted this writer with the task of preparing a catalogue of the weapons. Every opportunity of studying them leisurely and thoroughly was given. Owing to the conditions at the end of World War II, however, work had to be interrupted and the plan to publish the Catalogue as a monograph of the *Monumenta Serica, Journal of Oriental Studies of the Catholic University of Peking,* failed to materialize.

Meanwhile the Chinese government, having learned about the existence and importance of Mr. Jannings' collection and anxious to have it remain in the country, arranged with the collector that he part with it and that it be given permanent housing in one of the buildings of the National Palace Museum in Peking, where it would be exhibited as the Werner Jannings Collection. The transfer to the Palace Museum was effected on January 22, 1946.

During the following months, the writer, with the able assistance of the Museum staff under the direction of Professor Ma Heng who on returning from unoccupied China had resumed his position at the Palace Museum, had the pleasant task of arranging, in a secluded corner of the Forbidden City, the exhibit of the weapons, which was opened — concurrently with the exhibit of the ritual vessels, displayed in another gallery in Mrs. Eleanor Consten's arrangement — on October 10, the Double Tenth, 1946. Grateful acknowledgment is made of the receipt of a subsidy granted by the Chinese government for completing and rendering into English the text of the Catalogue, the publication of which by the Palace Museum was prevented by want of printing facilities as well as by other postwar shortages. The editor of the *Monumenta Serica,* P. Dr. Rudolph

Rahmann, S. V. D., then accepted the manuscript — which in the meantime was enlarged by the chapters on typology in the Introduction — and was taking steps toward its publication, when his scholarly institution was ordered to cease its activities and leave Peking because of the approach of the Communist armies and the impending siege of the city in the fall of 1948.

It is with deep gratitude that the hospitality and intense interest in these studies shown by Colonel Willis B. Sawyer, U. S. A. F., himself a distinguished collector of ancient weapons, are remembered. His observations and discussions of points of structure, function, or details of design were a source of infinite stimulation. In similar ways the writer is indebted to his friends, Professor Arthur F. Wright, Stanford University, and Professor James Robert Hightower, Harvard University, who moreover readily gave their help in improving the phrasing of the text.

The present publication became finally possible through a subsidy given by the University of Michigan from a fund established by Charles L. Freer for the furtherance of research and publications in the field of Oriental art.

For various advice and criticism, the writer's sincere thanks are due Professor Ludwig Bachhofer, University of Chicago, his former teacher at the University of Munich; Mrs. Wilma Fairbank; Mr. John A. Pope; Dr. Laurence Sickman, director of the William Rockhill Nelson Gallery of Art in Kansas City; and Professor A. G. Wenley, director of the Freer Gallery of Art in Washington.

Most of the cuts used for the plates were made, under the supervision of Mr. Hilmar Biedermann in Shanghai, at the expense of Mr. Jannings, whose kind permission to use them adds greatly to the obligation toward him.

Lastly the writer wishes to acknowledge thankfully the devoted and sensitive labor of designing done by Mr. George Lenox, of the University of Michigan Press.

M. L.

# CONTENTS

# ILLUSTRATIONS

*Figures in the Text*

## *Map*

# Introduction

# AXES

*Chapter I*

The axes of the earlier Chinese Bronze Age, with the inclusion of types commonly styled Ordos, display a greater variety of forms than do other classes of weapons. Some of the axes are rare, and not all of them are represented in this collection, which, however, contains several unique types and magnificent specimens; among these the huge broad axe (Cat. no. 13) ranks first.

Variegated and fascinating materials of study, the Chinese axe types known thus far reveal little of their origin and developments, their connections and age. Some types have ornaments which plainly link them with Shang or Chou sacrificial vases; they are easily, if vaguely, datable. Others are bare of decoration and therefore, if nothing is known about their provenance and archaeological context, hardly datable at all. Still others are decorated in much the same way as the Sino-Siberian knives, with simple geometric patterns; their setting should not be questionable. A few types defy any attempt at establishing their affiliations. Inscriptions of chronological import are very rarely seen. An inscribed pick in this collection (Cat. no. 82), datable within narrow limits, is for that reason of paramount importance, although it could be roughly dated by its décor. Scientifically excavated specimens have not come to our knowledge till now. Hence a specimen of battle-axe with a very long tubular socket, hailing from Anyang and acquired by the Toronto Museum, claims particular attention in that it was found together with Shang bronzes.[1]

The existing types may feasibly be divided into three main categories, according to their mode of hafting:

A   AXES WITH SHAFT-HOLES
B   AXES WITH TANG
C   SOCKETED CELTS

It is worthy of note that this division would to some extent apply also if — leaving aside for the moment plain pieces and existing exceptions — the décor styles were to be made our point of departure. The above categories would then predominantly show:

> A: GEOMETRIC PATTERNS ("NORTHERN" ORNA-MENT)
> B: SHANG-CHOU ANIMAL CONFIGURATIONS ("CHINESE" ORNAMENT)
> C: BOTH GEOMETRIC AND ANIMAL DESIGN

But such a scheme, of course, means simplifying what in fact is quite complicated. One must first subdivide and describe the widely differing types which are comprised in categories A and B before one can arrive at more clearly conditioned results with regard to the actual distribution of the two styles of ornamentation.

A: SOCKETED AXES

To the exclusion of specimens later than Western Chou, category A is composed of no less than twelve distinct types:

> A I: Long tubular socket; slender widening blade. See Fig. 1.
> A II: Long tubular socket; oval blade, the long axis of which is parallel to the shaft. See Fig. 2.
> A III: Moderately long tubular socket; oval blade, the long axis of which is at right angle to the shaft. See Figs. 3, 4, 5.
> A IV: Moderately long tubular socket; slender, straight, wedge-shaped blade with a round hole. See Figs. 6, 7; cp. Cat. no. 16.
> A V: Short tubular socket or shaft-hole; grooved blade, straight (Va) or widening (Vb). See Figs. 8, 9, 10; cp. Cat. no. 21.
> A VI: Shaft-hole or shaft-ring (shorter than the heel of the blade); straight, usually thin blade with longitudinal ribs. See Fig. 11; cp. Cat. no. 20.
> A VII: Shaft-ring; slender, widening blade with asymmetrical edge, resembling A I blades. See Fig. 12.
> A VIII: Moderately long tubular socket or shaft-hole; broad, widening blade. See Fig. 13; cp. Cat. no. 9.
> A IX: Shaft-ring (shorter than the heel of the blade); broad, short, widening blade. See Fig. 14.
> A X: Long tubular socket; dagger-axe blade with descending edge (*hu*). See Fig. 15; cp. Cat. no. 70.
> A XI: Shaft-hole or short socket; dagger-axe blade. See Figs. 16, 17, 18.
> A XII: Shaft-ring (shorter than the heel of the blade); dagger-axe blade (= the *ch'ü,* category III of the dagger-axes). See Fig. 19; cp. Cat. nos. 65-68.

The foregoing alignment, in that it treats the types as equals, is merely typological and descriptive, not historical, and shows nothing of interrelations or temporal sequence, let alone geographical data;

and insofar as it skips over lesser accessories and decoration, it may appear clumsy or even arbitrary. There are, moreover, some stray types which do not fit in. However that may be, all the main types of category A are included. It remains to try to extract some sign of life from the bare list.

*Types A I and A II* are obviously closely connected. Not only have they an extremely long (6-7 inches) socket in common, but also a slight bend of the socket toward the blade, though this is not always present (Figs. 1: A, C; 2: A). Such analogies cannot be casual, and one can take them as a proof that both types existed at about the same time.

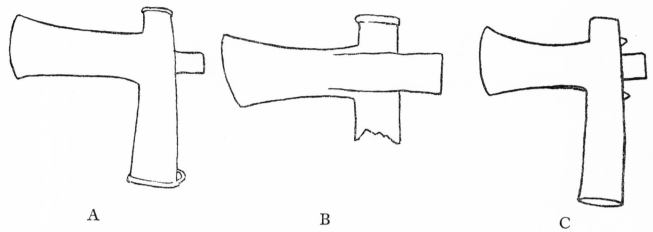

A                                    B                                         C

Fig. 1: *Axe-heads with tubular sockets (type A I)*.

A — Royal Ontario Museum, Toronto. After Umehara (ca. 1/3). B — Freer Gallery, Washington. After Umehara (ca. 1/3). C — Royal Ontario Museum, Toronto. After White (ca. 1/3).

The axe Fig. 1: C is the Toronto piece alluded to above, the Shang age of which seems warranted by its provenance from Anyang.[1] Fig. 1: A, B illustrate two variants of this rare type, which has been published by Umehara.[2] The one with a small loop near the lower rim of the socket is fairly similar to the other Toronto axe; the Freer Gallery fragment (Fig. 1: B) differs in that the blade has an asymmetrical edge and embraces the socket with a strengthening belt as though the bronze tube were the shaft itself. An asymmetrical edge, combined with a shaft-ring which most strikingly resembles the detail of the belt around the tube, recurs in a likewise scarce type, A VII (Fig. 7); even the shape of the squarish heel is the same in both cases. If the fragment Fig. 1: B were deprived of the tube extending upward and downward from the belt, what remains would be almost exactly in the form of type A VII.

The three pieces of the A I group are bare of ornament, unless the short spikes at the neck of the Toronto axe (Fig. 1: C) be regarded as such. These spikes are an interesting feature. W. C. White explained them as "relics of the axe-heel extending at the back in three

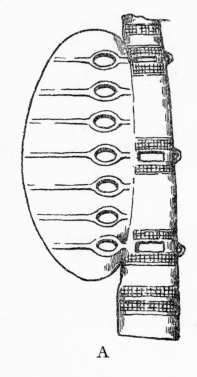

A

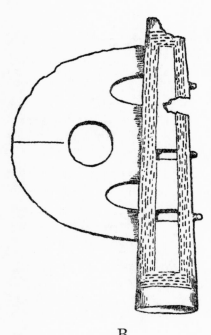

B

Fig. 2: *Oval-bladed axes with tubular sockets (type A II).*

A—Formerly in the possession of Huang Chün, Peking. After *Tsun Ku Chai Ku Ping Ching* (1/2). B—After *Chin Shih So* (ca. 1/2).

knobs" (including the square plaque in the middle), taking the whole as "an evolutionary development of the hafted dagger-axe."[3] Prototypes that could have led to the design of the spikes are unknown, however, while the squarish plaque undoubtedly has to do with the *ko* and kindred dagger-axes. I only know of a single instance in which a pair of knobs — rather than spikes — occupies the neck: an axe of A III type with an un-Chinese animal design on the blade, an axe not datable in itself (Fig. 4).

Secondary evidence for the Shang date of type A I is afforded by the very small group A II (Fig. 2: A, B). Several of these impressive and most peculiar axes bear ornaments such as are found also in many Siberian and some Shang knives: crosshatched fields and zigzags, in tectonic zonal arrangement; in one instance, there is a globular slitted jingle at the back of the socket.[4] A striking feature is the row of seven holes in the blade, surrounded by elevated margins and connected with the edge by thin ribs. A close parallel in *Hsi Ch'ing Ku Chien* (ch. 37), there defined as "Chou dance axe," shows these ribs tapering and pointed. It is the only piece which exactly corresponds to Fig. 2: A. There are three further related specimens depicted in *Hsi Ch'ing Ku Chien, Po Ku T'u Lu,* and *Chin Shih So,* presently to be described.

*A II variants.* The *Hsi Ch'ing Ku Chien* piece has a similarly long, apparently straight socket fitted with a jingle or rattle, as mentioned above, while the edge of the blade, which has only three round holes and no ribs, terminates in convolute spirals.[5]

The same blade form recurs in the *Po Ku T'u Lu* specimen, which, however, has ribs extending from the three perforations to the edge. The socket does not consist of a tube, but is divided into three superposed rings to receive the haft.[6]

Finally, the *Chin Shih So* variant (Fig. 2: B), very similar to Fig. 2: A with regard to the socket with three horizontal slots and small loops at level with the slots, shows a blade which differs considerably from all the foregoing examples. This blade has a wide central hole and two arched apertures at the base. A thin rib or "seam" connects the perforation in the middle with the edge. One of the authors of the *Chin Shih So* had seen that axe in 1821 in the collection of the then living descendant of Confucius and had made a drawing of it. He regarded the axe, which was found in Shantung, as a weapon rather than a dance-axe and thought it to be prior to the Ch'in-Han dynasties — thus consciously refuting the Han date assigned to the *Po Ku T'u Lu* specimen.[7]

An axe type with similar blade but with a tang instead of a socket will be described under category B VI below.

As to the extremely rare types A I and A II and their variants, one can generalize by saying that, when decorated, they do not bear ornaments other than geometric patterns common in "Sino-Siberian" ornamentation, while animal motifs of Shang or Chou style are absent. It is questionable, therefore, whether these stately types were used for ceremonial purposes — such as the Big War Dance at the royal ancestral shrine,[8] as the older Chinese catalogues would have it — and I rather agree with Feng Yün-p'eng's view stated in the *Chin Shih So* that these axes were true weapons. Distinguished by their extraordinarily long socket-tubes, these axes (at least the A I type) show a close filiation with the blade forms and structure of type A VII (Fig. 7) and with the shaft-ring structure in type A XII (Fig. 12), the very common Shang dagger-axe with shaft-ring (*ch'ü*). The *ch'ü* ordinarily is decorated with Shang animal motifs or carefully executed archaic glyphs and is never found with "Sino-Siberian" geometric patterns (allowance being made for grooved butts, as in Cat. no. 68). This contrast is interesting. The *ch'ü,* not supposed to represent a ceremonial weapon, has décor elements of the sacrificial bronzes. This can be explained in three ways: (1) there was no such thing as a hieratic décor; (2) the gorgeous axes A II are foreign; (3) these axes were obsolete at the time when typical Shang décor was fashionable. There is as yet no proof for the validity of any of these explanations, of course, and I shall revert to these questions later. For the present I only wish to add that the A I-II axes for all their stateliness impress one as being rather archaic; their long shaft-tubes are a little clumsy, and certainly uneconomical. It is not surprising, therefore, that nothing comparable is found in later types and that these long tubes should have vanished early.

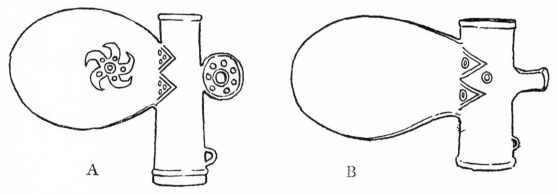

Fig. 3: *Oval-bladed axes with tubular sockets (type A III).*

A — Museum of Far Eastern Antiquities, Stockholm. After Andersson (1/2). B — Lu Mou-te Collection, Peking. After Umehara (ca. 1/2).

*Type A III* (Fig. 3: A, B), likewise rare, has a far shorter tube of oval or horseshoe-shaped section and a usually even width. The blade is oval or roundish, and in eight of the nine examples [9] known to me is decorated. As a rule, there is a protuberance at the neck of the socket: round or angular studs, knobs, a ring; animal figures occur (Figs. 4, 5), but squarish plaques apparently do not. The attractive design of this fairly sturdy type which usually is regarded as an Ordos type, is often accentuated by some simple tectonic ornament such as a pair of double angles at the juncture of blade and socket, while the wide space of the blade-oval receives some decora-

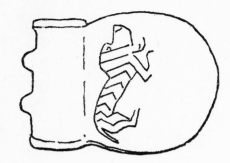

Fig. 4: *Round-bladed axe*
(*type A III*).

Museum of Far Eastern Antiquities, Stockholm. After Andersson (1/2).

Fig. 5: *Round-bladed axe*
(*type A III*).

Formerly possession of Huang Chün, Peking.
After *Tsun Ku Chai Ku Ping Ching* (1/2).

tion nicely adapted to the round: whorl-stars, concentric circles, or
diapers in one case, always delicately removed from the center toward the base. In a variant with a shorter socket set with two knobs
at the back (Fig. 4), an animal is incised along the base of the nearly
circular blade on either side: a tiger, and what appears to be a pig.[10]
The drawings are un-Chinese in style. So is the decoration of all of
these axes, in a way, and even the whorl-star is something different
from the stars and whorls on Shang bronzes.[11] This can be said also
of animals cast in the round on the socket in two specimens of type
A III. The one, reproduced in a rubbing in Huang Chün's *Tsun Ku
Chai Ku Ping Ching* (Vol. III), shows a tiger with its head turned
upward and its skin rendered by deep transverse furrows, the blade-
face being occupied by a five-pronged whorl-star (Fig. 5). The other
closely allied piece in the David-Weill Collection, Paris, was published by O. Janse, who likened it to Hallstatt types for its sculptural
adornment.[12] This piece is rough cast. The socket is short and has
no strengthening belts; the blade is decorated by crudely drawn concentric rings; the animal figure, a tiger to all appearances, hardly
surpasses in fineness its counterpart on Huang's axe. To embellish
weapons — hilts of daggers and sockets of axes in the first place —
with animal figures in the round is not specifically a Chinese idea.
On the contrary, such plastic decoration is rare in China,[13] whereas
by comparison it abounds in Central Siberia, Iran, the Caucasus,
and Mesopotamia. In the present case, moreover, realism and a
hearty sketchiness in the representation of the beasts make it obvious
that they originated somewhere outside the Shang sphere. Thus, this
group of oval-bladed axes might well be localized in the Ordos and
adjacent regions, consistent with recent tradition.

But there arises a problem. A specimen in the collection of Liu
T'i-chih, with approximately circular blade decorated with concentric rings in sunken design, and with a transversely grooved stud at
the back of the socket, has three inscribed Shang glyphs reading *"tsu
jih i* 且日乙, Ancestor Day I." This formula is common in short
dedicatory inscriptions on Shang sacrificial vessels. On weapons it is
not at all common. Except three Shang *ko* with series of names of
the same pattern [14] — conspicuously reminiscent of how ancestral
names are listed in Shang oracle bones — and a *ko* with the inscription *"tsu hsin,* Ancestor Hsin,"[15] there are to my knowledge no such
inscriptions on weapons. The axe inscription may be spurious. If so,
we are deprived of a valuable clue indeed for determining the age of
the axes in question and must look for other, unsuspicious factors to
make up that loss, for the axes A III are not in themselves datable.
The following observations taken together seem to make certain a
date for them toward the end of the IInd millennium B.C.

1) The Stockholm axe (Fig. 3: A), on account of the perforated
disk at the back of the socket, is indubitably linked with the slender
battle-axes A IV, wherein the same kind of disk constitutes the main

decoration of the blade. These battle-axes, as I shall presently show, probably date from before and around 1000 B.C.

2) The same disk motif appears on the socket of a dagger-axe of category A X (Fig. 15: B). The shape of that socket makes its close connection with type A III obvious. Rows of small knobs decorating the upper and lower rims of that socket further link it with an interesting socketed dagger-axe in the E. v. d. Heydt Collection (Fig. 16: B), which stands halfway between A X and A XI types and cannot be later than Shang. The ornament of a pair of double angles overlapping the socket at the juncture of the blade is common to both A III and A X types.

3) The socket of the Stockholm axe (Fig. 3: A), although shorter than those of the A I-II types of Shang age, comes very close to them. Hence, the A III axes must not be far removed in time from A I-II.

4) The A I types show affinities with the A VII shaft-ring axes, which are probably of Shang age.

5) As I shall point out below, the animal sculptures on a few of the A III axes are suggestive of being somehow affiliated with Persian (Luristan) types from the second half of the IInd millennium B.C.

These points seem to warrant later Shang as the latest possible date of the oval-bladed axes A III.

*Type A IV* (Fig. 6). Of this small and fairly uniform group of slender battle-axes, no more than seven examples are known up to the present, inclusive of one piece in this collection (no. 16, where the other six pieces are listed).

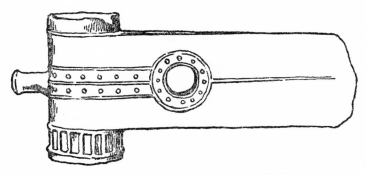

Fig. 6: *Slender battle-axe (type A IV)*.

Eumorfopoulos Collection, London. After Yetts (ca. 2/3).

Their stout wedge-shaped blades are comparatively long; they are straight and usually have a round hole in the middle. The blade embraces the socket which, thick-walled, projects above and below, the lower section usually being somewhat longer. From the neck projects a cylindrical, round-headed stud. The ever-recurring décor consists of a ring around the perforation and a double band running from the ring to the neck, both ring and bands being set with small knobs. Between the ring and the edge, which is slightly curved, goes a thin rib — emphasizing, but not influencing, structure. There are some minor divergencies from this general description. Thus, two lozenges interrupt the row of small knobs in the case of the Jannings piece no. 16.[16] Two specimens have blind perforations,[17] in another the disk framing the perforation is plain.[18] Some axes have the lower section of the socket fluted, similar to the Eumorfopoulos specimen (Fig. 6), while others have horizontal ribs instead or are plain.[19] Still, uniformity seems characteristic of this group, which excels in clear, simple, sober, structurally conceived, and elegant design.

Nothing much can be said regarding the provenance of these axe-heads. Most of them were acquired as stray pieces in Peking, where they used to be labeled "Ordos." Of a piece in his collection, Professor Yü Hsing-wu states that it came from Honan.[20] None of the specimens bears an inscription or any decorative element of unmistakable Shang character. Their archaeological context is unknown. This makes it very difficult to come to a decision about their date.

There is the round hole in the blade. It is a device used in Shang axes of all types, too commonplace to be of much use. However, the circumstance that this round hole is linked with edge and base or, rather, with the socket by some linear system deserves attention. The system recalls the way the blades of A II type are decorated: thin ribs issuing from the base, furcating to embrace the blade-holes and thence extending to the edge.[21] The rows of small knobs are a very primitive motif; yet, there are very few parallels to be found, and the few I know are, with one exception, Siberian or Northern.[22] As to the disk around the perforation, it was stated above that its recurrence in one of the oval-bladed axes (Fig. 3: A) and in one of the dagger-axes with down-curved edge (Fig. 15: B) irrefutably links these types with the present one, A IV. These scanty analogies do not suffice to establish a Shang date for this battle-axe species, but there seem to be no indications for a later, or much later, date. And this is corroborated by the structural properties of the type.

Among the *A IV variants,* poorer material on the whole, there is at least one piece, the provenance and date of which can be regarded as fixed past doubt. This piece belongs to a group of twelve weapons said to have been unearthed in Hsün-hsien (North-Honan),[23] which are now in the Freer Gallery.[24]

The Hsün-hsien axe (Fig. 7) stands halfway between A III and A IV forms. With the former it shares the longer socket, with the latter, the straight, strong, wedge-shaped blade. And while its scanty adornment of concentric circles calls to mind the concentric circles of A III axes (see note 9, nos. 5, 6), another element, the squarish heel projecting rearward from the socket, definitely connects this axe with A I, V, VIII types, in which this element regularly occurs. These several affinities clearly demonstrate that the Freer axe belongs to the ensemble here dealt with. Its date would carry weight therefore in any attempt to date the A IV and other, indirectly connected

Fig. 7: *Axe from Hsün-hsien.*
Freer Gallery (ca. 1/2).

groups. Since the Freer axe — in spite of its typological foreignness, a point stressed by John A. Pope [24] — proves to be connected
with unambiguously Chinese weapon types from Hsün-hsien on account of the motif of concentric circles,[25] there is every reason to
believe that it is contemporaneous with those weapons. They purport to belong to the very beginning of the Chou dynasty, because
of their style in general, the inscription "K'ang Hou 康侯" on one
of them,[26] and the provenance which is trustworthily attested by
Ch'u Te-i 褚德彝.[27] On this basis one can operate with a date around
1000 B.C. for the twelve weapons in the Freer Gallery, including
the axe. Hence, type A IV must be placed also around 1000 B.C. and
perhaps earlier. Earlier, because there must have been forerunners
of the Hsün-hsien axe, and because the A IV types are likely to be,
or to belong to, those forerunners.

A coarser variant which comes fairly close to the Hsün-hsien axe
is contained in the Jannings Collection (Cat. no. 17). It has no perforation and is bare of any ornament, but in the fashion of the A IV
types is provided with a stud at the back of the socket.

The Jannings specimen no. 18, though differing more widely, may
also be mentioned here. Its blade is comparatively broad and not
wedge-shaped; the socket, which is depressed oval in cross section,
has a small and short rectangular neck-plate. A round boss on the
blade is reminiscent of the blind perforations or circular ornaments
in the present group to which it is tentatively attached.

*Type A V.* Included in this group are axes with short sockets
or shaft-holes, the blades of which have longitudinal grooves, furrows, or ribs. Although stout, they do not equal the A IV type in size
or heaviness. There are two different forms (or subtypes):

   a) Oblong blades resembling A IV blades in outline and proportions; in the
   fashion of A IV their sockets have a stud or knob (Fig. 8)
   b) Widening blades, resembling A I and A VII types, with varying sockets that
   have a squarish plate instead of a stud (Fig. 9)

B. Karlgren has published three A Va specimens from the Stockholm collections, two of which are said to have come from Anyang.[28]
In one of them, the ribs start only from the juncture of blade and
tube; in the other one, the ribs are laid around the tube. The third
Stockholm piece is closely allied to the Port Arthur axe (Fig. 8),
regarding the provenance of which the Museum catalogue says only
"China."[29] The Jannings piece no. 21 may be counted as a variant
of this group, but it shows characteristics diverging from it (shaft-
hole, trapezoidal heel).

The Vb group is a loose assembly of a few heterogeneous types. To
a piece from Suiyüan (Fig. 9) described by Andersson,[30] with a socket
projecting downward only and with ribs embracing the socket, an
axe from Tsou An's collection may be added (Fig. 10). This axe,
published in a rubbing,[31] combines a relatively long shaft-tube with
a neck-plate resembling the same member in the Stockholm speci-

Fig. 8: *Axe with grooved
blade (type A Va).*

Port Arthur Museum. After the Museum
catalogue (ca. 1/2).

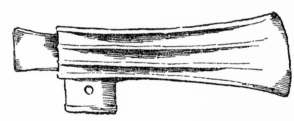

Fig. 9: *Axe with longitudinal
ribs (type A Vb).*

Suiyüan. Museum of Far Eastern Antiquities,
Stockholm. After Andersson (1/2).

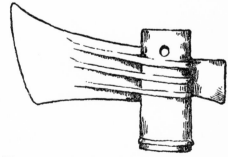

Fig. 10: *Axe with tubular socket
and longitudinal ribs.*

After *Chou Chin Wen Ts'un* (ca. 1/2).

men and with a remarkably shaped blade. In its outline, this blade shows affinities with both A I and A VII blades. This may be said also of the ribs which form strengthening belts around the socket and gradually sink in as they near the cutting edge. Structurally, types A I, VII, XII have much in common with the present design. Another variant was in Lo Chen-yü's collection.[32] It is an axe with almost straight blade and a short socket which tapers off, outwardly, on both sides; the blade margins engird the socket, and four ribs between the marginal ones run across from the squarish heel to the edge. Though rather heavy, this axe, terse, trim, and rigid of build, strikes one by its unstatic air. A piece in a Chinese collection, essentially similar to the Stockholm example (Fig. 9), bears an inscription of Shang script style, topsy-turvy, and perhaps doubtful.[33]

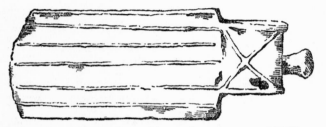

Fig. 11: *Axe with shaft-ring (type A VI)*.

Yūrinkan, Kyoto. After Umehara (ca. 1/2).

*The A VI group* (Fig. 11) is well represented by three specimens in the Yūrinkan Collection in Kyoto,[34] two in Port Arthur,[35] three in Stockholm,[36] and one in the Jannings Collection (Cat. no. 20). The Jannings piece is the smallest of the series, and it stands apart in that it has a shaft-hole as high as the blade itself. For the remainder, shaft-rings of lesser height are typical. The blades of these axes are uniformly thin and decorated rather than reinforced by a varying number of raised lines parallel to the axis. The shaft-rings are provided with studs throughout, something they have in common with the incomparably more shapely and solid A IV types as well as with most of the A Va types. It seems that the thin A VI axes are inferior in workmanship to any of the other classes. They are so primitive and crude that one might feel tempted to consider them as earlier than the finer axes (see Cat. no. 20). If these axes, on the other hand, hail from Anyang,[37] it would be difficult to assume that their inferiority — strikingly contrasted with Anyang's fabulous refinement — was not deliberate. There is a problem here, which presumably will be solved only by excavations. For one cannot be contented with explaining as burial gifts the present category, which has features of its own and does not look like a cheaper substitute for other types. But theorizing might lead far and to no end. It is sufficient to point to a special ornament found in them: thin ridges on the shaft-ring, crossing or meeting at an acute angle at the neck. Nothing like this is seen in other axes or weapons of whatever class, with the exception of a "Northern" pickaxe from Ta-t'ung (Shansi) with thin ridges crossing over the shaft-hole wall in exactly the same manner as in the A VI pieces.[38]

*Type A VII.* Reference has already been made several times to type A VII (Fig. 12), a slender axe with strongly asymmetrical edge, shaft-ring, and heavy squarish butt. The walls of the oval shaft-ring overlap the blade considerably, coming flush with the surface in the end: a trim and solid contrivance, which is also characteristic of the large and important groups A IX and A XII. The broad and prevailingly symmetrical A IX types are in fact so similar to our A VII specimen that the latter could well be classed as one of their subtypes. It is the blade-form — always taken into account in the present survey — which induces me to give this rare type a place of its own. This form proves akin to A I and A Vb blades. One of the A I axes, moreover, shows a strengthening belt around the socket, a belt overlapping the blade and gradually becoming flush with it: fundamentally the same constructional idea as that in the shaft-ring of the Sawyer axe (Fig. 12). Contact with the common Yin shaft-hole dagger-axe (A XII) is likewise thus established. This means that — as far as typologically founded dates are conclusive — A VII, A Vb, and A I types are probably all of Yin age. There is one pertinent A VII specimen in Tokyo University.[39]

Here the question arises whether those several interconnected groups mark stages of an evolutionary process, or whether they are approximate contemporaries during an inventive and productive age. An attempt to answer this question must be made, but one had better approach this problem anew after having concluded a survey of the manifold remaining types.

*Type A VIII,* excellently represented in this collection (Cat. no. 9), comprises only a few socketed axes with widening blades and pronouncedly curved cutting edges. With the exception of an outsider, and in conspicuous contrast with all foregoing models, these axes are at once recognizable as unadulterated Shang creations. They are lavishly ornate, bearing relief representations of the *t'ao-t'ieh* and other motifs familiar to us from Shang and Early Chou sacrificial vessels. It may be that these distinguished pieces were made for shows, parades, dances, festivals, sacrifices, processions, or for the exclusive use of princes, officers, or bodyguards, something that would account for their luxurious design. Still, all this would not explain the fact that these axes differ also structurally, and that there is not the slightest touch of such decoration, however simplified, reduced, or impoverished in the previously reviewed axes, which too are Shang age weapons. The present group, on the other hand, has all the more in common with the B IV types (with tang instead of tube or shaft-ring), which likewise do not exhibit ornamental features of "Northern" character, that is, geometric patterns, tectonically and thriftily applied.

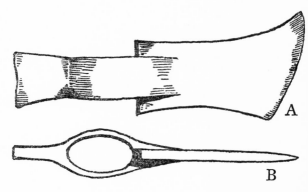

Fig. 12: *Shaft-ring axe with widening blade (type A VII).*

Sawyer Collection, Washington (ca. 1/2).

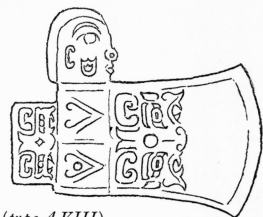

Fig. 13: *Early Western Chou axe (type A VIII).*
Rutherston Collection, London. After Umehara (ca. 2/5).

The Jannings specimen (Cat. no. 9) is not even overornate. Allied examples in the London collections Rutherston (Fig. 13)[40] and Raphael[41] surpass it. Each has its socket crowned by some plastic element: a human head with that curious sign on its cheeks, which in double rows covers the blade of the remarkable silvery dagger in this collection (Cat. no. 85); a fantastic animal in the case of the Raphael axe, the margins of which are furthermore elaborately wrought into elongated beasts in openwork technique — a detail, by the way, that also occurs in B II types. In Fig. 13, the shaft-hole does not exceed in length the base of the blade; otherwise it is so near the Jannings specimen (no. 9) that it seemed advisable to group it with the latter. There may be a difference in time. The Rutherston axe appears to be an Early Chou product, whereas the Jannings piece — with a rather divergent, much more vigorous *t'ao-t'ieh* in bolder relief — most probably is still of Shang age. As to the Raphael specimen, there can be no doubt that it is later than either of the two others; the date proposed in the *London Exhibition Catalogue* (no. 130: Period of the Spring and Autumn Annals) is, however, too late and should be replaced by "Western Chou." At any rate, these axes, being so late, do not contribute very much toward the elucidation of the Shang typology. They rather do so in a negative way. Their scarcity seems to mean that axes with shaft-tubes, decorated in unadulterate Anyang fashion, do not belong to the characteristic Shang inventory.

The aforementioned "outsider" is an axe in the Museum of Far Eastern Antiquities in Stockholm.[42] Supposedly hailing from North-China, this axe structurally resembles the Jannings specimen no. 9 very closely, save that its proportions are by comparison a little clumsy. Its decoration consists in nothing more than a round perforation encircled by a large bulging ring in the middle of the blade. The piece is hardly earlier than Chou I. Whether it should be connected with "Northern" types remains doubtful.

*Hsi Ch'ing Ku Chien* (ch. 37) contains one example of a fine, slender-bladed axe with a widening, curved cutting edge, the socket of which penetrates the wedge-shaped body of the blade as in the case of the battle-axe type A IV. But the whole silhouette, as well as the fact that the axe has a squarish neck-plate, suggests that it

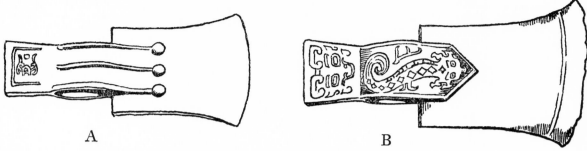

Fig. 14: *Shaft-ring axes with widening blades (type A IX).*

A — Sawyer Collection, Washington (ca. 2/5). B — Anyang. Museum of Far Eastern Antiquities, Stockholm. After Karlgren (ca. 1/2).

be grouped rather with the A VIII types. It deserves attention as perhaps the only piece in which an unmistakable Shang or Early Western Chou décor — a *t'ao-t'ieh* on the butt — is combined with a structure reminiscent of A IV and, significantly, close to A VIII types.

*The A IX types* have widening broad blades with curved cutting edges and shaft-rings (Fig. 14). They are closely related to the slenderer A VII axes and, due to the hafting-device, to A XII dagger-axes. Symmetrical types (Fig. 14: A) occur side by side with asymmetrical ones, the edges of which may be slanting (Fig. 14: B). As a rule, the pieces are decorated or are inscribed in pure Shang-Chou style. Similar blades and ornaments are found in the bulk of the much more numerous B axes, their tanged brothers. These tanged types are well represented in the Jannings Collection which, on the other hand, contains not a single example of the present group. Being well defined, this group requires no lengthy discussion, and references to published specimens are confined to a note.[43] A touch of sophistication in the asymmetrically designed types is felt. Indubitably of Shang age, the earliest phase of the Chinese Bronze Age according to present knowledge, they nevertheless reveal nothing in the way of real beginnings. Again one is bewildered by the absence of truly archaic, truly primitive tools. There is a certain narrowness, a lack of wider, deeper perspective in our material — diverse, rich, and peculiar though it be. The material shows a constant trait of similarity, interrelation, and propinquity, which nowhere opens a clear vista of primitiveness. Types which in some regards are farthest away from the Shang type A IX are the oval-bladed axes A II and A III: they are not primitive at all. The light, striped blades A VI do differ considerably, but they have shaft-rings like those of the type A IX. The rectangular neck-plates are a feature in the utterly different, long-socketed type A I. The lack of these squarish plates, and the presence of a stud or knob instead, might perhaps provide a clue as to where to seek types remote in time or in space.[44] One thus would have to count on the socketed axes with studs, A III, IV, Va, X. Whether it is possible to gain something by relying on them is a question taken up later.

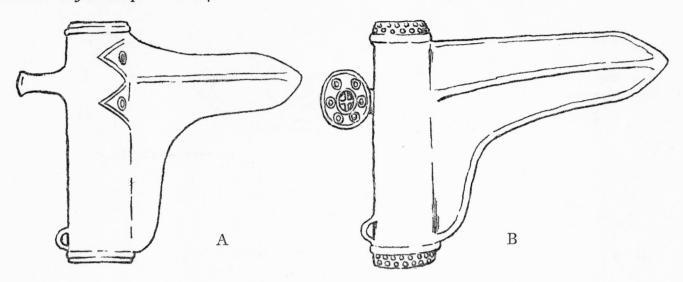

Fig. 15: *Dagger-axes with long tubular sockets (type A X)*.

A — Collection of Liu T'i-chih. After *Shan Chai Chi Chin Lu* (ca. 1/2). B — David-Weill Collection, Paris. After O. Janse (ca. 6/10).

The peculiar *dagger-axe type A X* is known to me in only four varieties. Two of them are in the collection of Liu T'i-chih (Fig. 15:A),[45] one in the David-Weill Collection (Fig. 15:B);[46] the fourth was in the possession of Huang Chün, Peking.[47] In all of these specimens the socket-tube is long enough to engage the entire length of the base of the blade, whose dagger-like horizontal pointed part is contiguous with an approximately vertical-edged prolongation downward, uniting with the main blade in a curved edge. (This form is considered at some length in Chapter III.)

The bare fact of the long sockets as well as ornamental features links these pointed axes with the A III and A IV types: the perforated disk in the David-Weill piece recurs in an A III axe in Stockholm (Fig. 3:A) and in the disks surrounding the blade-hole of the A IV battle-axes (Fig. 6); the double angles with little rings as fillings at the juncture of blade and socket appear in an axe-head of the Lu Mou-te Collection (Fig. 3:B). Attention has been drawn to the simple décor of rows of small knobs apropos of the A IV axes (see note 22). To complete the analogies, the sockets of the present group also show round studs at the back (Fig. 15:A) and a loop underneath. The relative date of the A X type is, therefore, not doubtful: it belongs to the same period as the A III and A IV axes. As a similar dagger-axe, with shaft-ring instead of a tube and with a Shang style character on its heel, in the Jannings Collection (Cat. no. 69; cp. ch. III, Dagger-axes, category III), shows this particular blade-form with down-curved edge existed already in the Shang period. Thus, the blade-form does not contradict what was learned from ornamental criteria, namely, that A X must be a Shang type.

It is significant, I think, that both the dagger-axe and axes with broad edge such as A I, VII, VIII, IX existed, as it were, in two versions: either with a long socket or with a narrow shaft-ring. The shaft-ring types seem to be more numerous, particularly in the case of the dagger-axes (*ch'ü*). It is in them that are found most often ornaments or inscriptions of Anyang style. This fact counts in an attempt at clarifying how the two versions were actually connected with each other chronologically and historically.

A stray type of dagger-axe with a long openwork socket in this collection (Cat. no. 70) is strongly reminiscent of the present small group A X. The piece purports to be of "Northern" origin and probably is younger than any of the four examples assembled under A X.

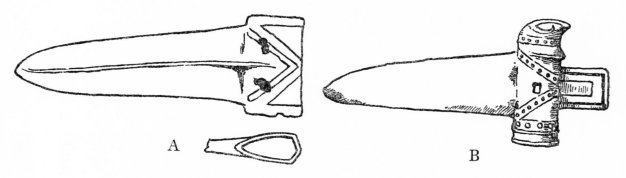

Fig. 16: *Dagger-axes with sockets (type A XI)*.

A — Freer Gallery; after Umehara (ca. 2/5); B — Baron v. d. Heydt Collection; after Griessmaier (ca. 2/5).

*Shaft-hole dagger-axes of the type A XI* are rarities. A pertinent specimen in the Freer Gallery seems to be unique in that its socket bears no rearward projection and hardly exceeds in length the width of the blade, which is rather thin (Fig. 16: A).[48] Its shaft-hole is roughly triangular in cross section — another uncommon feature. There is little in the way of ornament: an acute angle opening toward the blade, a motif recalling the juxtaposed angles in groups A III and A X (Figs. 3: A, B; 15: A). The motif recurs in the likewise singular axe in the v. d. Heydt Collection (Fig. 16: B), to which I have referred above for its ornamentation with little knobs.[49] According to V. Griessmaier's description, it is an Ordos weapon. The peculiarly helmeted socket has, however, a rectangular heel which goes well together with purely Chinese *ko* types, and the same may be said of the blade. Even so, the general appearance of the Heydt specimen is incompatible with its being grouped with Anyang finds. A third example, assuredly found in the Ordos Desert and resembling neither of the foregoing two, deviates pronouncedly from Shang types. Its shaft-hole is exactly as long as the blade is wide; ribs run over the socket, issuing from the plain, very long and broad heel. This dagger-axe, in the Museum of Far Eastern Antiquities, Stockholm,[50] has so little in common with genuine Shang type A XII that it would be difficult to assume that it depends on that category: the dimensions of the butt, the structure of the shaft-hole, the ribs, and the form of the blade never occur there in that form.

This again applies to a piece from Suiyüan in the same Museum

Fig. 17: *Dagger-axe with socket. Suiyüan.*

Museum of Far Eastern Antiquities, Stockholm. After Karlgren (ca. 1/2).

(Fig. 17).[51] It has a veritable shaft-tube and a triangular blade with a slight bend in it and is distinguished by three ribs uniting at the tip. The ribs run over the entire length to the heel, which is grooved between them. Finally, a fifth specimen, with an almost circular tube and a broad blade strengthened by a tapering, strong midrib (Fig. 18), was acquired by O. Karlbeck in Yü-lin-fu (Shansi) for the Stockholm Museum. Andersson, who published it, regards its Ordos origin as probable.[52] In fact it looks as un-Chinese as the previous specimens do, even though it is fitted with a squarish neck-plate in the fashion of Shang dagger-axes.

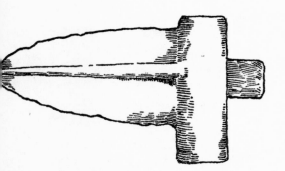

Fig. 18: *Dagger-axe with socket. Shansi.*

Museum of Far Eastern Antiquities, Stockholm. After Andersson (1/2).

This group (A XI) is made up of a few pieces that differ among themselves as widely as from Shang types in general. Although, as weapons, they are dagger-axes too, they cannot be shown to descend from Shang prototypes. Less refined, without the precision or meticulousness of Shang work, divergent in almost every structural detail, bare of the slightest trace of Shang ornamentation, and localized in China's northern borderlands, the A XI types should rather be taken as proof of the existence of an independent Northern facies. No one of these several types resembles another; yet they have something in common: a family likeness, so to speak. The fact of divergencies within the family also testifies to their originality. The more so since dagger-axes are much less at home, to judge by their scarcity, in the steppe region than they are in China proper. If they were derived from Chinese prototypes, stronger reminiscences of the prototypes would be expected than actually are known. I shall have to revert to this problem toward the end of the present chapter.

*Type A XII,* the *ch'ü,* a Chinese weapon par excellence, is included here to complete the schema (Fig. 19). It is more fully described in chapter III, Dagger-axes.

The hafting-device is essentially the same as in types A VII and A IX, and, as in this latter category, decorative patterns are of Shang style. There is a multitude of examples, for which Anyang is the accepted place of origin. The contrast with the preceding type A XI is striking.

The most interesting question regarding this particular type is whether it came into being at the same time as the tanged counterparts (*ko*), or, as many think, later, or perhaps earlier. Differences in time would in any case be very small, too small, perhaps, to be

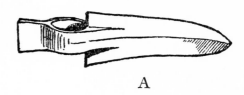 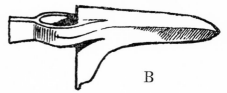

Fig. 19: *Shang dagger-axes with shaft-ring (type A XII).*
A — see Cat. nos. 65-68; B — no. 69.

accurately calculated by means of formal criteria. Still, this important question must be taken up once more, after the following discussion of the tanged axes.

Blades with down-curved edges, similar to A X types, but linked with A XII by virtue of their shaft-rings, exist in small number (Fig. 19: B). They, too, are treated in the chapter on dagger-axes. In Chou times, their blade form tends to supersede the blades without vertical edge; but, strangely enough, the shaft-ring seems to become obsolete, perhaps as early as the beginning of the Chou dynasty.

## B: TANGED AXES

The *tanged axes* are poorer in type variation than the shaft-hole axes. Existing types, moreover, are more homogeneous; they display unity in typological as well as ornamental features. Examples with un-Chinese-looking décor are scarce, as are plain pieces; both are far outnumbered by those types which bear Yin and Chou I style ornaments. It appears as though the pieces without décor save, perhaps, a round aperture in the blade, or the un-Chinese-looking ones occurred only in the group of symmetrically built types. Axes with Yin-Chou décor, on the contrary, prove to be practically all asymmetrically shaped, having the tang off the center and a slanting cutting edge. Symmetry, in these axes, seems to be restricted to an ornately designed model with a pair of animals occupying the margins of the blade (similar to a shaft-hole axe type mentioned above in group A VIII).

The dagger-axes with tang (*ko*), which, as a kind of tanged axe, are pertinent here, are separately treated in the chapter devoted to them.

Among the other axes, which are far less numerous than the *ko* extant, are found these six main types:

B I: Symmetrical, slender blades with tang placed in the middle axis. See Figs. 20, 21; cp. Cat. no. 19.

B II: Symmetrical slender blades with tang placed in the middle axis and with lateral lugs. See Fig. 22.
Subtype: Ornate axes of identical structure. See Fig. 23.

B III: Broad, short blades with broad tang. Occasionally of huge dimensions. See Fig. 24; cp. Cat. no. 13.

B IV: Asymmetrical blades with tang off center:
    a) Decorated with the motif of the open jaws, cp. Cat. nos. 4, 5, 6;
    b) Decorated with the motif of the curled dragon, cp. Cat. nos. 7, 8.

B V: Asymmetrical slender blades with tang off center. Occasionally a sharply slanting cutting edge. Decorated with circles and hanging triangles. See Fig. 25; cp. Cat. no. 12.

B VI: Blades of oval outline with the tips of the edge ending in inward bent volutes; tang off center. See Fig. 26.

B –: Sundry stray types. See Figs. 27, 28; cp. Cat. nos. 14, 15.

*Type B I.* In these axes, which are rather rare, the shoulders and the edge are usually of equal width, with the margins always concave. The tangs are straight and of varying lengths. Rarely they occur without a "splint-hole" in the tang or lashing-slots in the shoulders.[53] Most often the blade has a wide perforation in the center or near the base (Fig. 20).[54] Decoration, if there is any, consists in very simple geometric motifs, while typical Anyang ornaments are lacking.[55] It can be safely assumed that the wide perforation of the blade did not serve any practical purpose. In one case, a jade disk with central hole is inserted in the round aperture.[56] At times, convex buttons of shell were used to fill the aperture.

A hatchet similar to that in Fig. 21 was acquired by B. Laufer at Hsi-an (Shensi) in 1903. Meanders in three triangles at the butt and in narrow rectangles at the end of the tang, which might be claimed to reflect one ubiquitous Shang ornament, are hardly to be found so primitively applied in true Anyang art. Laufer's axe, moreover, is slightly asymmetrical, the axis of the blade diverging somewhat from that of the tang.[57] In this almost imperceptible or at least not at once noticeable bend in the median axis, a specimen bearing a Shang inscription in this collection (Cat. no. 19) is related to Laufer's. A small stop-ridge between the slots of specimen no. 19 is a feature which also distinguishes an axe in the Lu Collection (Fig. 21).[58] The Lu hatchet is thoroughly symmetrical. On the basis of the inscribed Jannings specimen, palaeographically datable around the end of the Yin dynasty, it would appear that these several pieces belong to the close of the Yin age, and that in them one can witness the appearance of the stop-ridge, later developed to a flanged bar, a process that has a parallel in the dagger-axes.

The hatchet Fig. 20, however, impresses one as being earlier. Its lack of sophistication becomes even more apparent when it is compared with typical Shang products. The wide hole in the blade must certainly be understood as an adaptation of the hole customary in stone and jade axes. I shall demonstrate this in the Catalogue below, under no. 14, a remarkable semicircular-edged specimen of tanged bronze axe which — more clearly than any early Chinese metal implement I have seen — makes one think of stone prototypes.

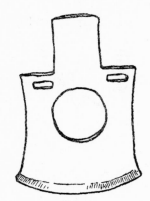

Fig. 20: *Axe of B I type.*

After Umehara (ca. 1/3).

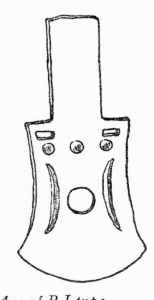

Fig. 21: *Axe of B I type.*

Lu Mou-te Collection. After Umehara (ca. 1/2).

This agrees well with the view taken much earlier by others, namely, that tanged bronze blades are translations into bronze of shouldered celts of stone.[59] In the case of other types, on the other hand, evidence as afforded by stone or jade materials rather points to the opposite: prototypes in metal, copies done in stone.[60]

This B I group consists exclusively of comparatively primitive pieces that cannot match the Anyang finds in refinement. Such, for instance, is the beautiful axe-head with the large *t'ao-t'ieh* on the blade in this collection (Cat. no. 11): superior in every regard, and probably later than the more primitive types with their static silhouette, this axe-head with its subtle asymmetry obviously belongs to another environment. Yet, basically, the type is the same as B I, and it is not probably later than around the end of the Shang. As a consequence, types as primitive as those in Fig. 20 and in the Catalogue no. 14 must be considerably earlier — provided they too are Chinese and not barbarian imitations. It must be remembered in this connection that such tanged axes have not hitherto been reported from the Steppe, Suiyüan, or the Ordos Desert. Localization in China proper thus being (theoretically) inevitable, the possibility of a greater age of the simple hatchets must be considered.

There are few pertinent published specimens not mentioned above.[61]

*Type B II* has much in common with B I: symmetry, slender blades widening toward the cutting edge, a round perforation in the blade. But instead of the shoulder with slots for lashing the tool to the haft, there appear two short lugs or wings projecting upward and downward from the base (Fig. 22).[62] This device, which is oftener found in the dagger-axes, has the advantage of not weakening the blade and at the same time prolonging the part which rests on the haft. Thonging was even more simple and solid this way. In the present example, a sunken ring takes the place of the blade perforation. The décor at the heel or *nei* is not clearly recognizable in the rubbing after which the drawing was made and therefore gives no clue as to the date of the axe. The sunken circle, however, recalls Hsün-hsien pieces of the Early Chou time (see above, under type A IV).

An undecorated piece of this type, with a wide round hole in the blade, was published by Umehara together with a specimen bearing a *t'ao-t'ieh* on the blade, a specimen which is, or was, in the Berlin Museum.[63] It stands halfway between B II and the ornate subtypes.

*B II Subtype.* In these ornate axes, the space between the lengthened lugs — now compounded by a flange running from end to end — and the strongly backward bent tips of the cutting edge is occupied by a pair of dragons. These dragons are in full round. With their turned heads they touch the shafting-wings; their claws grip the margins of the blade; their sinuous, slim bodies, sometimes set with a crest of pointed hooks, end in long tails which conjoin the tips of the edge in gracefully drawn volutes. The piece here chosen for illustration[64] (Fig. 23) was formerly in Dr. O. Burchard's possession.

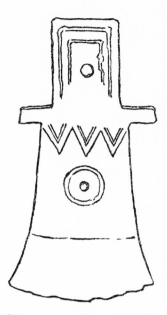

Fig. 22: *Axe of B II type.*

After *Tsun Ku Chai Ku Ping Ching* (1/2).

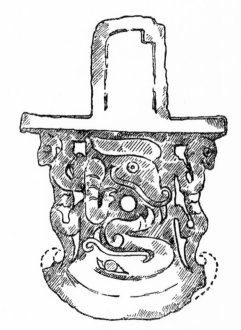

Fig. 23: *Tanged axe of B II ornate subtype. Chou I-II.*

After Umehara (3/5).

Fig. 24: *Broad axe with tang*
*(B III type). Anyang.*

Kishi Collection, Kyoto. After Umehara
(1/2).

The décor on the blade vividly reminds one of the ornate socketed
axe in the Raphael Collection referred to above (note 41): there
is nothing of Shang spirit in it; these half-animate, fragmentary,
somewhat uncouth batrachian figurations certainly take us down to
the end of the Chou I period, perhaps a little later.

None of these several axes[65] appears to be earlier than Chou I.
Shaft-supports in the shape of ears standing out above the tiger-like
masks on the blades are a noteworthy feature three of them display.
Such ear- or leaf-shaped supports also appear, as isolated elements, occasionally on dagger-axes (see Cat. nos. 46, 72). A less
pretentious version of shaft-support, consisting of simple rectangular
plates standing aslant, is seen in the Jannings specimen no. 15. The
ear-shaped supports possibly go back to Yin types.[66]

Very different from the rest of these tanged hatchets are those of
*group B III, the broad shapes.* There are no more than six pieces
hitherto published, which vary considerably among themselves.

1) A symmetrical blade with no tang but a narrow shafting-bar
instead that has one(?) long slot; decorated with a row of whorl-
circles along the base and triangles with ornamental fillings below,
executed in bold relief. Fragmentary(?). Width 140 mm(?).
A. Hellström Collection, Mölndal.[67]

2) A symmetrical blade with broad tang displaced toward the
upper shoulder, which has one slit while the lower one has two. The
blade is decorated with the motif of the fanged jaws, pierced through
in the middle, not occupying the entire width. The rear part of the
tang shows an animal mask in a narrow field. Width ca. 160 mm.
Y. Kishi Collection, Kyoto (Fig. 24).[68]

3) A symmetrical blade with slenderer tang, placed asymmetrically. Two slots in the shoulders. The motif of the fanged jaws in openwork, as in the above specimen, is here, quite exceptionally, combined with a human face, the several parts of which stand out in high relief. Heel decorated with a bird (?) design. Width 197 mm. H. J. Oppenheim Collection, London.[69]

4) A symmetrical blade with broad tang in center, decorated with a *t'ao-t'ieh* and two flanking dragon figures executed in openwork. A magnificent specimen, reportedly excavated near Anyang, and slightly larger and heavier than the axe in the Jannings Collection. Width 378 mm; weight 5850 gr. H. J. v. Lochow Collection, Cologne.[69a] See Fig. 72 A.

5) Blade with slanting cutting edge and asymmetrically placed tang. Three embossed circles with concentrically arranged knobs on them form a row along the base. Hanging triangles in flat design beneath the row. One Shang character — an animal pictogram — inscribed on the triangle in the center. The tang is short and plain. Width 320 mm. David-Weill Collection, Paris.[70] See drawing under Cat. no. 13 below, Fig. 72 B.

6) Axe no. 13 in this collection. Blade with slanting cutting edge, but with the tang placed in the middle axis. Width 370 mm.

It would be rash to try to arrange chronologically this small group of axes which, though typologically as well as stylistically nothing less than uniform, form a fairly united species. I do not propose to question whether they are all of Shang age or not, pro's being stronger than con's. It is worth noticing that the group is interconnected with B IV by the occurrence in two cases of the jaws-motif — peculiarly adapted to a frontally conceived face (3), a congelation, even forceful in expression, of harsh, trenchant, obvious, and disconnected elements. The fangs originally were designed for profile view, and in less obtrusive dimensions. The adaptation of the motif to a front view (3) surely must be understood as derived and, therefore, "late"; thus, the Oppenheim axe may be of Chou I age.[70] The other pieces, which show combinations of variously rendered circles and triangles, are related to group B V, the slender light axes with slanting edges.

Perhaps the most noteworthy feature of these axes is the formidable size and weight of some of them. Tools so large cannot have served as weapons. There were ritual executions in those times.[71]

*The B IV group* consists of axes with more or less strongly slanting cutting edge and asymmetrically placed tang. A subtype (a) is decorated with a pair of addorsed animal-heads in relief, the jaws of which unite in an arch in the middle of the blade. Teeth and fangs are rendered in lesser relief below that arch, the space between them often being pierced through — a feature not unlikely to be related to the round blade-holes of B I. As there do exist representations in jade or bronze of tigers with open jaws thus rendered, we must infer that the addorsed animal-heads with ears in the form of a recumbent C are meant to be tiger heads.[72] Examples of this group, which evidently is more developed than the naïvely symmetrical B I types, are numerous. In the Jannings Collection alone there are no less than three specimens (Cat. nos. 4, 5, 6), among which a heavy, almost mineralized one (no. 5) is most impressive. There is little doubt that that piece, as many others of the same group, was unearthed at Anyang. It is generally agreed — and there is no reason to contradict — that these axes are genuine Shang axes. For a list of related specimens see under Catalogue no. 4 below.

The motif of the open jaws recurs in two further extraordinary axe-heads of the Jannings Collection: the jade axe with bronze haft no. 2, and the magnificent bronze axe no. 10 on which the motif is a mere residue, an isolated element with no relation to the rest of the décor. Two more baroque variants in Swedish collections prove connected with our no. 10. Both have the shoulders decorated with birds with mighty beaks jutting forth from the silhouette, accompanied by two dragons confronting each other and facing the birds' tails in one case (Museum of Far Eastern Antiquities), and by the jaws-motif under an arch continuing in convolute spirals which touch the birds' heads in the other (Hellström Collection).[78] Sophistication and playfulness make these variants appear "late," as do stylistic properties reminiscent of Chou I sacrificial vessels.

*Subtype IV (b)* typologically diverges only in that the blades on the whole retain symmetrical shapes, while the tangs are always removed from the blade median. The décor is nothing but a variant of the open-jaws motif: a gaping dragon in profile, whose scaly body follows the curve of the edge and is bent back in a slightly angular volute so as almost to touch the fangs, the space within the figure commonly being in openwork.

Besides the two pieces in this collection (Cat. nos. 7, 8), one of which has a filling of black paste in the sunken parts which elsewhere are done in openwork (no. 7), six were previously published (see under Cat. no. 8 below).

The design seems not so conventionalized in these types as in the foregoing group, which, moreover, shows more asymmetrical shaping. There is not sufficient evidence for decisively answering the question whether IV b has to be regarded as earlier than, or contemporaneous with, IV a, but I think it unnecessary to consider IV b as possibly later.

*Type B V* musters a small body of fairly homogeneous examples. The tang does not always stand asymmetrically, while the cutting edges, with one exception, are slanting and more pronouncedly splayed than in any of the other categories. In some cases there are no shoulder-slits. Ornament, *au fond,* does not vary; execution does. A band with three circles, flat or with raised rim or embossed, goes parallel to the butt, and triangles with some fillings of hooks or angular spirals hang downward in series of three, pointing to the edge; but sometimes the outer triangles are cut by the margins.

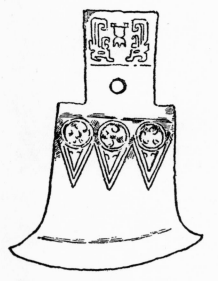

Fig. 25: *Axe of B V type.*

After *Ch'ih An Ts'ang Chin* (1/3).

The decoration makes it obvious that these types are closely connected with the broad axes in group B III, which seem to antedate —
though probably not very much — these slender B V types. It can
be taken for granted that they outlasted the Shang dynasty; at least
one example in a Peking collection (*Yen K'u*), although it was
excavated at Anyang, purports to be of Western Chou age.[74]

Including the one example of comparatively small dimensions
in the Jannings Collection (Cat. no. 12), there are all together six
specimens known thus far; they are enumerated under Cat. no. 12.

Apropos of the circular bosses on the Sumitomo axe, Karlgren
observed that "this décor element . . . is handed down from prehistoric times" (the Stockholm Museum owns a neolithic pottery
sherd from Kansu with some comparable ornament), and that it also
recurs in ritual vessels.[75] Whatever the pottery parallel implies, the
recurrence of really similar studded bosses on a vessel of Chou I
age [76] is of interest for our present purpose, because it corroborates
the Early Chou date of at least part of the B V types. It is not different with the motif of the whorl-circle: this element is likewise
present in Chou I bronze vases.[77] The fact that the *t'ao-t'ieh* accom-
panies such tenth century B.C. elements in these weapons (as in our
no. 12) precludes the year 1000 B.C. as the time for the vanishing of
the *t'ao-t'ieh*; the *t'ao-t'ieh* lingered on in certain types of weapons
as it did in ritual vessels.[78]

Very scarce are *B VI types,* which are more shapely than all the
other tanged axes. The blade is short and high; the edge forms
one continuous curve ending in inward bent volutes. Its butt widens
in correlation with the outline of these volutes and is prolonged by
wings. The lower of the wings is considerably longer, owing to the
fact that the shafting-plate (*nei*) is displaced upward. There is a
round hole in the blade center. One specimen of this type is in the
Royal Ontario Museum, Toronto [79] (Fig. 26), a second one, deprived
of its shafting-contrivance, was published by Huang Chün.[80] Umehara pointed out the resemblance of the Toronto axe to that contained
in *Chin Shih So* (Fig. 2: B), already discussed under A II variants
above.[81] Resemblance is even closer to the *Hsi Ch'ing Ku Chien* axe
with spiraling edge tips and a rattle at the back of the socket, also
mentioned above. The latter piece, however, in contrast to the
Toronto axe, has three blade-holes.

On the heel of the Toronto specimen (Fig. 26) there is some animal ornament which seems to be of Chou I age. This date would
appear to correspond with the whole shape of this axe type; exceptionally elegant, with a subtle diminution in size of the lower half of
the blade, and a developed construction of the shafting-bar set off
from the base by a ledge, this type shows features which are very
surprising when compared with the long-socketed oval axes A II,
and undoubtedly surpass in refinement B IV and V axes.

*Sundry types.* In connection with B VI and A II axes, a broad-
shouldered celt with three round holes in the blade, acquired by
Laufer in Hsi-an in 1903, is of particular interest [82] (Fig. 27). Evi-

Fig. 26: *Tanged axe of B VI
type. Chou I.*

Royal Ontario Museum, Toronto. After
Umehara (ca. 1/3).

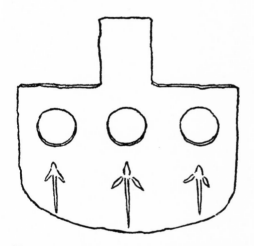

Fig. 27: *Broad tanged axe with
blade-holes.*

After Laufer (1/3).

dently this singular specimen is an archaic type, of striking simplicity. It reminds one not only of the oval axes with three or more round apertures in the blade, but also of the broad B III axes with round bosses instead of the apertures. The scanty décor recalls that found in the A II blade: ribs embracing the holes and extending to the edge (see Fig. 2: A above). Thus this stray specimen, in spite of its typological isolation, displays several features tending to link it with more than one of our categories. Is it too venturesome to think that it was a forebear of the broad axes with embossed circles (B III) in true Shang style? Did it stand in the same relationship to the oval-bladed axes with socket (A II) which do not quite fit in with Shang forms? Or was this piece of Laufer's nothing more than an impoverished, rustic replica of those gorgeous types — with one characteristic change, namely, the replacement of the tubular socket by the simpler flat process, the tang, familiar to the makers since Neolithic times? Perhaps this piece is not truly archaic, but was cast in the modest workshop of a small chieftain anxious to have imitations of luxuries he had seen in his suzerain's court. Although these questions cannot definitely be answered, and while the absence of lashing-slots and splint-hole might well be casual deficiencies rather than signs of great antiquity, the fact remains that this axe shows analogies with early types only; moreover, these several early types seem to converge in it.

A detail that should not be overlooked is the relatively long and narrow tang. Only class B I shows the tang in similarly slender proportions (Fig. 21). But the axe no. 14 in this collection also has a very slender tang (Fig. 28). In this detail, and in the wide perforation of the blade, this axe has something in common with Laufer's broad axe. Otherwise it is very different. The silhouette has a wonderful rhythm. It shows something that is hardly ever found in Chinese tools: an edge reminiscent of hammered edges. It is, however, not actually hammered, but cast in a rigorously designed mold. It cannot, of course, be accidental that the edge exactly forms half of a circle which touches the outer corners of the rectangular lashing-slots and the shoulders where the tang meets them. Still another trait distinguishes this axe, not seen in others: the gently convex surfaces. Such surfaces are characteristic of stone tools. Metal tools ordinarily are of even strength. So this stray type has typological qualities justifying a very early date, and it is therefore not surprising that it can be likened to stone hatchets rather than to the average Shang bronze axe. It is impossible not to assume that this handsome tool takes one back to a *pre-Anyang* stage.

Last, a stray type of tanged axe with broad, pointed blade with down-curved lower edge in the fashion of dagger-axes such as Fig. 19: B deserves to be mentioned. The piece, in the collection of C. A. Piek, Bussum, has a strange ornament in the shape of a reptile, the head of which was adapted to a common decorative element: a round boss with hollow center off the base. A vague but appropriate de-

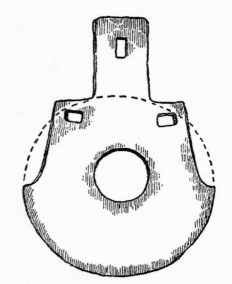

Fig. 28: *Axe with semicircular edge.*

Jannings Collection, Cat. no. 14 (1/2).

scription, "animal-like ornament," given in the catalogue of the Berlin Exhibition of 1929 (no. 46) was replaced by a more fanciful one, "leopard in relief," in the catalogue of the Burlington House Exhibition of 1935 (no. 177), where this peculiar piece was, moreover, dated too late ("Warring States") : its style is Western Chou. Partly for this reason, and partly because it is very much *sui generis,* this axe throws no light on the typology of the early stages. A small notch at the lower corner of its broad tang, on the other hand, is a detail worth noticing: there are many *ko* which display such an indentation together with apparent Shang ornamentation. It may well be that they, broadly speaking, are rather Chou I products (cp. the *ko* nos. 47 — with jade blade, 58 — with turquoise inlay, and 59 — with sunken design suitable for inlay, in this collection).

## C: SOCKETED CELTS

As regards the large group of *socketed celts* (C), to which this collection contributes nothing, the reader is referred to some general remarks in the chapter "Siberia in the Early Bronze Age."

Having finished the description of early axes with shaft-holes and tangs, I should like now to sum up the foregoing observations, adding some materials from outside China for comparison.

## SUMMARY

When the types described and tentatively dated in the preceding pages are arranged according to their decoration, they readily fall into three categories:

1) Unmistakable Anyang and Early Chou types;
2) Types which do not clearly reveal their dependence;
3) Northern ("Sino-Siberian") types.

The distribution of the various A types and B types within these three categories is as follows:

| Décor Style | A — Socketed Axes | B — Tanged Axes |
|---|---|---|
| Anyang-Chou | VIII. IX. XII. | II. III. IV. V. VI. |
| Undefined | I. Va. Vb. VI. VII. | I. |
| Northern | II. III. IV. X. XI. | |

From this table it is immediately obvious that tanged axes predominate in the Anyang-Chou category while they are completely lacking in the Northern one. It also reveals the prevalence, in the Northern group, of axes with long sockets or round studs.

If, on account of these studs or knobs in the A VI types and the long shaft-tubes of the A I types, we place them with the Northerners, only types A Vb, A VII, B I are left as undefinable neutrals, and the picture would be even more striking.

It was pointed out that the B I type is in line on the one hand with stone prototypes and on the other with Shang types; B I may therefore reasonably be shifted from the second category to the first, the Anyang-Chou décor category. The tanged B axes would then in their entirety go to the "Chinese" side.

As to A VII, a close relationship with both A I and A VIII was recognized; A VII holds an intermediate place between them. This position is strengthened, as it were, by A Vb (including the variant specimen Fig. 10), a variety which wavers between, or is in contact with, both the Anyang-Chou and the Northern categories.

With these several adjustments made on the strength of legitimate typological observations, the following modified grouping obtains:

| Décor Style | A — Socketed Axes | B — Tanged Axes |
|---|---|---|
| Anyang-Chou | VIII. IX. XII. | I. II. III. IV. V. VI. |
| Undefined | Vb. VII. | |
| Northern | I. II. III. IV. Va. VI. X. XI. | |

This implies that all the tanged types and some shaft-ring types are *Chinese* (Shang), while the long-socketed ones and the majority of the remaining shaft-hole axes are *Northern* (Ordos, Suiyüan, etc.).

This agrees exceedingly well with the fact that tanged axe types are practically absent in the northern borderlands of China and factually absent in Siberia and is quite in line with Orvar Karlbeck's thesis: "It would seem as if the Nomads who inhabited the region now known as Suiyüan, in Han and pre-Han times made exclusive use of socketed axes. When adopting Chinese forms they even went so far as to change the mode of hafting." [83]

One may venture a step further. Morphologically, the tang can be regarded as a feature derived from *stone* tools. Long sockets as well as shaft-rings, on the other hand, and particularly the round studs or knobs at the back of the sockets incontestably are features of *metal* tools; they can only have been conceived by metal-casters. This *aperçu* furnishes a clue to the distribution of the respective types, Chinese and otherwise, tabulated above: *metal types* with long sockets and studs or knobs are *Northern; stone types* are *Chinese*. The respective distribution then is clear: the tanged (Chinese) types are indigenous, broadly speaking, whereas the Northern types appear to be foreign intruders. Thus, the absence of tanged types in the northern borderlands becomes understandable.

In the light of this hypothesis, the question whether the *shaft-ring types* in general are earlier or later than the long sockets must be taken up again. I cannot undertake here a detailed investigation. It rather seems advisable to leave aside minute details, such as ornaments and their style and chronological order, and take the typological characteristics of entire groups as a point of departure. There are the types A VIII, IX, XII with sockets and shaft-rings, decorated in Anyang or West-Chou fashion. Is it possible that these Chinese types represent a stage earlier than the Northern types A I-IV, Va, VI, X, XI? Is it possible, particularly, that A IX — with affinities to the "neutral" type A VII — is on the whole earlier than, say, A I? Is there any verisimilitude in an assumption that the very long shaft-tube was either evolved from, or — not to insist on evolutionary filiation — at least preceded by, the shaft-ring?

Granted that an offhand decision is impossible, there seems to be nothing more unlikely than such an evolutionary course, which implies the growth of a narrow ring into a tubular socket of increasing length. A priori it is more reasonable to think of ring and socket as basically different contrivances. The one might, at a time, have supplanted the other for reasons hard to guess, technical, aesthetic, or economic. The ring-types are more numerous than those with long tubes. Should this be explained by the assumption that the latter were transient fashions, soon receding into oblivion because they either did not gain favor, or proved unwieldy or too expensive, or, requiring embarrassingly large molds, were difficult to make? The more natural conclusion would be that the more numerous ringed types must be later than the few and uncharacteristic long-socketed types.

The dagger-axes clearly reveal that the long sockets never played an important role and that the shaft-rings disappeared as early as the Chou I period.[84] The form which was maintained was the *tanged* blade. This shows convincingly that the shaft-hole dagger-axe was a temporary phenomenon. By analogy one may safely assume that the shaft-rings fared no better on broad-edged axes than on the far more common dagger-axes. Though including some Chou pieces, types A VIII and A IX prevailingly purport to be of Shang age: axes with short sockets or shaft-rings thus are of Shang age. But the extremely long-socketed type A I is also of Shang age. To assume that the extremely long sockets were only an interlude at the time when the ringed types were about to recede, toward the end of the Shang, would be in direct contradiction to the evolutionary trend displayed by the dagger-axes.

Secondly, there is the testimony of the décor of several A II axes, closely affiliated with the plain A I types by their kindred sockets. That décor, being Northern, does not fit in between Shang and Chou ornamentation. A II must therefore be regarded as either foreign or somehow non-Anyang, or earlier than the typical Anyang animal design. In either case A II is a determining factor in locating historically the axe type A I.

Finally, the A I type itself offers a hint. The Toronto Museum specimen, Fig. 1 : C, has two spikes above and below the squarish heel at the back of the socket. These spikes have no analogies in the Anyang axes, nor is there anything similar in the Northern materials, except perhaps some vaguely analogous knobs (Fig. 4). Since the décor of the axe Fig. 4 is evidently Northern, and knobs and studs appear to belong exclusively to tools of foreign stamp, it should not be surprising to find parallels farther west.

*West-Asian materials for comparison.* Persian axes of the IInd millennium B.C. show forms that can be paralleled. One finds there not only spikes at the back of the sockets (Fig. 29), but also the exceedingly long socket as such (Fig. 30). These two examples from Nihavand (south of Hamadan-Ecbatana) are datable, according to

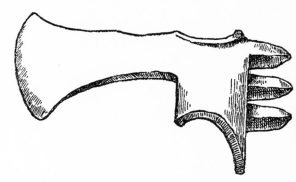

Fig. 29: *Axe, from Nihavand, Persia.*

After Dussaud.

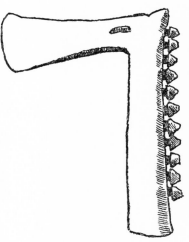

Fig. 30: *Horse-head axe, from Nihavand, Persia.*

After Dussaud.

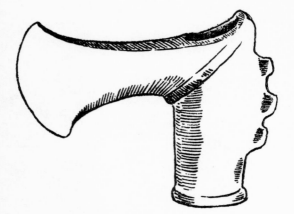

Fig. 31: *Axe. Luristan.*

Brussels Museum. After Speleers.

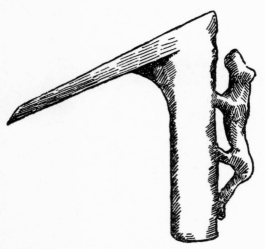

Fig. 32: *Socketed adze. Luristan.*

Museum of Fine Arts, Boston. After A. U. Pope.

Dussaud, "first half of the second millennium" and "c. 1500 at the earliest," respectively.[85] The former type, however, already occurs toward 2000 B.C. in Assur,[86] and the three spikes can again be traced back to the times of Sargon of Agade (first half of the IIIrd millennium).[87] The horse-head axe (Fig. 30) with its long socket represents a later development of the axe with three spikes, intermediary stages being known.[88] The long past and the wide distribution of the two Persian examples are facts which, when one compares them with shapes from as far away as China, deserve consideration: one has to do with forms persisting through more than a thousand years.

The possibility of discovering links between China and the ancientmost center of metallurgy, Mesopotamia, cannot offhand be denied, but chances to assemble strikingly similar specimens from both sides are, of course, slim. One must not regard as more than suggestive the parallel — unsatisfactory at that — between the Persian pieces and the Shang battle-axe (Fig. 1: C). It moreover remains to be seen whether there is anything in the way of parallels to other Chinese axe types.

In the case of group A II, one might perhaps remember the comparatively late semicircular or crescent-shaped axes of Western Asia, such as the Transcaucasian Amazon axes with their narrow sockets or, rather, shaft-rings which may have short spikes or a knob or girding ribs.[89] A plain piece from northeastern Georgia with shaft-ring and scalloped base (Berlin Museum) makes one think of the *Chin Shih So* variant (Fig. 2: B) mentioned with the A II types.[90] The same can even more justly be said of a rounded blade with two big holes from Susa [91] and related axes from Syria.[92] None of these Western objects, however, shows the central blade-hole of the Chinese types, and none of them impresses one as more than faintly reminiscent.[93]

It is somewhat different with type A III. The oval-shaped blade has, it is true, no parallels in Siberia and farther west or southwest. But the sockets may well be likened to the one or other Luristan piece, whether for the knobs (Fig. 31) or, what is more conspicuous, for the sculptural adornment (Fig. 32). The axe with the three knobs superposed at the bulging back of the socket (Brussels Museum [94]) has been said to date from around the middle of the IInd millennium B.C.[95] The remarkable adze with its very long shaft-tube in the Boston Museum [96] shows a feline beast cast in the round on the socket wall. The combination of tool and animal sculpture is something too specialized to be ignored in looking for analogies in East Asia, such as the Ordos axe (Fig. 5). The Boston adze is but a refined replica of Sumerian transverse edge tools, of which there is a specimen datable between 2219-2211 B.C. in Brussels.[97] It is likely, therefore, that its date is around the middle of the IInd millennium if not even somewhat earlier, for the animal (as well as the tool itself) appears to be more archaic than the plastic decoration on any other axe.

Hallstatt, which shows a late reflection of this kind of animal-adorned tool, cannot historically account for what is found in China's earlier Bronze Age. One may expect to come across really relevant material in Luristan and Iran, where these types likewise persisted throughout many centuries — though changing into some of highly intricate design (e.g., the Oxus Treasure axe in the British Museum [98]) which rather recall the elegant Chinese picks from around 500 B.C. in this collection (Cat. nos. 80, 81, 82) — and whence they wandered north to Turkestan and Central Siberia and eastward to China's northern confines. Still, the differences between Iranian and Chinese or Sino-Siberian finds remain profound. It is only generalities that may be compared. Details such as blade, socket, and animal figure are nowhere the same.

The studs at the back of A III and A IV sockets stand out as something obviously belonging to the art of the Northern metal-casters. In fact one meets the very same detail again in Persia. There is an excellent example of the shaft-hole axe in the Brussels Museum, described by Speleers [99] (Fig. 33). The blade and the angle it forms with the shaft are strongly reminiscent of the archaic Sumerian shaft-hole axe (which has no stud). I am not sufficiently conversant with Mesopotamian or Iranian antiquities to propose a date more exact than IInd millennium B.C. for that axe in Brussels. What matters is the type and the particular element of the round stud with its domed head, an element which exactly corresponds to the shape in the A IV axes. The blade form, on the other hand, differs strongly from the Chinese ones.

These several analogies between some of the Sino-Mongolian shaft-hole axes and Mesopotamian-Iranian types, to my knowledge not hitherto observed, are scarcely a convincing demonstration that there was lively contact between those widely separated areas. Apart from a few features — not isolated ones in either of the centers in question — there is, in fact, nothing much in the way of similarities there. Whether these analogies none the less have some weight cannot be decided from the restricted field of weapons alone, least of all from one particular type of weapon, but it seems worthwhile to do what is possible within that frame. The meager result of our searching vividly evokes what C. W. Bishop said about transmissions eastward from that old cultural hearth, Mesopotamia:

> There was of course no mass transference [of cultures or peoples] from the banks of the Euphrates and Tigris, or even the Oxus and Jaxartes, direct to those of the Hwang Ho. The process . . . is only beginning to be grasped in part. What must have happened was something like this. Certain culture traits, including the knowledge of bronze working and the use of wheeled vehicles, spread from southwestern Asia before the close of the 3rd millennium before the Christian era to the grasslands north of the Caucasus, the Elburz, and the Hindu Kush. There they underwent local modification and were then still further disseminated . . . to the river basins of Northern China. There they were able to take root and develop along special lines. . . .[100]

Fig. 33: *Socketed axe with stud. Luristan.*

Brussels Museum. After Speleers.

It remains to ask whether the dagger-axes with shaft-holes, types A X, XI, classed within our Northern group, have any counterpart among finds from farther west.

Under type A X are brought together four pieces with an apparently later variant from the Jannings Collection (Cat. no. 70); under type A XI are also five pieces. None of them shows the slightest trace of Shang origin. On the contrary, I am inclined to take those dagger-axes as distinct representatives of a Northern facies which, however intimately interwoven with Shang culture, does not depend on it. Its sources should therefore be sought in the West and, partly perhaps, in the North, but in the absence of parallels it would seem safest to assume that that facies was capable of producing forms of its own.

In Mesopotamia and Persia, dagger-axes seem to be missing, while picks of rectangular cross section occur early. Their shape is entirely different from types A X, XI.[101] Another kind of pick is extremely common in Minusinsk and Western Siberia. It always has a socket-tube, which meets the round or faceted blade with usually tetrahedral point near the middle of the blade length.[102] Parallels to these Minu-

Fig. 34: *Fragment of socketed dagger-axe. Altai.*

Museum Minusinsk. After Aspelin (1/2).

Fig. 35: *Sumerian axe from Kish A.*

After Childe (1/4).

sinsk picks are fairly rare in China and in the regions to the north;[103] moreover they belong, on the whole, to a later period than 1000 B.C. and so are irrelevant for the present purpose. A few comparable objects, however, do occur in Western and Central Siberia. They have a dagger-like blade with or without a midrib, a round socket, and a characteristic lug at the back.[104] A fragment from the Altai region[105] has a blade which closely resembles that of the v. d. Heydt specimen (Fig. 34; cp. Fig. 16: B), which is a Northern type but not quite dissimilar to genuine Shang dagger-axes, at least as far as the blade form is concerned. The other Siberian dagger-axes are different from Shang types in every regard; it is again a Northern type, the Shansi specimen in Stockholm (Fig. 18), which comes relatively close to them. All in all, the Siberian analogies are scanty and poor, the pickaxe having been the weapon preferred by the Siberians.

Whether an axe type with shaft-hole and squarish butt which was found in Kish A (Fig. 35) has genetically to do with the much later Chinese dagger-axes is as yet impossible to decide.[106]

For category A X (Fig. 15), I am unaware of anything comparable from outside China. The peculiar shape of the down-curved blade is so widely used in Chinese dagger-axes, both *ch'ü* and *ko,* that it would seem unwise to separate the A X types from them, even though they are not decorated in Shang style.

So one finds a perplexing situation regarding the Northern dagger-axes. The seemingly most natural and least forced conclusion would be to declare A X and XI as *derivatives of Chinese prototypes,* which are superior in number, form, and workmanship. But immediately there arises a serious difficulty: the derivatives do not resemble the prototypes. And how should the strange fact be explained that only socketed types found their way to the steppe folk, and that none of the common shaft-ring types or tanged types ever traveled with them. Nor do they show the faintest trace of the common Shang décor. Hence, this hypothesis is unsatisfactory from the outset.[107]

The alternative explanation is to regard the Northern types as *native to the steppe.* There is ample material to support it: other weapons, small sculpture, bronze kettles, ceramics, in brief, all those obviously non-Chinese remains which occur there. The difficulty here is that dagger-axes were not a weapon typical of the nomads, though Tallgren held otherwise as regards the Scyths.[108] With a view to the Siberian types mentioned above (note 104), he suggested Western origins,[109] which — ever lurking or manifest in many of the Siberian forms — must be of course duly taken into account, however scanty the finds.

Another possible hypothesis, free from the obvious weak points of the others but also shaky, would be to ascribe to a *pre-Anyang stage* those alien-looking types which I have called Northern. It is true that no metal age site antedating Anyang has yet been discovered, but metalmaking must have started somewhere a little earlier. It is in this regard that the archaic types among the tanged axes must be considered as representing a pre-Anyang stage, as I suggested above (B Axes, sundry types). The shaft-hole types would then take their place in the picture: the long sockets were the initial stage, giving way to the shaft-rings and flat tangs which alone survived in the end. This neat explanation — though supported by the evidence of other archaic types (A I, II versus A VII, VIII) — leaves unanswered the problem of a well-developed type, the long-socket dagger-axe, standing at the beginning of an evolutionary series, for the long sockets could not have evolved from an indigenous stone tool environment as could a flat axe, a shouldered celt, or any metal tool molded after stone prototypes. I therefore leave the enigmatic A X and XI categories, and turn back to the axes in general.

The last chance to arrive at a sound theoretical explanation is to combine the questions which, put one by one, seem unanswerable.

The result of this typological investigation as presented in tabular form suggests that the ornamentation of most of the shaft-hole axes is not in Shang-Chou style. The inference must be that they are either *earlier or foreign.* Foreignness accounts more satisfactorily for two matters: (1) the absence of primitive types or, in other words, the "sudden appearance" in China of the manifold early socketed axe types; (2) the rarity and final disappearance of sockets in the Chinese weapon par excellence, the *ko,* indicating a deep-rooted predilection for the old, traditional practice of tang-hafting. But foreignness ought to be verified by valid earlier parallels from abroad; if possible, their way of transmission should be established. The results of an attempted verification are frail. Yet, with regard to some features, namely, the coincidence of sockets with rearward studs or with animal sculpture, a few Persian forms are extant, which give some background for those traits which are specifically inventions of metal-casters.

Thus, for the pertinent types (A I, II, III, IV) one may think of some Iranian strain which, passing first through Turkestan and southern Siberia, then farther east between the Altai and T'ien-shan ranges to Kansu and Suiyüan, finally — though distorted and disguised — no longer applicable to whole shapes, reached the Yellow River, where perhaps a still essentially Neolithic culture obtained. That strain must have mixed with elements from more northerly sources, as the Pontus and North Caspian, the Semipalatinsk and Kazakhstan steppes, and certainly also with some elements native to the Siberian forest zone with its hunter traditions of hoary age but still recognizable in metal tools of the Krasnoyarsk and Minusinsk regions.

The settled peoples in North-China soon were in possession of the secrets of the caster's art and in no time surpassed in skill their less gifted neighbors, who remained none the less formidable foes, with efficient equipment which came to them from developed centers in the Ancient East. The Chinese probably adhered to their own repertory of stone tools or stone weapons as far as it proved feasible to copy them in metal, for among the axes with tang there are types and shapes which are absent among the herdsmen's, while they closely resemble Neolithic stone axes. It may be that even the oval blades of the flamboyant A II axes were derived from stone or jade blades. Laufer's three-holed primitive shouldered axe of bronze (Fig. 27) is suggestive of being stone-derived, and I know of one round jade axe with two bore-holes, which when hafted as an axe (it could be hafted as a club as well) would be a fair model for an A II axe.[110] Tanged axes of B I type likewise give the impression of being descendants of stone blades with wide perforations.

As to the question of the origin of the dagger-axe, the presence of several socketed pieces (A X) and a few with shaft-holes (A XI) as against almost countless pieces with shaft-ring (A XII, *ch'ü*) or tang (*ko*) is intriguing. If those A X and XI types are Chinese, they must be forerunners of the common types, products of an experimental stage preceding the bulk of the Anyang products. If they are regarded as foreign, the long sockets of A X and the non-Anyang décor would be accounted for. But about all one can say is that the sockets in either case seem to belong to a foreign strain. And what about the blades? Siberia offers little in the way of analogies; in China, this particular blade form (Fig. 19) abounds. Are there stone archetypes in China, as in the case of some B types? Alas, the ingenuous question opens an abyss of incertitude and controversy. Stone blades of dagger shape are plentiful indeed (e.g., Cat. nos. 47, 48), but they are understandably absent in Neolithic context, since daggers had not been conceived in stone. It is probable that extant specimens of jade and marble or other stone blades of dagger-axe shape all were manufactured after metal forms, as were the marvelously chipped daggers of Egypt or Europe.[111] An errant sturdy *ko* of stone in Stockholm[112] and some conspicuous finds from Yang-t'ou-wa (South Manchuria)[113] are not sufficient proof to the contrary. Before the dagger of metal existed, it was made of bone rather than stone. There existed in China some kind of antler axe — precursor, in Europe, of some type of shaft-hole axe[114] — converging perhaps in the Bronze Age dagger-axe. In Kansu, Andersson has found a fine deer antler axe with asymmetrically cut tip in a Painted Pottery site; in the Lung-shan Black Pottery site (Shantung), similar antler axes came to light.[115] Still, in whatever direction one searches, there is no coherent picture of how things actually developed. Any simplification seems arbitrary, hazardous, and unconvincing.

Thus, this summary is rather a discussion of problems. Some light, I believe, is gained by the separation of most of the tanged types with their Shang-Chou décor and stone implement affinity (B group) from most of the shaft-hole types (A group) with their Northern décor.

## NOTES: CHAPTER I   AXES

[1] W. C. White, *Illus. London News,* April 20, 1935.

[2] S. Umehara, "Note on Bronze Tools and Weapons," p. 95, Fig. 3.

[3] White, *op. cit.*

[4] Zigzags: *Hsi Ch'ing Ku Chien,* ch. 37; axe with jingle, *ibid.*

[5] *Ibid.*

[6] The *Po Ku T'u* axe (26:50) presumably was the model after which an awkward jade "axe" in the *Ku Yü T'u Lu,* ch. 28 = Laufer, *Jade,* p. 41, Fig. 1, was copied. Typical misunderstanding on the carver's part: the shaft-rings of the bronze type have become senseless extensions at the base of the jade blade, except the lowermost one, which is clearly recognizable as a socket in the *Po Ku T'u* drawing.

[7] *Chin Shih So, Chin So,* ch. 2. Cf. Fr. Hirth, in *T'oung Pao,* 1896.

[8] *Li Chi, Ming T'ang Wei,* 10; tr. Couvreur, I, p. 731.

[9] The nine specimens of the axe type A III are:

1. Whorl-star on the blade, socket with disk and loop; Museum of Far Eastern Antiquities, Stockholm. Andersson, "Hunting Magic," Pl. X:2 = Fig. 3:A.

2. Whorl-star, socket with round stud and loop; Eumorfopoulos Collection, London. Yetts, *Catalogue,* no. A 146, Pl. LIX.

3. Whorl-star, socket with angular stud and loop; Liu T'i-chih Collection. *Shan Chai Chi Chin Lu,* 11:20; *Hsiao Chiao Ching Ko,* 10:106a.

4. Whorl-star, socket with tiger sculpture. Rubbing in *Tsun Ku Chai Ku Ping Ching,* vol. III = Fig. 5.

5. Concentric circles, socket with tiger sculpture; David-Weill Collection, Paris. O. Janse, in *BMFEA,* 2 (1930), Pl. III:2.

6. Concentric circles, socket with transversely grooved stud; Liu T'i-chih Collection. *Shan Chai Chi Chin Lu,* 11:31 =

*Hsiao Chiao Ching Ko,* 10:110b. This piece is inscribed *"tsu jih i."*

7. Plain blade, socket with angular stud and loop; Lu Mou-te Collection, Peking. Umehara, "Note on Bronze Tools," Pl. 4:2 = Fig. 3:B.

8. Sunken lozenges on the blade, socket without either stud or loop; Captain Mayer Collection, Stockholm. Andersson, "Selected Ordos Bronzes," Pl. 4:2.

9. Animals incised on the blade faces, two knobs at the back of the socket; Museum of Far Eastern Antiquities, Stockholm. Andersson, "Hunting Magic," Pl. 10:1a-b = Fig. 4.

[10] See note 9 above, specimen no. 9.

[11] Whorl-stars, on the other hand, do occur in Anyang: there are buttons of shell thus shaped, as, for instance, two three-pronged examples reproduced in H. G. Creel, *Birth of China,* Pl. VII.

[12] See note 9 above, specimen no. 5;

O. Janse, "Quelques antiquités chinoises d'un caractère Hallstattien."

[13] A gorgeously decorated axe — allied with type A VIII — purely Chinese in design, has a plastic animal on top of the socket; Umehara, *Shina Kodō Seika,* VII, 98 B = W. P. Yetts, *Burlington Mag.,* LIX (1931). Later examples are *ko* with shaft-tubes overtopped by plastic bird-figures, such as no. 75 of the Jannings Collection. In the presence of the abstract and intricate design of the first-mentioned axe, the alien character of the tiger sculptures on the two A III axes becomes manifest.

[14] *Meng Wei Ts'ao T'ang, chung:* 1-3; *Chou Chin Wen Ts'un,* 6/1:68-69. These pieces were in Lo Chen-yü's collection and were reproduced in various books, perhaps without having been subjected to a critical, direct examination. Offhand, one would think that a scholar of Lo Chen-yü's standing and experience could not well have been victimized by a forgery. My hesitation to trust the inscription of the *Shan Chai,* oval-bladed axe (note 9 above, no. 6) may be unfounded, in which case the Shang date of the A III axes would be epigraphically ascertained.

[15] *Chou Chin Wen Ts'un,* 6/1:70a.

[16] A comparable ornament, that is, lozenges combined with meander patterns, is on a long-socketed celt in the Kyoto University collections; Egami and Mizuno, *Inner Mongolia,* Pt. II, Pl. 35:4. The celt, however, appears to date from a later period than the Jannings axe no. 16.

[17] Janse, "Hallstattien," Pl. III:1; *Shuang Chien I Chi Chin, hsia:* 47.

[18] Umehara, "Note on Bronze Tools," Pl. IV:1.

[19] See the list under Cat. no. 16 below.

[20] *Shuang Chien I Chi Chin, hsia:* 47, text.

[21] Comparable decoration with a round hole in the blade, surrounded by a ring with radial strokes, occurs as far south as Tongking; see O. Janse, "Un Groupe de bronzes anciens," p. 115, Fig. 11, Pls. XII-XIII: dagger-axes with a long socket — if these obtuse-edged blades may be called "dagger-axes."

[22] F. R. Martin, *L'Age du Bronze au Musée de Minoussinsk,* Pl. 21:13, a dagger-handle. Egami and Mizuno, *Inner Mongolia,* Pt. II, Pl. 41:3-4, handles of knives; Pl. 42:2, handle of a knife. G. v. Merhart, *Bronzezeit am Jenissei,* Fig. 50 = Pl. VI:6, a socketed celt from Ladeiki near Krasnoyarsk; *ibid.,* Fig. 51, a socketed celt from Irbit (Perm). These two celts show rows of small knobs in an arrangement and size which agree perfectly with axes of A IV type. It is interesting to note that the Ladeiki celt, a local product, is rather isolated with regard to its décor of knobs, and that these knobs do not appear in Minusinsk celts either, while they are common in the East-Russian Ananino types. Cf. *ibid.,* p. 85.

The exception, a Chinese example, is a fine slender chisel(?) with a transverse double row of knobs below two superposed animal masks; *Yeh Chung P'ien Yü,* II, *shang:* 40.

[23] For the archaeological significance of the Hsün-hsien site, cf. Creel, *Birth of China,* p. 246 ff.; Yetts, "An Early Chou Bronze"; J. A. Pope, *Freer Catalogue,* p. 94.

[24] *Freer Catalogue,* Pl. 49, no. 34.13.

[25] A *ko* in the Freer Gallery with a circle inlaid with mother-of-pearl; *Freer Catalogue,* Pl. 48, no. 34.8. A kind of *ko* from the same set with a shallow circular depression, *ibid.,* Pl. 48; no. 34.5. Two *ko,* with a round depression in one case, concentric circles in the other; *Hsün-hsien I Ch'i,* fol. 20 and 21.

[26] A kind of knife-halberd belonging to the set in the Freer Gallery; *Freer Catalogue,* Pl. 47. K'ang Hou in all probability refers to Wei K'ang Shu 衛康叔, younger brother of Wu Wang, enfeoffed in Wei in the beginning of Ch'eng Wang's reign; cf. Chavannes, *Mém. hist.,* IV, p.

189 ff., and the discussions quoted above, note 23.

[27] Ch'u Te-i's statement is translated on p. 91 in the *Freer Catalogue.*

[28] B. Karlgren, "Some Weapons and Tools," Pl. 5, no. 31, Pl. 6, nos. 32, 33.

[29] *Ryojun Hakubutsukan Zuroku,* Pl. 9:1.

[30] "Hunting Magic," Pl. 10:6.

[31] *Chou Chin Wen Ts'un,* 6/2:113 b.

[32] *Hsüeh T'ang so ts'ang Ku Ch'i Wu T'u,* fol. 14 b.

[33] *Shan Chai Chi Chin Lu,* 11:25 = *Hsiao Chiao Ching Ko,* 10:107 b.

[34] Umehara, *Anyang Treasures,* Pl. 18: 5-7.

[35] *Ryojun Hakubutsukan Zuroku,* Pl. 9:2-3.

[36] Karlgren, "Some Weapons and Tools," nos. 28-30.

[37] Both Umehara and Karlgren classify their pertinent examples as Anyang finds.

[38] Egami and Mizuno, *Inner Mongolia,* Pt. II, Pl. 35:7.

[39] Harada and Komai, *Shina Koki Zukō,* Pt. I, Pl. 5:2.

[40] O. Sirén, *A History of Early Chinese Art,* I, Pl. 58 = Umehara, "Note on Bronze Tools," Pl. 4:7 = Harada and Komai, *Shina Koki Zukō,* Pt. I, Pl. 5:4.

[41] Umehara, *Shina Kodō Seika,* VII, Pl. 98 B = Yetts, in *Burlington Mag.,* LIX, p. 76 = *London Exhibition Cat.,* no. 130.

[42] Janse, "Un Groupe de bronzes anciens," p. 114, Fig. 10 (right). The bulging ring with an open center may not be a genuine "Northern" motif. It recalls eyes thus shaped in Chinese apotropaic masks and even weapons, such as, for instance, an axe with a pair of such "eyes" in *Yeh Chung P'ien Yü,* III, *hsia:* 11.

[43] H. Rivière *et al., Collection Osvald Sirén,* Pl. 4:18. Karlgren, "Some Weapons and Tools," nos. 35, 36, 37 (= Fig. 14 B). *Po Ku T'u Lu,* ch. 26:49. S. Umehara, "Note on Bronze Tools," Pl. 5:1 (Rutherston Collection), 5:2 (Franz

Hopp Museum, Budapest), 5:3 (Royal Ontario Museum, Toronto): three plain pieces. The shaft-ring is placed axially in the case of the Toronto and Rutherston specimens, which latter closely resembles the Sawyer axe (Fig. 14 A) in outline and proportions, while its blade is plain. An axe similar to both the Rutherston and Sawyer specimens, and like the latter decorated with three round bosses, is in the Mukden Museum—or was, when I visited it in December, 1940. An axe similar to Karlbeck's (Fig. 14 B) but with turquoise-incrusted heel is in the Asano Collection, Osaka; see Umehara, *Anyang Studies*, Pl. 45:1.

[44] It has always been felt that "Anyang" presupposes a long period of evolution, and recently Karlgren went so far as to say that "Anyang is sure to represent not the first phase but at least the second, possibly the third or fourth of the Chinese Bronze Age" ("Some Weapons and Tools," p. 104 note), without however pointing out what kind of materials there are in support of earlier stages.

[45] *Shan Chai Chi Chin Lu*, 11:27 and 26 (= Fig. 15 A); also in *Hsiao Chiao Ching Ko*, 10:109 a-b.

[46] O. Janse, "L'Empire des Steppes," Pl. V:13 = Fig. 15 B.

[47] *Tsun Ku Chai Ku Ping Ching*, vol. II.

[48] Umehara, "Note on Bronze Tools," Pl. 12:5 = Fig. 16 A.

[49] V. Griessmaier, *Sammlung Baron E. v. d. Heydt*, no. 80 = Fig. 16 B.

[50] Karlgren, "Some Weapons and Tools," no. 204.

[51] *Ibid.*, no. 205 = Fig. 17.

[52] "Hunting Magic," Pl. 10:3 (p. 241) = Fig. 18.

[53] A small hatchet without splint-hole or slots is in the Harbin Museum. It has a perforation with a raised margin in the middle of the blade; the corners of the shoulders are filled with three knobs on either side; below the perforation there is a

transverse band from which three pointed ribs extend to the cutting edge. The cutting edge is a little broader than the butt.

[54] Umehara, "Note on Bronze Tools," Pl. 5:4 (drawing; no indication regarding the owner of the piece) = Fig. 20.

[55] An asymmetrical variant in *Ch'ih An Ts'ang Chin*, 35, has a *ya-hsing*-framed inscription on its rather broad heel, purporting to be of Yin age. The inscription in the cross-cartouche probably reads *yin* 尹, not *fu* 父 as proposed in that catalogue.

Another variant with an inscription is the no. 19 in this collection, a piece which again on account of some typological properties proves to be later than the basic B I types.

[56] *Yeh Chung P'ien Yü*, II, *hsia:* 22 = Karlgren, "Some Weapons and Tools," no. 54. The piece is slightly asymmetrical and is provided with a long stop-ridge between the shoulder-slits. Karlgren's remark: "Big round hole in the blade, probably for some precious stone" (p. 105) almost touches the truth, for there is actually a jade ring let in that big hole. This fine specimen found its way, if I remember correctly, into the Museum für Asiatische Kunst in Bamberg.

[57] Laufer, *Jade*, p. 74, Fig. 12.

[58] Umehara, "Note on Bronze Tools," Pl. 4:3.

[59] Laufer, *Jade*, p. 74 ff. Shouldered celts from China having been unknown then, Laufer refers to Pegu, Cambodia, Central India, where such celts widely occur. In 1931, Menghin still had to base himself mainly on these materials to which he added, as a remarkable novelty, finds from Korea; cf. *Weltgeschichte der Steinzeit*, p. 297. In the meantime, China and its northern borderlands have yielded further material.

Jehol: I. Yawata, *Contribution to the Prehistoric Archaeology of Southern Jehol*, Fig. 9; T'ung Chu-ch'en, in *Li-shih yü K'ao-ku*, I (Mukden, 1946), Pl. I:21. A

peculiar type with broad, short, almost oval blade with well-worked tang (a hoe?) was published by E. Licent, who christened that piece "hallebarde"; provenance: Hata, Jehol; Licent, *Les Collections néolithiques du Musée Hoangho Paiho de Tientsin*, Pl. 41:5 = P. Teilhard de Chardin and Pei Wen-chung, *Le Néolithique de la Chine*, p. 40, Fig. 22.

Shansi: C. W. Bishop, *The Neolithic Age in Northern China*, Pl. 3:5.

Honan: Andersson, in *BMFEA*, 15, Pl. 24.

S. Manchuria: *Select Specimens of Antiquities in the Archaeological Seminary, Tokyo Imp. University*, no. V (1931), Pl. 9.

Sino-Mongolian borderland: characteristic types of very broad axes, reproduced by Andersson in *BMFEA*, 15, Pl. 25, cf. p. 58.

Thus, as regards possible stone prototypes, there is no need to look for materials from far outside China.

[60] See, for instance, the jade blades of *ko* and spearhead types in the Jannings Collection, Cat. nos. 24, 47, 48.

[61] *Ryojun Hakubutsukan Zuroku*, Pl. 8:6, axe decorated with a trapezium filled with rows of small knobs. *Shan Chai Chi Chin Lu*, 11:29-30, blade with longitudinal furrows. *Chou Chin Wen Ts'un*, 6/2:116 a-b, two plain axes with round holes in the blades. Umehara, *Anyang Treasures*, Pl. 19:1, plain blade with wide perforation and particularly broad tang.

[62] *Huang Chün, Tsun Ku Chai Ku Ping Ching*, vol. III.

[63] Umehara, "Note on Bronze Tools," Pl. 4:5. A very similar axe in *Chou Chin Wen Ts'un*, 6/2:117; the interpretation of the inscription *ibid.* v° is misleading.

[64] Umehara, "Note on Bronze Tools," Pls. 5:10 and 6:2.

[65] See *ibid.*, Pl. 6; O. Kümmel, *Jörg Trübner zum Gedächtnis*, Pls. 23, 24.

[66] *Yeh Chung P'ien Yü*, III, *hsia:* 2 = *Yen K'u Chi Chin, hsia:* 1.

[67] *Yeh Chung P'ien Yü,* I, *hsia:* 10 b = Karlgren, "Some Weapons and Tools," no. 56.

[68] Umehara, *Anyang Treasures,* Pl. 24: 1.

[69] W. Cohn, "Eine frühe Hellebarden-klinge" (*OZ,* 1934, Pl. 34) = *London Exhibition Catalogue,* no. 267 = Karlgren, "Some Weapons and Tools," no. 55. Cohn as well as Karlgren is inclined to place this axe in the Shang period.

[69a] Sammlung Lochow. *Chinesische Bronzen,* II, no. 15.

[70] *London Exhibition Catalogue,* no. 197 = *Commemorative Catalogue,* Pl. 18. See *infra,* Cat. no. 13, Fig. 72.

[71] de Groot, *Religious System of China,* II, pp. 721 ff.; Maspero, *La Chine antique,* p. 214 f.; C. Bishop, "The Rise of Civilization in China with Reference to Its Geographical Aspects," p. 618; H. G. Creel, *Studies in Early Chinese Culture,* p. 214 ff.; *idem, Birth of China,* p. 204 ff.; A. Waley, *The Way and Its Power,* p. 85; L. C. Goodrich, *A Short History of the Chinese People,* p. 15; W. Eberhard, "Lokalkulturen im alten China," I, 74 f.

[72] There are many *t'ao-t'ieh* representations, on the other hand, in which the same C forms must be interpreted as horns, the ears being unmistakably indicated below them.

[73] Karlgren, "Some Weapons and Tools," nos. 41, 42.

[74] *Yen K'u Chi Chin, hsia:* 2. The author and collector, Liang Shang-ch'un, states that that axe dates from the beginning of the Chou dynasty and that it had been unearthed at Anyang in 1940. Most uncommon, an incised or cast character on the tip of the *nei* interferes with the animal mask which occupies the *nei;* the character intersects the left ear of that mask. Stylistically, the axe actually belongs to Western Chou age.

[75] Karlgren, "Some Weapons and Tools," p. 104, no. 38. Karlgren refers to a four-legged *Ting, Shang Chou I Ch'i T'ung K'ao,* Fig. 129. I doubt that this

*Ting* is of Shang age, as Jung Keng proposes, *ibid.,* I, p. 307, no. 133. The décor of two snakes uniting in one head occurs in Early Chou bronzes, e.g., the *Fang I* in the Freer Gallery (*Freer Catalogue,* Pl. 21). Moreover, the round bosses — again combined with that snake-motif — are found on another, very similar four-legged *Ting* with Chou inscription (*Shan Chai Chi Chin T'u Lu,* 43-44; cf. Karlgren, "New Studies," p. 23 and Pl. 29, no. 26: the *Tso-ts'e Ta Ting,* of Chou I age).

[76] The second square *Ting* mentioned in note 75.

[77] As, for instance, in the famous *Kuei* of the Malcolm Collection, London; Yetts, "An Early Chinese Bronze" = *Shang Chou I Ch'i T'ung K'ao,* Fig. 259.

[78] Cf. Bachhofer, *A Short History of Chinese Art,* p. 36.

[79] Umehara, "Note on Bronze Tools," Pls. 4: 6, 5: 8.

[80] *Tsun Ku Chai Ku Ping Ching,* vol. III.

[81] Umehara, "Note on Bronze Tools," p. 96.

[82] Laufer, *Jade,* p. 75, Fig. 13, an outline drawing which says nothing about the strength, the height of the relieved parts, or other details.

[83] O. Karlbeck, "Notes on the Archaeology of China," p. 201.

[84] Cp. chapter III, Dagger-axes, category III.

[85] R. Dussaud, "Haches à douille de type asiatique," Pl. 42: 2 and 1 = Figs. 29 and 30. A later date, viz., around 1000 B.C., was proposed for the long-socketed axe (Fig. 30) by E. Dullo, "Die kaukasischen Äxte der Bronzezeit," p. 116f.

[86] Assur, stratum E; Berlin Museum für Vor- und Frühgeschichte. Cf. *ibid.,* p. 104. This axe is typologically earlier than that from Nihavand.

[87] Representations on seal cylinders; cf. *ibid.,* p. 101. An actual specimen of an axe with three spikes and a pick-like blade, ascribed to the IIIrd millennium B.C., was found in Ur: *ibid.,* Fig. 10: 7.

[88] An axe from Nihavand with seven spikes and pertaining shaft-foot mounting; R. Dussaud, "Haches à douille," p. 249, Fig. 7.

[89] Cf. G. Nioradze, in *ESA,* VII, Figs. 3 a-c: three Georgian Amazon axes, c. 10th to 8th cent. B.C. — F. Hančar, in *ESA,* IX, Fig. 16 e. — W. M. Flinders Petrie, *Tools and Weapons,* Pl. A VI: 172. — E. Dullo, "Die kaukasischen Äxte der Bronzezeit," Fig. 6: 1-3.

[90] Dullo, *ibid.,* Fig. 6: 3.

[91] J. de Morgan, *L'Humanité préhistorique,* p. 127, Fig. 54: 2. This axe evidently is a primitive forerunner of the Syrian axe mentioned in note 92 below.

[92] *British Mus. Quart.,* IV, 4 (1930), Pl. 40 a = R. Dussaud, "Haches à douille de type asiatique," p. 253, Fig. 13. This beautiful axe with a confronted pair of lions, half in relief, half in the round, in recumbent position on the socket, dates from before 1500 B.C. The animal décor connects it with Persian types such as listed in note 98 below.

[93] The question of the origins of the round-bladed axes with two holes at the side of the median, of the type illustrated in Fig. 2 B, demands a special investigation that cannot be undertaken here. The pertinent examples from Persia and Susa quoted in notes 91 and 92 do not represent all the known varieties from Hither Asia. The axe type with blade-holes occurs early in Mesopotamia; cf. L. Woolley, *Ur Excavations,* vol. II, *The Royal Cemetery,* Pl. 224 U. 9687. W. M. Flinders Petrie, *Tools and Weapons,* Pl. 74: 171, brings a pertinent specimen from Central Syria, which instead of a shaft-tube has a narrow shaft-ring, the neck of which is prolonged so as to attain the length of the blade width; at the back it is provided with a round stud. Without its peculiarly prolonged neck, the piece would rather closely resemble the Amazon axe types referred to in note 89 above; Petrie (*ibid.,* p. 10) thinks that there is a connection with the Amazon axes. Dus-

saud, on account of a Phoenician character inscribed on the Syrian example, dates it "13th c. B.C."; cf. *Syria,* XI, p. 249, n. 1. With reference to Chinese designs I wish to draw attention to a detail of that Syrian axe: the blade wings form open angles to lean on the wooden shaft when it is inserted. This device is not unknown in China; cp. a dagger-axe of A XII type with descending lower edge fitted with superposed wings as shaft-supports, *Yen K'u Chi Chin, hsia:* 36, no. 50.

The *Chin Shih So* (*Chin So,* ch. 2) contains another interesting specimen of round-edged shaft-hole axe, acquired at Loyang in 1841, illustrated for the read-

er's convenience. I am unable to propose a date for this piece, which is also depicted in Laufer's *Jade,* p. 44, Fig. 5, and erroneously taken for a tanged hatchet by Laufer. What in the first place interests us here is an undeniable affinity to the Amazon axes from Transcaucasia and the earlier Mesopotamian, Iranian, or Syrian types with two blade-holes which preceded them.

[94] L. Speleers, in *Bull. Musées Royaux d'Art et d'Histoire,* May, 1933, p. 64, Fig. 15.

[95] E. Dullo, "Die kaukasischen Äxte der Bronzezeit," p. 114.

[96] A. U. Pope, *A Survey of Persian Art,* IV, Pl. 51 D. The date there given is IInd to Ist millennium B.C.

[97] L. Speleers, "Nos nouveaux bronzes perses," p. 61, Fig. 8: "Portant une dédicace au nom de Gimilsin, roi d'Ur (2219-2211), sa date ne fait aucune doute." The years of his reign, according to Ed. Meyer,

*Geschichte des Altertums,* I, 2, par. 415, would have been 2386 or 2384-2378 B.C.

[98] Van (Armenia): axe of early shape with strongly slanting lower mouth of the socket, on which in relief and full-round is a lion attacked by a dog. *British Museum, Guide Ant. Bronze Age* (1920), p. 176, Fig. 187 = Rostovtzeff, *Iranians and Greeks in South Russia,* Pl. 11 e = Dussaud, in *Syria,* XI, p. 250, Fig. 8. IInd millennium B.C.

Hamadan-Ecbatana (NW. Persia): axe with winged lion in relief, the fore part of the beast with its head turned downward forming the socket. *British Museum, Guide,* p. 176, Fig. 188 = Rostovtzeff, *op. cit.,* Pl. 11 b. Achaemenid.

Oxus Treasure: axe with complicated configuration of three animals, partly in relief, partly forming the body of the blade itself.

Rostovtzeff, *op. cit.,* Pl. 11 = Sirén, *History of Early Chinese Art,* II, Pl. 19 D. — Obviously developed from types such as the foregoing.

Luristan: axe with lion figure in relief on the socket and the base of the blade. David-Weill Collection. A. U. Pope, *A Survey of Persian Art,* IV, Pl. 52 C. — Later than the Van axe, but earlier than the Hamadan axe. Probably latter half of the IInd millennium.

Luristan: fragment of an axe-halberd with iron blade and bronze socket with the figure of a crouching lion. Brussels. *Bull. Musées Royaux,* III, 3 (1931), p. 82, Fig. 13. First half of the Ist millennium B.C.

[99] L. Speleers, "Nos nouveaux bronzes perses," p. 63, Fig. 14.

[100] C. W. Bishop, "The Rise of Civilization in China with Reference to Its Geographical Aspects," p. 625.

[101] Stele of Naram-Sin, first half of IIIrd millennium: one of the king's weapons. Cf. L. Delaporte, *Mesopotamia,* p. 69 and p. 31, Fig. 4. Ur: IIIrd millennium (?), pick with three spikes at rear; Dullo, "Die kaukasischen Äxte der Bronze-

zeit," Fig. 10:7; cf. Fig. 10:8. Nihavand, IInd millennium: a pick almost identical with that from Ur; *ibid.*, Fig. 12:12. Luristan, late IInd millennium (?): picks of a shape similar to those from Ur and Nihavand, save that they have a vertical crest and a strong horizontal process at the back of the socket; Speleers, "Nos nouveaux bronzes perses," in *Bull. Mus. Royaux,* IV, 3, Fig. 12: A, B, C. A piece with transverse edge — adze-shaped: *ibid.*, Fig. 13 A.

[102] F. R. Martin, *L'Age du Bronze au Musée de Minoussinsk,* Pl. 8; Tallgren, *Collection Tovostine,* Pl. VI: 5 and 10, the latter specimen being of iron.

[103] M. Loehr, "Chinesische Pickeläxte." A rare type of shaft-hole pick of different shape does occur in China: *Shan Chai Chi Chin Lu,* 10:44, a specimen with early Chou inscription *"hou* 侯*."*

[104] A. M. Tallgren, "Svärdstavar från Ural och Sibirien," Fig. 6: Minusinsk, 2 and 4: Tomsk, 3: Tobolsk; Fig. 4 = *idem, Coll. Tovostine,* p. 50, Fig. 50. The lugs at the rear of the West-Siberian examples are also known in Minusinsk types, e.g., a socketed axe with a straight, wedge-shaped blade recalling A IV and Va axes, but apparently isolated in Minusinsk. See F. R. Martin, *L'Age du Bronze au Musée de Minoussinsk,* Pl. 7:2 = Karlgren, "Some Weapons and Tools," Pl. 34, no. 191.

[105] J. R. Aspelin, *Antiquités du Nord Finno-Ougrien,* p. 60, Fig. 239.

[106] V. G. Childe, *The Most Ancient East,* p. 178, Fig. 74 a = Fig. 35.

[107] It is the conclusion drawn by Karlgren, "Some Weapons and Tools," *passim.*

[108] "Je me figure en effet que l'arme à forme de pic est devenue de bonne heure nationale chez les Scythes, et sous les influences grècques." Tallgren, *Coll. Tovostine,* p. 51.

[109] *Ibid.,* p. 50.

[110] Unpublished. E. A. Voretzsch Collection, Colmberg. The piece strongly resembles greenstone axe-clubs of New Caledonia, but was acquired by Dr. Voretzsch in China, as a Chinese artifact.

[111] Peake and Fleure, *Priests and Kings,* Fig. 1; *idem, The Way of the Sea,* Fig. 48 d. — M. C. Burkitt, *Our Early Ancestors,* p. 113, Pl. 12:1, 3.

[112] Andersson, "An Early Chinese Culture," Pl. V:1 = Karlgren, "Some Weapons and Tools," Pl. 40:250. Karlgren discusses that stone tool, *ibid.,* p. 133 f., with reference to the view held by C. W. Bishop and H. G. Creel that it is a stone reproduction of a metal form; Karlgren says that that is a mere guess. To invalidate it, he points out that the model after which that stone tool has been made cannot be shown. The same, however, then holds true for the metal blades as well, the extant specimens of which are not any closer to the supposed prototypes in stone. Thus, Karlgren gives no cogent proof either. I hold with Creel and Bishop. The stone tool makes the impression of a typical product of the transitional stage between the Neolithic and Early Metal ages.

[113] T. Kanazeki *et al., Yang-T'eou-Wa,* Pls. 12:1-2; 45:1, 2, 4, 6; 58:6-7. This site near Port Arthur, excavated in 1933, yielded a series of lancet-shaped, mostly rhomboid blades with more or less narrowing butt, perforated with double-conical bore-hole. They are well ground but of lesser fineness than Anyang pieces. It is a material which must be seriously considered as possibly genuine stone shapes in dagger form. The authors, however, and rightly I think, are very cautious and admit that they are at a loss to determine whether those stone daggers were made after stone or bronze models, either of which would have come from the Hwang-ho region; *ibid.,* p. 78.

[114] Cf. V. G. Childe, *The Dawn of European Civilization,* Figs. 5 (Lyngby axe) and 7 (Ertebølle antler axes). — L. v. Marton, "Dolchstäbe aus Ungarn," Fig. 3:2 (Kestölc).

[115] Andersson, "The Site of Chu Chia Chai," Pl. 13:1. — Lung-shan: *Ch'eng-Tzu-Yai,* Pls. 48:5, 48 a:5.

# SPEARHEADS

*Chapter II*

As in the case of other bronze weapons, China's soil has thus far not yielded any really primitive spearheads — those types with more or less leaf-shaped blades, flat or thickened, with or without tang. There is not one example of the kind, so common in the Near East, which could be taken for a dagger as well as a spearhead, depending on the way the piece was hafted. All of the numerous finds of Chinese Bronze Age spearheads show socketed types. This fact is unquestionably significant.

There is, however, a considerable wealth of types among the materials from the IInd millennium B.C. Comparing them, one can even establish a relative sequence that goes back, with the earliest of them, as far as the thirteenth century — there is no knowledge of spearheads older than those from the Yin sites near Anyang.

The widest divergence in Anyang types is illustrated by Figs. 36 A and 36 E. The first has a relatively small leaf-shaped blade and a long, round, tapering socket which goes through to the tip and is provided with two loops above the mouth of the socket. In the second one the blade is relatively large, and the edges are drawn downward as lateral flanges along the shaft-tube so as to include the two loops, which here actually are two holes in the prolonged edges; the socket is much shorter and stops below the center of the blade, which is marked by a sunken field repeating the outline of the blade. These differences make it obvious that a development has taken place, leading from the unsophisticated structure of the former head with its stem and blade being clearly separable entities, to the much more differentiated type Fig. 36 E with its several parts so interdependent that it is impossible to say exactly where the one ends and the other begins, the whole now being a homogeneous unit.

Another change that can be observed is the replacement of the round socket by a rhombic or squarish one. Angular sockets are, of course, no *sine qua non* in the later types,[1] but it seems that they do not occur in the early, or earliest, spearheads, and may thus be

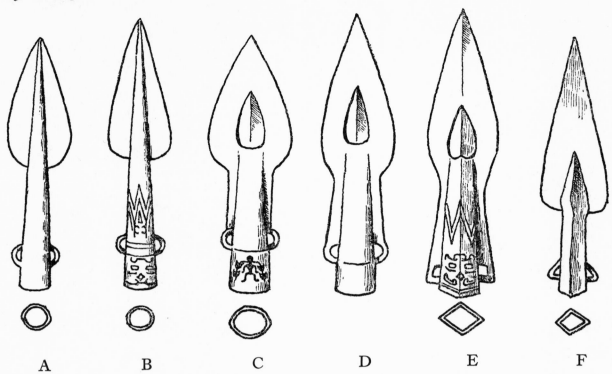

A     B     C     D     E     F

Fig. 36: *Various types of Shang spearheads.*

A — Kyoto, Yūrinkan; after Umehara. B — Academia Sinica; after Li Chi. C — unpublished specimen from the author's collection. D — Kyoto, Yūrinkan; after Umehara. E — Jannings Collection, no. 26. F — formerly in the possession of Huang Chün; after *Yeh Chung P'ien Yü* II (A ca. 1/3, B — F ca. 3/10).

taken as an additional criterion. The very archaic-looking type Fig. 36: F, for the same reason, cannot be grouped with the early specimens, and this can be verified by the following arguments.

The three examples Fig. 36: C, D, E form a self-evident sequence that teaches us something. They show the gradual unfolding of the lateral flanges or counterforts, although perhaps not in the earliest stage. In the beginning, the flanges just meet the loops without infringing on their formal independence and thus revealing themselves as a new element. In Fig. 36: D, they meet the loops so as to form a coherent outline with them, widening to the extent needed. Eventually, in 36: E, the loops as such have gone and are replaced by angular holes in the flanges. These have now become dominant also in that they affect the outline of the blade itself: looking back to 36: C, a certain abruptness in the silhouette there, and an increase in smoothness, fluidity, and length here are quite obvious.

A detail worthy of attention is the way the loops are fashioned in Fig. 36: F, forming triangles rather than semicircles. Fig. 36: E, which has rough, rectangular holes, shows that the round loops gave way to cornered ones, which were usually triangular. The probable reason is this: the flanges, once having taken in the loops, end in an acute angle with horizontal base (Fig. 37). The outline thus given no longer harmonizes with rounded orifices. Consequently they were cut so that they fitted in, repeating the outer angle of the flanges, but curved back to the socket-wall lest the opening should become too long. The lance-head Fig. 36: F, while not flanged, shows loops exactly shaped after the pattern just described. It is a form which can have been derived only from types such as Fig. 37. Hence, the seemingly archaic type 36: F must be later than the types 36: C, D, E.

Whether Fig. 36: A is an older type than the rest is a question that cannot definitely be answered yet. Still, the fact remains that its blade form is different not only from any of the types 36: C-E, but also from the specimen 36: B, which otherwise is very similar. The silhouette of 36: B, nearing a triangle, is more common[2] than that of 36: A, but this latter is not quite isolated either. There was excavated in Anyang a type which also has a leaf-shaped blade; it shows a strong ridge, and its lower part apparently is strengthened by a roof-shaped reinforcement (Fig. 38: B). Li Chi published two specimens of this type without assigning a specific date to them.[3] Another interesting spearhead with leaf-blade is contained in Lo Chen-yü's *San Tai Chi Chin Wen Ts'un* (20:34a). It has a peculiar feature in that the loops are placed quite low, at the very mouth of the socket (Fig. 38: A). The piece gives the impression of being even more primitive than the types 36: A and 38: B.

To return once more to Fig. 36: B with its approximately triangular blade, it may not be overlooked that it bears a décor which is almost identical with that of 36: E. It would be safe to assume, therefore, that both belong to the same period, although the former seems to represent a type which existed before the latter. The type may have survived after the invention of the spearheads with lateral counterforts; perhaps they served different purposes, as weapons used by chariot fighters, foot soldiers, or hunters. Further evidence is required, then, to place the type 36: B.

None of the Shang spearheads listed is datable, unless by typological methods which will not lead far in terms of years or centuries. Palaeography may become helpful one day, when developed into a subtler instrument of research. It is here sufficient to point to the different script styles in the examples Fig. 36: C and F,[4] which tend to confirm their relative places. In the case of 36: F, moreover, two *ko* with the same inscription are known.[5] These *ko* are not very early pieces, resembling as they do specimen no. 64 attributed to the end of the Shang or the beginning of the Chou dynasty. The *ko* are another argument in favor of the relative late date of the type 36: F. But even for the type 36: E (= Cat. no. 26), the Shang date, though not improbable, is by no means certain.

## THE QUESTION OF THE ORIGINS

Before passing on to a short discussion of some typical Chou forms of spearheads, one may give a thought to the question of what the small assembly of specimens here presented in drawings means. What can they tell about China's Bronze Age?

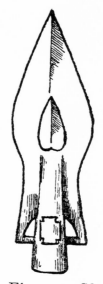

Fig. 37: *Shang spearhead.*
After *Shuang Chien I Chi Chin T'u Lu* (ca. 1/4).

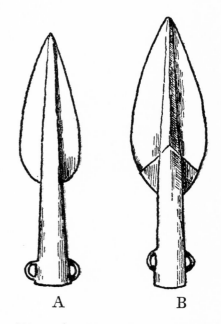

A                    B

Fig. 38: *Two Shang spearheads.*

A — After Lo Chen-yü. B — Academia Sinica; after Li Chi (ca. 1/3).

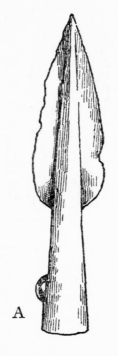

A

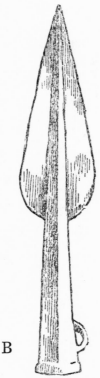

B

Fig. 39: *Two spearheads from Pokrovsk (lower Volga).*

After Rykov (2/5).

Li Chi, in a paper on five types of Yin-hsü bronze tools, has advanced the idea that the Shang spearheads may have been brought to China from abroad. He based this on the fact that past evolutionary processes are "clearly written" in the physiognomy of these spearheads and that these processes are not traceable within China. He even alludes to Britain as the ultimate source of socketed spearheads with loops.[6] Two pieces from North-China, which Li Chi, for lack of more convincing material, suggests should be regarded as possibly autochthonous prototypes — namely, a Yang-shao stone point and a tanged bronze dagger — are in fact irrelevant.[7] W. C. White also holds that the Shang spears were "not probably indigenous to China."[8] This conclusion seems perfectly natural. The absence in China, as mentioned above, of truly primitive forerunners makes it difficult not to argue so. The only way out would be to assume that socketed blades were an *ad hoc* invention of the Shang, or that there did exist more primitive forms one somehow never chanced to find: assumptions that lead nowhere. Spontaneous invention of the socketed tool would still require knowledge of an advanced casting technique and an acquaintance with valve molds, and to suppose that these technical contrivances should have been acquired without some precognition of the products made in them would seem wholly ill-advised.

There are, on the other hand, no finds reported from adjacent regions which could serve to establish satisfactorily a source for the spearhead and a route by which it could have reached China. In contrast to other tools (knives, daggers, socketed celts), spearheads are conspicuously rare among the Ordos-Suiyüan and Minusinsk materials, and Karlgren justly observed that the spearheads play a very modest role in the cultural remains of the nomads.[9] The few specimens known from there, moreover, do not compare favorably with what we have from China.[10] It is only as far west as South Russia, Eastern Russia, and West Siberia that spearheads were found which can be paralleled with Chinese ones.

The most striking instances of which I know are specimens unearthed near Pokrovsk (Lower Volga) from tombs of Khvalynsk culture. They resemble Shang types in their blade forms, their long stems of roundish or rhombic section, and their whole proportion, but differ in that they have only one eyelet (Fig. 39).[11] The Pokrovsk barrows also contained a more slender head with a slitted socket and two pin-holes instead of loops.[12] Both types are current in the Seima cemeteries (Central Russia),[13] while the first one recurs in a variant, also known from Seima, in one of the two silver lances of the hoard find from Borodino (Bessarabia).[14] In Tomsk (West Siberia), a mold for a spearhead similar to the Borodino piece was found, which on the reverse side is arranged for casting socketed celts of Seima design (Fig. 67).[15] Celts of this design spread eastward to Minusinsk.[16] Thus, a secondary relation of the Russian spearheads just mentioned with Central Siberia is established. But there is also a primary one.

The second spear-blade from Borodino has a peculiar trait in the way the socket is trifurcated, forming two small, short prongs between which the main one rises and extends into the median ridge. Regarding this particular type, Tallgren has stated: "*En Ukraine, on ne peut rattacher à ce type qu'une lance en argent du trésor de Borodino. La trouvaille de Seima contient des lances semblables, et on en trouve aussi à Perm, dans la Sibérie Occidentale, et dans les steppes de Minoussinsk.*"[17]

Undeniably one has to do here with a well-interconnected group of remains from approximately contemporaneous cultures or local offshoots of one culture — Seima, Borodino, Pokrovsk — linked with the Yenisei through the Andronovo culture in Kazakhstan and Southern Siberia, and datable no later, I think, than around the middle of the IInd millennium B.C.[18] The fact that these spearheads on their way east were accompanied by socketed celts of Seima style — which spread to Minusinsk and, although no longer in identical shapes, to the Ordos region and North-China — is significant in that the Shang spearheads, in consequence, are not isolated. This fact suggests that the Shang spearheads were connected with the Russo-Siberian group.

Greater wealth and refinement on the Chinese side, it is true, are opposed to an explanation that implies Siberian priority. But, if China were the giver, should not some reflection of specifically Chinese forms or ornaments reasonably be expected to have appeared among the Siberian finds? Up to the present, none has been observed. Hence one faces here in a small sector a phenomenon as puzzling as that of the Chinese Neolithic painted ceramics being superior to most of the West Asian and Black Earth painted potteries, with which they inevitably must be linked. Archaic stages seem not to be represented in China. These wares appear "suddenly," as if transplanted from a foreign ground, and yet display unrivaled workmanship. And the very same phenomenon is seen in the knives of the Shang and, in some way, in their bronzes in general.

CHOU SPEARHEADS

To draw a coherent picture of the typological changes during the Ist millennium B.C. is, for lack of materials as well as reliable data, still impossible.

In the Chou I period, types such as Fig. 36 E and Fig. 37 lingered on. It is therefore not easy to decide whether 36 E (Cat. no. 26) is of Shang or Chou I age, while its *t'ao-t'ieh* décor at least precludes a date later than the tenth century.[19] There are two further specimens, however, the Chou date of which cannot be questioned. One, formerly in Lo Chen-yü's collection, bears a Western Chou inscription in the almond-shaped middle field of the blade.[20] The other has a décor of broad, angular meanders in low relief, covering the flanges and the lower part of the blade, rudely cutting through it horizontally on a level with the top of the rhombic socket, which moreover shows a *ya-hsing*-framed inscription. This décor is probably not earlier than Late Western Chou, and definitely is not Shang, as asserted by the author of the *Ch'ih An Ts'ang Chin*.[21]

Something new turns up in a meagerly represented category of very slender blades with long, oval shaft-tubes not provided with loops. It appears as though this category was derived from the types just mentioned, because it retains the almond-shaped field in the blade, whereas counterforts and eyelets have disappeared. The almond-shaped contour, however, has undergone a change, becoming heart-shaped or arrow-shaped, and finally cut open at the base. Thus were developed the inward bent hooks and, eventually, spirals, as in the Catalogue no. 25 piece, which, because of its flanges, is a suggestive, if baffling, eccentric. Fig. 40 shows several variants of this category, just enough to permit of theorizing about the evolutionary process dimly revealed by them, but too few in number to be suited for typological treatment.

At any rate, these few examples comprise so many contradictory elements that without a further supply of allied specimens there is little hope of proper assessment. The type Fig. 40 A, in spite of the volute design which theoretically is farther away from the almond-shaped field, may be earlier than the other three pieces in that it has the lateral counterforts, the element linking it with Shang and Early Chou varieties. As to the socket, which is round in this case and thus differs from the prevailing rhombic ones of those Early Chou varieties, a similar specimen in the Tuan Fang Collection[22] proves to be a valuable supplement; it not only has a squarish socket but also more hooklike prongs, nearing the forms shown in Fig. 40 B, C. The Tuan Fang specimen, moreover, is quite reassuring with regard to actual variations within one special, very characteristic type, Fig. 40 A, distinguished by its heaviness and solidity and somewhat clumsy proportions.

The examples Fig. 40 B, C, D are all of lighter build, and their elongated silhouettes make it obvious that they form a category of their own. The most conspicuous feature in them is the absence of flanges and loops. As to the blades, B and C resemble each other closely, while D stands apart not only on account of its barbed blade with an arrowhead-shaped field, but also because of the concave cut of its socket, a feature which became essential only in Eastern Chou and later types. However, D (Cat. no. 27) cannot be that late, for except for this detail it has nothing at all in common with those later fashions. The Ramet specimen (40 C) is of importance in that its socket is decorated. Unfortunately, the piece — known by the Burlington House Exhibition of 1935, where it was given too late a date (Warring States) — has never been adequately published; I am unable, therefore, to ascribe to it a more exact date which would be of use in arranging the present group, and I wish to leave open the question of the accurate chronological relationship between them. As to the beginnings of these slender javelin types, Chou I would seem

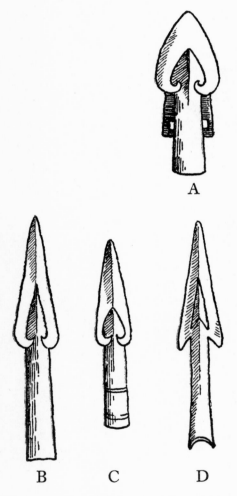

Fig. 40: *Spearheads of Western Chou age.*

A — Jannings Collection, no. 25. B — Yūrin-kan, Kyoto; after Umehara. C — Paris, Collection Mme Ramet; London Exhibition no. 176. D — Jannings Collection no. 27 (ca. 1/4).

an appropriate period if one keeps in mind that the flanged type preceding them was then still in use. A specimen in a Peking collection
may be adduced here since it bears on the chronological issue. It is
inscribed with two characters regarded as Shang by the owner.[23]
This specimen, evidently akin on the whole to my series, adds a new
trait in that it lacks the distinctive design of the hooked prongs below
the almond-shaped field. It is typologically earlier in this respect,
and the outline of its blade even recalls the approximately triangular
blades of Shang age, such as Fig. 36 B and F. Of slender proportions like Fig. 40 B, C, D, and likewise devoid of loops, this piece
dates perhaps from the close of the Shang-Yin dynasty, and at any
rate antedates, as a type, the three other examples.

As to the spearheads of Eastern Chou times, only a glimpse of
their evolution can be presented to the reader. The few available
specimens are commonly devoid of chronological pointers, and the
forms tend to become more and more standardized. The resulting
monotonousness makes them unpromising for typological purposes,
but a chiefly typological approach is still necessary for lack of excavations, closed finds, and epigraphical *points d'appui*.

Decoration seems to become more rare. The production of spearheads may have increased with the growing population and size of
the standing armies, and mass fabrication coupled with a demand for
effective and soberly designed — if elegant — weapons may have led
to decrease in ornamentation. Even so, some unobtrusive adornment
still is found in the finer pieces and provides some clue to their order
on stylistic grounds.

The basic shape remains the same as in Western Chou times (Fig.
40 B, C, D) : a very slender blade combined with a long tube that
usually has no loops. A specimen in Liu T'i-chih's collection with a
*ya-hsing*-framed one-character inscription (Western Chou) perhaps
gives a hint of how shapes developed. The blade is comparatively
long and looks as though the inward-bent prongs had been straightened out, joining the tube a little lower than in previous types.[24]
Blade and socket are no longer contrasted; the structure moves further toward greater unity. In the piece just mentioned a division is
still discernible in that the socket penetrates visibly into the body of
the blade.

In a type such as Fig. 41 A — an exceedingly slender ogival head
with a median ridge stopping short below the point where the edges
end — blade and socket have coalesced into one body. This body
flattens and widens above the socket proper and so forms edges; it
tapers at the tip to form a point. It is a perfectly united structure;
there is no longer any question of discernible component parts. The
specimen Fig. 41 A has an inscription of two characters which have
not been deciphered but palaeographically look to be earlier than
Eastern Chou, though less archaic than "Shang-Chou," as has been
suggested.[25] This piece has a concave cut socket-rim — like that of
Fig. 40 D above — and shows a new feature in a very small loop

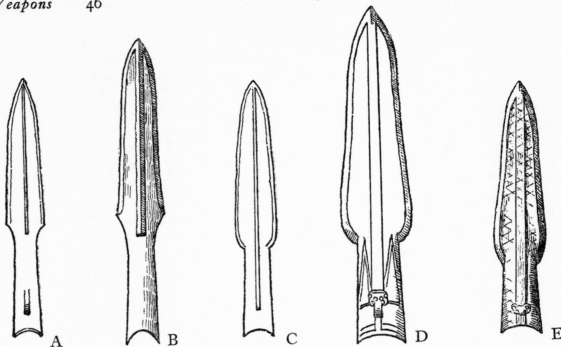

Fig. 41 : *Some types of Eastern Chou spearheads.*

A — Peking, Li T'ai-fen; after *Ch'ih An Ts'ang Chin.* B — Jannings Collection, no. 28. C — Jannings Collection, no. 29. D — Tokyo, Marquis Hosokawa; after *Shū Kan ihō.* E — David-Weill Collection, Paris; after Janse.

placed medially. One here sees the type which was to rule supreme throughout the Eastern Chou period but which seems to have already existed in the latter part of Western Chou, provided one can trust and correctly evaluate the date of the two glyphs. Fortunately, there is at least one variant specimen in *San Tai Chi Chin Wen Ts'un*[26] which is likely to confirm the early date of this type, hitherto more often than not regarded as a Warring States type.

To give a comprehensive account of the developments during the Eastern Chou period would demand a detailed investigation that cannot be undertaken here. In this preliminary attempt to systematize the presentation of some essential features, it will suffice to state in brief that subsequently a tendency becomes apparent which leads to *lengthened blades* and correspondingly *shortened sockets* (Fig. 41 B, C, D). This observation is based on the sparse decorative elements found in those later spearheads, and more particularly on an important piece in Marquis Hosokawa's collection, which is inscribed with the name of a Yüeh 越 ruler (Fig. 41 D). It is the same name which appears on the turquoise-incrusted guard of sword no. 97 (q.v.). Kuo Mo-jo is inclined to identify the name with that of a Yüeh sovereign who was murdered, according to the *Bamboo Annals,* in the year 376 B.C. It is likely, therefore, that the spearhead dates from about 376 or at any rate from the first half of the fourth century B.C.[27]

The broad-faceted edges of this specimen (Fig. 41 D) gently, almost imperceptibly curve and join the tube in a flexure which perfectly answers to the outline of the tip. The tip is tetrahedral, the sloping facets of the stout, elegantly cornered midrib being flush with the facets of the edges. The midrib is drawn down to a point near the aperture — which again is concave — and its end is marked by a miniature animal-mask of Huai style. The zone below the mask is occupied by two confronted, vividly curved animals in frames which accentuate, and depend on, the structure and outline of the whole, while a pair of acute triangles with ornamental fillings rises above the animals, reaching the inner courses of the edges at the point where the latter issue from the socket. The inscription, executed in gold wire hammered into *fossae,* shows the intricate and dainty lineament which the "bird script" requires. The proportions are very different from those of the earlier shapes, the socket part measuring no more than 28 per cent of the entire length, as against 40 per cent in Fig. 41 A, 41 per cent in 41 B, 34 per cent in 41 C, and even 47 per cent in the specimen from a Peking collection mentioned (note 23).

Fig. 41 B is a diagram of the beautiful, plain, evenly oxidized spearhead no. 28 in the Jannings Collection, a description of which is given in the Catalogue. This piece evidently has much in common with both A and D of Fig. 41. It is difficult, on the other hand, to decide whether it stands midway between them or is closer to the former so that it should be regarded rather as a refined variant. Fig. 41 A undeniably has quite similar proportions and, notably, the same kind of spine that ends a little below the recess of the edges. But even so, 41 A appears stiff, inanimate, uninspired, and somehow naïve by comparison with the truly noble silhouette of 41 B, a piece of much superior design: spruce, sharp, strangely sleek, urbane, so to say. These qualities depend upon a few improvements which should not go unnoticed: the transition between the blade and the tube, which here is emphasized by a delicate overwidening; the fine swing in the contour resulting therefrom; the strength given to the median ridge; and last but not least the greater accuracy and technical skill. These qualities, I wish to add, have nothing whatsoever to do with usefulness or efficiency; they are of purely aesthetic import and reveal some intellectual effort. Still the question of the relative age of the piece 41 B remains to be answered. I admit I have no satisfactory solution for the present, but I estimate that the type will be found to be not much younger than 41 A, while appreciably older than 41 D, and that it dates from the period of the *Spring and Autumn Annals* (Chou III).

Fig. 41 C (Cat. no. 29; counterpart in Osvald Sirén's collection) unquestionably represents a stage between Fig. 41 B and D. It resembles D fairly closely, but its edges are straight; it is related to D in much the same way as 41 A is to 41 B. Again, it is not yet possible to say how far 41 C is removed in time from the other types. The date "376 B.C." of 41 D, however, is likely to imply a date toward the end of Chou III or early in Chou IV for the type 41 C.

The David-Weill specimen (Fig. 41 E) is of particular interest in that its surface is covered by a nielloed diaper pattern.[28] The same pattern distinguishes the blade of the sword no. 101 in the Jannings Collection, and thus this sword — in spite of the fact that the diapers are done by etching — is approximately coeval with the spearhead. In view of the very close resemblance of this spearhead to Marquis Hosokawa's, which is datable "376 B.C.," one may assume that a date of early fourth century applies for both the David-Weill specimen and sword no. 101.

## NOTES: CHAPTER II SPEARHEADS

[1] Squarish sockets were made in the late Shang and early Chou periods, thereafter they went out of fashion. Later, sockets of oval or lens-shaped cross section prevailed. Cp. Cat. nos. 25, 27 ff.

[2] Examples in Karlgren's "Some Weapons and Tools," nos. 1-5. Nothing of this kind, however, is in the Jannings Collection.

[3] *Yin-hsü T'ung Ch'i Wu Chung*, Pl. I: 2; *Anyang Fa Chüeh Pao Kao*, II, Pl. IX opp. p. 239, drawing p. 245. The same pieces in Karlgren's "Some Weapons and Tools," nos. 7, 8.

[4] The inscription on the spearhead Fig. 36 C is tolerably clear in the drawing; that on the specimen Fig. 36 F is reproduced in *Yeh Chung P'ien Yü*, II, *hsia:* 18 and by Karlgren, "Some Weapons and Tools," no. 2.

[5] *Yeh Chung P'ien Yü*, I, *hsia:* 1-2. H. G. Creel, *The Birth of China*, Pl. XII.

[6] *Yin-hsü T'ung Ch'i Wu Chung*, pp. 84-88. Regarding British types assumed to have reached South-Russia, cf. V. Gordon Childe, *The Bronze Age*, p. 93. — In *Anyang Fa Chüeh Pao Kao*, IV, p. 576, Li Chi briefly says that bronze casting, the spearhead, and the socketed celt are definitely linked with Central and Western Asia (確與中亞及西亞有關者爲靑銅業, 矛, 銎頭銹, 等.).

[7] The large Yang-shao arrowhead, in J. G. Andersson, "An Early Chinese Culture," Pl. VI: 8. — The bronze dagger, in *Ch'iu Ku Ching She Chin Shih T'u*, ch. 2: 1 (referred to below, under Cat. no. 88), is not a "Hsia," but a Western Chou weapon. Neither of these pieces has anything whatsoever to do with spearheads.

[8] W. C. White, *Illus. London News*, April 20, 1935, Fig. 5.

[9] Karlgren, "Some Weapons and Tools," p. 125, note. Cf. A. M. Tallgren, *Coll. Tovostine*, p. 48, note 3.

[10] E.g., F. R. Martin, *L'Age du Bronze au Musée de Minoussinsk*, Pl. 25: 3, 5; Tallgren, *Coll. Tovostine*, Pl. 7: 10; V. Radloff, "Sibirskiya drevnosti," Pls. 18-19 (quoted after Karlgren, "Some Weapons and Tools," p. 125 note).

[11] P. Rykov, "Die Chvalynsker Kultur der Bronzezeit," spearheads Figs. 19: 1 and 20: 1 = Fig. 39 B and A.

It should be mentioned in this connection that a Shang spearhead with only one eyelet figures in J. M. Plumer's *An Exhibition of Ancient Chinese Ritual Bronzes Loaned by C. T. Loo*, Pl. 33: 8. But one might doubt whether that piece was not originally provided with two loops. The Catalogue text is not helpful by stating "Bronze Staff Head (*sic*) with ring on handle to hold tassel."

Another instance of an apparently early spearhead with a single loop placed immediately below the blade — unusually high above the mouth of the socket, which strongly tapers — is reproduced in *Chou Chin Wen Ts'un*, 6/1: 89 a.

[12] Rykov, *op. cit.*, Fig. 24: 1.

[13] Tallgren, in *MAGW*, LXI, p. 87; *idem*, "La Pontide préscythique," Figs. 76: 6 and 78: 14. For the date, see the chapter on Siberia below.

[14] For literature on the Borodino find, see the chapter on Siberia, note 34. Tallgren's earlier view that the hoard dates from around 1500 B.C. (cf. Ebert, *RLV*, II, p. 121) is supported by E. Dullo, in *PZ*, XXVII, p. 151.

[15] Cp. the chapter on Siberia, note 117.

[16] Tallgren, "KBrZ NOR," p. 188 ff.; G. v. Merhart, *Bronzezeit am Jenissei*, p. 70 ff.

[17] Tallgren, "La Pontide préscythique," p. 134; *idem, Miscellanea Archaeologica, ESA*, VI, p. 178, Fig. 6, p. 179 (lance head of Seima-Galich type in the Perm Museum); A. Heikel, "Antiquités de la Sibérie Occidentale," Pl. 12: 15 (lance head from the Irbit Lake, in the Yekaterinburg Museum).

[18] See the chapter on Siberia, below.

[19] Bachhofer, *A Short History of Chinese Art*, p. 36, holds that the *t'ao-t'ieh* vanishes around 1000 B.C., soon after the fall of the Shang. As already said above (ch. I, note 78), I cannot bring myself to apply so strict a date to every type of weapon that has a *t'ao-t'ieh* mask on it.

[20] *Meng Wei Ts'ao T'ang*, chung: 22. The inscription also in *Chou Chin Wen Ts'un*, 6/1: 88 a.

[21] *Ch'ih An Ts'ang Chin, Hsü Chi*, 37. The inscription possibly is a later addition; the piece itself is unquestionably authentic.

[22] *T'ao Chai Chi Chin Lu*, 3: 48. Cf. Cat. no. 25, below.

[23] *Ch'ih An Ts'ang Chin*, 40. A counterpart in *Yen K'u Chi Chin, hsia:* 47, no. 61; the text says that in 1939 three identical specimens were excavated in Anyang.

[24] *Shan Chai Chi Chin Lu*, 10: 46 = *Hsiao Chiao Ching Ko*, 10: 69 a. This spearhead has two loops.

[25] *Ch'ih An Ts'ang Chin*, 42.

[26] *San Tai Chi Chin Wen Ts'un*, 20: 40 a; cf. *ibid.*, 41 a-b.

[27] *Liang Chou Chin Wen Tz'u Ta Hsi, K'ao Shih*, Fig. 3; text, *ibid., pu-lu:* 1-2. — *Shū Kan ihō*, Pl. 54. Cf. Cat. no. 97 *infra*, where the inscription of this spearhead is briefly discussed.

[28] O. Janse, "Le style du Houai et ses affinités," Pl. 53: 2.

# DAGGER-AXES

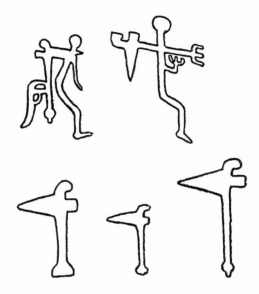

Fig. 42: *Shang pictographs showing dagger-axes.*

*Chapter III*

The dagger-axe in its various forms — being the most widely used type of weapon — was characteristic of Bronze Age China. These axes were common from the latter part of the IInd millennium B.C. till the end of the pre-Christian era, and their very existence throughout that long span not only makes it obvious that they were the preferred weapon of the Chinese, but also suggests that there were no radical changes in the mode of warfare during those more than thousand years.

This weapon resembles the European Early Bronze Age halberd (*dolchstab*). It was hafted at right angles to a relatively thin stick which was thickened and bent back at the upper end. That the stick was thickened on top can be ascertained by the traces of patina on many specimens. The backward curve, on the other hand, is attested only by the shape of the shaft in Shang pictographs (Fig. 42) and a miniature model in jade of the David-Weill Collection [1] (Fig. 43). Both top-heaviness and curve are understandable as devices for rendering the stroke more formidable and directing it more securely, and both, too, have analogies among recent primitive weapons from Oceania or Africa.

There were two modes of hafting. The more common way was to insert the tang or shafting-plate (*nei* 內 ) through a cleft in the wooden stick, and to fasten it further by thongs or cord lashings. In the other way, the stick was forced through a shaft-hole or, rather, shaft-ring which was shorter than the width of the blade (cp. Fig. 19). Instead of such rings, though rarely, shaft-tubes or sockets of some length also occurred (cp. Figs. 15-18). The shaft-ring types appear concurrently with tanged types as early as Shang, but seemingly failed to gain favor, being practically absent among Chou types. The two hafting devices were used indiscriminately with the same blade types; neither was bound to a definite form of the blade. Unless future discoveries prove contradictory, hafting by means of rivets — characteristic of the European dagger-axes — was unknown.

Fig. 43: *Jade miniature model of hafted ko.*

David-Weill Collection. After Janse (1/1).

There is a considerable wealth of shapes, which may conveniently be reduced to the following basic types:

    I. Broad triangular blades with tang (*k'uei*)
   II. Slender blades with tang (*ko*)
  III. Slender blades with shaft-ring (*ch'ü*)
  IV. Slender blades with descending edge (*ko*)

These types — neglecting transitional forms — can be further classified according to the following details: symmetrical or asymmetrical build; the position of the tang (*nei*) in relation to the axis; form and décor of the *nei;* the angle of the shafting-bar; the formation of the down-curved lower edge or *hu* 胡. It goes without saying that these formal or structural differences purport evolutionary stages or, to put it otherwise, that the typological order established with the help of these differences has a bearing on chronology.

The aforementioned four basic types may be briefly described and — with inclusion of transitional forms — examined for their respective chronological places.

I. BROAD TRIANGULAR BLADES WITH TANG, *K'UEI* 癸戉

This type is characterized by a triangular outline of the blade, which often has a very broad base, by a prevalence of symmetrical shapes, a rectangular *nei,* and, as a rule, a round perforation in the blade. This perforation, which is found in all variants of the type, is only rarely omitted, but the rare exceptions show that it was not a structural necessity.

The simplest form is that of Fig. 44: 1, a flat blade with midrib and two slits in the base, above and below the tang, which is placed symmetrically. A somewhat more developed form, probably not appreciably later than the first one, is the crested blade of rhombic section, likewise of symmetrical design (Fig. 44: 5, 6, 7; cp. Cat. no. 43). The tangs are provided with variously shaped holes for riveting(?), lashing, or attaching tassels. A further group is distinguished by blades with a strengthening shield at the base, which also encloses the perforation; the blades are ribbed (Fig. 44: 9, 10; cp. Cat. no. 44), or crested (Fig. 44: 8) as is the extremely broad specimen in the Eumorfopoulos Collection with its tang placed in the upper half of the base. A round boss may replace the perforation (Fig. 44: 11), or the shield may be adorned with an animal-mask (Fig. 44: 15 = Cat. no. 45). In a category of blades with midrib and rounded points, the shield, including the perforation, appears merely as a kind of decoration (Fig. 44: 12, 13, 16). An individual case is a specimen with the perforation off the point of the shield (Fig. 44: 14).

Particular features of the category with decorative shields are slanting shaft-supports (Fig. 44: 13 = Cat. no. 46), and short lugs in prolongation of the base for attachment by thongs to the shaft — an old and widespread device, but quite exceptional within this group

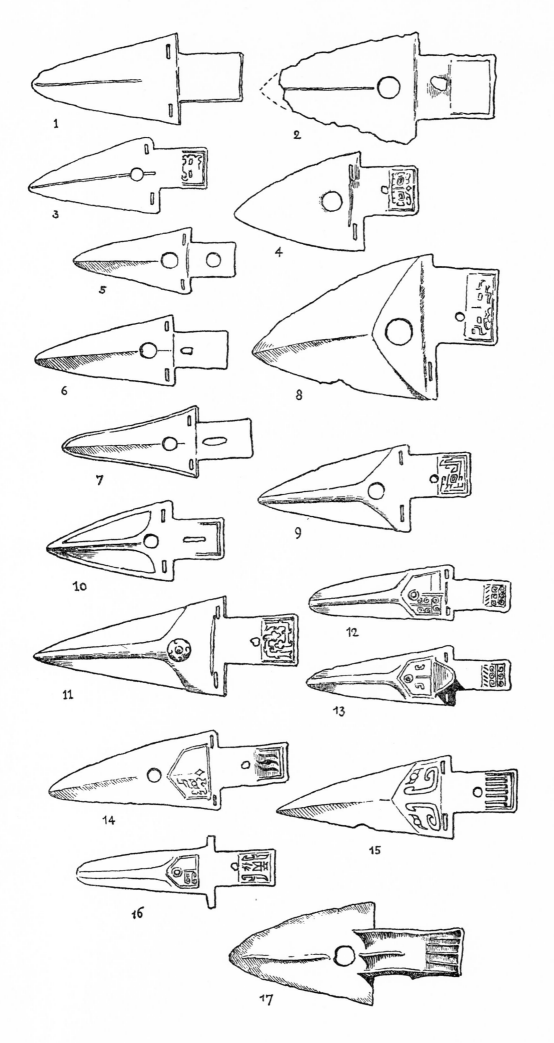

Fig. 44: *Variants of the dagger-axe type I (k'uei)*.

1, 5, 7 — Lu Mou-te Collection; after Umehara (ca. 3/10). 2 — David-Weill Collection; after Umehara (ca. 3/10). 3, 12, 14 — Kishi Collection, after Umehara (1/4). 4 — Liang Shang-ch'un Collection; after *Yen K'u Chi Chin T'u Lu* (1/4). 6, 9, 13, 15 — Jannings Collection Catalogue nos. 43, 44, 46, 45 (1/4). 8 — Eumorfopoulos Collection; after Yetts (not to scale). 10 — Fujii Collection, Yūrinkan, Kyoto; after Umehara (1/4). 11 — Yü Hsing-wu Collection, after *Shuang Chien I Chi Chin T'u Lu* (1/4). 16 — after Lo Chenyü, *San Tai Chi Chin Wen Ts'un* (ca. 1/4). 17 — Museum of Far Eastern Antiquities; after Karlgren (1/3).

(Fig. 44: 16). By virtue of these particulars and, at the same time, of the no longer really triangular outline of the blades, these *k'uei* rather closely converge with the following class (II), wherein the short wings or lugs are common, and shaft-supports not too rare. This subtype hence holds a place between the basic types I and II, but evidently having been derived from type I it is feasible to group it with type I.

A broad-bladed variant with obtuse point and shaft-supports also belongs here, represented by a specimen deprived of its *nei* (Hellström Collection), and two complete specimens in the collections of Marchese Taliani (unpublished) and of Professor Yü Hsing-wu.[2]

Finally, a type with very broad blade and without reinforcement of the base should be inserted here (Fig. 44: 4) as throwing light on the otherwise isolated Eumorfopoulos specimen; whether the blade of the former is flat or profiled cannot be determined from the reproduction.[3]

*Age of type I.* The examples in Fig. 44 almost exhaustively represent the extant variants of this type.[4] In contradistinction to this handful of triangular blades there are hundreds of examples of types II, III, IV. This numerical discrepancy certainly counts in judging their relative ages. Type I is rare, and its rarity most likely is due to the fact that it was in use for only a short period before going out of fashion. As to the other categories, it is known that they were used from the Shang period down to the end of the Chou without any revolutionary changes. This leads to the assumption that the *k'uei* must be placed before the other types and perhaps was a forerunner of the commoner *ko* types.

It should be asked whether this assumption is compatible with the structural characteristics and the décor of the type. The same question was once, long ago, taken up by Ch'en Chieh-ch'i 陳介祺 (d. 1884), noted collector and archaeologist, who came to the following conclusion: "The décor of the *ch'ü* is throughout more ancient than that of the *ko*" 瞿文皆古于戈[5] (*ch'ü* being the triangular blade here called *k'uei*). Likewise, Umehara defines the type as "archaic *ko*" 古式戈, placing it at the head of his typological scheme.[6] The décor (Fig. 44: 2-4, 8, 9, 11-16) in fact demands an early date. But the priority of the type does not by any means follow, for all the elements which are here, such as the meander, *t'ao-t'ieh,* whorl-circle, and turquoise incrustation, cannot be separated from those in category II. Inscriptions too, scanty though they be, connect the *k'uei* types with the Shang material from Anyang having analogous inscriptions. Thus, one eventually turns back to the shapes of the blades: the predominance of symmetrically built specimens, the simplicity of the *nei,* the absence of wings (with the exception of Fig. 44: 16), and the unquestionable affinity of the more developed subtypes to category II shapes all clearly point to the greater age of type I.

No proof, however, is afforded by these considerations, and it should not be overlooked that another question arises at the moment when type I is placed at the beginning of the dagger-axe series: whence came this type? Obviously, it is not a translation into metal of a stone tool; stone tools of comparable shape, moreover, are not known thus far. A remarkable circumstance is the absence in this group of any "Northern" ornament and of shaft-hole types, with the exception of one stray specimen from Shih-chia-chuang (Hopei) in the Museum of Far Eastern Antiquities, Stockholm [7] (Fig. 44: 17). This circumstance means that these tanged blades must be regarded as autochthonous Shang types, although their genesis is still obscure.[8]

*Nomenclature.* The nomenclature of the various dagger-axe types is far from being uniform. This fact was lamented by the author of the *Liang Lei Hsien,* Wu Yün 吳雲, who for the present type decided on the name *k'uei* 戣, on the basis of an inscription occurring on such a type.[9] Tsou An, Lu Mou-te, and Umehara used the same name [10] and the *Ch'ing I Ko so ts'ang Ku Ch'i Wu Wen* (1:17) even tries to justify it in a lengthy discussion of the question whether or not this type is identical with the *k'uei* of the *Shu Ching.* Nevertheless, there is so far no certainty that this type was actually or exclusively called *k'uei* by the ancients, even though the character is epigraphically traceable in the following four variants: 戣, 戣, 鐆, 戣.[11] The very same character also occurs on dagger-axes of different design,[12] while the *Shu Ching* passage mentioning a *k'uei* in correlation to a *ch'ü* 瞿 reveals *au fond* only that there have been weapons so named.[13] As a consequence, type I also was considered as representing the *ch'ü.*[14] Another designation, the general term *kou-ping* 勾兵, "hook-weapon," also occurs.[15] However, most scholars who have dealt with the subject have thought it necessary to have a term stressing the differences between this weapon and the *ko;* for the same reason the name *k'uei* is used here.

## II. SLENDER BLADES WITH TANG, *KO* 戈

For this category, which is rich in variants, a slender blade in combination with lugs (shafting-wings) and tang (*nei*) is the characteristic element. In the earlier variants the *nei* is placed in the middle axis (Fig. 45: 1, 2); in the later variants the *nei* is on a level with the upper edge (Fig. 45: 4, 6). With the passage of time, the blades deviate more and more from the nearly symmetrical archetypes toward gently curved shapes with the tip bent downward (Fig. 45: 7). The cross sections vary: rhomboid (crested) blades are frequent; midribs occur, which sometimes are very broad (Fig. 45: 2); exceptionally, a reinforcement occupying almost the entire surface of the blade appears (Fig. 45: 4); convex blades of lens-shaped section are favored at an early date and maintained for a long time (Fig. 45: 3, 7).

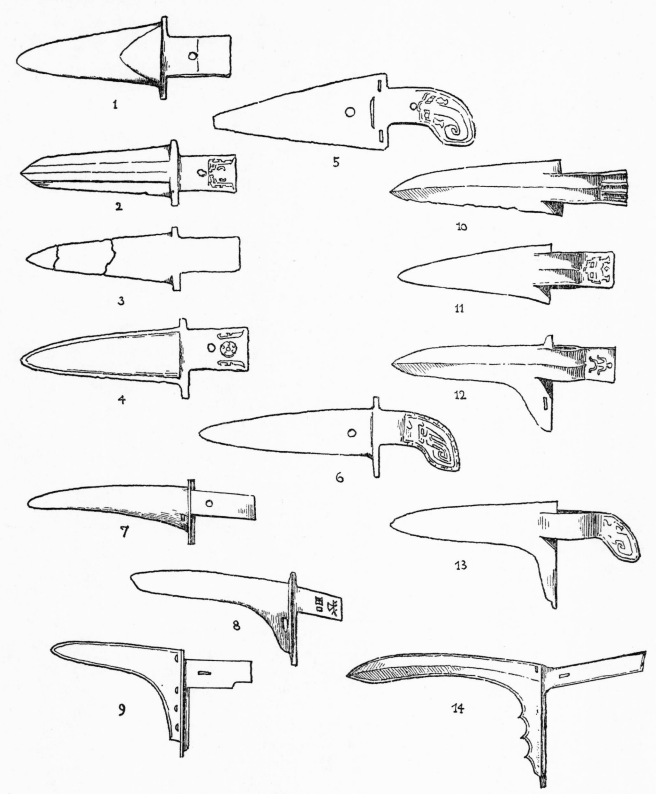

Fig. 45: *Variants of dagger-axe types II, III, IV (ko, ch'ü).*

1, 2, 4, 6, 7, 9, 10, 11, 12, 14 — Jannings Collection; Catalogue nos. 49, 50, 53, 61, 71, 74, 68, 66, 69, 79. 3 — Anyang; after *Anyang Report*, Vol. III, Pl. 5:3. 5 — Yü Hsing-wu Collection; after *Shuang Chien I Chi Chin T'u Lu, hsia*: 12. 8 — Hsün-hsien, Grave 42; after *Hsün-hsien I Ch'i*, fol. 25. 13 — formerly Bohlken, Berlin; after a photograph (all 1/4).

The shafting-plates or *nei* in the beginning have a simple squarish form. Later variants exhibit rhombic forms, that is, the angles shift in accordance with the asymmetrical trim of the whole (e.g., Fig. 45: 7, 8). Parallel with the angular *nei,* rounded ones come into being probably as early as the Shang period (Cat. nos. 58, 59), and some which are rounded and down-curved (as Fig. 45: 5, 6, 13). Rounded *nei* being practically absent in category I, a specimen in Professor Yü Hsing-wu's collection[16] (Fig. 45: 5) combining the triangular *k'uei* blade with a down-curved *nei* constitutes a remarkable exception; this specimen must be assigned to the types transitional between I and II and might with equally good reasons be linked with category I. The same holds true for a blade with turquoise inlay in the Jannings Collection (Fig. 45: 1 = Cat. no. 49): it would fit in the end of the *k'uei* series or in the beginning — but not later — of the *ko* series.

*Age of type II.* On the whole, the style of the *nei* decoration points to Shang and Early Chou periods. Archaeological evidence for the dating of the various subtypes, however, is at present scanty. Thus far, no more than two pieces of scientifically excavated specimens of Shang date have been published. They were found in tombs 18.2 and 18.3 near Hsiao-t'un (Anyang), opened in October, 1929. While the first grave did not yield any other funerary gift than the *ko* — a type with rectangular *nei* attached somewhat below the upper edge (Fig. 45: 3) — the second one contained some ceramics, two stone implements, and one oracle bone in addition to the *ko*, which has a rounded down-curved *nei* (as in Fig. 45: 6 = Cat. no. 61). It is the oracle bone on which the date of both tombs depends, but stratigraphic evidences are lacking.[17]

Less poor are the results of excavations — again confined to one single place — of Chou I-II burials at Hsin-ts'un 辛村 in the vicinity of Hsün-hsien 濬縣 (Northern Honan).[18] The finds made there have been only partly published, and for the *ko* do not include any accurately datable piece. Yet they are important in that they show, though vaguely, what there was after Shang and before Chou III. According to Kuo Pao-chün's report, fifty-five unbroken specimens and twenty-seven fragmentary ones were collected from these graves, which had been disturbed by robbers. No more than eight pieces belong in category II, whereas category IV is represented by sixty-two with short vertical edges (*hu* 胡) and another six with long *hu.*[19] Thus, there is ample evidence that types with a short *hu* were dominant at that time, that the heyday of the "classical" stage of type IV had not yet come, and that the models of type II had already been obliterated. These latter, therefore, cannot have survived very long after the Chou conquest. With all due reservations one may suppose that their lifetime was over by the end of the Chou I period.

Epigraphy does not contradict this; it rather points to an even earlier date for category II; however, there are no inscriptions to furnish any exact date.

*Nomenclature. Ko* 戈 is the designation most widely adhered to. The brothers Feng used it, and so did, later, Lo Chen-yü, Li Chi, and Jung Keng.[20] Umehara, for the sake of preciseness, added "archaic" (*koshiki*) to it, stressing the dissimilarity of the types with vertical edge.[21] Ch'eng Yao-t'ien defined examples of category II as *kou-ping* 勾兵, leaving open the question whether or not they should be identified with the *ch'ü* 瞿 in one of the *Shu Ching* chapters.[22] And the term *ch'ü* still lingers in more recent Chinese works dealing with this subject.[23] Li Chi, however, has justly pointed out that, not knowing what kind of weapon is hidden behind the *Shu Ching* term *ch'ü*, one cannot properly evaluate it.[24] His objection must not induce one to give up the use of a term which as such is suitable for a practical discrimination between the existing types; but since *ch'ü* has not only failed to gain general recognition, but also is used for shaft-ring types (III), it remains too ambiguous a term for the present case. It thus seems logical to cling to the conventional name *ko,* which, it is true, does not claim to be precise, but is a convenient designation for the simple tanged blades, inasmuch as it agrees with the forms of the dagger-axes represented in Shang pictographs (Fig. 42). The ancient character *ko,* and hence the name *ko,* must not be separated from those pictographs which in the question of nomenclature are of equal significance with later texts or commentaries.

### III. SLENDER BLADES WITH SHAFT-RING, *CH'Ü* 瞿

The blade forms resemble those of category II, and rhomboid blades with the median accentuated by a narrow ridge or a crest prevail. As in category II, slightly curved blades outnumber the straight, a fact observed already by O. Karlbeck.[25] They are hafted by means of a ring-socket pointed oval in section. This ring, attached in the middle of the heel of the blade and overlapping it, has an approximately square neck-plate (Fig. 45: 10). The type is briefly discussed in connection with socketed axes (ch. I, A XII).

In contrast to the other basic types, this one is poor in variants. A certain vacillation with regard to the degree of symmetry seems to be all that this beautiful type has to offer if approached typologically. The shafts were surprisingly thin: to judge from the specimens in the Jannings Collection, shaft-hole measurements do not exceed widths of 25-30: 20 mm (Cat. nos. 65-68).[26] Consequently, the sticks cannot have been very long.

Too rare in relation to the basic type to justify a separate category, the variant of the shaft-ring blade *with vertical edge* (Fig. 45: 12, 13) may be inserted here as category III a. Here appears (possibly toward the end of the Shang) the downward prolongation of the base, provided with a cutting edge which in a curve joins the lower end of that prolongation: the *hu* 胡 ("dewlap"), most characteristic element of the *ko* in its later, definite shape. It is a contrivance aiming at a rigid hafting by means of a considerably lengthened support with an additional slot for lashings. Apropos of this shape, the presence of the same kind of blade with descending edge and correspondingly long socket among the axes of "Northern" cast (ch. I, type A X) should be called to memory. The historical relations of the latter type (Fig. 15 above) to the present one are of far-reaching importance, but how the analogies must be interpreted is not clear as yet.[27]

*Age of type III.* The specimens appearing in the market or hitherto published are labeled Anyang finds and are generally considered to be Shang relics.[28] The Anyang excavations carried through by the Academia Sinica had not yielded, according to a statement by Li Chi, any such specimen up to 1933.[29] In the finds derived from the so-called Tomb of the Elephant published by Bishop White, however, the type is represented together with examples of categories I and II.[30] One may safely assume, therefore, that the shaft-ring types actually belong to Shang times and coexisted with the other two types. Ornamentation on the butts likewise speaks in favor of this remote age.

A question less easy to answer is how long the type existed. To all appearances there are no specimens with ornaments in the style of the Chou II-III periods. Rather, it seems as if the type had hardly survived the Shang dynasty — with the possible exception of some stragglers.

The subtype with vertical edge (III a) can only be understood with reference to the basic type (III). It typologically presupposes the latter and thus, on the whole, should be a little later. The shape of the *hu* offers a parallel to the early forms in category IV. But, for some reason or other, subtype III a did not gain ground, but soon disappeared, presumably together with the basic type.

*Nomenclature.* Like the preceding two types, the present one does not correspond to the *ko* as described in the *K'ao Kung Chi,* and once more there arises uncertainty as to proper nomenclature. Hence one finds the terms: *chi* 戟, *mao* 矛, *shu* 殳, *k'uei* 叕,[31] while some writers choose the name *ch'ü* 瞿.[32] For the sake of clear discrimination, I follow suit in calling this type *ch'ü,* although there seems to be no evidence — epigraphical or otherwise — that this name was the one used by the ancients.

## IV. SLENDER BLADES WITH DESCENDING EDGE, *KO* 戈

This type, the *ko* proper, combines a horizontal blade (*yüan* 援) with a vertical one (*hu*) which in a curve goes downward from the lower edge of the *yüan* to the end of the prolonged base. Hafting is done with the help of the shafting-plate (tang, *nei* 內) passing horizontally through the wooden shaft at level with the main blade. Along the base there are holes or slits for lashings (Fig. 45:9).

This particular form of the dagger-axe — apparently not found outside China — reigns during almost the whole of the Ist millennium B.C. During that long period, the unassuming primary shape underwent manifold changes and refinements, and the bold and elegant creations of the Warring States period unmistakably show, by the attention and inventiveness then at work, the important role the *ko* continued to hold. Although the later variants do not bear much resemblance to their archaic forerunners, they remain, in principle, faithful to them, and, notwithstanding occasional extravagances, the optimal solution (Fig. 45:9 may be regarded as an example) once attained remained a standard never abandoned till the beginnings of the Han.[33] The traditional principle was violated by a single innovation only: in the Chou IV period there are types with *sharpened nei* (Fig. 45:14), weapons which are intrinsically different in nature from the normal types.

The few specimens of category IV in this collection do not provide an ample survey of the development of the *ko,* and the drawings given only serve to illustrate the main stages in the long history of this type. There is no urgent reason, moreover, to treat this subject broadly here.[34]

*Age of type IV.* There is no reliable *point d'appui* as yet to decide whether this model existed already under the Shang. The Tomb of the Elephant did not contain it.[35] In the Anyang reports it is represented by an isolated specimen that was bought at Anyang and cannot safely be dated.[36] There are, on the other hand, III a types fitted with the vertical edge which apparently date from Shang times.[37] One can only assume that the simpler types with tang and vertical edge (IV) are at least not later than the ringed types with vertical edge (III a), and that the simpler types must also have been there in the Shang period. Yet, since new Anyang reports which perhaps will give a final answer to this question are to be written before long, it is pointless to theorize about the matter. Li Chi ascribes type IV (with short *hu*) to the "Shang-Chou" transitory period.[38] All one may safely say at present is that type IV was not characteristic of Shang.

This, too, is partly corroborated by the inventory of the *Hsün-hsien* tombs dating from Western Chou: these tombs were not poor in examples of type II; they included *ko* with short *hu* (early stage of type IV), while *ko* with long *hu* were all but absent.[39] The specimen (Fig. 45:8) inscribed "Ch'eng Chou 成周" from Hsün-hsien (Grave 42) may be taken as an average example of the early form of type IV, with only one shafting-slot in the prolonged base. The same burial (Grave 42) also furnished a *ko* without *hu,* the blade being curved throughout (similar to Fig. 45:7) and provided with shaft-supporting flanges standing aslant.[40] Sun Hai-po regards the *Ch'eng Chou Ko* as a relic of Duke Wu of Wei 衞武公, who in the forty-second year of his reign (771 B.C.) undertook an expedition against the Ch'üan Jung 犬戎 in order to relieve the House of Chou.[41] Now, Ch'eng Chou, the city built by Ch'eng Wang 成王 on the Lo River, certainly was a station on that expedition, and Tomb 42, which belongs to the largest of that necropolis, certainly was a prince's.[42] Yet it is quite unwarranted to assume that it was Duke Wu's burial place, or that the event of the year 771 should be connected with that *ko*. To me an earlier date seems much more likely: another *ko* inscribed "Ch'eng Chou" is placed in the beginning of the Chou time by Jung Keng,[43] and the aforementioned piece without *hu* from Grave 42 shows an animal-head ornament which is not later than Chou I. It thus appears justified to date the type shown in Fig. 45:8 about Chou I-II.

Two *ko* from the lavishly equipped Tomb of Hsin-cheng 新鄭 in Central Honan — residence of the ancient feudal state of Cheng which existed till 375 B.C. — are examples from a closed find ranking next in age. In general appearance and blade shape these two pieces are not unlike Chou I-II types, but they no longer have the small lugs (or shafting-wings) extending beyond the upper edge, and the *hu,* which still is short, is not drawn down in a curve but springs back at right angle; shafting-slots are lacking.[44] There is no general agreement about the date of this important find. Among a hecatomb of bronze vessels only one bears a decipherable inscription, and this inscription has given no definite clue as to the originator.[45] A reliable conclusion will be arrived at as soon as the style of the vases and sundry finds can properly be valued.[46] For the time being one may well operate on the basis of Kuo Mo-jo's date of the burial, 680 B.C., as the least forced hypothesis, and, though with reserve, think of a date "before 680 B.C." for the whole of the inventory. Hence one may assume, dependent on a final decision concerning the Hsin-cheng find, that around 700 B.C. the "classical" Chou *ko* (Fig. 45:9) had not yet been developed.

Here some specimens may be briefly described which, on account of their inscriptions, bear on the chronology of category IV.

1) *Ko* of a prince of Liang (梁伯戈), a small state situated in North Shensi, extinguished in 641 B.C. according to the *Ch'un Ch'iu.*[47] It has a rare form: a base prolonged upward, with a consequently broad-heeled blade that rises slightly. The *hu* is short, and is provided with two slits. The *nei* projects at level with the axis of the straight, angularly pointed blade. There are shaft-supports in the shape of animal-heads. Provided that the date "before 641 B.C." holds true, this relatively archaic weapon again seems to show that the "classical" *ko* type had not yet appeared in the first half of the seventh century.

The "classical" type is represented by some *ko* in the Yü Hsing-wu Collection, which belong to the Chou III period (first half of the fifth century B.C., at the latest).

2) *Ko* of Duke Luan of Sung 宋公䜌 (= Ching Kung 景公, 516-453 B.C.).[48]

3) A *ko* from Wu 吳 (before 473 B.C.).[49]

4) *Ko* of King Yen Chang of Ch'u 楚王酓璋 (488-432 B.C.).[50]

5) *Ko* of Viscount Hu of Hsü 鄦伯虎.[51]

6) *Ko* of Chia Tzu of Ts'ai 蔡加子 (before 477 B.C.).[52]

The first three of these specimens have gold-wire inlay inscriptions in the capricious ductus invented by that restless time; they include characters difficult to decipher. All these five *ko* show the criteria of the standardized Chou design: a rising, often slightly curved blade with a steeply drawn and sharpened vertical edge which recedes at right angles to the shafting-bar jutting out below; the *nei* projects somewhat underneath the upper edge of the blade; there is one lashing-hole in the upper corner of the blade, two vertical slots in the *hu,* and a horizontal slot in the *nei.* The blades are faceted, and some of them have a rhombic cross section.

The novelty of a *sharpened nei* is encountered first, to my knowledge, in a *ko* which, judged by the style of its inscription, dates from about the same period as the preceding examples, that is, from about the end of Chou III.[53]

The oldest example of the less frequent, handsome model with *dented lower edge* (as in Fig. 45:14) also belongs to that time. It is a *ko* from Ch'en 陳,[54] a state annexed by Ch'u in 478 B.C., so that the piece in all probability is anterior to that year. The very long shafting-plate with rounded lower edge and sharpened facets almost imperceptibly rises; it clearly is a precursor of the type here illustrated (Cat. no. 79), with its more decidedly rising but likewise very slender *nei.*

Some further variants dating from Chou IV (between 323 and 221 B.C.) are referred to in the Catalogue under no. 79. They are less slenderly built than the earlier specimens, without, for that matter, appearing clumsier.

Two inscribed *ko* from Ch'in 秦, bearing the name of the famous Lü Pu-wei 呂不韋 and the date "5th year" (of Shih-huang-ti: 242 B.C.), are in the tradition of the classical type. Both, however, are equipped with extraordinarily long vertical edges, which factually are nearly as long as the blade proper and have altogether four slits for thongs. Their *nei* are sharpened.[55]

Another two Ch'in pieces with dates corresponding to the years 222 and 218 B.C. — the earlier one having been excavated at Lo-lang 樂浪 (Korea) — do not have such extremely long *hu;* they are quite artless, sleek, shapely types with sharpened *nei,* surprisingly conservative, on the whole.[56]

Finally, a dated *ko* from the Earlier Han dynasty may be mentioned. Typologically striking by the unparalleled length of its *nei* which almost balances the blade,[57] it rather shows, as to the rest, affinities with models earlier than those typical of Chou IV. This phenomenon demonstrates that a standardized type of the *ko* with long *hu* has maintained itself down to the close of the Ist millennium B.C., a type perfected since the seventh, certainly in the sixth century, but eventually traceable back to the earliest Chou and beyond.

NOTES: CHAPTER III    DAGGER-AXES

[1] O. Janse, "Le style du Houai," Pl. 53: 4 = Fig. 43.

[2] The Hellström piece, *London Exhibition Catalogue*, no. 169; apparently identical with the specimen formerly in Wannieck's possession: Umehara, "Note on Bronze Tools," Pl. 10: 2. — The Yü piece, *Shuang Chien I Chi Chin, hsia:* 9.

[3] *Yen K'u Chi Chin, hsia:* 14, no. 19 = Fig. 44: 4.

[4] Further specimens of *k'uei* dagger-axes, category I: *K'ao Kung Ch'uang Wu Hsiao Chi, HCCC*, ch. 537: 48 b-49 a; *Ching I Ko*, ch. 1: 15-16; *Shan Chai Chi Chin Lu*, ch. 11: 1; *Liang Lei Hsien*, 8: 5-6 = *Chou Chin Wen Ts'un*, 6/1: 65, 74, 76; *Cheng Sung T'ang Chi Chin T'u, chung:* 54 = *San Tai Chi Chin Wen Ts'un*, 19: 21 b (triangular blade with forward-bent lugs; Early Chou); *Hsiao Chiao Ching Ko*, 10: 76a (transitional type between categories I and II); Collection Sirén, *Ars Asiatica*, VII, Pl. 8: 17 (a later variant of the basic type, with slender blade, rounded and notched *nei*, and an animal-head in relief at the base, dating probably from late Western Chou time. The *nei* has a scalloped heel similar to that of the Yü Hsing-wu specimen listed in note 2 above).

[5] *Fu Chai Ts'ang Ku Mu*, vol. *hsin-ssu*, fol. 37a. Ch'en Chieh-ch'i here dates a similar type, even "Hsia."

[6] Umehara, "Shina no seidōki-jidai ni tsuite," *Shina Kodō Seika*, VII, and in *Shina Kōkogaku Ronkō*, p. 132. — *Idem*, "Note on Bronze Tools," Pl. 12.

[7] Karlgren, "Some Weapons and Tools," no. 249, text p. 133.

[8] Karlgren, *ibid.* p. 132 ff., came to the following conclusion: "It is impossible, on the basis of the An-yang materials alone, to answer the question, whether these elongated axe types (= category II) were derived from broader types, namely the broader triangular axes (= category I) . . . by a gradual narrowing of the blade, or whether the latter, on the contrary, are a modification of the former, by a gradual broadening of the base of the blade; or, as a third alternative, whether classes . . . (= category II) on the one hand and class . . . (= category I) on the other represent quite independent types."

[9] *Liang Lei Hsien*, 8: 5-6.

[10] Tsou An, *Chou Chin Wen Ts'un*. Lu Mou-te, *Chung-kuo Shang Ku T'ung Ping K'ao*. Umehara, "Note on Bronze Tools," p. 117, following Lu Mou-te; *idem, Shina Kodō Seika*, VII; *idem, Anyang Treasures*.

[11] Cf. *Ku Chou P'ien*, 26: 6.
鐶: *T'ao Chai Chi Chin Lu*, 2: 21 = *Chou Chin Wen Ts'un*, 6/1: 8 b; *Hsiao Chiao Ching Ko*, 10: 46.
癸: *Hsiao Chiao Ching Ko*, 10: 83 a (it is not absolutely certain that 癸 stands for 戣, the graph may be a name as well).
戣: *Liang Lei Hsien*, 8: 5 = *Chou Chin Wen Ts'un*, 6/1: 65.
戣: *Meng P'o Shih Hu Ku Ts'ung Pien, chin-lei*, no. 9, quoted after Lu Mou-te, *op. cit.*, p. 292.

[12] On *ko* types from the Warring States period; see note 11 *s.v.*

[13] *Shu Ching, Ku Ming*; Legge, *Chinese Classics*, III, p. 556.

[14] E.g., *Shan Chai Chi Chin Lu*, 11: 1; *Yen K'u Chi Chin, hsia:* 14; Ch'en Chieh-ch'i, see note 5 above.

[15] E.g., Lo Chen-yü, *Cheng Sung T'ang Chi Chin T'u, chung:* 51-53; *Meng Wei Ts'ao T'ang, chung:* 1. Yü Hsing-wu, in *Shuang Chien I Chi Chin, hsia:* 9 and 13. Sun Hai-po, in *Hsün-hsien I Ch'i*, 20-21.

[16] *Shuang Chien I Chi Chin, hsia:* 12.

[17] Li Chi, *Fu Shen Tsang*, pp. 449-50, 463; referring to Grave 18.3, he says that "stratigraphic conditions do not permit us to recognize its age" 由地層上就沒法看它的時代性. *Ibid.*, Pls. 10, 12.

[18] For Hsün-hsien, see the titles quoted in ch. I, note 23.

[19] Kuo Pao-chün, *Hsün-hsien Hsin-ts'un*, p. 184. Reproductions of selected *ko* types from various graves: Sun Hai-po, *Hsün-hsien I Ch'i*, fol. 20-26.

[20] The Feng brothers, in *Chin Shih So*. Lo Chen-yü, *Hsüeh T'ang so ts'ang Ku Ch'i Wu T'u*, 15a (戈類) and *Cheng Sung T'ang Chi Ku I Wen*, 11: 20-21a (diverging from the catalogues referred to in note 15 above). Li Chi, *Fu Shen Tsang*, and *Yin-hsü T'ung Ch'i Wu Chung*, p. 81, Fig. 1. Jung Keng: *Sung Chai Chi Chin Hsü Lu, hsia:* 126-27.

[21] Umehara, *Anyang Treasures*, Pls. 15: 1, 16, 21: 1; *idem, Anyang Studies*, Pl. 36: 1.

[22] *K'ao Kung Ch'uang Wu Hsiao Chi, HCCC*, ch. 537: 42 b, with reference to the *Shu Ching* passage — cf. note 13 above.

[23] Tsou An, *Chou Chin Wen Ts'un*, 6/1: 77 b-78 a; *Yen K'u Chi Chin, hsia*, fol. 4 sq.

[24] Li Chi, *Fu Shen Tsang*, p. 467.

[25] O. Karlbeck, "Ancient Chinese Bronze Weapons," p. 203.

[26] Cf. *ibid.*, p. 202.

[27] See the discussion toward the end of ch. I.

[28] Li Chi, *Yin-hsü T'ung Ch'i Wu Chung*, pp. 82-84. — Umehara, *Anyang Treasures*. — Liang Shang-ch'un, *Yen K'u Chi Chin, hsia:* 15, 17 sq. — Regarding the provenances of these shaft-ring types, Karlbeck remarked that he knew specimens from Shansi and Shantung besides those from Honan; *op. cit.*, p. 203.

[29] Li Chi, *Yin-hsü T'ung Ch'i Wu Chung*, p. 83.

[30] W. C. White, in *Illustrated London News*, April 20, 1935, pp. 639-41.

[31] *Chi: K'ao Kung Ch'uang Wu Hsiao Chi, HCCC*, ch. 537: 44 b sq. — *Mao:* Liu Hsin-yüan, *Ch'i Ku Shih*, 10: 34-35. — *Shu: Chou Chin Wen Ts'un*, 6/1: 79 a. — *K'uei: Yen K'u Chi Chin, hsia:* 17 sq.

[32] Feng, *Chin Shih So, Chin So,* 2: 1-2. — Lu Mou-te, *Chung-kuo Shang Ku T'ung Ping K'ao,* p. 293. — Li Chi, *Yin-hsü T'ung Ch'i,* pp. 82-84, Fig. 5:5. — Umehara, *Anyang Treasures,* Pl. 21:2.

[33] Cf. below, note 56: two specimens similar to the "classical" *ko* type, dated 222 and 218 B.C., show that the slenderer Chan-kuo forms did not entirely supersede older forms of relatively thickset proportions.

[34] A more comprehensive representation of the evolution of the *ko* still would have to base itself mostly on typological comparison and epigraphical evidences. Specimens with datable inscriptions are scanty and late; for the periods Chou I-III safely datable material and closed finds are wanting. Trustworthy chronological results, therefore, which would bear on the Chou chronology of the weapons in general are not to be expected at present. The specimens contained in the Jannings Collection also do not offer anything new within this category.

[35] Cf. W. C. White's article quoted above, note 30.

[36] Li Chi, *Fu Shen Tsang,* Pl. 5:4.

[37] Cf. category III a above, and the remarks under Cat. no. 69.

[38] Li Chi, *Fu Shen Tsang,* p. 471.

[39] About the numerical relation of the *ko* with long *hu,* cf. above, under category II. — Kuo Pao-chün, *Hsün-hsien Hsin-ts'un,* p. 184.

[40] Sun Hai-po, *Hsün-hsien I Ch'i,* fol. 23-24. — The contrivance of the slanting shaft-supports is seen, for instance, in Cat. no. 72.

[41] Sun Hai-po, *ibid.,* fol. 25 b. — About the expedition against the Jung, see *Shih Chi,* 37; Chavannes, *Mém. hist.,* IV, p. 193. The well-known story of the abused smoke signals and the vain cry for help of King Yu: *ibid.,* I, pp. 284-85; Maspero, *La Chine antique,* pp. 64-65.

[42] Short description of the tomb: Kuo Pao-chün, *op. cit.,* p. 171, no. 42.

[43] *Sung Chai Chi Chin T'u Lu,* fol. 32, text fol. 21 a; inscription also reproduced in *Cheng Sung T'ang Chi Ku I Wen, pu-i, chung:* 32 b.

[44] Reproduction of the Hsin-cheng *ko*-axes: best in *Hsin-cheng I Ch'i, hsia:* 137-38; further in *Hsin-cheng Ku Ch'i T'u Lu,* Pl. 55; drawing of one piece in *Cheng Chung Ku Ch'i T'u K'ao,* 8:2.

[45] The date of the Hsin-cheng Tomb. — The decipherable inscription belongs to a rectangular pan, and it says that the piece was the property of the royal prince Ying-tz'u 王子嬰次. Wang Kuo-wei identified this prince with Ying-ch'i 嬰齊, a younger brother of King Chuang of Ch'u 楚王莊 (613-591 B.C.) on the argument that he was the only Ying-ch'i who corresponds to the wording of the inscription, viz., the son of a king. The unexpected fact of a Ch'u prince's property being found in a Cheng tomb is explained by Wang Kuo-wei thus: the pan, after the battle of Yen-ling 焉陵 (575 B.C.) lost by Ch'u, found its way to Cheng with war spoils. Accordingly, the Cheng tomb had to be dated "after 575 B.C." Cf. Wang Kuo-wei, *Wang Tzu Ying-tz'u Lu Pa* 王子嬰次廬跋 *Kuan T'ang Chi Lin,* ch. 18:6 b, and Pelliot's summary in *T'oung Pao,* 1924, 256 sq. Reproductions of the bronze pan and of the inscription are contained in the catalogues mentioned above, n. 37. — Wang's main argument, however, cannot be regarded as unshakably valid, for the feudal lords, as Wang Kuo-wei himself has once pointed out in a short article, were not rarely honored with the title "king" by their subjects or descendants; cf. *Ku chu-hou ch'eng wang shuo* 古諸侯稱王說 "on the title 'king' used for the ancient feudal princes," in *Kuan T'ang Pieh Chi, pu-i,* fol. 9 b.

Kuo Mo-jo, on the other hand, is convinced that the name in the inscription refers to a Cheng prince for the simple reason that the tomb is situated within the old Cheng territory; and since there was a prince Ying of Cheng 鄭子嬰 (693-680), he identifies with him the Ying-tz'u (or, Ying-ch'i) of the inscription. The expression "king's son" is easily understood, he says, if one remembers that Cheng then was at the peak of its power, while its relations to the Chou court were not at their best. With regard to Wang's proposal of the Yen-ling battle, Kuo wittily objects that it took place in the hottest season of the year, in the sixth month, so that to carry a charcoal fire-pan would have been quite unnecessary and not understandable. Cf. Kuo Mo-jo, *Liang Chou, K'ao Shih,* 182 a sq. — The weak point in Kuo's interpretation is that tradition knows of a Ying whereas the inscription speaks of a Ying-tz'u. But for that matter Kuo justly remarks that abbreviations of such names are not infrequent in the literary tradition.

A third attempt, undertaken by Kuan Po-i, starts from a new decipherment of the character "ying." Kuan proposes to read T'ui 頹 instead of Ying, and to identify that person with Tzu T'ui 子頹, son of King Chuang of Chou 周莊王. The tomb is considered by Kuan to be that of Duke Li of Cheng 鄭厲公, who in 673 B.C., together with King Hui of Chou 周惠王, had put aside that Tzu T'ui, and had died a month later. His obsequies, after a curiously long delay, only took place in the twelfth month of the same year. Kuan Po-i, *Cheng Chung Ku Ch'i T'u K'ao,* 7:13 b sq. — Kuan's theory fits into tradition very nicely, suits the "royal prince," and easily explains how one (or many) of the bronzes from the Chou treasury came into the possession of a duke of Cheng. Yet Kuan's theory, too, has its weak side, and that at the outset. Deciphering the character "t'ui," he takes into account several strokes which undoubtedly do not form component parts of the graph in question, but chanced to get there somehow later; for these strokes are placed quite inorganically and lack the ductus of the script. Kuan's reproduction (*op. cit.,* 7 : 13a) fails to show this so clearly as do the renderings in *Hsin-cheng I Ch'i* (*hsia:* 130a) or *Hsin-cheng Ku Ch'i T'u Lu,* Pl. 54 b.

On the connections between the Chou and the Cheng state, the temporary exile of King Hui of Chou, the death of Tzu T'ui and that of Duke Li, we find information in the *Tso Chuan* (Chuang, 21st year); Legge, *Chin. Classics,* V, pp. 98-101; briefly in the *Bamboo Annals* (Chou Hui Wang, 2nd year), Legge, *Chin. Classics,* III, *Proleg.,* p. 162. Cf. also *Shih Chi* 42 — *Cheng shih-chia;* Chavannes, *Mém. hist.,* IV, pp. 461-62; *Kuo Yü, Chou Yü,* 1 : 10 b-11 a.

[46] The Hsin-cheng bronzes are not homogeneous in style, and the date here adopted, "before 680 B.C.," seems to be surprisingly early for some pieces and late for others. This date constitutes, it is true, a *terminus ante quem,* the actual age of each of the finds still having to be determined.

In fact an analysis undertaken by L. Bachhofer in his *Short History of Chinese Art* (pp. 41-42) of what he calls the "Hsin-cheng style" reveals that "the oldest group of bronzes from Hsin-cheng definitely resemble works of the late 9th and 8th century," whereas the characteristic patterns of the "Hsin-cheng style" still occur in part of the seventh century B.C.

Whether the dagger-axes should be linked with the earlier or the later materials within this frame is impossible as yet to say, because they have no ornaments. I am inclined to date the Hsin-cheng *ko* not long before 680, around or somewhat before 700 B.C., on the assumption that it is not very likely that antiquated, old-fashioned models of so common a weapon would have served as funerary gifts.

[47] *Ferguson Catalogue,* p. 998 *s.v.* Kuei-fang ko 鬼方戈. The best reproduction is found in Lo Chen-yü's *Cheng Sung*

*T'ang Chi Chin T'u, chung:* 63-64. For the inscription, cf. Wang Kuo-wei, *Liang Po Ko Pa* 梁伯戈跋 in *Kuan T'ang Pieh Chi, pu-i:* 17 b, and *Kuei-fang K'un-i Hsien-yün K'ao* 鬼方昆夷玁狁考 in *Kuan T'ang Chi Lin* 13 : 1 b-2 a. Kuo Pao-chün, though not decidedly, expresses some doubt as to the authenticity of the inscription; cf. *Ko Chi Yü Lun* 戈戟餘論 in *Bull. Acad. Sin.,* V/3, p. 315. — The downfall of the Liang state is reported in two words in the *Ch'un Ch'iu* (Hsi Kung, 19th year), somewhat more in detail in the *Tso Chuan;* Legge, *Chin. Classics,* V, pp. 175-77.

[48] Reproductions of these five *ko* in *Shuang Chien I Ku Ch'i Wu, shang:* 43-47, in the same order.

Sung Kung Luan: Luan was the personal name — preserved only in the *Tso Chuan* (Chao, 25th year, 11th month; Legge, *Chin. Classics,* V, pp. 707, 711) — of Duke Ching of Sung when crown prince. *Tso* writes 欒, the inscription, abbreviated, 縊. The same form of abbreviation occurs in the inscription of a tripod lid: *Hsieh Shih K'uan Chih* 9 : 6; Karlgren, "Yin and Chou," C 125; *Liang Chou Chin Wen Tz'u Ta Hsi, K'ao Shih,* 185 b.

[49] The Wu *ko* was assigned to King Kuang of Kung Wu 攻吳王光 by Yü Hsing-wu (*Shuang Chien I Ku Ch'i Wu, shang:* 44). Kuang is the name of King Chu-fan's 諸樊 second son who reigned as Ho-lü 闔廬 (514-496). In this Yü partly follows Jung Keng, who has treated this inscription and established the right interpretation of Kung Wu = Wu, in his *Niao Shu K'ao Pu Cheng* (*Yenching Hsüeh Pao,* XVII). The certainly not far-fetched equation Kuang = Ho-lü, and the dating within narrow limits resulting therefrom, have been doubted by Shang Ch'eng-tso: the arrangement of the characters, he thinks, demands a different interpretation, and instead of wang 王 "king" he reads kung 工 "fecit"; cf. *Shih*

*Erh Chia, Shuang:* 3-5. — Shang's reasons are not enough to prove that Jung Keng's reading, which has for itself the greater verisimilitude, must be wrong. As to the date implied, should Jung Keng's and Yü Hsing-wu's opinion be discarded, we only need replace "between 514-496" by "before 473 B.C.," the year Wu ceased to exist (*Shih Chi* 31; Chavannes, *Mém. hist.,* IV, p. 32), so that there is practically no difference.

[50] As to the third *ko,* with an inscription running in two columns over blade and *hu* (which is broken off at the lower part), the name of King Chang 璋 of Ch'u guarantees a date between 488 and 432 B.C. Chang is identical with Ch'u Hui Wang 楚惠王 (cf. *Shih Chi* 40; ed. Ku, II, 310; Chavannes, *Mém. hist.,* IV, p. 380 sq.). The particular form of the name, Yen Chang 酓璋, recurs in two inscriptions, namely, on a sword and on a bell from the fifty-sixth year of that king's reign; and the connection of the name with a longer reign than that attained by any other Ch'u ruler makes the attribution absolutely certain. Bell inscription: *Hsieh Shih K'uan Chih,* 6:7; *Liang Chou, K'ao Shih,* 165 b. The sword: *Ch'u Ch'i T'u Shih,* fol. 9, text fol. 4b; *Shih Erh Chia, Tsun,* 28 b sq.; for the inscription cf. also T'ang Lan, *Shou-hsien so ch'u T'ung Ch'i K'ao Lüeh,* in *Kuo Hsüeh Chi K'an,* IV/1, 1934. The sword is mentioned under Cat. no. 93 below (4).

[51] The Hsü *ko.* — The small state of Hsü 鄦 — in the inscription briefly 無, while book texts have the writing 許 — still existed in 481 B.C., but perished about the beginning of the Warring States period; cf. Karlgren, "Yin and Chou," p. 61 *s.v.* Hü.

[52] The fifth *ko* originates from Ts'ai, a fief erected after the advent of the Chou. Situated at first in Southeastern Honan, finally in Northern Anhui, Ts'ai was definitely annihilated by King Hui of Ch'u (cf. note 50 above) in 447 B.C. (*Shih Chi* 35; ed. Ku, II, p. 215; Chavannes, *Mém. hist.,* IV, p. 162). It is likely that this *ko* still dates from the sixth century B.C.

[53] Reproduced in *Chou Chin Wen Ts'un,* 6:17; cf. *Ferguson Catalogue,* p. 994 *s.v.* Yüan Cheng Ko 趄貞戈. For the inscription, see Shang Ch'eng-tso in *Shih Erh Chia, Shuang,* fol. 5 b. The script type is very similar to that of the Wu *ko* (*ibid.,* fol. 3-4; note 49 above), and the piece may therefore date from around 500 B.C.

[54] *Ch'en Tzu Chao Ko* 陳子召戈: *Chou Chin Wen Ts'un* 6/1:26 b; *Hsiao Chiao Ching Ko* 10:39 b with the reading "Ch'en Tzu I 翼"; mentioned under Cat. no. 79 below. — The Ch'en state, in present-day Honan, existed till 478 B.C. (*Shih Chi,* 36; Chavannes, *Mém. hist.,* IV, p. 182).

[55] *Lü Pu-wei Ko: Chou Chin Wen Ts'un* 6/1:1 and 3 — two different specimens. The first one is identical with that in *Shan Chai Chi Chin Lu,* 10:37. Contrary to what the *Ferguson Catalogue,* pp. 999-1000, states, the second one is not identical with *Shan Chai,* 10:35. The duality of an inscription referring to a Lü Pu-wei on two fairly similar specimens of *ko* must, of course, arouse suspicion. Only the first *ko* is, according to its pedigree, above suspicion: it was in the collection of Ch'en Chieh-ch'i in Wei-hsien, and has been reproduced already in *Ch'i Ku Shih* (10:29 b) and *Fu Chai Chi Chin Lu* (ch. 4). — Lü Pu-wei held office from 247 to 237 B.C.; cf. Chavannes, *Mém. hist.,* II, pp. 101, 112; Giles, *Biographical Dictionary,* p. 1455.

[56] Reproduced in *Shū Kan ihō,* Pl. 55; Sekino, Yatsui *et al., Rakurō-gun jidai no iseki,* text Figs. 201-3: photograph, detail, and diagram of the hafting of the Lo-lang specimen from 222 B.C.

[57] *Tu Chien Ko* 杜堅戈, dated Chien-p'ing 建平 2nd year = 5 B.C. Reproductions: *Hsiao Chiao Ching Ko,* 14:5 b; Jung Keng, *Han Chin Wen Lu,* 6:10 b.

# KNIVES AND DAGGERS

## Chapter IV

The first bronze knife of Shang age excavated at Anyang — an isolated specimen of inconspicuous design, and the only one to appear in the *Preliminary Reports* — became known in 1930.[1] It did not sensibly influence the then prevailing opinion that the Shang apparently had no knives. Three years later, in an article on several types of bronze tools from Yin-hsü, Li Chi described it together with a second Anyang knife of widely different design.[2] The first piece, which is fairly small, has a short and relatively broad blade slightly upcurved at the tip; its back, markedly thickened and nearly straight, is prolonged into a tang (Fig. 46 A). The other knife is more refined. It has a continuously curved, broadened back and handle, and the handle ends in a ring; the edge of the blade, jutting forth in an elegant angle, repeats the curve of the back (Fig. 46 B).

Li Chi at once pointed out that the ring-handle form must be inseparably connected with the Chou knife-shaped money, the "Ch'i knives 齊刀" (as they are called on account of the character 齊 often inscribed on them), and he also presented a theory on the origin of these knife types. Yin-hsü, he said, offers no instance of any comparable tool of premetallic age, whereas Kansu as well as Northern Manchuria yielded bone knives with flint edges such as the one from Chu-chia-chai 朱家寨 published by Andersson.[3] The bone knife would account for the shape of the cross section of the bronze types: the broad back, having no *raison d'être* in a metal tool, would easily be understood as a residue of the strong bone haft studded with thin flint flakes.[4]

To this may be answered that to regard such a composite tool of Tardenoisean appearances as a forerunner of the bronze knives would be justified, not by its structure, but rather by the mere fact that it too was a knife; moreover, the broad back of the bronze specimens is required to make good the lack of rigidity of their thin blades. Having thus reasoned on the question of possible prototypes, Li Chi mentions similarities found in the West and notably in Siberia, without pronouncing himself definitely on interdependence or priority.

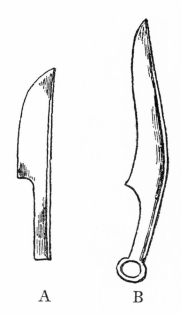

A          B

Fig. 46: *Two Shang knives from the excavations at Anyang.*

After Li Chi (ca. 1/3).

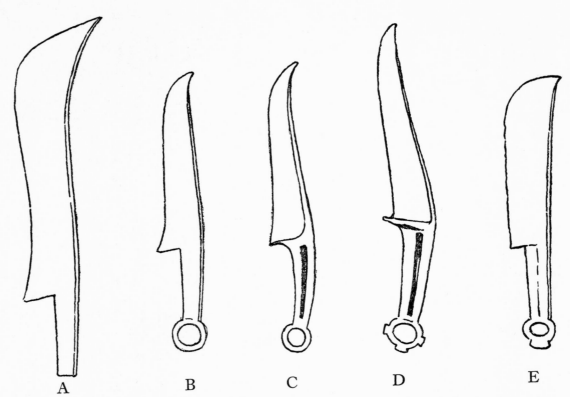

Fig. 47: *Shang knives from Hsiao-t'un (Anyang).*

Royal Ontario Museum, Toronto. After White (ca. 1/4).

A further series of Shang knives was made known by Bishop White in 1935.[5] These pieces were found in the Tomb of the Elephant, or in tomb-shafts in the vicinity of it, east of the village of Hsiao-t'un 小屯 near Anyang (Fig. 47).

A knife with a remarkably outlined blade of convex edge and steeply updrawn, strongly recurved point, but with the same broadened back extending into a tang, figures among them (Fig. 47 A), a very elegant type which is not found outside China. Another specimen closely resembles the ring-handled one mentioned above, save that the base of the blade forms a right angle with the hilt (Fig. 47 B). Something new is encountered in two curved knives with cast handles: hollow handles, oval in section and slitted throughout the length, meeting the blade in different ways and crowned by ring-pommels which may bear small knobs set at ninety-degree intervals (Fig. 47 C, D). The last specimen in that series diverges a little in shape; it has a strangely broad blade that widens toward the tip; the ring is very narrow and is set with a large knob; the back is straight (Fig. 47 E). It is true that these specimens, which are in the Toronto Museum, were not excavated by experts but found, associated with Shang bronzes, in an area abounding with remains of Shang age; having parallels, moreover, in the two examples described above (Fig. 46), their Shang date cannot well be doubted.

Umehara's contributions to our knowledge of the Anyang site in his magnificent albums, *Anyang Treasures* and *Anyang Studies,* are surprisingly meager with regard to knives, limiting themselves to two examples of tanged blades of slender shape, which stand roughly midway between the types Figs. 46 A and 47 A.[6] Another knife, a ceremonial tool, was reproduced by H. J. Timperley with some important Anyang discoveries. It resembles Fig. 47 A, but is enriched by an indented crest along the back and typical Shang ornaments of early style on the blade.[7]

There is another category of Shang or Early Chou knives, namely, that with *animal-heads* as pommels. They are very favorably represented in this collection by the unique, heavy dragon-head knife (Cat. no. 32), two curved knives with horse-heads (Cat. nos. 33 and 34), and a ceremonial knife with a large, broad, and heavy blade, the handle of which is terminated by a horse-head somewhat different in style (Cat. no. 40). The two horse-heads 33 and 34 have parallels in horse-head finials from Anyang in the Toronto Museum, where there is also kept a knife with a harnessed horse's head of the same provenance and age.[8] Knives purporting to hail from Anyang and having their handles crowned by elk- or ram-heads were published by G. Ecke in 1940.[9]

These scanty materials have increased substantially by Karlgren's publication of Anyang weapons in the Stockholm Museum.[10] Among them are almost all of the types listed thus far, with a dozen curved, ring-headed knives of comparably crude make and bare of any decoration, and four more elaborate pieces: (1) one with a ring set with three studs (like Fig. 47 D and Cat. no. 39); (2) a jingle-hilted one with remarkably recurved blade (Fig. 48); (3) one terminated by the head of an animal, probably a horse; and (4) a fragmented blade, the handle of which shows an ibex-head pommel and a small crested bird sitting on top of the grip.[11]

More allied types have been unearthed at Anyang during the later campaigns of the Academia Sinica,[12] including a remarkable specimen of curved knife with slitted grip and horse-head (Fig. 49) mentioned in Karlgren's paper. Since these pieces are the only ones to have been excavated under supervision of the Academia staff, they hold particular interest. One is not on thoroughly safe ground with the rest of what is presently available, and its evaluation will partly depend on those Academia finds, although some further evidence for the Shang age of the knife types dealt with here is afforded by early bronze inscriptions showing pictographs of knives of kindred design.[13]

PROBLEMS CONNECTED WITH THE SHANG KNIVES

All the specimens from Anyang described or referred to above — except types for ceremonial use such as Fig. 47 A, and, with regard to its singular dragon-head, the knife no. 32 in this collection — have

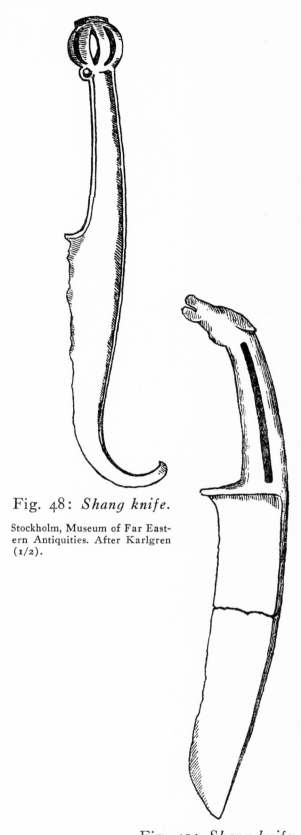

Fig. 48: *Shang knife.*

Stockholm, Museum of Far Eastern Antiquities. After Karlgren (1/2).

Fig. 49: *Shang knife.*

Nanking, Academia Sinica. After Karlgren (ca. 1/2).

more or less faithful counterparts among the materials from the Ordos Desert, Suiyüan, Inner Mongolia, and Central Siberia. Left without information as to their Anyang origin, I should assign those knives to the steppe cultures in the northern and northwestern borderlands of China proper, for knives with arched or recurved backs, slitted handles, pommels shaped as rings, animal-heads, and animal-figures abound there, and, in the case of early pieces, the simple geometric motifs found also in Shang examples embellish their hilts: parallel lines grouped in transverse bands, herringbone patterns, saw-teeth or serrated bands running longitudinally or transversely, rows and fields of dots or squares (Fig. 50).[14]

The presence of this sober and primitive but not in the least ungainly repertory characteristic of Sino-Siberian or Northern art in the midst of Anyang's gorgeous, sometimes bizarre décor of curves and hooks and spirals arranged to patterns utterly different in rhythm and subject, and never encountered in nomadic art, confronts one with the question whether these knives with geometric ornament are an invention of the Shang or the property of the nomads.

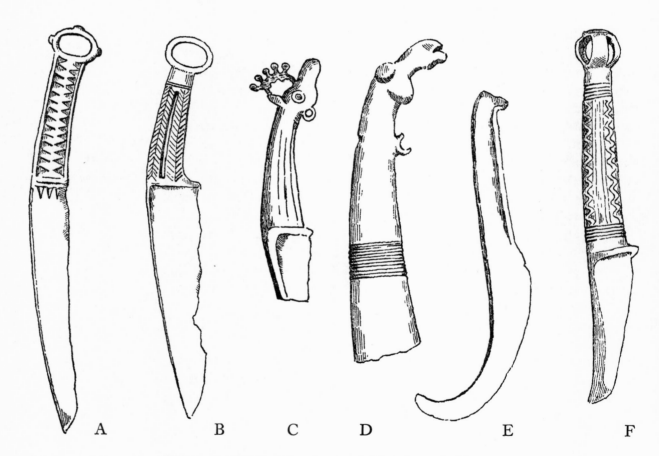

A          B          C          D          E          F

Fig. 50: *Some Siberian and Northern knife types.*

A—Znamienka (Minusinsk); after Martin. B—Ordos; after Egami and Mizuno. C—Karasuk (Minusinsk); after Teploukhov. D—Ordos, Larsson Collection; after Andersson. E—Suiyüan; after Egami and Mizuno. F—Mongolia, Stockholm Museum: after Karlgren (not to scale).

The same question arises again when the few *daggers* said to have
come from Anyang are compared with the many that are known
from the Steppe. There are, to my knowledge, no more than three
specimens labeled "Anyang," viz., dagger no. 89 with the rattle,
and two daggers in Stockholm with straight blades and with hilts
overtopped by awkwardly conventionalized, doubled or trebled animal-heads bent sideways.[15] The latter two pieces do not look like
Anyang things — even if compared with those animal-head knives
from that site which in style as well as subject least resemble typical
Shang decoration — while they strongly remind one of Ordos forms.
And, regarding the dagger no. 89 with its simple geometric ornament, parallels likewise are found only among Siberian and related
materials. All in all it is rather difficult to accept these daggers as
genuine Shang products, and further evidence will have to be sup-
plied by excavations to have the question of their origin and localization settled.

However, a few early daggers of obvious Chinese design (ornamentation and facture), such as nos. 85 and 86 in the Jannings Collection, do not show the slightest connection with the ambiguous
types just mentioned. These daggers with human faces on them differ
from the Siberian forms also in that they have no guard and grip
but a flanged, perforated tang instead, a device which apparently
never occurs in Siberia. The existence of such an independent [16]
Chinese type is highly significant. It bears out that the "Northern"
or Siberian daggers, although more numerous and widespread,
are something apart, distinct from purely Chinese daggers. In the
same way, during the following centuries, Ordos and related types of
daggers persist concurrently with those of unmistakably Chinese
(Chou) design (e.g., no. 92). Since these tanged Chinese daggers [17]
cannot have been derived from Siberian prototypes or Anyang types
allied with the Siberian, one might presume that there were forerunners, still unrecognized, from the Shang dynasty or from outside.
One touches on a problem here that seems to constitute a parallel to,
and to be linked with, that of the tanged short swords which (as is
shown in the chapter on swords below) are not related to the Scythian
*akinakes* and its precursors or anything Siberian, but rather precede
the *akinakes* and have their roots either in early Chinese tanged daggers or somewhere outside.

As to the main question which remains to be answered — that is,
whether the knife and dagger types from Anyang which occur in
variants in the steppe lands ultimately came from China, from Siberia, or, perhaps, from a Northern cradle influencing both Shang
and Central Siberian art — various elements which are not covered
in this chapter have to be taken into account. I have tried to sum them
up in chapter VI.

A discussion of the problem would presuppose a valid typology of
the Northern materials, which is wanting as yet.[18] Thus, theorizing

about the question of the origins of the Sino-Siberian knives would not lead beyond the line attained in the analysis of the axe types (ch. I). The arguments need not be repeated. I only wish to emphasize that the sheer fact of analogous conditions in a different class of weapons is very significant. There is an unconformity, too: unlike the knives, the axes that seem strangers in Anyang do not occur in Minusinsk.

The dagger was not, it seems, a favored weapon in ancient China, to judge by the scantiness of the finds, but there are considerable typological diversities to be observed, as would be expected to occur during the many centuries of the Bronze Age. However, I am still unable to trace a development which might have led from the tanged types, such as no. 85, to a much later variety with cast, richly decorated hilts, represented by no. 92. In the Chou III period, to which this specimen may belong, daggers with beautiful openwork scabbards were in fashion. Few of these scabbards have survived, and extant daggers which were sheathed in them display rather feeble blades unfit for serious use.[19] The dagger of this kind was evidently a mere accessory to the gala dress of the great, whose descendants later presumably replaced it by the fine short sword.

NOTES: CHAPTER IV    KNIVES AND DAGGERS

[1] *Anyang Fa Chüeh Pao Kao*, II: Li Chi, Pl. 9:2.

[2] *Ts'ai Yüan-p'ei Anniv.*, vol. I: Li Chi, *Yin-hsü T'ung Ch'i Wu Chung*, pp. 90-91, Pl. 1:6, 7.

[3] Andersson, "Preliminary Report on Archaeol. Research in Kansu," p. 13.

[4] Li Chi, *op. cit.*, in note 2, p. 91.

[5] W. C. White, in *Illus. London News*, April 20, 1935, Figs. 16-18.

[6] Umehara, *Anyang Treasures*, Pl. 17: 3-4.

[7] H. J. Timperley, in *Illus. London News*, April 4, 1936, Fig. 7.

[8] H. Kühn, "Chronologie der Sino-Sibirischen Bronzen," *IPEK*, XII, Pl. 57: 5, 6, 8.

[9] G. Ecke, "Über einige Messer aus Anyang," Figs. III, IV, V.

[10] Karlgren, "Some Weapons and Tools of the Yin Dynasty," *BMFEA*, 17.

[11] *Ibid.*, nos. 156, 157 (L. Clarke Collection), 160, 161, 161a, 162-66, 168-70; my enumeration (1)=172, (2)=173, (3) = 174, (4) = 180.

[12] Cf. Shih Chang-ju's *Yin-hsü tsui chin chih chung-yao fa-hsien* ("Recent discoveries at Yin-hsü"), pp. 17-20, 23, 50, 68, Fig. 5:40, 53, 54; Fig. 6:17; Fig. 16:2, 6 = Pl. 11:3, 4; Fig. 22:59. Altogether seven knives from three burials and one dwelling pit.

[13] Chewon Kim, "Über eine Gruppe chinesischer Messer," *OZ, XIV*, pp. 60-64.

[14] Illustrations in Fig. 50 after the following sources: A: F. R. Martin, *L'Age du Bronze au Musée de Minoussinsk*, Pl. 11:6. — B: Egami and Mizuno, *Inner Mongolia*, Pt. II, Corpus III, "Knives," A 2. — C: Teploukhov's drawing = Salmony, *Sino-Siberian Art*, Pl. III = Egami and Mizuno, *op. cit.*, Fig. 26:2 = Karlgren, "Some Weapons and Tools," no. 234. — D: Andersson, "Hunting Magic," Pl. 5:2. — E: Egami and Mizuno, *op. cit.*, Pl. 6:1. — F: Karlgren, "Some Weapons," no. 216.

[15] Karlgren, "Some Weapons," nos. 182, 183.

[16] In view of resemblances that have been said to exist between some Chinese and Luristan bronze things, it should at least be noted that there occur daggers in Luristan which have flanged hilts, and which may well be compared to the Chinese types in question. Cf. A. U. Pope, *A Survey of Persian Art*, vol. IV, Pls. 54 C, 55 A, B — the latter two items datable between 1123 and 1113 B.C. as shown by S. Langdon, *ibid.*, pp. 279 ff.

[17] In addition to the daggers with flanged tang, such as the nos. 85 and 86 below, there are other Chinese *tanged daggers* without flanges, which also go back to the days of the Early Chou. I have dealt with them in the Catalogue under no. 88; three examples: *Shan Chai Chi Chin Lu*, 11:3 b, *Ch'iu Ku Ching She*, 2:1, Janse, "Epées anciennes," Pl. 11:7. One further specimen, said to have come from Hsün-hsien (south of Anyang), is in Colonel W. B. Sawyer's collection; M. Loehr, "The Earliest Chinese Swords and the Akinakes," p. 136, Fig. 11. It is this small series of simple tanged daggers and a not much larger group of tanged short swords which lead me to believe that the Chinese swords are autochthonous; cp. ch. V, "Swords."

[18] A first attempt was made in my "Ordos Daggers and Knives," First and Second Parts, 1949 and 1951.

[19] One specimen of this kind, in the collection of A. Hellström, Mölndal, Sweden, is reproduced with an *akinakes* and its beautiful openwork scabbard from the Marquis Hosokawa collection, Tokyo, in Egami and Mizuno, *Inner Mongolia*, Pt. II, p. 34. Drawings of two daggers of this category, *ibid.*, Corpus II, Daggers, nos. 42, 43. The foregoing pieces may not illustrate the feebleness of the blades as strikingly as did two pieces which I happened to see in Peking; one of them was in a sheath of purely Chinese design in openwork, stylistically belonging to the Chou III period at the latest.

# SWORDS

*Chapter V*

In China, the sword is a loiterer. It not only appears late, it also has remained rather stationary as to its shapes. There are relatively primitive types, but no such highly developed ones as the Mörigen type or the Hallstatt slashing sword,[1] and the hilts especially show, on the whole, a surprising uniformity. The shapes, on the other hand, are pleasant and well built, and they are so distinctive that offhand it would seem more plausible than not to assume their independence. Independence, however, is just the quality outright denied them, it being taken for granted that the Chinese sword came from the West, most often the Scythian *akinakes* being regarded as its ancestor. The prevailing view has been that the sword was brought to China, with a host of other elements found in the decorative art of that time, around the middle of the Ist millennium B.C.[2]

But, since several inscribed specimens show that the Chinese sword from around 500 B.C.[3] is of the fully developed type (Fig. 51 D), an earlier date has to be assigned to their forerunners with the hollow hilt (Fig. 51 C) and a much earlier one to the comparatively primitive blades with tang as in Fig. 51 B. These three main types are contrasted with a typical *akinakes* of bronze from Kamenka (Kiev Govt.), which probably goes back to the seventh century B.C.[4] and is thus certainly among the earliest specimens of its kind. It is obvious that it resembles none of the Chinese swords. The question of the absolute age of these latter as warranted or suggested on epigraphical grounds, as well as of their typological order, has been treated extensively in the Catalogue below (nos. 87, 88, 93, 97). It will suffice, therefore, to state that according to our present knowledge the following dates are valid:

    Fig. 51 B — with tang, from the eighth-seventh centuries B.C.
    Fig. 51 C — with hollow handle, from the sixth century B.C.
    Fig. 51 D — with ringed solid handle, from about 500 B.C.

It must be remembered that these dates only indicate lower limits, that they are fortuitous, and that datable specimens are insufficient in number to permit of establishing a neat chronological sequence. There is, however, no typological gap between types such as Fig. 51 B and C, a transitional design having been recognized.[4a]

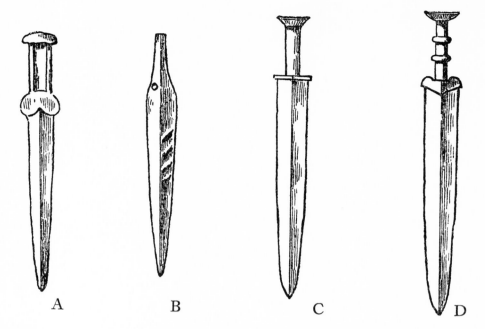

Fig. 51 : *A — Scythian akinakes from South-Russia. B, C, D — three types of Chinese swords.*

A — after *The Cambridge Ancient History*, Vol. II, Pls.
B, C, D — after specimens in the Jannings Collection (not to scale).

No sword was ever excavated at Yin-hsü (Anyang).[5] Thus, the tanged blades of the seventh or eighth century represent the oldest Chinese swords extant. They resemble typical *akinakes* (Fig. 51 A) no more than do the better known hilted types. Was there, then, any connection between the *akinakes* and the Chinese swords?

## THE *AKINAKES*

The Scythian short sword from South-Russia, Iran, and Siberia seems to go back to the seventh century B.C. In the beginning, bronze specimens occur, soon to be replaced by iron ones and by some of bronze and iron combined.[6] The *akinakes* is not a native of South-Russia. Swords were practically unknown to the regions north of the Pontus before the Scyths invaded them,[7] and the several examples of daggers known from pre-Scythian times are entirely different.[8]

In ancient Mesopotamia and the Caucasian cultures, the sword, in contrast to tanged daggers which spread over the whole of Hither Asia and also reached South-Russia, did not play an important role.[9] Luristan[10] and the Talysh[11] had splendid short-hilted swords of bronze in the Late Bronze and Early Iron ages, which again are strikingly different from anything Scytho-Siberian or Chinese.

Really close affinities to the *akinakes,* however, are found in Central Siberia and in the Suiyüan-Ordos region. N. Toll summarized the relation as follows:

> We can demonstrate that the South-Russian *akinakes* and the Minusinsk daggers are very similar to each other. The difference between these two groups consists mainly in the material, which in South Russia almost unvaryingly is iron, in the Minusinsk Steppe however is preferably bronze, or bronze and iron. In

South Russia, a tendency to replace the short thrusting dagger by the slashing sword is clearly recognizable, while the dagger of the Minusinsk Steppe unchangeably retains its old short form. . . . Among the Minusinsk daggers, on the other hand, we find types which are entirely absent in the Black Sea habitat of the Scyths. In general, the variety of forms in the Minusinsk daggers is perhaps greater than that of the Scythian *akinakes*.[12]

Even so, basing himself on G. v. Merhart,[13] Toll declines the idea of any direct contact between Minusinsk and the Scythian culture. But the apparently sudden and conspicuously wide distribution of the *akinakes* over Turkestan, Northern Persia, the Northern Caucasus, and South-Russia in the sixth century requires the assumption of a foregoing development somewhere in the nomadic world. This mysterious somewhere, Toll proposes, might be looked for not far from Mesopotamia.[14]

Many suggestions have been made as to the center of Scythian art — which need not a priori be the same whence the *akinakes* sprang — and they have been taken up in the following way by E. H. Minns:

As the nomads came across the metal-working tribes of the Krasnoyarsk-Minusinsk areas, perhaps other settled metal-workers in the Altai, they had their things copied in metal, and likewise later employed Chinese, Iranians, or western Asiatics, and Greeks. Great authorities have wished to put the origin of the nomad style in various places according as they thought each of these influences was fundamental.[15]

Swords cannot, of course, have been among the things of wood, stone, horn, or bone copied in metal, and one may safely assume that they were passed to the nomads from some sedentary folk skilled in bronze casting. The existence in the early Bronze Age of daggers in and around the Yenisei basin and among the Sino-Siberian bronzes is known. The early daggers do not resemble the *akinakes,* whereas the later ones do. If it were possible to prove — as I think it is — that the *akinakes*-like Siberian dagger had been developed from those early types, one would not hesitate to regard the Minusinsk-Krasnoyarsk and adjacent regions as the true home of the *akinakes.* The extent to which the Ordos province had an active part is a question that may be left open for the present; on the whole, one may think of a parallel evolution. A sketch will better serve to illustrate the change from the Karasuk[16] type of dagger of the later IInd millennium B.C. (Fig. 52 A, B) to the type of the advanced Bronze Age (Fig. 52 C-F),[17] a change which, of course, must have taken place before the seventh century B.C. when the *akinakes* had spread westward.

Although what I said above regarding the genesis of the *akinakes* is still hypothetical, some observations made by Merhart may be adduced in support of my point. Regarding the dagger from Monok (Abakan Steppe) shown in Fig. 52 A, with a kind of guard formed by characteristic incisions at the heel of the blade, he remarks that this type underwent changes which by way of reduction of the incisions led to forms very much nearer the typical daggers of the full Bronze Age kurgans. And, referring to the latter (types such as

52 E), Merhart says: "The guard does not conceal a certain connection with that of the *akinakes,* though very often it is narrower."[18] Earlier, Minns had noted that "these early inhabitants of the Jenisei developed a dagger with a curious heart-shaped guard and a well-defined knob at the end of the haft, which type is found in Scythic tombs and on the monuments of Persepolis."[19] That the shapes evolved in the same environment — Central Siberia and Suiyüan taken as a unit — included broad, rounded guards most closely resembling those of the genuine Scythian *akinakes* is demonstrated by an example from the Kishi Collection (Fig. 52 F), which was then unknown to Merhart.

So much seems clear: the Scythian sword migrated from East to West, no matter whether it can be traced back to the earliest daggers of the Karasuk stage in Central Siberia or corresponding types in the territory farther southeast. The characteristic roof-shaped or heart-shaped guard is common throughout the whole nomadic realm from the Yenisei to Suiyüan, with several predominant basic types, and in endless varieties which conspicuously contrast with the monotony found in the *akinakes* from Persia, the Euxine, or Ananino (Kama-Volga region).

If the *akinakes,* as I believe, came into being in that part of the nomadic continuum which borders China in the north, is it not likely that its influence should all the more have made itself felt in China, where there apparently was no form of sword, native or foreign, during the IInd millennium B.C.? The typical Chinese swords of Bronze Age fashion (Fig. 51 C, D) are without counterparts among the nomadic daggers or swords. They are of an entirely different structure. Moreover, they are preceded in time by a so-to-speak atypical short sword (Figs. 51 B, 53 D-F), for which again no models are to be found among the Scytho-Siberian remains. With this particular kind of sword I shall deal briefly.

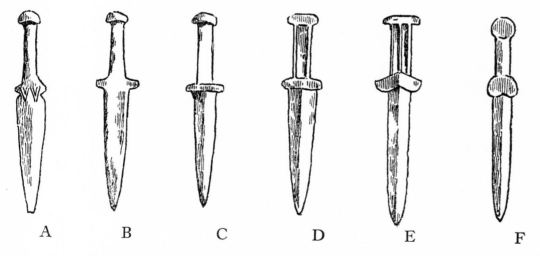

Fig. 52: *Daggers from Minusinsk (A-E) and the Ordos (F).*

After v. Merhart, F. R. Martin, Egami and Mizuno (not to scale).

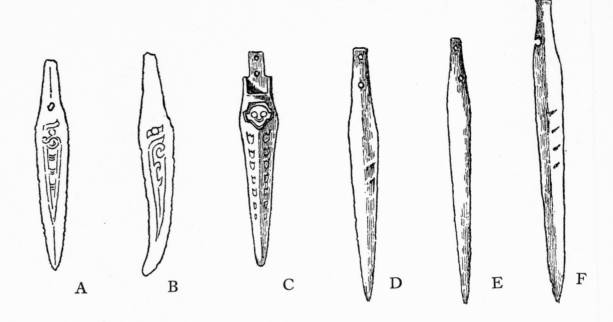

Fig. 53: *Chinese tanged daggers (A-C) and short swords (D-F).*

A—*Shan Chai Chi Chin Lu.* B, E—Stockholm Museum; after Janse. C, F—Jannings Collection, nos. 85 and 88. D—*Ch'iu Ku Ching She Chin Shih T'u.* (B, C, ca. 1/4; A, D-F, 1/4.)

## THE EARLY, ATYPICAL CHINESE SHORT SWORD WITH TANG

This rare category is represented in the Jannings Collection by the blade no. 88 (Fig. 53 F). Some of the examples referred to in the Catalogue under no. 88 are here shown in a series illustrating the typological position of this category.

The characteristic features of the swords of Fig. 53 D-F are these: a leaf-shaped blade, continuously tapering from the base; a tapering tang with perforations, engaging the full width of the base; a more or less rounded midrib or ridge; transverse slanting ribs (in the case of D and F). None of these features is encountered in Ordos, Siberian, or Scythian weapons, whereas some daggers of purely Chinese design (judged by their ornamentation) of Western Chou age (A, B, C) do exhibit them. Thus, one has good reasons for considering these "atypical" long daggers or short swords as likewise purely Chinese products, evolved from the early daggers; and so peculiar a detail as the slanting ribs recurring in D and F may even be taken as a definite proof for that. It might be argued, on the other hand, that the — possibly spellbinding — motif of the hand with a snake-head, which appears almost ubiquitously on these tanged swords (cp. under no. 88 below), has something foreign about it. Heine-Geldern indeed regards this type as a Western, ultimately European, intruder of the ninth, possibly the tenth century B.C.[19a] The way the ornaments are executed moreover recalls the sloping cut technique, common in Scythia. Nevertheless, the close relation with the Chinese daggers remains an undeniable fact, and this means that the Chinese archaic sword has nothing whatsoever to do with the *akinakes*.

This tanged, leaf-shaped blade is a rare type.[20] Presumably, it also was a short-lived one, soon replaced by another model: the sword with the hilt cast in one piece with the blade. One must, however, not think of a sudden change as having taken place. It rather seems that the shape of the tang first underwent a modification in that it became more slender and, in structure, more decidedly set off from the blade.[21] Afterward, a kind of hilt without a guard developed.[22] Finally, the grip-plates, which till then had been indispensable, were superseded by a cast handle.

THE SWORD WITH HOLLOW HANDLE

The median crest or the median rib could not offer the means of securely connecting the handle with the blade. A device had to be invented, and was, in the form of a rhombus-shaped plate long enough to cover the breadth of the blade, and broad enough to engage the width of the handle (Fig. 54). This hollow-handled type of sword, which takes one back at least to the sixth century B.C. (see no. 93), also shows a marked difference with regard to the blade. The latter now has parallel edges, with a slight reduction of the width in the lower third, and the edges are very accurately ground to facets; a section would, in general, show a narrow rhombus. The hilt widens a little on top, where it is trimmed to a commonly horizontal, plain ring. The hollow is sometimes filled or covered by a disk of turquoise, glass (see no. 93), bronze,[23] or other substances. In the rest, there is no decoration at all.

This sword, although it would have served mainly for thrusting or piercing, still was, regarding the structure of the hilt's attachment to the simple rhombus-guard, a comparatively fragile weapon. Consequently, its length in general is moderate, rarely exceeding 450 mm.[24] The fact of its occurrence in fairly large numbers, on the other hand, suggests that it had been a favorite type which seemingly did not vanish at once when the "classic" type began to appear. Not paying attention here to subtypes or minor variants of either hilt-shapes or blade-forms, I wish only to emphasize that the development of the "classic" type may be understood as an attempt to overcome the structural weakness of the hollow-handle sword by strengthening the guard, the element on which the juncture of blade and hilt depends.[25]

THE SWORD WITH RINGED SOLID HANDLE

The "classic" Chinese sword has the heel of the blade reinforced by a more or less broad guard which is thicker and slightly wider than the blade. From a saddle between the rounded shoulders of the guard the stout, solid handle rises, with ring-rolls and a pommel in

Fig. 54: *The hilt of the hollow-handled sword.*

the shape of a generally conical disk (Fig. 51 D; nos. 94-99). This type usually is heavier and tends to be longer than the hollow-handled one, while the form of the blade remains essentially the same as before: the edges are parallel, and the lower third commonly narrows to form a slender ogive. The blades are nearly always rhombic in section, but sometimes the crest protrudes more markedly, making the courses appear hollow (as in the case of the beautiful rapier, no. 102). In contrast to the hollow-handle category, the present one is often decorated at the guard with a kind of animal-mask and some ornament on the upper face of the pommel; the effect of these ornaments is not seldom heightened by incrusted turquoise particles (nos. 97, 98, 102).

This type made its appearance around 500 B.C.; epigraphically datable specimens — on which we have to base ourselves exclusively for lack of archaeological evidences — do not, for the time being, lead farther back. Thus it seems as if the older type with the hollow handle was predominant for only a short while; but we must keep in mind that epigraphical dates are, as was said already, quite casual, and that they only mark *termini ante quos*.

It would be interesting to know how the ring-handle sword came into being. Transitional types such as in Fig. 104 under no. 97 do exist, suggesting that the "classic" type was evolved from the hollow-handle type. However, these intercategorical specimens are still insufficiently known and the few known ones do not constitute a typological series that would demonstrate the supposed evolution convincingly. Even so, what those several transitional shapes suggest, namely, the autochthonous creation of the most representative Chinese sword type, must be seriously considered. Olov Janse was convinced that the transformation had taken place.[26]

NOMENCLATURE

The Chinese designations for the several parts of the Chou sword as described above are as follows (Fig. 55):

| | | | |
|---|---|---|---|
| Pommel | *shou* | 首 | "head" |
| Handle | *heng* | 莖 | "stalk" |
| Lashings | *kou* | 維 | "cord" |
| Guard | *la* | 臘 | .....[27] |
| Median ridge | *chi* | 背 | "spine" |
| Courses at each side of the median ridge | *tsung* | 從 | "lengths" |
| Blade | *shen* | 身 | "body" |
| Facets | *o(ngo)* | 鍔 | "edge"[28] |
| Edge | *jen* | 刃 | "edge" |
| Point | *feng* | 鋒 | "point" |

What the *K'ao Kung Chi,* the oldest source dealing especially with the Chou sword, says is little and not unambiguous, so that a reconstruction based on it led to such a fallacious shape as was contained in E. Biot's translation (II, 496). True understanding of that lapidary text only was attained when Ch'eng Yao-t'ien 程瑤田 in his *K'ao Kung Ch'uang Wu Hsiao Chi* went over it again, comparing the scanty data with extant Chou swords. He thus notably corrected the interpretation of the expression *"la kuang 臘廣"* — which had previously always been regarded as denoting "the width of the blade" — by pointing out that it must refer to the guard.[27]

How long the shapely type of the "classic" bronze sword did live is not yet exactly known. Janse called attention to the fact that in Lo-lang, the Chinese Han period settlement in Korea, bronze swords are outnumbered by iron ones; his conclusion was that around the beginnings of the Han dynasty bronze swords had gone out of fashion.[29] No new excavations that might shed some light on the question have since been undertaken.

IRON SWORDS

In this collection, iron swords are represented by a single specimen, fragmentary at that, which does not add to our knowledge (no. 103). Sabers of either bronze or iron, increasingly occurring toward the beginning of the Han dynasty, are not represented at all.

The characteristic traits of the iron blades as compared with those of bronze are their length and solidity, making them the superior weapon. It is a matter of course, therefore, that the bronze types receded to the background as soon as the iron types appeared. Whether this was already the case when the new material as such became known is open to question; studying iron objects of Chou date, one rather gets the impression that iron, in the beginning, was used preferably for things lovelier than weapons, since iron belthooks and the like, plated with gold foil and dating back to a time as early as the fifth century B.C., have been found.[30] No iron sword has thus far been discovered that could be dated so early. And, corroded and decayed as they are, none can be dated by means of an inscription.

Rostovtzeff, in his *Iranians and Greeks in South-Russia,* credited the Sarmatians with having brought to China a whole series of weapons:

> . . . the Chinese adopted not only their scale and ring armour from the Sarmatians, their heavy spears, and their conical helmets, but their arrows with the characteristic triangular head, their short ring-headed daggers, . . . their horsetrappings, which during the Han and succeeding dynasties are purely Iranian, and last but not least their *long* swords, in which the guard, the pommel and the bottom of the scabbard are of jade, just as in South Russia of the Sarmatian period.[31]

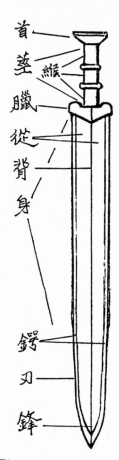

Fig. 55: *The "classic" Chou sword and its parts.*

We have seen that helmets, heavy spearheads, and ring-pommel daggers existed as early as the Shang dynasty; triangular arrowheads were common in China since premetal ages; the swords were developed, as I tried to demonstrate above, independently from those of the nomadic world, and early assumed — at least in individual cases — considerable lengths. There is no need to look for sources far away to account for the presence of long swords in China, and much in the same way as W. P. Yetts stated that he failed to find evidence of contact between the Sarmatians and China as far as horse-trappings are concerned,[32] I do not see how to verify the supposed Sarmatian influence in the case of the sword.

In literature, the sword plays a role from the Warring States period onward, while it is not mentioned in the earlier classics such as the *Shu Ching* or the *Odes*. Such omission is quite significant as regards the age of the sword as a weapon, and we do well to remember that palaeography down to Western Chou offers no instances of the character "sword" either. Of passages referring to datable events which mention swords, those of the *Tso* and *Kung-yang Commentaries* to the *Spring and Autumn Annals* seem to go back farthest: the *Tso Chuan* to the tenth year of Duke Hsi (650 B.C.) with the account of a man's suicide in answer to his ruler's reproaches;[33] the *Kung-yang Chuan* to the twelfth year of Duke Chuang (682 B.C.).[34]

Later sources, reveling in sword legends that seem to have arisen during the Warring States period, do not hesitate to ascribe to remote antiquity swords endowed with marvelous qualities. There must then have been an atmosphere fostering the growth of sword myths, for there are tales of connoisseurs with unerring judgment;[35] of saltimbancos capable of juggling five swords simultaneously;[36] of curious smiths;[37] and of praiseworthy blades of fabulous value[38] or those of ill portent.[39] There were princes who liberally entertained desperadoes willing to display their swordsmanship in earnest until they fell under the quicker opponent's thrust — at the rate of over a hundred a year.[40] No wonder that a weapon cherished and perfected as was the sword of late Chou time — which probably was never carried by the common soldier — so gained in esteem that swordless kings and heroes of the past became quite unimaginable. An enthusiastic scholar finally drew up a catalogue of famous swords of the rulers of all the known dynasties, beginning with the Hsia: a *Record of Knives and Swords, Ancient and New*.[41] Less pretentious as a document, less thrilling than the many stories of wonderful blades, but of human and literary worth is Ssu-ma Ch'ien's anecdote of Prince Chi-tzu of Wu 吳季子, who gave his precious sword to one who had coveted it but who passed away before he could receive it.[42]

NOTES: CHAPTER V    SWORDS

[1] E.g., V. G. Childe, *The Bronze Age,* Fig. 8: 10, 12.

[2] O. Janse, "Epées anciennes," pp. 97-99. — Harada and Komai, *Shina Koki Zukō,* I, p. 22. — Egami and Mizuno, *Inner Mongolia,* Pt. II, p. 29. — L. C. Goodrich, *A Short History of the Chinese People,* p. 27. — L. Bachhofer, *A Short History of Chinese Art,* p. 46. Earlier writers held that the bronze sword did not date back beyond the Han dynasty; cf. Laufer, *Chinese Clay Figures,* p. 215.

[3] See the materials discussed under Cat. no. 97 below.

[4] After *The Cambridge Ancient History,* Pl. I, p. 257a. The piece "cannot well be later than 7th c. B.C.," *ibid.,* III, p. 198.

[4a] A specimen in the Li T'ai-fen Collection, Peking; *Ch'ih An Ts'ang Chin,* fol. 65. Cf. M. Loehr, "The Earliest Chinese Swords and the Akinakes," pp. 139, 137, Fig. 13.

[5] Expressly stated by Harada and Komai, *Shina Koki Zukō,* I, p. 21, and by Komai in *Tōyō Rekishi Daijiten,* IV, p. 100.

[6] In the Pontic region, the iron sword is the rule, whereas in Siberia (Minusinsk, in the first place) bronze remains in favor even after the beginnings of the Iron Age about the seventh century B.C. Cf. Borovka, *Scythian Art,* p. 75; N. Toll, "Bronzedolche der Sammlung Zichy," p. 186. — For the Pontus (Kuban), we may assume that iron was widely in use at the time when the Scyths arrived, its beginnings being around 1000 B.C., according to A. V. Schmidt, *ESA,* IV, p. 21.

[7] A. M. Tallgren, "La Pontide préscythique," p. 202, regarding swords says: "Elles n'appartiennent pas au mobilier archaïque populaire de l'Europe orientale. On n'en trouve que dans les cultures des Sarmates, Goths et Vikings. Mais là aussi, elles sont de grandes raretés. L'épée de bronze à deux tranchants était une arme de Mycènes et de l'Europe Centrale, septentrionale et occidentale, mais pas de l'Orient."

[8] Cf. Tallgren, *ibid.,* Figs. 88 and 109: daggers with broad, oval, leaf-shaped blades with midrib widening at the heel, cast in one piece with the hilt that forms a longitudinal oval eye. They belong to the later Bronze Age. The pieces in *ibid.,* Fig. 88, form part of the Sosnovaya Maza hoard (Saratov Govt.) which, according to Tallgren, dates from 900 B.C. A small dagger of exactly the same type in the Minusinsk Museum is reproduced in a drawing in Tallgren's *Collection Tovostine,* p. 42 (= Fig. 59 B), where he refers to some more related specimens from Minusinsk and the Urals.

[9] Cf. Childe, *The Most Ancient East,* p. 226. Those tanged daggers are of far earlier age than the types mentioned in note 8 above.

[10] A. U. Pope, *A Survey of Persian Art,* IV, Pl. 54 C; 55 A, B.

[11] J. de Morgan, "La Préhistoire orientale," III, Figs. 198, 249, 251.

[12] N. Toll, "Bronzedolche der Sammlung Zichy," *ESA,* IV, p. 186 f.

[13] *Bronzezeit am Jenissei,* p. 17.

[14] Toll, *op. cit.,* p. 187 f.

[15] E. H. Minns, "The Art of the Northern Nomads," p. 13.

[16] The dagger type is included in Teploukhov's typical inventory of the Karasuk stage. Cf. his "Essai de classification" in *Mat. po Etn.,* IV/2, or the reproduction in A. Salmony's *Sino-Siberian Art,* Pl. 3.

[17] Sources from which our text Fig. 52 A-F is taken: A: v. Merhart, *Bronzezeit am Jenissei,* p. 59, Fig. 34; B-E: F. R. Martin, *L'Age du Bronze au Musée de Minoussinsk,* Pls. 23: 10, 9, 7, Pl. 22: 10; F: Egami and Mizuno, *Inner Mongolia,* Pt. II, Corpus III, Daggers, no. 37.

[18] *Bronzezeit am Jenissei,* pp. 60 and 56.

[19] E. H. Minns, *Scythians and Greeks,* p. 246 f.

[19a] R. Heine-Geldern, "Das Tochararproblem und die pontische Wanderung," p. 229.

[20] In addition to the specimens listed under no. 88, the reader is referred to three related pieces published in my article "The Earliest Chinese Swords and the Akinakes," p. 135, Figs. 2, 3, 8.

[21] Cf. O. Janse, "Epées anciennes," Pls. 11, 13, 14.

[22] The unusual type, *ibid.,* Pl. 12: 2, with a hilt but without a guard, and Pl. 9: 3, 4, flat-tanged short blades with a round

pommel on top of the flat handle, seems to point in that direction. Cf. also the specimen mentioned in note 4a.

[23] O. Janse, "Epées anciennes," p. 72, Fig. 1.

[24] *Ibid.*, p. 73, we read of exceptionally long pieces of 725 mm.

[25] This function of the guard as a structural part is, of course, not to be generalized. Guards of jade or of bronze attached to iron tanged blades of the late Chou or Han time do not influence at all the solidity of the structure.

[26] "Epées anciennes," p. 97. For the problem of the transformation of the hollow-handle type into that with broad guard and solid handle, cp. the remarks under Cat. no. 97 below.

[27] As to the term *la* (*lieh?*) 臘, the *Chou Li K'ao Kung Chi* text runs as follows: 臘廣二寸有半寸。兩從半之 (*Shih San Ching Chu Su*, ch. 40, fol. 7 b). As in Biot's translation, this term has commonly been taken in the sense of "blade"; so, for instance, in *Ch'iu Ku Ching She Chin Shih T'u*, ch. 1:4. Ch'eng Yao-t'ien, however, has observed that the Commentary erroneously explained 臘謂兩刃 "*la* (or *lieh*) means the two edges" (*Chu Su, ibid.*), and that *la* actually refers to the guard. Cf. *K'ao Kung Ch'uang Wu Hsiao Chi, HCCC*, ch. 538:6 b last column. — In Karlgren's *Grammata Serica* (637 j) one still finds the following entry: "*La*, loan for *idem* part of sword blade (from ridge to edge) (*Chouli*)."

[28] The differentiation between *o* (*ngo*) = "facets" and *jen* = "cutting edge" may seem risky, for both terms were probably used rather indiscriminately. Ch'eng Yao-t'ien indeed explains the term *o* 鍔 in *Chuangtse* (*Shuo Chien P'ien* 說劍篇) by *jen* 刃 "edge"; *K'ao Kung Ch'uang Wu Hsiao Chi, op. cit.*, 1 b.

[29] "Epées anciennes," p. 93. See the discussion under Cat. no. 97.

[30] E.g., T. Nagahiro, *Taikō no kenkyū*, Pls. 28 and 46. For the date of early, spatula-shaped belt-hooks with rectilinear design such as found on iron specimens,

cf. L. Bachhofer, "Bronze Figures of the Late Chou Period," p. 324 f.

[31] M. Rostovtzeff, *Iranians and Greeks in South Russia*, p. 204, cf. p. 129.

[32] W. P. Yetts, "The Horse: A Factor in Early Chinese History," *ESA*, IX, p. 254 f.

[33] Legge, *The Chinese Classics*, V, pp. 156-57.

[34] *Shih San Ching Chu Su*, ch. 7:8a; *Harvard-Yenching Index*, I, p. 60.

[35] E.g., *Yüeh Chüeh Shu*, quoted *TSCC*, *ts'e* 764, ch. 288, fol. 2 a:2-3; *Hanfeitse*, ch. 7, fol. 13 b, quoted *TSCC*, *ibid.*, fol. 1 b:1-2.

[36] *Lietse, Shuo Fu* 8:8 a, quoted *TSCC*, *ibid.*, fol. 1 b:1.

[37] *Wu Li Lun*, quoted *TSCC*, *ibid.*, fol. 3 b:2; *Sou Shen Chi*, quoted *TSCC*, *ibid.*, fol. 1 b:2 (variant rendering of that story in *Wu Yüeh Ch'un Ch'iu*, quoted *TSCC*, *ibid.*, 1 b:2-3).

[38] *Shih Chi* 97, 陸賈傳, ed. K'ai Ming, I, 0229.1; quoted *TSCC*, *ibid.*, fol. 3 b:2. — *Yüeh Chüeh Shu*, quoted *ibid.*, fol. 2 a:2-3 (the value here given of a certain sword in the possession of King Kou-chien of Yüeh exceeds that of two villages with markets, 1000 good horses, and two cities of 1000 households). Referring to another sword of the same provenance, we elsewhere learn of much less moderate figures: 30 villages with markets, 1000 fine horses, and two cities of 10,000 households each (*TSCC, ibid.*, fol. 2 a:1).

[39] Such an ill-famed sword from Yüeh was Yü-ch'ang 魚腸, said to be predestined for parricide or slaying sovereigns; *Wu Yüeh Ch'un Ch'iu*, quoted *TSCC*, *ibid.*, fol. 2 a:1.

[40] *Chuangtse, Shuo Chien P'ien*, ch. 10, first passage; quoted *TSCC*, *ibid.*, fol. 2 b:2.

[41] The *Ku Chin Tao Chien Lu* 古今刀劍錄, included in *Han Wei Ts'ung Shu*.

[42] *Shih Chi* 31: *Wu shih-chia*, ed. K'ai Ming, I, 0122.1; Chavannes, *Mém. hist.* IV, p. 15 f. — Cp. the sword of Wu Chi-tzu's son, discussed under Cat. no. 93 (1).

# SIBERIA IN THE EARLY BRONZE AGE

*Chapter VI*

Having dealt with various types of early metal weapons from China, I time and again observed a complete lack of primitive types. Hence the question inevitably arises whether these might not be found outside China. Comparing early Chinese forms with corresponding materials from more westerly countries, I did not, however, arrive at a clear-cut and generally applicable result. The several principal classes of weapons rather seem to suggest varied origins, indigenous or otherwise, as shown in the following table.

| TYPES | PROBABLE ORIGINS |
|---|---|
| Shaft-hole axes | Northern. Ultimately Mesopotamia? |
| Tanged axes | China. Stone prototypes? |
| Socketed celts | Russia — Siberia. |
| Spearheads | Russia — Siberia? (no Northern elements recognizable). |
| Tanged dagger-axes | China. |
| Socketed dagger-axes | China. Shaft-holes Northern? |
| Knives | Northern types and Chinese types. |
| Tanged daggers | China (Early Chou?). |
| Hilted daggers | Early types Northern. Chou types independently Chinese. |
| Swords | China (derived from Early Chou daggers). |

This is not a clear picture. There are types which are not traceable outside China. Others may have come from sources far away in Western Asia, but undergone changes en route so that it is difficult to come to a conclusion. Only in the case of cultures in immediate contact with the Northwest, broadly speaking, do identical shapes occur. One of the reasons why possible relations between China and Turkestan — Iran — Luristan cannot be traced satisfactorily is that information on the intermediate regions of Mongolia, Dzungaria, Kazakhstan, and Russian Turkestan is scanty.[1] Therefore, I am not able to pronounce with assurance in the case of such weapon types as seem to be foreign but are absent in Minusinsk.

Thus, archaeological proofs for ancient links between China and Mesopotamia-Iran are not afforded. On the other hand, one cannot gainsay the probability of these ancient centers with their IVth millennium metallurgy having been somehow instrumental in the rise of China's bronze industry, not only because the latter is much younger — taking us back no farther than around 1300 B.C., according to present knowledge — but also because Chinese artifacts in themselves favor the hypothesis that there had been borrowing of well-developed types. Primeval types, such as the flat celt and the triangular dagger, current in Egypt, Babylonia, and Sindh,[2] have not been found in China thus far. Sudden beginnings and rapid growth to utter refinement are the salient features, riddleful and always striking, of China's first metal age. In taking into account the tremendous difference in age, occasional resemblances of Chinese and West Asian materials — as in the case of some axe types — deserve to be noted.

Rather incomprehensible is the fact that the Chinese metal age started so late. Dead reckoning based upon that difference of 2,000 and more years in the beginnings might induce us to push back by a couple of centuries the dawn of metalworking in the Far East. C. W. Bishop thought that the use of copper began around 2100 B.C. in extreme northwestern China,[3] and some time after 2000 B.C. in northern China,[4] but he did not indicate what kind of finds he had in mind. To my knowledge there are no materials suggestive of a date that early. Even the few metal objects from late Painted Pottery sites in Kansu and Jehol are unlikely to antedate appreciably, if at all, Anyang, which by and large remains the earliest Chinese Bronze Age site. Anyang (Yin-hsü), as was established by Ch'en Meng-chia[5] and, independently, by B. Karlgren,[6] had been the residence of the *Shang-Yin* dynasty from 1300 to 1028 B.C., while the *Chou* began their rule in 1027 B.C., the date in accordance with the (authentic) *Chu Shu Chi Nien* or *Bamboo Annals*. The date hitherto upheld for P'an Keng's removal of his capital to Yin (Anyang) was, according to the "orthodox" chronology, 1401 B.C. Thus, for the time being, we must accept the perplexing fact that China took to metallurgy very late.

Departing from the date 1300 B.C., Karlgren calculated that Siberian influences on China were not possible because objects comparable to Chinese ones were later than 1300 in the Yenisei region around Minusinsk. The analogies are "animal style" artifacts, which in Teploukhov's classification of the Minusinsk metal cultures[7] appear around 1000 B.C. The question of the animal style is a detail that will be touched upon later. My foremost concern is the chronology of the Siberian metal age in general.

To evaluate properly historical relations between China and her neighbors north and west, one must keep western Asia in mind. No matter how humble their civilization might have been in comparison to that of the Shang, the herdsmen of the Eurasian steppes had had contacts with the splendors of urban life in western Asia from very early times, and had acquired knowledge of metal and weaponsmithy. In a quarter nearer the cradle, far west in the Steppe, South-Russia, one finds testimonies of the early contact of the Steppe folk with Mesopotamia and Anatolia: the great kurgans north of the Caucasus, Tsarskaya (Novosvobodnaya), Maikop, Kostromskaya, Psebaiskaya, Vozdvizhenskaya, Andriukovskaya, Kelermes, Konstantinovskaya, Ul, and others, dating from the IIIrd and IInd millennia B.C. The date of these barrows, especially of Tsarskaya and Maikop, is of interest because it bears on the chronology of Siberia.

THE AFANASIEVA STAGE

For the simple reason that the region of Minusinsk archaeologically is better known than are other parts of Siberia, one had best start there, but I wish to make it clear from the outset that Minusinsk alone will not provide a picture representative of the whole of Siberian prehistory. The Yenisei basin to the north of the Altai and Sayan range lies outside the main steppe thoroughfare and will thus probably not have been reached by all movements in the open grasslands to the south. The Minusinsk-Krasnoyarsk basin, where, for instance, Stone Age painted pottery is absent but which in very remote times already sheltered settled folk,[8] rather was intimately connected with the Eurasian Forest Zone cultures. Nevertheless, Minusinsk affords valuable clues as to what occurred in the steppe belt.

Before a palaeolithic background with Aurignacian (Malta, near Irkutsk[9]) and Magdalenian features (Tomsk; Afontova Hill near Krasnoyarsk; several stations around Minusinsk[10]), offering many analogies to finds made in Russia, there is a sequence of chalcolithic and metal age cultures which again show that remote corner of Siberia well interconnected with southwestern and western formations in Turkestan and South and Central Russia. The first of these cultures, according to S. A. Teploukhov, is the *Afanasieva* culture from the verge of the IIIrd millennium B.C., named after Afanasieva Hill near Bateni on the left bank of the Yenisei, downstream from Minusinsk.[11] The graves, covered with stones, contain contracted or at any rate flexed skeletons, rough clay pottery (pit-comb ware), ceramics with plaster applied for decoration or coated with copper. Ergological remains are of stone and bone; a slender shouldered celt seems to belong to the typical tools. Bones of domesticated animals such as horse, ox, and sheep were found, evidencing Afanasieva man's experience in cattle breeding and his acquaintance with the horse. An important feature is the kind of shell made into beads and worn around the neck and the wrist. This species of shell occurs in the Aral Sea, whence it must have been imported.[12] More recent discoveries in Khorezm brought to light a neolithic culture on the southern shore of Lake Aral, the *Kelteminar* culture, which proved closely connected with the Afanasieva stage.[13] Ornaments in Kelteminar were in part also made of imported shells, such as occur in the Red Sea, the Arabian Gulf, and the Persian Gulf. Imposing are the wide connections revealed by flint tools and ceramics: Russian archaeologists observed resemblances to neolithic stages in Central Russia (Kama River region), the Urals, Southern Siberia, and Northern India.[14] *Anau,* due south, at the foot of the Iranian Plateau, may have played an active part in the shaping of the Kelteminar culture.[15]

THE ANDRONOVO STAGE

In Turkestan, an early bronze culture, distinct from that of Anau,[16] rose in apparently close connection with the Steppe from the Ukraine to South-Siberia: the *Tazabagyab* culture. Parallel with it, perhaps a little later, the first bronze phase in Minusinsk is found: the *Andronovo* culture, named after a burial site excavated near Andronovo in the district of Achinsk.

Andronovo designates, as Tallgren says, a rich and powerful civilization which has left objects, large, heavy, and magnificent.[17] The tombs lie under low tumuli often surrounded by a stone fence. Stone cists occur, but wooden chamber constructions are more characteristic, with contracted skeletons, lying sideways. In addition to coarse pottery, a finer ware appears, decorated with triangles and lozenges, meander and swastika — tidy geometric designs. Of course there are stone tools in the graves. Beads of stone, sard, copper, and animal teeth are common. Pendants, spirals, temple rings of silver, arm rings of bronze recalling Caucasian ornaments, copper pendants with gold inlay testify to wealth and refinement. Metal tools, in the Minusinsk region, comprise daggers with a primitive cast hilt (Fig. 66 D) and socketed celts of Seima type (Fig. 56); farther southwest, Andronovo graves yielded also spearheads (Fig. 39) and shaft-hole axes (Fig. 62). In pits containing funeral food, bones of horse, ox, and sheep were discovered as well as wheat in large quantity. In one case, a dog had been interred with his master — a feature apt to recall vividly what A. R. Burn has said on the good companionship of man and dog.[18] Textiles, too, occur.[19]

If any culture in the West did convey elements likely to promote metalworking in North-China, it must have been the Andronovo culture. One therefore cannot but go somewhat into detail, to ascertain, if possible, facts regarding its expansion, filiations, and age, and become acquainted with its character and properties as far as weapons are concerned.

EXPANSION OF THE ANDRONOVO CULTURE

Excavations in Kazakhstan were made by P. S. Rykov near the Soviet Farm Gigant in the Karaganda district, approximately halfway between Tazabagyab at the Amu-Darya and Minusinsk; a large

Andronovo settlement was uncovered.[20] Another was unearthed in Alexeyevka on the Tobol River by B. N. Grakov: a town and a large cemetery belonging to the Andronovo facies.[21] To the northeast, the culture is traced in the Yenisei region. It thus must have covered the whole of South-Siberia from the southern Urals — where Tallgren, presumably in consideration of Grakov's discoveries, presupposes its center — to Minusinsk. It can safely be assumed that there were extensions eastward along the upper Irtysh River and by way of the Dzungarian Gap,[21a] reaching Mongolia somewhere around Kobdo; and farther south perhaps, guided by the Ek-Tagh Altai range toward the north bend of the Yellow River, some communication through the later Hsiung-nu territory seems not unlikely. At any rate, if contact was made with China through the northwestern *barbaroi,* it was not necessarily or exclusively from or via Minusinsk, a secondary hearth off the main route.

In the west, one meets this culture at the Lower Volga (Saratov, Khvalynsk; spearheads, Fig. 39).[22] It is widely scattered in the Central Russian Forest Zone around the Upper Volga, and splendidly represented by the finds from Galich, Seima, Turbino, Korshunovo-Sloboda, Yarlikly.[23] Farther north stray finds are recorded, among which a socketed celt of Seima type from Ustsysolsk (Fig. 56 B) may be mentioned.[24] Related types are known from Finland, where they are not isolated phenomena but are associated with Andronovo pottery (Hankasalmi).[25] The Russian Arcticum, where traces of this culture are encountered, may have been, as Tallgren thought, a sphere of interest of the Andronovo civilization.[26] Along the Kama River, connections crossing the Urals did exist (Verkhne-Kizil; peat-bog finds of Shigir and Gorbunovo).[27]

The Ukraine certainly was connected with that civilization, and perhaps had her active share in it; Tallgren supposes the Seima celt to have originated in the Ukraine.[28] Lastly, Bessarabia must not be forgotten: thence came the hoard find from Borodino[29] near the mouth of the Dniester, with its superb stone battle-axes (see Fig. 63).

Thus, embracing the immensely vast stretches of the northern steppe and no small part of the parklands and forests farther north, and, as has been said, connected with the Tazabagyab bronze culture south of Lake Aral, Andronovo is likely to represent the Siberian Bronze Age in its prime. The sheer fact of its huge expansion bespeaks a radiating power which makes it more probable than not that effects were felt as far as Mongolia and China.

It might justly be asked whether Andronovo with its wide dispersion actually was a unity. Taken in the broad sense of the *Early Bronze Age of the Steppe* I think it was. From the point of view of Shang-Yin or pre-Shang China it does not matter if "Andronovo," as a term, includes locally distinct formations that may overlap in time. In the case of China, unity is not afforded either, and "Shang" means something quite different when applied to North-Honan,

Jehol, or Kansu. In short I wish to stress that I take "Andronovo" as a term comprising various local strains, and that to narrow it down to a special facies would be inadequate for our purpose.

The fundamental question, namely, does Bronze Age Minusinsk depend on China or on the West, is answered to some extent by its relations with Russia and Turkestan, stated in a general way. However, proofs of contacts ought to be given by pointing out particular objects of unmistakable Andronovo character recurring both in Minusinsk and the West. They should be types so specific that their recurrence must mean actual relationship or dependence. There are several types which answer this requirement; we shall deal with them presently.

## ANDRONOVO AND SOME LATER TYPES OCCURRING EAST AND WEST

The socketed celt is common in Europe, Siberia, and the Far East, but absent in Egypt, Mesopotamia, and Iran, and almost unknown in Anatolia.[30] This distribution indicates, as C. G. Seligman stated in 1920, that the socketed celt reached China by a trans-Siberian land route, and not south of the Himalaya or by sea;[31] Andersson thought it possible that the Chinese socketed celt (*pen* 錛) was derived from stone adzes of Yang-shao type,[32] but concrete proof was added in neither case. It is true that evolutionary phases preceding the socketed celt in Europe (flat celt/flanged celt/palstave/winged celt) were not found in China, but this will not do; for the idea of that rigid evolutionary order — implying that all socketed axes should accordingly belong to the Late Bronze Age — has been abandoned,[33] and it might even be argued that the Chinese had been quicker inventors, skipping evolutionary stages dear to Western prehistorians. As lack of primitive metal types is a general feature in China, that argument would have to stand against very unpropitious odds.

Untrammeled by such questions, Tallgren, in 1937, wrote these lines:

> It may, perhaps, be appropriate to mention that it is in this [Andronovo] civilisation somewhere in Eastern Europe [possibly in the present Ukraine] that the *origin of the socketed axe* should be sought. . . . The flat axe with raised borders is not rare in the Ukraina and it probably gave rise to the Seima socketed axes, the edged axe and the lower part of the cloven handle of wood having been copied in bronze. If this hypothesis is correct, the axe of the Seima type is one of the first and oldest types of socketed axe in the world. In any case the upholders of the Seima-Andronovo civilisation were very skilled in all kinds of technical work, rich and active traders and colonisers. In the Russian forest zone, perhaps, it represents a foreign dominion that vanishes, though by no means without leaving traces, before the Scythian invasion of the steppes in the 7th century B.C.[34]

It is exactly this venerable tool which Teploukhov had assigned to his Andronovo stage in Minusinsk, confirming that it had wandered there from Seima. The relations between the Seima celt — then still considered a Finnish local form called Pielavesi type — and its Finnish relatives had been clarified by Tallgren in 1911; he recog-

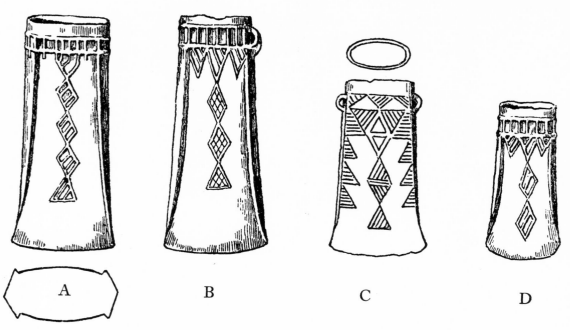

Fig. 56: *Seima celts from East-Russia and Central Siberia.*

A — Seima; after Tallgren (1/2).  B — Ustsysolsk; after Sidorov (2/5).  C — Viatka Govt., after Merhart (not to scale).  D — Bieisk, Minusinsk Govt.; after Martin (2/5).

nized that this type had reached Finland from the Kama-Volga region, and that there must have been connections with Siberia.[35] Later, the "outspoken west-east movement of the genuine Seima type" from Central Russia toward Minusinsk was established by v. Merhart, who also felt that it might be the oldest among the Minusinsk socketed axe types.[36] Fig. 56 A-C shows three typical Seima celts from Russia: A — from Seima itself (Oka River, Novgorod Govt.), B — from Ustsysolsk, far north in the Vychegda River region (Vologda Govt.), C — from the Viatka River region (Viatka Govt.); [37] Fig. 56 D is a counterpart from Bieisk, southwest of Minusinsk.[38] Finds made in Perm, Tobolsk, Omsk, and Tomsk (mold,[39] Fig. 67) indicate that the occurrence of the type in Minusinsk cannot be accidental.[40] It is unnecessary to describe in detail these pieces; their typology has no bearing on the matter.[41] A characteristic trait — ledges along the four corners which together with the gently beveled lateral faces account for the distinctive cross section (Fig. 56 A) — is maintained in the Minusinsk specimen. Similarity of the decorative schemes is striking.

The meaning and import of the foregoing with regard to China is as follows. Socketed celts of Seima pattern do not occur in China, nor do celts with Chinese (Shang) décor occur in Minusinsk. The inference can only be that the socketed celt did not wander to Minusinsk from China, and this is firmly corroborated by the demonstrable migration from Russia. This statement is by no means revolutionary, for other writers have held so before.[41a] But the subject has not been seriously taken up thus far in Western literature, and Japanese experts, who went furthest into detail, did not go very far in linking up their material with the West chronologically.[42]

Naturally, the question arises whether the socketed celt did not travel to or from China in another guise than that styled Seima. Perhaps we might be able to find out by way of copious typological investigation, for types derived from Seima celts, robust, shorter, simplified in decoration, occur at the Yenisei as well as north and south of the Great Wall. I cannot undertake such investigations here, which would tax the reader's patience heavily, but propose to give other demonstrations instead. There are two kinds of tools which serve this purpose excellently and which we may discuss in brief.

The first of these tools is another socketed axe type, the distinctive feature of which is asymmetrical build: from below the rim, one of the faces (the under face when hafted) slopes strongly toward the edge; the sloping plane which meets the upper part of the round socket wall in an arch may be hollowed or even broken open. This type is so specialized that its recurrence indicates connections between the respective areas, however distant they may be from each other. Indeed its distribution appears to be much the same as in the case of the Seima celt: Southern and Eastern Russia, Minusinsk; but we can add Suiyüan, North-China, and Yünnan.[43] A kindred form had been in use in the Seventh City of Hissarlik,[30] a circumstance which counts for the chronological side of the matter. Of the examples assembled in Fig. 57, I wish to stress those from Minusinsk[44] (C), Suiyüan (D), and North-China (E), because they clearly reveal interconnections between Central Siberia and China.

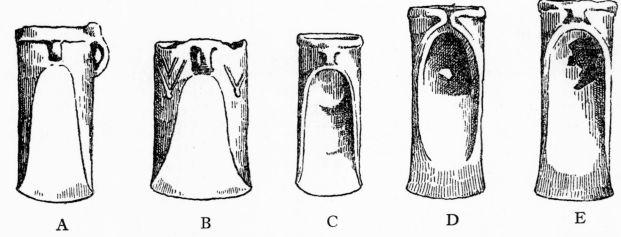

|  A  |  B  |  C  |  D  |  E  |

Fig. 57: *Socketed celts (adzes) from South-Russia, East-Russia, Siberia, Suiyüan, and North-China.*

A — Sosnovaya Maza, Saratov Govt.; after Tallgren (1/2). B — Viatka Govt., Museum Kazan; after Merhart (not to scale). C — Uty, Minusinsk, Museum Minusinsk; after Martin (ca. 1/3). D — Suiyüan, Kyoto University; after Egami and Mizuno (ca. 1/2). E — North-China, Museum Stockholm; after Janse (1/2).

The Sosnovaya Maza specimen [45] (A) is typologically interesting in that it has one loop above the arch of the sloping plane and another at the right side. Merhart is undoubtedly right when explaining this peculiar property as a transitional mode;[46] the following types have only one loop in the middle of the lower face, as is practical and reasonable for this transversely edged tool. The Sosnovaya Maza type is, for that matter, earlier than the Viatka and Minusinsk types (B, C). This agrees with the fact that in Minusinsk there occur only such types with median loop or no loops at all: a cogent reason for assuming that they came from the west. Two pieces from the Sosnovaya Maza hoard have the same décor as the celt from Hissarlik-Troy: vertical zigzags (Fig. 58). Since the type as such is an intruder in the Troad from Europe, this coincidence means that the prototypes in Europe must antedate Troy VII b, "the squalid town"[47] which followed Priam's city. It may be necessary, therefore, to revise the date proposed by Tallgren for the hoard in question, to wit, "around 900 B.C.,"[48] and to place it tentatively around the fall of Troy in the twelfth century B.C.[49]

Fig. 58: *Socketed celt from Troy VII b, reconstructed from a mold (1/3).*

After Dörpfeld–Götze.

A merchant's hoard — comprising no less than fifty-five sickles, the socketed celts mentioned above, a few clumsy knives, and hollow gouges — Sosnovaya Maza contains in addition some *daggers* of a type which occurs also somewhat farther west, in the Kharkov and Voronezh governments, and much farther east, in Minusinsk. Their blades are leaf-shaped and strengthened by a strong midrib so widened at the base that it engages the entire width of the hilt, which is cast in one piece with the blade; the hilt forms an oval eyelet (Fig. 59).[50] This form, which seems to be entirely foreign in Central Siberia and is there represented by only two pieces,[51] irrefutably supports the assumption that in Minusinsk we have to do with predominantly western strains, and definitely so in the case of this dagger type and the socketed axes connected with it.

Another subtle detail which is apt to furnish evidence for links should not be passed over in silence. On the Viatka adze (Fig. 57 B) there is a simple ornament of boxed triangles, the outer ones having small round knobs at their tips. Exactly the same fashion appears on a heavy Suiyüan celt with two loops and widened mouth in the Kyoto University Collection,[52] a shape which is encountered among the Minusinsk celts.[53] In Minusinsk, that shape purports to belong to the first stage of the "Kurgan culture" around or soon after 1000 B.C. — which is in harmony with what I said regarding the probable age of the Sosnovaya Maza hoard. The time of the arrival at China's northern confines of that particular type of socketed adze (Fig. 57 E) cannot be later, of course, than the first phase of the "Kurgan Period" — much later than the Andronovo culture with the Seima celt. What matters, however, is substantial proof for contacts rather than chronological calculation, and I believe that the two different groups of socketed celts discussed above can be regarded as sufficient proof.

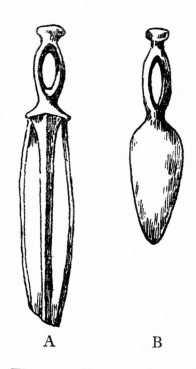

A                    B

Fig. 59: *Daggers from South-Russia and Minusinsk.*

A — Sosnovaya Maza (1/4); B — Minusinsk (1/2). Both after Tallgren.

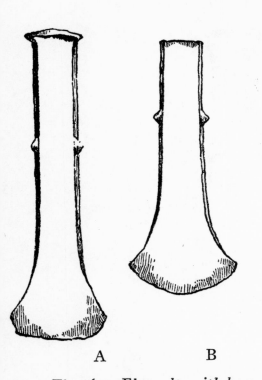

A          B

Fig. 60: *Flat celts with lugs.*

A — Ta-t'ung, Shansi; after Egami and Mizuno (2/3). B — Lecchum, West Georgia; after Nioradze (not to scale).

A second tool testifying to the historicity of eastward transmissions is the *flat celt with lugs*. This type was widely used in the Near East, Anatolia, Armenia, and the Caucasus in the first place; it seems to be at home where the socketed celt was not. The first Far Eastern variants to become known were a few pieces from Suiyüan published by Egami and Mizuno, who immediately pointed out that these pieces must be understood as derivatives of West-Asian types.[54] As parallels to a celt from Ta-t'ung (Shansi) in the Tokyo University collections (Fig. 60 A) and a similar one in Kyoto, acquired in Peking, they gave examples from Persia, Anatolia, Kerch, Italy, Hallstatt, and Troy VII, which is once more represented by a mold.[55] The closest resemblance, however, with regard to the very short lugs, mere bosses indeed, seems to occur in Transcaucasia (Fig. 60 B).[56] These flat celts with lateral lugs, hafted transversely, flourished in the latter half of the IInd millennium B.C.[57] Flat axes of copper or bronze being conspicuously absent in the Far East, it is natural to take the two isolated Suiyüan specimens as offshoots of their western relatives. It is particularly noteworthy that this type is lacking in Minusinsk, and apparently is not common in Russia.[58]

As I have tried to show in chapter II, there is some likelihood that the Shang *spearheads* go back to prototypes such as occur in the Pokrovsk barrows of the Lower Volga. We thus would be referred to the same environment, the Andronovo culture and its affiliations in South and Central Siberia, where the socketed axes just discussed led us. Since it is not doubtful, according to authorities in the field of Russian and Siberian prehistory, that these socketed axes migrated from Russia eastward and not vice versa, and since there is not only a loose, general connection of the spearheads with that same cultural background given, but also the most concrete proof for it — a mold combining socketed celt and spearhead, found in the region of Tomsk (Fig. 67) — it may be rather safely assumed that the spearhead actually came to China by way of Siberia.

As was found in examining existing analogies between China (Anyang) and Minusinsk, these analogies are limited to the types which I termed "Northern." Since these types seem foreign when compared with true Shang art, and since no traces of the latter are found in Minusinsk where "Northern" forms, on the other hand, abound, it is hardly conceivable that this limited repertory should have originated in Anyang and thence have been transmitted to Minusinsk.[58a] Under these circumstance we cannot gain very much by comparing Anyang types with Minusinsk types, and we had better examine the factor on which any decisive answer ultimately depends: the chronology of the Siberian Bronze Age. This task will occupy us in an excursus on the date of the Andronovo culture and the Russian metal age.

THE DATE OF THE ANDRONOVO CULTURE

As was said already, the term "Andronovo" is used here in a sense less strict than specialists in Russian archaeology might perhaps approve, but recent usage of the compound "Andronovo-Seima" might render such lack of precision excusable. For the question we are concerned with in the first place is whether there was a Bronze Age culture in Siberia earlier than Anyang. We have seen that the Andronovo civilization covered a huge area indeed, bespeaking extraordinary expansive energies. In Siberia, however, it is not in itself datable. Dates ascribed to it invariably are based on parallels in South-Russia, whereon dates for Central and Eastern Russia likewise depend. To make things worse, South-Russia again does not offer independent chronological evidences for the early metal age. Its chronology had to be constructed with the help of analogies in Europe, the Aegean world, Anatolia, and Mesopotamia, requiring a vast system of correlations, comparison of countless objects and their settings, and careful evaluation of yet dimly divined connections and events — a painstaking and extensive undertaking. Eminent scholars, fortunately, have ventured upon that task, and the results of their labor have made it possible that today an approximate chronology of prehistoric South-Russia is at our disposal. In it uncertainties are still involved, and figures still differ considerably. So do the figures adopted for the Andronovo period. Vernadsky, relying on Russian authorities, broadly speaks of the first half of the IInd millennium B.C.; [59] Tallgren's date is 1400/1300 — 1100/1000 B.C.; [60] Grousset followed Tallgren; [61] Minns favors a date around 1500 B.C. [62]

For the present purpose, the shorter way would be to take for granted the dates proposed by Russian scholars, V. A. Gorodzov, S. A. Teploukhov, and S. V. Kiselev for Siberia's early metal age: [63]

| Stage | Gorodzov | Teploukhov | Kiselev |
|---|---|---|---|
| Afanasieva | 3000-2000 | ca. 2000 | 3rd-early 2nd mill. |
| Andronovo | 2000-1500 | 1800-1400 | 1700-1200 |
| Karasuk | 1500-1000 | ca. 1000 | 1200-700 |

For Andronovo, these figures harmonize relatively well, while there is an alarming discord as regards the subsequent Karasuk culture. In Teploukhov's scheme, the first phase of the Minusinsk Kurgan culture begins also around 1000 B.C. Thus, there is some inconsistency apparent in his chronology, which — in common with the fact that it deviates also from Gorodzov's — makes it difficult to accept these figures unquestioned. I shall try to find a way to verify their estimates with the help of Russian parallels.

CHRONOLOGY OF THE RUSSIAN EARLY METAL AGE

Guided by those implements from Andronovo which demonstrably came from Russia — the Seima celt, an archaic dagger type not previously mentioned (Fig. 66), spectacle-spirals [64] — our questioning must center on the age of the Seima finds and allied materials.

In Central Russia, metal first appears during the *Fatyanovo* period, named after a site discovered in the seventies of the last century in the region of the Upper Volga (Kostroma and Yaroslav Govts.).[65] The Fatyanovo culture "discloses the rise of a warlike food-producing society in the forest zone where the food-gathering economy of peaceful hunters and fishers had hitherto ruled." [66] It is characterized by beautifully worked stone battle-axes and corded ware, found under low barrows with contracted skeletons. Globular vessels, related to both European globular amphorae and their South-Russian forerunners from Novosvobodnaya (Tsarskaya), are common.[67] Among copper tools — still rare and believed to be imported — a certain shaft-hole axe type is interesting in that it recurs in Seima and Galich (Fig. 62), and constitutes a chronological *point d'appui*.[68] While obvious connections of Fatyanovo with the Central European Single-grave culture and its ceramics and battle-axes are variously interpreted, it seems an accepted fact that metal had been brought to Fatyanovo from the Kuban, by way of the Volga vale.[69] Hence the equation, ever maintained by Tallgren,

Fatyanovo = Novosvobodnaya, Maikop

— the two great tumuli most representative of what is now called the Early Kuban Culture.[70] As to the absolute age of Early Kuban, the approximate equation

Early Kuban = Hissarlik II-V

is safe, perhaps conservative.[71] Notwithstanding these parallels, Tallgren was not ready to abandon another one, namely, the Mycenaean shaft-graves, and, to provide for chronological contact of Maikop and Mycenae, he suggested a scheme "Fatyanovo = Middle Minoan I-II = Troy II-V = 2000-1700 B.C.," which does not do full justice to the above equations.[72]

The date for Early Kuban was low as long as it was calculated by means of comparisons with the Aegean and Europe including Scandinavia. Much higher dates were advocated by those who threw the weight of more recently excavated materials from Mesopotamia and Anatolia into the dispute. Rostovtzeff, Frankfort, Contenau arrived at dates around 2500 B.C. and earlier.[73] A. V. Schmidt, pointing out that Tsarskaya (Novosvobodnaya) is more archaic than Maikop, went even further and established a differentiated sequence [74]:

Early Kuban    = 3000-2500 (Tsarskaya; Maikop;
  Kostromskaya),
Middle Kuban = 2300-1600 (Konstantinovskaya;
  Kurgan VIII Andriukov-
  skaya; Ul?),
Late Kuban    = until 1000 B.C.

But this somewhat expanded chronology experienced a modification. In consideration of new Anatolian finds from Ahlatlibel (south of Ankara) and Alaca Höyük (north of Boghazköi),[75] the beginnings were taken back to 2600 B.C., and the subsequent periods brought down a little, commencing 2100 and 1500, respectively. Such are the figures accepted by F. Hančar[76] and by V. G. Childe, who gave reasons why Tallgren's figures in this case are irrelevant.[77] A further reduction was recommended by C. F. A. Schaeffer,[77a] who places

Early Kuban = 2400-2000 B.C.,

clearly within the frame of the date now adopted for Hissarlik-Troy: Troy II-V = 2600-1900 B.C.[78] Hence, the absolute date of the Fatyanovo culture cannot be appreciably later than Troy II-V, and with

Fatyanovo = 2500-2000 B.C.

we at last have a starting-point whence to approach the stages of more immediate concern for us. I wish to note that Gorodzov's date,[79] Fatyanovo = 3000-2000, coincides as to the lower limitation, which should not be taken too strictly.

## SEIMA

On various occasions it has been observed that the finds from Seima, Galich, and allied ones which I comprise under Andronovo, must not be separated from the later Fatyanovo.[80] Consequently, Andronovo might well take one back to some time not long after 2000 B.C., as in fact is contemplated by Gorodzov and Teploukhov. Minns places Seima around 1500 B.C.,[81] while Tallgren, on various occasions, insisted on a somewhat lower date, i.e., 1400-1300 B.C. Among the finds made at Seima, stone tools are fairly numerous: silex arrowheads with flat base and with short stems have the lead; arrowheads of quartz occur; two finely worked saws of silex, a dagger of slate presumably made in imitation of copper daggers, and minor stone implements were found. Copper and bronze tools are, on the whole, of archaic type: thirty flat daggers or fragments of such; five daggers with hilts of the design shown in Fig. 61; flat celts, chisels, awls of commonplace early fashion. Of chronological import are the spearheads. One type is identical with that from Pokrovsk (Fig. 39); another was derived from, or at any rate is most closely related to, the beautiful silver lances from Borodino[29] and recurs, likewise in silver, in the Turbino treasure;[23] a third type has a slitted socket, a device known during Middle Minoan III (1700-1550 B.C.) in the Aegean.[82] Furthermore, two copper shaft-hole axes of a genre

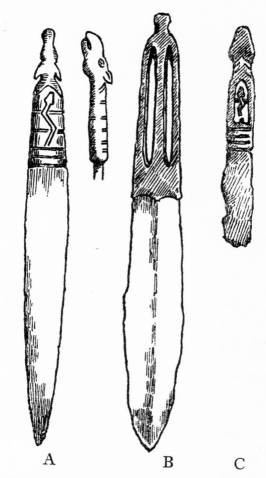

Fig. 61: *Daggers from Seima (A, B) and Galich (C).*

After Tallgren. A—1/2, B—2/5, C—1/4.

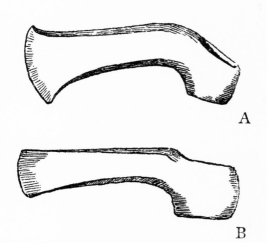

Fig. 62: *Russian shaft-hole axes.*

A—Galich; after Aspelin-Tallgren (ca. 1/3). B—Seima; after Childe (1/3).

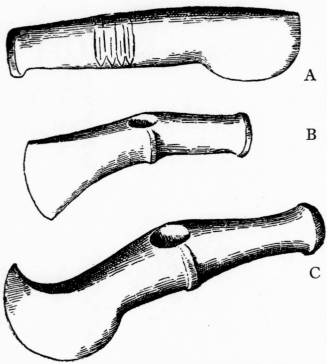

Fig. 63: *Stone battle-axes from Fatyanovo  (A)  and  Borodino  (B, C).*

A — Velikoye Selo, Fatyanovo region; after Äyräpää (ca. 2/5). B — (ca. 1/3). C — (ca. 2/5), after v. Stern–Tallgren.

confined to southeastern Europe with the exception of Greece, widely found in Russia but only rarely in Siberia, were discovered, which have analogies in Fatyanovo and the Galich treasure (Fig. 62). Said to be of Transylvanian origin [83] and absent in all the Hungarian later Bronze Age hoards, this axe type goes back to about 1800 B.C. in Russia, according to Tallgren.[84] John Nestor, on account of their Balkan parallels, refers these Central-Russian axes to the seventeenth century B.C.[85] It may, however, not be overlooked that there are prototypes in the Near East which are of hoary age, being assigned to about 3000 B.C.[86]

Thus, it would be justifiable to operate with a date about 1700-1500 B.C. for Seima, which is exactly within the frame of Gorodzov's and Teploukhov's for Andronovo, that is, "Seima in Siberia."

BORODINO

While no stone battle-axes are reported found in Seima, which thereby is devoid of an outstanding Fatyanovo feature, stone battle-axes of superb shape accompany the two silver lances, a tanged silver dagger with gilded midrib, a rhombus-head silver pin plated with gold ornaments, and three limestone maceheads of globular and ovoid form of the Borodino Treasure, found in 1912 near the Dniester estuary.[87] Of the four stone axes and fragments of another two, one with elegantly curved edge (Fig. 63 C) is of exemplary refinement; the others are of the pattern shown in Fig. 63 B. The lower part of the cutting edge of the former recurs in Fatyanovo specimens (Fig. 63 A).[88]

Understandably the composition and nature of this hoard led to its homogeneousness being questioned. But it is not even known whether it was perhaps a grave find. On the analogy of some wonderful battle-axes of greenstone and lapis lazuli [89] in Treasure L from Hissarlik II c (approximately 2400-2300 B.C.), however, and on the evidence of the precious objects themselves, it seems more likely than not that the Borodino find was a treasure. This would leave more freedom regarding the dates of the single objects. The absence of any object of copper or bronze should be noted. The inference may not be that we have to do with pre-Bronze Age remains, but that we are confronted with some heirloom of princely milieu, perhaps purloined and hidden. In any case, the lances with their peculiarly furcated socket are linked with similarly designed bronze lances that formed part of the earthly possessions of the Oka foresters and dune dwellers from Seima. It would seem appropriate to allow that the distinguished Borodino types preceded their humbler relatives. In absolute figures they would be somewhat earlier than Seima, for which I have adopted a period around 1700-1500 B.C.

One of the limestone maces from Borodino has oval protuberances on its ovoid body (Fig. 64 A), reminiscent of a pinhead form current in South-Russia during the Bronze Age, and also known in the Caucasus; an example from Kazbek illustrates the point very well.[90] This resemblance can be casual, but there occur maceheads with four spikes on spheroid or ovoid bodies in Koban (Northern Caucasus), as well as stone heads with four knobs.[91] A stone mace from Agha-Evlar (Talysh) comes very close to the Borodino specimen.[92] A piece similar to it, but worked in semiprecious stone and pear-shaped, was found in Perm.[93] Much older precursors were discovered in Susa I, IVth millennium).[94] Stone clubs, generally speaking, were an almost ubiquitous weapon of Hither Asia, and as such are well represented in Troy from the deepest layers onward.[95] According to Tallgren, stone maces were encountered in many catacomb-tombs of South-Russia.[96] This fact permits of a lower date limit for the apparently archaic Borodino example: Middle Kuban (2100-1500). We thus arrive, in the broadest manner, at a date compatible with that given by the spearheads.

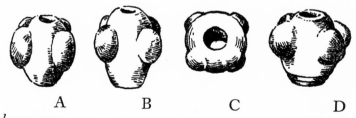

A        B        C        D

Fig. 64: *Stone maceheads with protuberances.*

A — Borodino. B — Caucasus; after Ebert, *RLV*, VI, Pl. 91. C — Talysh; after H. de Morgan (1/3). D — Susa I; after J. de Morgan.

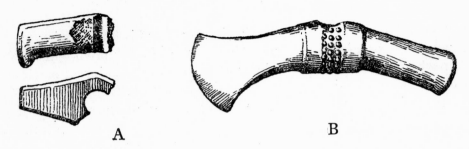

A          B

Fig. 65: *Fragment of stone battle-axe from Troy II-V* (1/3) *and greenstone battle-axe from Troy IIc* (1/4).
After Dörpfeld–Götze.

Important and intriguing is the question of how the battle-axes of the Borodino hoard should be dated. Answers will vary fundamentally according as one thinks it possible that the South-Russian battle-axes were derived from Scandinavia and Germany, or assumes the reverse process, which certainly is favored by chronology; I incline toward regarding Anatolia as the common source of the European types generally (while Anatolia in turn is indebted to Mesopotamia). The fact of the occurrence of splendid stone axes in Troy II weighs heavily in assessing the Borodino pieces, the more so since more primitive stone axes with widening edge were found also in Troy I and in Thermi I-II (Lesbos).[97] A fragment from Troy II-V (Fig. 65 A) could be mistaken for a Fatyanovo type: the end of the hammer has a downward prolongation[98] (cp. Fig. 63 A). Clumsier stone axes with perforation but edges not exceeding the body's width belong to the common inventory of IIIrd millennium Anatolian and more eastern sites. A slender and high-bodied, true battle-axe was acquired by de Morgan in 1899 from a site laid in ruins by Hammurabi and never reoccupied.[99] At Tepe Musyan (northwest of Susa), a pertaining fragment probably of Susa II age (ca. 3000 B.C.) was found; clay models and perforated stone axes of similar shape from Ur add another millennium to the lifetime of the battle-axe in the Near East.[100] In Macedonia, to return to quarters closer to Borodino, stone battle-axes of South-Russian character[101] were ascertained to be of Early Macedonian (Bronze) Age, roughly parallel to Troy II-V.[102] I need not go into detail; it will suffice to have made it clear that the Trojan battle-axes are not an isolated phenomenon requiring explanation by Nordic analogies. Metal types of Asian origin surround these stone axes from the beginning (Russia: Vozdvizhenskaya), challenging the stoneworker's skill. Borodino, at the northwestern littoral of the Pontus and not far from the Hellespont, must inevitably be compared with Troy. Offhand, its seems more likely than not that the Bessarabian Treasure should be linked with Troy rather than with stations as far away as Denmark. But some scholars explained Borodino by analogies from the Baltic, and hence came to advocate dates as late as between 1500 and 1000 B.C. or even the Hallstatt Period. As a consequence, they had to regard these excellently worked pieces as a "late revival" of neolithic forms, and to make reservations for a higher age of specimens associated with Ukrainian painted pottery;[103] in short, they incurred chronological difficulties that can be overcome only by dating the Borodino axes earlier.

The close similarity of the Trojan battle-axes as such does not exclude that there are formal differences which forbid linking them directly with the Borodino axes. However, intermediate examples from Russia are recorded which would seem to warrant connections between the Trojan and South-Russian battle-axes.[104] Notably, the type with transverse belt around the perforated section of the body, and with cylindrical hammer is known in Russia, as are ornamented axes too.[105] Parallels to the Borodino specimens were listed by Äyräpää (Europaeus).[106] A greenstone axe from Lugansk (Donets region) came from a catacomb-grave, a grave type — probably introduced from the Aegean — common during the Middle Kuban period (2100-1500). To the same period belongs a decorated boat-axe from Talnoye (Uman, Kiev Govt.). A very small, stout, richly carved axe was found with five pairs of arrow-straighteners near Horozheno (Kherson Govt.). The ornaments on this small axe — longitudinal ridges with herringbone striae between them, zigzags, and boxed triangles — recall the décor of the Borodino silver lances, according to Äyräpää (who consequently dates this axe Late Kuban). But the arrow-straighteners are characteristic of the Middle Kuban catacomb-graves — as the Finnish scholar expressly states, contradicting his date chosen in consideration of factors of no greater importance, as I believe.[107] In Yatskovitsa near Kiev a battle-axe which can be compared to the simpler Borodino axes came from a pit-grave with hammerheaded pins and pottery more primitive than that usually encountered in catacomb-graves: a find suggesting the earlier part of the Middle Kuban period.

It remains to mention that the axe with splayed and upcurved edge (Fig. 63 C) has counterparts as far east as Samara,[108] and that this particular blade form — resembling Sumerian hanging curved blades, as Childe pointed out[109] — undoubtedly links Fatyanovo with Borodino historically. Hence a date corresponding to the later Fatyanovo stage might be considered. But this would not be sound: Fatyanovo's date itself depends upon southern parallels so much that it would perhaps be affected by any date ascertainable for Borodino. This date, to sum up our scanty data, is earlier Middle Kuban (2100-1500) at best. Undeniable kinship with the Trojan battle-axes (ca. 2400-2300), however, makes it quite probable that the axes are earlier rather than later. The early date should be defended even if there is no definite proof for it at present — much as Äyräpää holds that battle-axes of stone were known in South-Russia during Early Kuban, although there are no finds thus far.[110]

A circumstance which appears reassuring is that the dates of the lances, the clubheads, and the battle-axes all point to the first half of the IInd millennium B.C., while it is not possible to attain more finely graded stages. For the remaining objects, I am unable to draw into consideration the silver dagger, reproductions accessible to me being not clear enough to permit recognizing details. The rhombus-head *pin* from Borodino shows a symmetrically arranged configuration of curves, which was likened to the design of an interesting stone battle-axe fragment from Popovka (Kiev Govt.).[111] This fragment, apart from S-curve motifs worked in raised lines, is distinguished by a peculiar crest surmounting the edge and by knobs projecting from the lateral faces. A comparable axe was found in Bulgaria.[112] The ornamental design on a unique chisel of the Kunderevich Collection, Kiev, may be grouped with the pin and the Popovka axe.[113] These relations, although not providing for a date, make it questionable whether one has to rely on the Mycenaean shaft-graves for obtaining a date for Borodino.

Borodino may thus well have preceded Seima; its battle-axes may be earlier than the spearheads and lead us back to some time near 2000 B.C., not too widely separated from Troy II. Schaeffer assigns the hoard to the first half of the second millennium B.C.[113a]

POKROVSK

Battle-axe and spearhead of Borodino-Seima type recur in fine specimens in tombs excavated in the vicinity of Pokrovsk (Saratov Govt., Lower Volga). From these tombs came various objects which link them with Seima: the spearheads described above (ch. II, Fig. 39); a type of tanged dagger (Fig. 66 B) which is also characteristic of Siberian Andronovo (Fig. 66 C, D); arrowheads of silex, with even base or short stem; pottery;[114] flat adzes of bronze. The latter, as well as certain ceramics, are indicative of relations with the period of the catacomb-graves, according to Rykov;[115] in tombs of the Poltavka Group — closely allied with, but somewhat older than, the Khvalynsk culture of Pokrovsk — even hammerheaded pins occur.[116] These analogies with Borodino and Seima on the one hand, with catacombs on the other, require, for at least part of the Pokrovsk timber-graves, a date no later than toward the end of the first half of the IInd millennium B.C., slightly earlier than assumed by Rykov, who submitted a date around "the middle of the IInd millennium and later."[117]

The important mold from *Tomsk,* published by Tallgren, combines the Borodino spearhead type with a Seima socketed celt type (Fig. 67).[39] The mold thus confirms in the safest manner that spearhead and celt are coeval and had made their way to Siberia together. The dagger accompanied them, as finds from the Upper Tobol and Vozkresensk (district of Yekaterinburg; Fig. 66 C) show.[118]

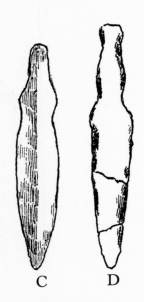

A        B

C        D

Fig. 66: *Tanged daggers of Seima-Andronovo type, Russia and Siberia.*

A — Seima (1/2); after Tallgren.  B — Pokrovsk (ca. 2/3); after Rykov.  C — West Siberia (ca. 1/3); after Heikel.  D — Minusinsk; after Teploukhov.

Fig. 67: *Mold for socketed celt of Seima type and spearhead of Borodino-Seima type. Tomsk.*

After Tallgren.

The cursory view of some stations and finds in Russia given in the preceding pages will perhaps be sufficient to show how closely Central Siberia and Russia were connected during that stage which, termed *Andronovo,* represents Siberia's Early Bronze Age. Affinities between Russia and Siberia are such that one must abandon the idea of slowly working transmission and corresponding retardation, and rather take them, as Menghin had pointed out, as a unity.[119] Owing to archaeological conditions, the more southerly route is less or not at all known at the present time. Chronology, too, is thereby affected. I see no way to assign to derivatives of Seima style in Siberia a date earlier than ca. 1700-1600 B.C.

THE KARASUK STAGE

This stage, named after a tributary of the Yenisei, followed upon the Andronovo period in Minusinsk and adjacent regions to the south and west and east.[119a] Cattle-breeders were the upholders of the Karasuk culture, and they buried their dead in stone-slab chambers not covered by barrows (habit of the Andronovo folk) and fenced by squarish stone settings instead of circular ones.[120] Types of tools appear, among which only the socketed celt clearly reveals itself as developed from the Seima celt, while others show evolutions independent from Russia and — for the first time now — analogies with Suiyüan and North-China. These types are the following: a broad dagger with a guard obtained by incisions at the heel of the blade, with hollow grip and a pommel shaped as ring, domed cap, or rattle (Fig. 50 A, B, F), knives with arched backs and geometric décor, sometimes with animal-head pommels (Fig. 50 C, D), but oftener with mushroom-like caps and rings of various shapes. Round mirrors with a simple loop in the center or with a straight handle belong to this stage, as well as humble adornments and globular vessels of copper or bronze, which have counterparts in the pottery. The Karasuk people, following Andronovo custom, erected huge, crude stone pillars with strange designs on them in their graveyards in the Minusinsk steppe. Less abundant, these monoliths occur also in the Orkhon and Kara-Irtysh regions; in the Altai, representations of the dagger type characteristic of this stage were found on such monuments by J. G. Granö.[121] Two of the Minusinsk stelae are crowned by sculptured heads of mountain sheep (argali), which, according to Hančar, mark the first beginnings of the Eurasian animal style in the Altai-Sayan area.[121a] A stone pestle with a ram's head and a whetstone terminated by a bull's head, both from near Minusinsk, are most strongly reminiscent of the bronze knives with animal-head knobs.[121b]

Nothing much can be said as yet regarding the typological order and sequence of the weapons and tools of that stage, but it seems that there was vivid life and working because the finds are numerous and the forms diversified and because by the tenth century B.C., the initial stage of the Minusinsk Kurgan culture (= Tagar culture), the dagger form that was to be the ancestor of the Scythian *akinakes* was well developed (cp. Fig. 52). It is possible but not at all certain that the primitive Andronovo dagger (Fig. 66) was gradually changed into the characteristic Karasuk dagger. Ornaments of Seima-Andronovo kind occasionally found on pieces which appear to stand midway between both would favor that idea. The assumption that it was daggers of bone which might rather account for the Yeniseians' novelties can be dismissed: not only are blade and hilt in their essential parts inconceivable in bone, but they are obviously smithy-work or caster's. Some time must have gone by before the Karasuk dagger finally took shape, and some more time before this shape became obsolete again or was, in other words, ousted by the *proto-akinakes* (cp. Fig. 52 D). Since daggers of the developed Karasuk type are fairly numerous, their lifetime cannot be assumed to have been very short. Chronological inferences are these: Working back from the Tagar *proto-akinakes* of about the tenth century we may count a span of nine or ten generations, say 270 to 300 years, for the latter's formation, the flourishing time of the Karasuk dagger, and the transition period preceding it. An admittedly crude calculation, which is based on the typological range briefly outlined in chapter V above and on the fact that the true *akinakes* was developed before the seventh century B.C., it does point toward the time around 1300 B.C. for the beginnings of the Karasuk period.

This date, well before 1000 B.C.— as in Teploukhov's estimate, which K. Jettmar already found rather too low [121c]— is supported also by Karasuk analogies in Anyang. H. Kühn was the first to draw the conclusion that the "Sino-Siberian style" is of Shang age, because it appears side by side with the "Shang style" in Anyang.[122] Kühn's observation applies to Karasuk, where the elements — daggers, knives, chisels or gouges, socketed celts, geometric décor — which we find in

Anyang are assembled. The question whether these elements are Siberian or due to the Shang again arises.

Fabulous wealth, superior technique, accuracy and spiritedness of form, and the presence of unheard of shapes and dimensions of ritual vessels of bronze in Anyang not only justify, but demand this question. Moreover, the validity of the chronology adopted for Siberia might be challenged. Actually, some adaptations and elaborations may become necessary. But I do not think that a revolutionary change will take place. Karasuk would come down at best to around 1200 B.C., the date upheld by Kiselev, if the elements it has in common with Anyang were thence derived. But, one might not stop there; a pre-Anyang stage might be postulated to account for Anyang's stupefying metallurgical refinement. Then, what about the role of Siberia? As I am inclined to surmise the existence of a pre-Anyang metal stage within present-day China's confines, my reply to this is in the following considerations.

ANYANG AND NORTHERN STRAINS

An analysis of Shang bronzes and bronze implements shows a style dominant of which there is no trace in the neolithic pottery of China, except a few geometric motifs of the Painted Pottery and the Black Pottery.[123] Motifs dominant in the bronze décor are animal configurations, sharply outlined, spiky of look, of a distinct rhythm resulting from alternating angles and curves. The evolution of this style can be observed, according to L. Bachhofer, in the White Pottery, which links the later Lung-shan or Black Pottery with the bronzes.[124] The White Pottery so decorated was found only in Anyang and therefore dates from 1300 B.C. and after. Consequently, the animal style dominant in the decoration of Shang weapons would date from some time after 1300 B.C. Nothing similar to this Shang style was ever traced in Siberian or "Northern" objects.

In striking contrast, Siberian or Northern ornament appears in the midst of the Shang world of Anyang. Seen from Anyang, the inference can be threefold.

1) The Northern style constitutes the remnants of an earlier one ejected by the vigorously unfolding new Shang style. Historical interpretation: People who were the upholders of a pre-Anyang metal culture were driven northward and settled around Suiyüan, where they continued to make their tools and ornaments as before, scarcely influenced by the Shang. Another interpretation: The vanishing Northern style was the pre-Anyang style of the Shang themselves, who merged with a people powerfully influencing and reshaping Shang art.

2) Or, the Northern style was but an intruder from the north or northwest, genuinely foreign. Historical interpretation: Northern nomadic folk in connection with groups farther west throughout Si-

beria, possessing a style of their own, were in contact with the Shang, and reflections of their art are found in Anyang in the guise of superior craftsmanship.

3) Or, the Northern style and the Shang style are two aspects of the artistic genius of one culture. This may be interpreted ethnically (foreign admixtures) or sociologically (Northern style profane, Shang style hieratic — as conceived by Karlgren [125]).

Archaeological conditions seem to support the second inference. The Northern style, insofar as it is geometric and of the beginning Bronze Age, is inseparably connected with the Siberian Seima-Andronovo facies, and its pre-Scythian animal art is accounted for by the vast reservoir of epipalaeolithic traditions in the Eurasian Forest Zone.[126] The inner unity of that zone impressively manifests itself by such analogies as the elk-head pommels of knives or daggers, or animal-head maces and other implements such as were found in Finland, Central Russia (Seima: Fig. 61 A), Minusinsk (Karasuk: Fig. 50 C), Suiyüan,[127] and even Anyang.[128] One does well to remember in this connection that the habitat of the reindeer embraced the Minusinsk steppe and Tannu-Tuva (Uryankhai), but never stretched as far south as Suiyüan, let alone Anyang.[129] Thus, the mere presence of the reindeer as an art motif clearly reveals the origins of that formation which I — not to identify it plainly with Minusinsk or Siberia generally — call Northern, to stress its profound difference from Shang art.

The main reason why "Northern" — a vague and hybrid term — must not be identified with "Siberian" is given in the fact that the weapon types comprised under "Northern" are not all met in Minusinsk. Whether Southern Siberia and Turkestan will provide materials likely to prove a western Asian provenance of such Northern types as are not represented in Minusinsk, remains to be seen. It is the shaft-hole axes and shaft-hole fitted dagger-axes which would come under this category. Types well represented in Minusinsk are the Seima celt and distinct series of daggers and knives almost identical with those from Suiyüan. The fact that the Seima celt and the Borodino-Seima spearhead are associated in their original home and in Siberia (Tomsk mold) strongly suggests that the comparable Anyang spearhead came from that source, although Minusinsk has nothing much to show in this case.

In addition, the term "Northern" is vague in chronological regard, in that it has a connotation of earliness or, to put it more exactly, of a *pre-Anyang stage*. The weapons of the Northern group are not only foreign in the Shang milieu by virtue of their décor, they are also typologically early throughout. Therefore, one must consider them as possibly older than Anyang, the more so since some of them (shaft-hole axes; dagger-axes with sockets or shaft-rings) go out of fashion early. At the same time, this pre-Anyang metal stage — not hitherto actually discovered at a particular site — would go some length to explain Anyang's extraordinary technical *niveau*. *Anyang* and *Kara-*

*suk* are on the same level phaseologically, and in all probability chronologically too. The difference is that Anyang is rich and immensely superior in its material culture, which has inherited late neolithic city refinement. But, which stage in China corresponds to *Andronovo?*

If I am not mistaken in placing some types of weapons earlier than Anyang-Shang because they do not fit in later, it always shows that they, when decorated, have no Shang features. Their décor is geometric, like that of the Black Pottery, the early White Pottery, certain Painted Wares of Kansu, and incised ones from Ssechuan,[130] and like typical Andronovo pottery, the Seima celts and their Siberian derivatives, and all the ornaments on Siberian and Suiyüan-Ordos early daggers and knives. That means that our Northern or, perhaps, pre-Anyang patterns would belong to a stratum — grossly outlined by this incongruous society — wherein the Shang animal pattern plays truant. Notwithstanding the differences at the root, in their substrata and growth, some geometric veneer may have created a temporary unity of the then living cultures of Inner Asia and North-China. This period, the inner complexity of which is revealed in but small part by the weapons, would correspond to the Andronovo world farther west.

NOTES: CHAPTER VI    SIBERIA IN THE EARLY BRONZE AGE

[1] Thanks to A. M. Tallgren's articles, reviews, critical summaries, and bibliographies in *Eurasia Septentrionalis Antiqua* (*ESA*), the student is at least aware of activities and new perspectives in the field of Russian and Siberian prehistory and archaeology, and the respectable amount of information known to be hidden in Russian publications out of reach will lessen readiness to judge *ab ignorantia.*

[2] V. G. Childe, *The Most Ancient East,* p. 225.

[3] C. W. Bishop, "The Rise of Civilization in China with Reference to Its Geographical Aspects," p. 623.

[4] *Ibid.,* p. 625.

[5] Ch'en Meng-chia, *Hsi Chou Nien Tai K'ao,* p. 22.

[6] B. Karlgren, "Some Weapons and Tools," pp. 114-21.

[7] S. A. Teploukhov, "Essai de classification des anciennes civilisations métalliques de la région de Minoussinsk," *Mat. po Etn.,* IV, p. 2. — Diagrams of the "ideal inventories" of the successive stages are, with the exception of the two ancientmost ones, reproduced in A. Salmony's *Sino-Siberian Art,* Pls. III-IV. The complete diagrams in reduced size, accompanied by a very brief summary, are contained in E. Golomshtok's article, "Anthropological Activities in Soviet Russia," pp. 320-21. — Teploukhov, "Ancient Burials in the Minusinsk District," *Mat. po Etn.,* III, p. 2.

[8] For palaeolithic finds from the Yenisei River, cf. G. v. Merhart, "The Palaeolithic Period in Siberia"; short note in W. Jochelson's *Archaeological Investigations in Kamchatka,* p. 23 ff. — Near Biriusina traces of settlement have been found in calcareous caves, and there is reason to believe in the continuity of local cultures from the Old Stone Age to the Neolithic; cf. G. Vernadsky, *Ancient Russia,* I, p. 25. Cf. note 10 below.

[9] Malta: a site where mammoth-ivory Venuses of Aurignacian type were discovered in 1918 by M. M. Gerasimov. Cf. Golomshtok in *Amer. Anthropologist,* XXXV, p. 314; M. C. Burkitt, in *ESA,* IX (1934); *Tōyō Kōkogaku,* p. 263; Tallgren, in *ESA,* VIII, p. 196.

[10] E. Golomshtok, *op. cit.,* p. 316; Jochelson, *op. cit.,* p. 24, quoting B. E. Petri, *The Siberian Palaeolith* (*Sibirskii Paleolit,* Irkutsk, 1923) and *idem, The First Traces of the Pre-Historic Man in Siberia* (Chita, 1922), mentions the discovery by Petri of several stations on the loess near Irkutsk belonging to the Upper Palaeolithic epoch. Petri is convinced that they are related to the Magdalenian, "but with many special characteristics."

[11] Teploukhov, *op. cit.,* note 7 above.

[12] G. Vernadsky, *op. cit.,* I, p. 25. Regarding shell ornaments from Afanasieva tombs, V. Altman (see note 13) gives the exact localization: "shells of a type encountered only at the issue of the Amu-Daria."

[13] Short account by V. Altman, "Ancient Khorezmian Civilization," in *JAOS,* LXVII (1947), pp. 81 ff. — S. P. Tolstov, *Drevnosti Verkhnego Khorezma. Vestnik Drevnei Istorii,* I (1941), pp. 155-84. *Idem,* "The Early Culture of Khwarizm," *Antiquity,* LXXVIII (1946), pp. 92-99.

[14] Altman, *op. cit.,* p. 82.

[15] Vernadsky, *op. cit.,* p. 25.

[16] Altman, *op. cit.,* p. 82.

[17] Tallgren, "The Arctic Bronze Age," p. 44.

[18] A. R. Burn, *Minoans, Philistines, and Greeks*, p. 108.

[19] Cf. Teploukhov's diagram (note 7 above); Vernadsky, *op. cit.*, pp. 37-38; Tallgren, "The Arctic Bronze Age," pp. 43-44, quoting his reviews of Teploukhov's and Griaznov's fundamental works in *ESA*, III, pp. 187-88, and the bibliography for the Minusinsk region by S. V. Kiselev, in *Sovietskaya Etnografiya* (1935), Nos. 4-5, p. 206 ff.; for textiles, *Problemy GAIMK* (1934), No. 2, p. 92.

[20] Vernadsky, *op. cit.*, pp. 37-38.

[21] Tallgren, "The Arctic Bronze Age," p. 44 note. M. P. Griaznov, *Pogrebeniya bronzovoi epokhi v zapadnom Kazakhstane. Kazaki*, II (1927). Cf. Grivtsov — Grakov, in *ESA*, IV, pp. 116-25.

[21a] Since this was written, Andronovo burials and settlements in the Arp and Chuisk river valleys, Northern T'ienshan, have become known through reports made by A. N. Bernshtam; his "Osnovnye etapy istorii kultury Semirechya i Tyanshanya," was made accessible to me in a translation kindly undertaken by Mrs. Kathleen Price. Other articles by Bernshtam are listed in K. Jettmar's "Archäologische Spuren von Indogermanen in Zentralasien," p. 253.

[22] Tallgren, in *MAGW*, LXI (1931); R. Grousset, *L'Empire des Steppes*, p. 33; P. Rykov, "Die Chvalynsker Kultur der Bronzezeit."—V. V. Holmsten, in *Trudy Sektsii Arkheologii Ranion*, IV (*Gorodzov Anniv. Vol.*); P. Rykov, *"K voprosu o kulturakh bronzovoi v nishnem Povolshe,"* in *Izv. Kraeved. Instituta*, II (1927); *idem*, "Arkheologicheskie razvedki i raskopki v Nishne-Volshskom krae," in *Zhurnal N.-V. Inst.*, Saratov (1929).

[23] Galich (Kostroma Govt.): A. M. Tallgren, "Die Kupfer- und Bronzezeit in Nord-und Ostrussland," abbr. "KBrZ NOR," pp. 25-91; *idem*, "The Copper Idols from Galich and Their Relatives," *Studia Orientalia*, I (1925); *idem*, "La Pontide préscythique," p. 136, Fig. 77;

*idem*, "Caucasian Monuments. The Kazbek Treasure," *ESA*, V (1930). — Mentioned by V. G. Childe, *The Dawn of European Civilization*, p. 161, Fig. 84.

Seima (Novgorod Govt.): V. A. Gorodzov, *Kultury bronzovoi epokhi v Srednei Rossii. Otchet Ross. Istor. Museya* (Moscow 1914). Tallgren, in *Finskt Museum*, XXII (1915); *idem*, in *MAGW*, LXI; v. Merhart, *Bronzezeit am Jenissei*, p. 19; Childe, *Dawn*, p. 201, Fig. 103.

Turbino (Upper Kama): A. V. Schmidt, *FUF*, XVIII, pp. 1-14; Tallgren, *FUF*, XX; *ESA*, XI, p. 44 note.

Korshunovo-Sloboda: Spitsyn, *Zapiski RORAO*, V, 1, p. 109; Tallgren, *ESA*, XI, p. 44.

Yarlikly: Smolin, in *Vestn. nauchn. obsh. tatarovedeniya*, IV (1926), p. 75; Tallgren, *loc. cit.*

[24] A. Sidorov, "Tüllenaxt von Ustsysolsk," *ESA*, VI (1931), pp. 173-74. Tallgren, "The Arctic Bronze Age," p. 17, Fig. 32.

[25] Tallgren, *ibid.*, p. 43, Fig. 60.

[26] *Ibid.*, p. 44.

[27] *Ibid.*, p. 44. — Verkhne-Kizil: *ESA*, III, p. 122 ff. Shigir: cf. *ESA*, X, p. 163.

[28] Tallgren, "The Arctic Bronze Age," Figs. 61, 62, pp. 45-46.

[29] Borodino (Bessarabia): E. v. Stern, in *Mat. Arkh. Ross.*, XXXIV; Ebert, *RLV*, II, p. 121; Tallgren, in *MAGW*, LXI, pp. 85-86; *idem*, "La Pontide préscythique," pp. 140-42; J. Nestor, "Zum Stande der Vorgeschichtsforschung" in *Rumänien*; Reinecke, in *Germania*, IX (1925); E. Dullo, "Die kaukasischen Axte der Bronzezeit"; A. Äyräpää, "Über die Streitaxtkulturen in Russland," p. 74 ff.

[30] Montelius, *Archiv f. Anthr.*, XXI, p. 16; Déchelette, *Manuel d'archéologie*, II, p. 254. Although practically absent in Asia Minor, an isolated socketed celt — or, to be exact, the mold for a socketed celt — has been found in Troy VII. See W. Dörpfeld, *Troja und Ilion*: A. Götze,

*Die Kleingeräte*, p. 405, Fig. 405 = Fig. 58.

[31] "Bird-Chariots and Socketed Celts in Europe and China," *JRAI*, L (1920), pp. 153-58.

[32] Andersson, "An Early Chinese Culture," p. 6, Pl. 4. *Idem*, "Children of the Yellow Earth," pp. 209-12.

[33] Peake and Fleure, *The Horse and the Sword*, p. 92.

[34] Tallgren, "The Arctic Bronze Age," pp. 45-46.

[35] Tallgren, "KBrZ NOR," pp. 183-90.

[36] *Bronzezeit am Jenissei*, pp. 69 ff., 96.

[37] Sources for Fig. 56: A — Tallgren, *MAGW*, LXI, p. 88; cross section, "La Pontide préscythique," p. 135, Fig. 76:2. B — A. Sidorov, "Tüllenaxt von Ustsysolsk," *ESA*, VI, p. 173 f., Fig. 1 = Tallgren, *ESA*, XI, p. 17, Fig. 32. C — v. Merhart, *Bronzezeit am Jenissei*, p. 74, Fig. 39: drawing, making up blurred portions of décor of the original, which is in the Anthropological Museum of Moscow University.

[38] Martin, *L'Age du Bronze au Musée de Minoussinsk*, Pl. 3:7 = Fig. 56 D.

[39] Tallgren, *Coll. Zaoussailov*, Figs. 27, 28; quoted after Merhart, *op. cit.*, p. 73, n. 17. *RLV*, IX, Pl. 240 B = Fig. 67.

[40] Merhart, *op. cit.*, p. 73.

[41] Whatever the typological order of the Russian Seima celts, it does not alter the fact that they are the oldest types appearing in Minusinsk. In regard to relations with North-China, the Seima prototypes are however not necessarily those found in the Minusinsk area; I think it possible that more southerly quarters, say around Semipalatinsk, will yield materials even more directly elucidating transmissive movements with China as their goal. This would be in accordance with v. Merhart's surmise that the Semipalatinsk Steppe may have been the cradle of another important socketed celt type, the *schwere Sechskantbeil* (heavy hexagonal celt), which is also found in the Far East (Egami and Mizuno, *Inner Mongolia,*

Pt. II, *Corpus I,* "Socketed Axes and Chisels," B 14-16): Minusinsk was not its original home; cf. v. Merhart, *op. cit.,* pp. 96-97.

[41a] E.g., R. v. Heine-Geldern, "Das Tocharerproblem und die pontische Wanderung," p. 231: "Die grosse Masse der chinesischen Tüllenbeile gehört . . . mit jenen der Mongolei, Sibiriens und des östlichen und mittleren Russland in eine grosse Gruppe, ist dagegen mit den Beilen Mitteleuropas und des skandinavischen Gebietes nur ganz entfernt verwandt."

[42] Umehara, "Note on Bronze Tools," pp. 104-6; Egami and Mizuno, *Inner Mongolia,* Pt. II, pp. 5-16.

[43] Suiyüan: Egami and Mizuno, *op. cit.,* Pl. 36:14 = Fig. 57 D. North-China: O. Janse, "Un groupe de bronzes anciens propres à l'Extrême-Asie Méridionale," p. 107, Fig. 6 = Fig. 57. E. Yünnan: Janse, *ibid.,* Pl. 7:4a.

[44] Martin, *L'Age du Bronze au Musée de Minoussinsk,* Pl. 6:8=Fig. 57 C.

[45] Tallgren, "La Pontide préscythique," Fig. 88:7 = Fig. 57 A.

[46] *Bronzezeit am Jenissei,* pp. 89-90.

[47] Childe, *The Dawn of European Civilization,* p. 46, credits Central European barbarians, the Lausitz people, with having brought to Troy the socket axe type in question, because the pottery appearing in Troy VII b is allied to Lausitz pottery. The socketed axe as such points also in that direction: some area of the Lausitz culture, Peake and Fleure say, may have been the original home of the socketed axe; *The Horse and the Sword,* p. 92. Tallgren's view is different, as we have seen (see note 34 and text).

[48] "La Pontide préscythique," p. 154.

[49] It goes without saying that the type which was brought to Troy from Europe (cf. note 47) must be older in Europe than in Troy. Troy VII b, the city which took the place of the Homeric Troy, commenced after the fall of the latter, that is, according to traditional chronology based on Eratosthenes, some time between 1194

and 1184 B.C. This date, however, is regarded as absolutely worthless by A. R. Burn, who likewise rejects Eusebios' date 1172 B.C. and suggests the years from 1120 to around 1100 B.C. instead; *Minoans, Philistines, and Greeks,* pp. 48-66. J. L. Myres, on the other hand, defends the traditional chronology: *Who Were the Greeks?* Cf. Peake and Fleure, *The Horse and the Sword,* pp. 1-2, 146. — That the city sacked by the Achaians was not Hissarlik VI but VIIa seems definitely ascertained; see Childe, *Dawn,* pp. 35, 45. Thus, to date in the twelfth century B.C. the socketed axes of the type recovered in Troy VIIb seems perfectly legitimate — even if Burn's date of around 1100 B.C. were accepted; otherwise I should not hesitate to operate with a date as early as "late 13th c. B.C." A detail which may not be overlooked in the case of the Sosnovaya Maza types is the second loop, on the lower face of the axe; it is a detail which appears to define the typological and, consequently, chronological place of these types between Troy VIIb and those Russian and Siberian forms which have only one loop, on the lower face, and have done away with the lateral loop which alone is found in the Troy specimen. This is the second reason for the conservative estimate "12th century" for Sosnovaya Maza. — Kiselev (*Drevnyaya istoriya yuzhnoi Sibiri,* p. 105) mentions the Sosnovaya Maza hoard as a characteristic example of the Khvalinsk group of bronzes of the late Andronovo period (1700-1200 B.C.).

[50] Sosnovaya Maza (Saratov Govt.): Tallgren, "La Pontide préscythique," Fig. 88:2 and 1 = Fig. 59 A; Kharkov: *ibid.,* Fig. 109:10; Voronezh: *ibid.,* Fig. 109:11.

[51] Tallgren, *Coll. Tovostine,* p. 42, Fig. 43 A = Fig. 59 B. With reference to this dagger, Tallgren says: "L'original, conservé au Musée de Minoussinsk, provient du vill. de B. Khabyk . . . Je connais . . . un autre exemplaire originaire des steppes de Minoussinsk. En outre il y

en a deux semblables provenant de l'Oural, 4 du dépôt de fondeur de Saratov, Sosnovaia Massa, et un de Kiev. Il est possible que ce type remonte au poignard plat de l'âge du cuivre. . . ."; *op. cit.,* p. 42.

[52] Egami and Mizuno, *Inner Mongolia,* Pt. II, Pl. 35:1.

[53] Martin, *L'Age du Bronze au Musée de Minoussinsk,* Pl. 1:7.

[54] Egami and Mizuno, *op. cit.,* Pl. 39:6 and 8=Fig. 60 A; text pp. 16-18. Discussing these pieces in "Das Tocharerproblem und die Pontische Wanderung" (p. 230), Heine-Geldern stresses similarities to Hallstatt B and C types (with broadened neck) and proposes a date, therefore, of around 800 B.C.

[55] *Ibid,* p. 17, Fig. 10:3 = W. Dörpfeld, *Troja und Ilion:* A. Götze, *Die Kleingeräte,* p. 405, Fig. 406. Cf. R. v. Heine-Geldern, "Archaeological Traces of the Vedic Aryans," p. 5 f.: "Not older than 1200 B.C."

[56] G. Nioradze, in *ESA,* VII (1932), Fig. a = Dullo, in *PZ,* XXVII (1936), p. 89, Fig. 9=Fig. 60 B. Heine-Geldern ("Archaeological Traces," p. 6) stated that this type "may be inferred almost with certainty to belong here to the 12th century B.C."

[57] E. Dullo, in *PZ,* XXVII, p. 95, inclines to date this sort of flat celt or adze toward the end of the Bronze Age, the Iron Age in Transcaucasia beginning around 1100 B.C.; while Heine-Geldern's corresponding date is "between 1200 and 1000 B.C.," as shown in his "Archaeological Traces," pp. 6-7.

[58] Cf. Tallgren, "KBrZ NOR," p. 116, first paragraph.

[58a] Cf. M. Loehr, "Weapons and Tools from Anyang and Siberian Analogies."

[59] G. Vernadsky, *Ancient Russia,* I, pp. 37-38.

[60] Tallgren, "The Arctic Bronze Age," pp. 42-43: "The second chronological stage in the East Russian Bronze Age . . . reveals an indigenous civilisation that is indebted chiefly to the southeastern Andronovo civilisation, with its centre about the southern Urals, and the contemporary civilisation of the graves with wooden chamber constructions on the steppes east of the Black Sea. It belongs to the latter half of the IInd millennium B.C., about 1300-900 B.C."

*Idem,* "Studies of the Pontic Bronze Age," p. 105. Tallgren here proposes the following scheme:

I.   The Fatyanovo graves=MM I-II = 2000-1700

II.  The catacomb graves=MM II-LM I = 1800-1500

IIIa. Graves with timber construction = 1400-1100 (Galich)

IIIb. Late graves with timber construction =1300-1100 (Seima)

He adds: "Much greater ages, however, have been suggested by others. Possibly the absolute chronology of groups IIIa and IIIb may be correct, although the lower limit should be about the year 1000 B.C. and the so-called Andronovo formation east of the Volga should be added to the facies of culture that are contemporary with each other (IIIa and IIIb), as one of the most important cultures during the period in question. On the other hand, groups I and II . . . probably begin somewhat earlier and represent a longer period than I have suggested."

[61] R. Grousset, *L'Empire des Steppes,* p. 32.

[62] E. H. Minns, "The Art of the Northern Nomads," p. 19.

[63] E. Golomshtok, "Anthropological Activities in Soviet Russia," pp. 316 (Gorodzov) and 319 (Teploukhov). S. V. Kiselev, *Drevnyaya istoriya yuzhnoi Sibiri,* pp. 99-105; map p. 69.

[64] These several types form part of the Andronovo inventory of Minusinsk, according to Teploukhov's diagram; *op. cit.,* note 7 above.

[65] Fatyanovo: A. A. Spitsyn, "Mednyi vek v verkhnem Povolzhe" (St. Petersburg, 1903), in *ZRORAO,* V, pp. 77-93; *idem,* "Novyya svedeniya o mednom vek

v srednei i severnoi Rossii," *ibid.*, VIII, 1905. — V. A. Gorodzov, *Kultury bronzovoi epokhi v srednei Rossii, Otchet Ross. Istor. Museya* (Moscow, 1914). A. M. Tallgren, "KBrZ NOR," p. 45 ff.; *idem,* "Fatjanovokulturen i Centralryssland," *FM,* 1924; *idem,* "La Pontide préscythique," 87-88; *idem,* in *MAGW,* 1931, p. 94; *idem,* in *ESA,* XI (1937), p. 42; *idem,* "L'Age du cuivre dans la Russie Centrale," in *SMYA,* XXXII (1922). — Aarne Äyräpää, "Über die Streitaxtkulturen in Russland," *ESA,* VIII (1933), pp. 96 ff., 123 ff., 154. — V. G. Childe, *The Dawn of European Civilization,* p. 160 ff., 200 ff. Peake and Fleure, *The Steppe and the Sown,* p. 48 f.

[66] Childe, *op. cit.,* p. 160.

[67] There has been, and still is, much controversy regarding the origin of the Fatyanovo globular pots as well as that of the stone battle-axes. Cf. M. C. Burkitt, *Our Early Ancestors,* p. 154 ff.; C. Dawson, *The Age of the Gods,* pp. 261-78. Regarding Fatyanovo pottery such an authority as A. Äyräpää (Europaeus) — recognizing that the Single-grave People came to Jutland from outside the Baltic area — holds that Fatyanovo ceramics must be explained as "eine Entartung der Kugelamphoren-Keramik" (*ESA,* VIII, p. 154), implicitly refuting the thesis that its roots had been in South-Russia. Others, like G. Nagy (*Arch. Ertesitö,* 1913), J. L. Myres (*Cambridge Ancient History,* I, p. 84: remark on the hemispherical pots of clay as the pottery of prairie folk), and Childe (*Dawn,* pp. 166-69) defend with good reasons South-Russia as the cradle whence both the battle-axe and the globular amphorae spread north and to the Baltic. Peake and Fleure flatly state that these pots "clearly originated on the steppe"; *The Steppe and the Sown,* p. 48; cf. p. 28 f.

[68] The Fatyanovo shaft-hole axe of copper is an isolated find made in that cemetery in 1909; Tallgren, "KBrZ NOR,"

pp. 47, 69. Its form is the same as that from the Galich Treasure (cf. note 23; Fig. 62 A), according to Tallgren. The Seima shaft-hole axe differs a little. — Dates proposed on account of parallels among Transylvanian axes are "about 1700 B.C."; J. Nestor, "Zum Stande der Vorgeschichtsforschung in Rumänien," p. 89; E. Dullo, in *PZ,* XXVII, p. 156 f. This agrees fairly well with Tallgren's view about the earliest East Russian Bronze Age: 1700-1400 B.C. — with Fatyanovo contemporary with the earlier part and, possibly, older (*ESA,* XI, p. 42). But Tallgren assigns a much lower date to Galich and Seima, i.e., 1400/1300-1100/1000 B.C. (*ibid.,* pp. 43-44, 105). — The shaft-hole axes here considered are rather common in Russia; cf. "KBrZ NOR," p. 56 ff; Dullo, in *PZ,* XXVII, pp. 154 ff.

[69] Cf. Tallgren, "KBrZ NOR," p. 84 f., 91, 216 f.; *idem,* "La Pontide préscythique," p. 88; Childe, *Dawn,* p. 161.

[70] Tallgren, "KBrZ NOR," p. 210; *idem,* in *MAGW,* LXI (1931), p. 94.

[71] "KBrZ NOR," pp. 207-10; *idem,* in *SMYA,* XXXII; cf. v. Merhart, *Bronzezeit am Jenissei,* p. 18.

[72] "La Pontide préscythique," p. 142; *idem,* "Studies of the Pontic Bronze Age," p. 105.

[73] M. Rostovtzeff, in *Revue archeologique,* XII (1920); *idem, Iranians and Greeks in South Russia,* pp. 19-31, with the conclusion that "the finds of Troy and the finds of the Kuban, though akin, are not contemporaneous, the Kuban finds being much older," p. 31. *Idem, The Animal Style in South Russia and China,* pp. 18-19, pointing out a strong influence from Sumerian art, and hinting at a correspondingly early date. — H. Frankfort, *The Sumerian Question,* p. 52 ff., speculating on the possible antecedence of Early Kuban before Ur; cf. *ESA,* XI, p. 106. — G. Contenau, *Manuel d'archéologie orientale,* III, 1564-75. For further relevant writings, see *ESA,* XI, p. 105.

[74] A. V. Schmidt, "Die Kurgane der Stanica Konstantinovskaja," *ESA,* IV (1929), pp. 9-21.

[75] Ahlatlibel: H. Z. Koşay, *Türkiye Cümhuriyeti Maarif Vekaletince Yaptirilan Ahlatlibel Hafriyati, Türk Tarih, Arkeol, ve Etnogr. Dergisi,* II (Istanbul 1934). — Alaca Höyük: R. O. Arik, *Les Fouilles d'Alaca Höyük, Rapport préliminaire sur les travaux en 1935* (Ankara 1937), p. 119. H. Z. Koşay, *Ausgrabungen von Alaca Höyük, Ein Vorbericht über die im Auftrage der Türkischen Geschichtskommission im Sommer 1936 durchgeführten Forschungen und Entdeckungen* (Ankara 1944), p. 177: "Es ist anzunehmen, dass diese kupferzeitliche Kultur in Alaca Höyük durch eine aus dem Nordosten [Caucasia, Kuban] kommende Kultur stark beeinflusst worden ist." Cf. F. Hančar, "Alaca Höyük," *WBKKA,* XII (1938), who — listing amazing similarities in burial customs and material culture in general — rejects the idea of direct connections between Alaca and Early Kuban, and draws attention to the existing differences.

[76] F. Hančar, "Alaca Höyük," pp. 30-34: 2400-1900 B.C. as the time of the early metal stage of both Alaca Höyük and Kuban. *Idem, Urgeschichte Kaukasiens von den Anfängen seiner Besiedlung bis in die Zeit seiner frühen Metallurgie* (Wien-Leipzig, 1937).

[77] V. G. Childe, *Dawn,* pp. 146-55. Cf. Peake and Fleure, *The Steppe and the Sown,* p. 31 f.

[77a] *Stratigraphie comparée et chronologie de l'Asie Occidentale,* Tab. IX.

[78] S. S. Weinberg, "Aegean Chronology: Neolithic Period and Early Bronze Age," in *AJA,* LI/2 (1947), pp. 165-82. Blegen, in *Proc. Prehistoric Soc.,* 1938, p. 221; quoted by A. Kühn, *IPEK,* XII (1938), p. 176.

[79] *Amer. Anthropol.,* XXXV (1933), p. 316.

[80] Tallgren, when first analyzing the Galich Treasure in "KBrZ NOR,"

stressed its indissoluble connection with Fatyanovo; *op. cit., passim.* Later, he came to separate them widely, i.e., by approximately three to four centuries (cf. *ESA*, XI, p. 105 f.) although admitting that "Fatyanovo, on the other hand, has certainly something in common not only with Galich etc., but also with early Unetice [Aunjetitz], and in the southeast with Tsarskaya, i.e. Early Kuban."

Albeit, continuity or even contiguity of Fatyanovo and Andronovo-Seima strains is not gainsaid by Tallgren: "Les objets métalliques sont très rares dans les tombes (de Fatyanovo). Par contre, on en a découvert dans les grandes trouvailles de Galitch et de Seima, qui sont essentiellement une suite de la culture de Fatianovo et se rattachent aux cultures du Kouban et du Volga inferieur" ("La Pontide préscythique," p. 87). Cf. G. Vernadsky, *Ancient Russia,* I, p. 24, observing that copper and bronze things appear in the later Fatyanovo graves, without there having been any forceful interruption. Similarly, Childe, *Dawn,* p. 161.

[81] Minns, "Small Bronzes from Northern Asia," *Antiquaries Journ.,* X (1930), p. 7.

[82] H. R. Hall, *The Civilization of Greece in the Bronze Age,* p. 88, Fig. 100. Childe, *Dawn,* p. 31, Fig. 15. Cf. Tallgren, "La Pontide," p. 195.

[83] E. Dullo, in *PZ,* XXVII, p. 154 ff. Cf. Tallgren, "KBrZ NOR," p. 66.

[84] Tallgren, *ibid.,* 56-69; *idem,* "La Pontide préscythique," 167-71.

[85] Nestor, "Zum Stande der Vorgeschichtsforschung in Rumänien," *Ber. Röm. Germ. Komm.,* XXII (1932), p. 89.

[86] Tepe Khazineh (near Musyan): *Mém. Dél. Perse,* VIII, p. 146, Fig. 308. — Tepe Gawra: Speiser, *Excavations at T.G.* (1935), Pl. 48, quoted after *PZ,* XXVII.

[87] Borodino: E. v. Stern, in *MAR,* XXXIV. Tallgren, in RLV, II, p. 121, with bibliography. *Idem,* "La Pontide

préscythique," pp. 140-42. *Idem,* in *MAGW,* LXI. E. Dullo, in *PZ,* XXVII, p. 151. Nestor, *op. cit.,* note 85 above. Äyräpää, in *ESA,* VIII, p. 74 ff.

[88] Tallgren, "KBrZ NOR," p. 46, Fig. 41 = Äyräpää, in *ESA,* VIII, p. 17, Fig. 7 = Fig. 63 A.

[89] Dörpfeld, *Troja und Ilion,* I: Götze, *Die Kleingeräte,* p. 374 f., Figs. 323-26. E. Dullo, in *PZ,* XXVII, Figs. 14-15. N. Åberg, *Das nordische Kulturgebiet in Mitteleuropa während der jüngeren Steinzeit,* II, Fig. 212.

[90] Tallgren, "Caucasian Monuments," *ESA,* V, p. 135, Fig. 42.

[91] E. Chantre, *Recherches anthropologiques dans le Caucase,* II, *Atlas,* Pl. 6 bis: 4-5 (bronze); Ebert, *RLV,* VI, Pl. 91: i (stone) = Fig. 64 B.

[92] H. de Morgan, in *Mém. Dél. Perse,* VIII, p. 321, Fig. 724 = Fig. 64 C.

[93] Mentioned by Tallgren, "La Pontide préscythique," p. 132; reproduced by J. R. Aspelin, *Antiquités du Nord Finno-Ougrien* (Helsingfors 1877), Fig. 627.

[94] J. de Morgan, "La Préhistoire orientale," III, p. 50, Fig. 61 = Fig. 64 D.

[95] Dörpfeld: Götze, *op. cit.,* I, pp. 323, 377.

[96] Tallgren, "La Pontide préscythique," p. 132.

[97] Dörpfeld: Götze, *op. cit.,* I, p. 322, Fig. 255. Childe, "Eurasian Shaft-hole Axes," *ESA,* IX (1934), p. 162.

[98] Dörpfeld: Götze, *op. cit.,* I, p. 376, Fig. 331 = Fig. 65 A. I am not aware that attention has been drawn to this remarkable analogy Troy-Fatyanovo by previous investigators.

[99] J. de Morgan, "La Préhistoire orientale," III, p. 100, Fig. 144.

[100] Musyan: *Mém. Dél. Perse,* VIII, p. 86, Fig. 116. Ur: Childe, "Eurasian Shaft-hole Axes," p. 159.

[101] The Russian "Absatz-Streitaxt" (heeled battle-axe): cf. Tallgren, "La Pontide préscythique," p. 115, Fig. 68: 1 = *ESA,* VIII, Fig. 56; "Pontide," Fig. 68: 5 = *ESA,* VIII, Fig. 50. Chantre,

*Recherches anthropologiques en Caucase,* I, Pl. 1:9 = *ESA,* VIII, Fig. 53.

[102] Hagios Mamas (Macedonia): Childe, *Dawn,* p. 82, Fig. 41, after *BSA,* XXIX.

[103] Äyräpää, in *ESA,* VIII, p. 89 note.

[104] N. Åberg took them for intermediate types, accounting for his theory that the Trojan axes were dependent on European forerunners of not purely Jutlandish cast. His date for the Borodino axes — several centuries earlier than those from Troy — is an inconsequence brought about by coupling them with the rest of the find as belonging in Montelius' II, and is hardly made good by the remark that "trotzdem scheint der Zeitunterschied allzu gross zu sein," and that these axes "als Kultwaffen ihre typologischen Züge Jahrhunderte hindurch haben bewahren können." Åberg, *Das nordische Kulturgebiet,* p. 109 and Figs. 209-11, 212-13. Cf. Äyräpää, *ESA,* VIII, p. 74, who gives further examples to be grouped with the Trojan and Borodino axes, but does not separate himself from Åberg's view, except for the remark that it is hardly thinkable that more simple specimens of Borodino type are all as late as the latter; *ibid.,* p. 79.

[105] Cf. Äyräpää, *ibid.,* pp. 79-80.

[106] *Ibid.,* p. 75 ff.

[107] *Ibid.,* p. 81 f.

[108] *Ibid.,* p. 77, Fig. 82.

[109] Childe, *Dawn,* p. 160.

[110] Äyräpää, "Über die Streitaxtkulturen in Russland," pp. 85-87.

[111] *Ibid.,* pp. 82-83, Fig. 87.

[112] *RLV,* II, Pl. 98 e: stone axe from Gorsko Kalugerovo.

[113] Published by Tallgren in *ESA,* VI, p. 179, Fig. 5. The décor of that object may well be compared to the curvilinear design of the Borodino pin and the Popovka battle-axe.

[113a] *Stratigraphie comparée et chronologie de l'Asie Occidentale,* pp. 244, 441, n.

[114] For Pokrovsk, see P. Rykov, "Die Chvalynsker Kultur der Bronzezeit,"

*ESA,* I, pp. 51-84; Tallgren, "La Pontide préscythique," pp. 72 ff., Figs. 48-54.

On the basis of the pottery finds made, P. Rykov analyzed the Khvalynsk Culture as a complex wherein the culture of the older timber-lined graves and a culture characterized by a particular ceramic vessel type met; this complex developed under influences from Seima and the Caucasus. Out of these complex conditions grew, he says, a cultural unity, which is revealed by the uniformity of the décor. Rykov, *op. cit.,* p. 57.

[115] Rykov, *ibid.,* Fig. 21:1; p. 59. Ceramics related to those of the catacomb-graves are broad vases with flat bottoms, such as *ibid.,* Fig. 7.

[116] P. Rau, "Neue Funde aus Hockergräbern des Wolgadeutschen Gebiets," *ESA,* IV, p. 41 ff. The pin was found in Kurgan VI, grave 9, on the Kalmückenberg near Boaro, lower Volga; *op. cit.,* Fig. 8. According to F. Hančar, this pin is the easternmost one recorded thus far; "Die Nadelformen des Kaukasusgebietes," *ESA,* VII, p. 121.

[117] Rykov, *op. cit.,* p. 61.

[118] Tobol: O. Grivtsov-Grakov, in *ESA,* IV, p. 119, Fig. 3. Vozkresenzk: A. O. Heikel, "Antiquités de la Sibérie Occidentale," p. 59, Pl. 12:16 = Fig. 66 C.

[119] ". . . die Andronovakultur, mit der die Kultur der Holzkammer-Gräber und die Chvalynsker Kultur zwischen Don und Uralfluss so nahe verwandt sind, dass man sie als Einheit auffassen kann." O. Menghin, *Weltgeschichte der Steinzeit,* p. 453.

[119a] For Karasuk, valuable information and bibliographies will be found in J. H. Gaul's "Observations on the Bronze Age in the Yenisei Valley, Siberia," pp. 183-85, and in K. Jettmar's "The Karasuk Culture and Its South-Eastern Affinities," pp. 123-26, to which has to be added S. V. Kiselev's book, *Drevnyaya istoriya yuzhnoi Sibiri* (1951). Briefer discussions in Loehr, "Ordos Daggers and Knives, . . . Second Part: Knives," pp. 130-38; Jettmar, "Archaeologische Spuren von Indogermanen," pp. 239-43, 247-49; Hančar, "The Eurasian Animal Style and the Altai Complex," pp. 171-75.

[120] See Teploukhov's diagram; note 7 above.

[121] J. G. Granö, "Archäologische Beobachtungen von meinen Reisen in den nördl. Grenzgegenden Chinas," *Journ. Soc. Finno-Ougr.,* XXVI, Pl. 9:30; cf. Tallgren, "Inner Asiatic and Siberian Rock Pictures," *ESA,* VIII, Fig. 25, p. 191.

[121a] F. Hančar, "The Eurasian Animal Style and the Altai Complex," p. 173 f. Cf. Tallgren, "Some North-Eurasian Sculptures," p. 118.

[121b] *Ibid.,* p. 119, Figs. 8, 9.

[121c] Jettmar, "The Karasuk Culture," p. 121.

[122] H. Kühn, "Chronologie der Sino-Sibirischen Bronzen," *IPEK,* XII (1938), pp. 162-65. Cf. Karlgren, "Some Weapons and Tools," p. 122.

[123] M. Loehr, "Zur Chronologie der älteren chinesischen Bronzen," *OZ* (1936); idem, "Neue Typen grauer Shang-Keramik," *Sinolog. Arbeiten* (1943), Pl. 1.

[124] L. Bachhofer, *A Short History of Chinese Art,* pp. 26-27. As to Bachhofer's observation that in the second style of the White Pottery decoration "the meander and the other motives are set slantwise," it may not be out of place to recall the fact that meanders, swastika-patterns, or similar geometric figurations filling the main friezes in *Andronovo* pottery are also set slantwise. Cf. *RLV,* XIII, Pl. 92 B.

[125] Karlgren, "Some Weapons and Tools of the Yin Dynasty," p. 131.

[126] Cf. Borovka, *Scythian Art,* p. 77; Minns, "The Art of the Northern Nomads," p. 14 f.

[127] Andersson, "Hunting Magic," Pl. 1:1, Pl. 5:2.

[128] G. Ecke, "Über einige Messer aus Anyang," Pl. A:III.

[129] Minns, *op. cit.,* note 126 above: p. 13 and map.

[130] Cf. D. C. Graham, "A Preliminary Report of the Hanchow Excavation," *West China Border Research Soc.,* VI (1934), Figs. 9, 11, 17, 19, 25, 32.

| Approximate dates B.C. | RUSSIA | | SIBERIA | CHINA |
|---|---|---|---|---|
| | EAST and CENTRAL | SOUTH | | |
| 2600 | | | | |
| 2500 | FATYANOVO | | AFANASIEVA | |
| 2400 | | EARLY KUBAN | | |
| 2300 | | NOVOSVOBODNAYA MAIKOP | | |
| 2200 | | | | |
| 2100 | | | | |
| 2000 | | MIDDLE KUBAN | (*First Copper*) | |
| 1900 | | | | |
| 1800 | SEIMA | BORODINO | | |
| 1700 | GALICH TURBINO | | ANDRONOVO (*Early Bronze*) | |
| 1600 | | LATE KUBAN | (*Seima celt; Tomsk mold*) *Geometric style* | "NORTHERN" EARLY ORDOS |
| 1500 | POKROVSK KHVALINSK | | | (*Bronze tools, geometric style*) |
| 1400 | | | KARASUK | PRE-ANYANG |
| 1300 | | | (*Early animal style; primitive mirrors*) | (*Geometric*) ANYANG (1300-1028) |
| 1200 | SOSNOVAYA MAZA | | | (*Shang animal style*) |
| 1100 | | | | |
| 1000 | | (*Iron*) | TAGAR I (*Proto-akinakes, bronze*) | |
| 900 | | | | HSÜN-HSIEN |
| 800 | | SCYTHS | | |
| 700 | | | TAGAR II (*Iron*) | HSIN-CHENG |
| 600 | ANANINO | | ALTAI: MAIEMIR PHASE | |
| 500 | | | | CHIN-TS'UN |
| 400 | | | ALTAI: PAZYRYK KURGANS | |
| 300 | | SARMATAE | | |
| 200 | | | | |
| 100 | | | | |

*Archaeological Time Chart*

| Dates B.C. | | | |
|---|---|---|---|
| 1027 | WESTERN CHOU | (1027-771 B.C.) | YIN-CHOU STYLE |
| 1000 | CHOU I | (1027-928 B.C.) EARLY W. CHOU | |
| | | | WESTERN CHOU STYLE |
| 900 | CHOU II | (927-771 B.C.) LATE W. CHOU | |
| | | | "MIDDLE CHOU" STYLE |
| 800 | EASTERN CHOU | (770-221 B.C.) | |
| | CHOU III | (770-ca. 450 B.C.) EARLY E. CHOU (CH'UN CH'IU, 722-481 B.C.) | HSIN-CHENG STYLE |
| 700 | | | |
| | | | LI-YÜ STYLE (?) |
| 600 | | | |
| | | | HUAI STYLE |
| 500 | | | |
| | CHOU IV | (ca. 450-221 B.C.) LATE E. CHOU (WARRING STATES, 481-221 B.C.) | CHIN-TS'UN STYLE |
| 400 | | | |
| 300 | | (END OF CHOU, 256 B.C.) | |
| 200 | TS'IN HAN | (221-207 B.C.) (206-A.D. 220) | |

Note: Dates before 841 B.C. are estimates. The initial year, according to the *Bamboo Annals,* was 257 years before the death of Yu Wang (771 B.C.), hence 1027 B.C. The year 928 B.C. corresponds to Mu Wang's last year, which marks the first century of Chou rule. The dates of the styles are crude estimates of the respective beginnings.

*Chou Chronology and Sequence of Styles*

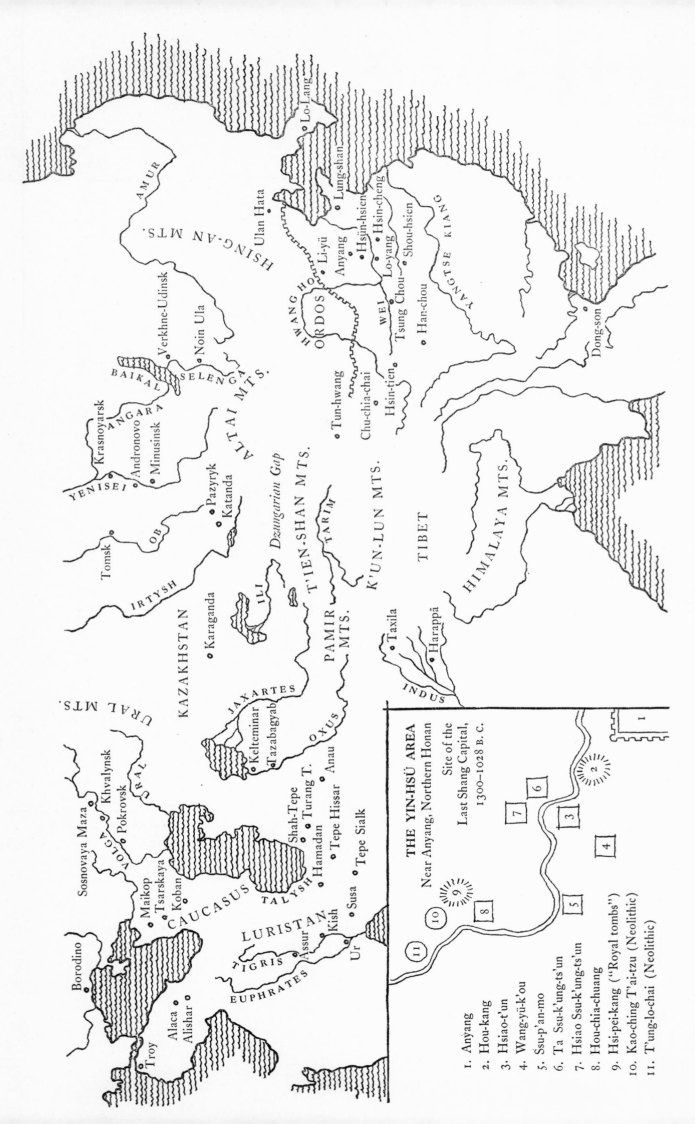

Archaeological Sites of Western, Central, and Eastern Asia

THE YIN-HSÜ AREA

Near Anyang, Northern Honan

Site of the
Last Shang Capital,
1300–1028 B. C.

1. Anyang
2. Hou-kang
3. Hsiao-t'un
4. Wang-yü-k'ou
5. Ssu-p'an-mo
6. Ta Ssu-k'ung-ts'un
7. Hsiao Ssu-k'ung-ts'un
8. Hou-chia-chuang
9. Hsi-pei-kang ("Royal tombs")
10. Kao-ching T'ai-tzu (Neolithic)
11. T'ung-lo-chai (Neolithic)

*Catalogue*

# CATALOGUE

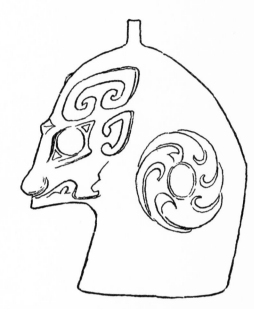

Fig. 68: *Helmet from Grave 1004, Hou-chia-chuang.*

(Ca. 1/5.)

(*I*) BRONZE HELMET

Casque type, with horizontal base and square opening for the face, covering the forehead, cheeks, and neck. The crest, which ends in the middle of the back, is surmounted by a short vertical tube. The front is in the form of an animal mask: two grooved, bent horns in relief, two oval eyes, ears, and a nose from which the crest rises. The helmet is slightly deformed, notably at the fore-front and lower rear parts. Breaks seem to occur over the whole piece, which has been repaired in a way that does not permit one to trace the nature and extent of the damage. Allegedly found in Hou-chia-chuang 侯家莊 to the west of Anyang (Northern Honan). Shang. Pl. I.

Height 235 mm; length of fore-front edge 115 mm; lower width 230: 190 mm; weight ca. 1800 gr.

A similar casque with broader frontal opening, bare of any décor, is in the Archaeological Collection of the Kyoto University (K. Hamada, *Select Specimens,* Pl. 46).

Another specimen which shows an animal mask combined with large whorl-circles on the cheek-plates — ornaments of pure Shang style — has been unearthed at Hou-chia-chuang, in the southern passage of one of the smaller graves in the immediate vicinity of the so-called Royal Tombs. The results of these excavations, carried through by the Academia Sinica in 1934 and 1935, have not yet been published. Shorter accounts were given by Pelliot, "The Royal Tombs"; H. J. Timperley, "The Awakening of China in Archaeology"; and S. Umehara, "Hou-chia-chuang."

Fig. 68 has been taken from Umehara's article. The origin as well as the decoration of that helmet leaves no doubt that it belongs to Shang times. The slightly varying form of the present specimen may not be overlooked, insignificant though it be with regard to any chronological difference. Horns of the same design as those on the helmet, moreover, also occur on a fragment of a marble *ts'ung* 琮 (symbol of the earth) with a ram's head, which in all probability dates from the Shang (Sirén, *History of Early Chinese Art,* III, Pl. 1; Umehara, in *Kōkogaku Zasshi,* XXII, 595).

### (2) JADE AXE IN BRONZE HAFT (*YÜEH*)

The blade, of a brownish gray stone stained green by bronze oxide near the haft, has slightly convex faces with a fine polish that yet leaves some of the natural unevenness on one side. The lateral edges, not entirely regular, are slightly rounded; the cutting edge is symmetrical in section. The bronze haft has two short wings at the socketed part which are not found among bronze axes of the same type. The haft also has two small square holes behind the socket of only 5 mm depth, and a larger round hole which, when the tool was mounted, lay just behind the wooden shaft. On the neck, which is slightly narrower than the fore part, is a décor of an animal mask not fully discernible under the crust of grayish green oxide that has spread over the bronze. Shang.                                    Pl. II.

Length 165 mm; weight 210 gr.

The way the stone has been worked does not show that overrefinement of so many Shang jade pieces which underwent an elaborate, even rigorous working process. The craftsman was satisfied with a sufficiently rubbed and smoothed piece which still reflected something of its crude original state.

There is a counterpart of this rare type in the David-Weill Collection, Paris (S. Umehara, *Shina Kodō Seika,* VII, Pl. 91 B; Sirén, *History of Early Chinese Art,* I, Pl. 17).

### (3) JADE AXE IN BRONZE HAFT (*YÜEH*)

Fig. 69: *Detail of the décor of the axe no. 3.*

Broad blade of grayish jade discolored into a creamy white on one side, with somewhat irregular convex faces. A double-cone perforation near the base cuts into the neat round cavity of a bore-hole that was begun but never completed. The narrow lateral edges are not polished; the cutting edge, fairly straight, shows sharply faceted grinding on both sides. The bronze haft with the two wings (as mentioned above, no. 2) is decorated by two symmetrical animal-heads above open jaws bristling with teeth. The end of the perforated shafting-plaque (or tang) again is occupied by a square-framed animal mask — most probably that of a tiger (Fig. 69). The sunken parts of the ornament contain a reddish brown paste. Bronze patina of a dull greenish brown tone, partly covered by a crust of green oxide. Shang.                                    Pl. II.

Length 178 mm; weight 280 gr.

The following factors lead me to suppose that the cutting edge has lost its original shape, having been resharpened at an early date: (1) the edge is not rounded as it usually is; (2) the grinding margins have not been smoothed over; (3) the shaping of the corners lacks the usual technical perfection; (4) finally, the polish is different from that of the rest of the surfaces. Thus, the question arises whether the cutting edge had perhaps been worn out, or, in other words, whether this weapon actually had been used — contrary to what one would expect in the case of a ceremonial weapon, which it undoubtedly was.

How the jade blade is fastened remains somewhat problematical. In the center it obviously only reaches the outer edges of the teeth. It is to the right and left of the semicircular jaws that the blade enters into the haft. The patina, however, prevents one from clearly making out this detail.

Perforated axes occur in both jade and bronze. A specimen exactly parallel to this type has not yet appeared.

### (4) HEAVY BRONZE AXE (YÜEH)

Rounded cutting edge, an asymmetrically placed tang (*nei*), and, correspondingly, unequally long shafting-slits in both shoulders. A broad relief band strengthens the base of the blade, showing the motif of threatening open jaws with large fangs between two animal-heads in sunken lineament; the eyes and the horns plastically stand out. The *nei* is decorated with a square animal mask (*t'ao-t'ieh*), inlaid with turquoise particles that partly are lost. On the reverse side a whorl-circle with fine indentations appears in its stead, again stripped of most of the turquoise (Fig. 70). Beneath that circle is an incised character. The patina is of a bright grayish green with some copper-red, overlaid by corrosions of a darker color. On that part which would pass through the haft, the patina apparently has been artificially heightened. Near the edge, the metal has bulged and swollen in the process of oxidation. Shang. Pl. III.

Length 228 mm; weight 870 gr.

Specimens of similar type and comparable size occur in two Japanese collections, Asano, Osaka, and Kishi, Kyoto (S. Umehara, *Anyang Studies*, Pl. 45 : 2; *Anyang Treasures*, Pl. 22). Cp. also *Shuang Chien I Chi Chin*, hsia, 45; *Ch'ih An Ts'ang Chin*, 33; *Yeh Chung P'ien Yü*, I, hsia 8, 9, 10; II, hsia 20.

The character inscribed would read, according to Takada, *ch'eng* 成 (*Ku Chou P'ien*, 87 : 11), which is hardly correct. More probably it is a shortened form of *k'o* 克, "able," "to vanquish."

### (5) HEAVY BRONZE AXE (YÜEH)

Rounded cutting edge and asymmetrically placed tang (*nei*), similar to but heavier than no. 4. The shoulder-slits have burst and are nearly hidden under an exuberant patina. The process of corrosion has violently expanded, warped, and burst open the bronze, so that the now rugged surface has entirely lost its metallic character. Color: fairly uniform dull malachite-green with blackish spots and earthy concretions. The shaft has left behind some wooden fiber saturated with bronze oxide. Shang. Pl. IV.

Length 208 mm; weight 1050 gr.

So complete a decomposition of the metal as in the present case is rarely to be observed. A series of fragments of bronze vases and halberds acquired at Anyang years ago by Dr. Herbert Mueller,

Fig. 70: *Décor on the reverse side of the axe no. 4.*

Peking, displays the same degree of corrosion, which seems to be characteristic of a certain site, or stratum, of Hsiao-t'un (Anyang). Presumably, it is the river bank site briefly surveyed and described by O. Karlbeck, "Notes on the Archaeology of China," p. 195.

## (6) HEAVY BRONZE AXE (*YÜEH*)

Similar to nos. 4 and 5 but differing in the pattern of the *t'ao-t'ieh* on the tang and in the jaws-motif, which here is openwork. The fangs thus produce an all the more menacing impression. A peculiar feature is the extraordinarily wide hole in the tang. Rough patina in manifold colors and shades of green, grayish green, bluish gray, and brown-violet. Blunt edge, marred by oxidation. Shang.     Pl. V.

Length 216 mm; weight 664 gr.

An allied specimen of unique proportions, i.e., a very broad and short blade, is in the Kishi Collection, Kyoto (Umehara, *Anyang Treasures*, Pl. 24:1). Another likewise relatively broad specimen, which shows a human face above the jaws, was on exhibition in London in 1935-36 (Cat. no. 267; H. J. Oppenheim Collection; cp. Introduction, ch. I, Axes, group B III, specimen 3).

The jaws of the tiger — that is what the motif presumably means — play an important role in the theriomorphic design of Shang art, without necessarily being tied to the representation of the tiger itself. Examples are offered by small jade sculptures, or in the ornamentation of sacrificial vessels; and some fantastic animal-heads on carved bones in the Royal Ontario Museum, Toronto, and in the collection of the King of Sweden (*Anyang Treasures*, Pls. 78:1; 79:1) could — regarding jaws and fangs — have served as models for the designs on these axes.

## (7) BRONZE AXE (*YÜEH*)

Rounded edge and asymmetrically placed tang (*nei*), rectangular shoulder-slits, and a round perforation in the *nei*. The blade is decorated with the figure of a coiled reptile, or dragon, which occupies half of the surface and whose contour fits in the outline of the blade. Its head — with jaws and fangs — is turned back; a row of characteristic scales covers its body, and along the dorsal line runs a crestlike band of strokes alternating with T-shaped figures. (A pattern familiar from the crests or flanges that bronze vases often have, where it appears to be a mere ornament devoid of organic meaning.) The design of the animal is done with bold incised lines filled with a black paste. On the *nei* appears an ornament wherein — in contrast of techniques — the design rises in *cloisons* above the hollowed ground, framed by a simple scale-band on three sides. Smooth, uniform dull green-gray and apple-green patina with some rough spots, notably at the neck. Shang.     Pl. VI.

Length 185 mm; weight 460 gr.

In regard to decoration and its technique, this specimen is unique (but compare the following type). The black filling, the pigment and medium of which have not been analyzed so far, occurs now and then on sacrificial vases. The scales on the animal's body are an ornament or a symbol which is often found in Shang and Early Chou animal design. In succession or alternating with different elements they appear on tigers and dragons in carved bone (Umehara, *Anyang Treasures,* Pls. 74: 3; 82; 91: 1, 2, 3, 7) or in jade (Salmony, *Carved Jade,* Pl. 21: 5; Pelliot, *Jades archaïques,* Pl. 17: 1, 42:6). Frequently, these scales occur as an isolated sign on the necks of dragons, snakes, and particularly birds in bone glyptics (Umehara, *op. cit.,* Pls. 87: 1, 88: 1, 4; 89: 3, 91: 5, 97: 1-4). Conspicuous examples of scales, furthermore, are added by a bronze *tsun* in the form of an owl in the Sumitomo Collection (*Senoku Seishō,* I, 33), by a jade bird — on the wing (Pelliot, *op. cit.,* Pl. 26: 1), and by that famous bronze in the shape of a tiger or tigress with a human figure — below the eyes of the beast (*Senoku Seishō,* II, 68 = Koop, *Early Chinese Bronzes,* Pl. 16). In many of these instances, the symbolic character of that sign is obtrusive, and the more so when it appears "unmotivated" and cannot be explained, therefore, as a conventionalized rendering of some real motif. Salmony defined these scales as cowry shells or abbreviated signs meaning cowry (*Carved Jade,* p. 33), and, consequently, a symbol of fertility. The form of the character "cowry" as demonstrated in the early epigraphy, however, is substantially different (cf. *Ku Chou P'ien,* ch. 99: 1-4). One glyph that actually shows a pair of such scales is thus far unintelligible (Jung Keng, *Chin Wen Pien, fu-lu, shang* 21a). Finally, attention is called to the remarkable dagger in this collection, in which a double row of these scales appears on the blade (no. 85), and to the decoration of the axe with dragons (no. 10).

## (8) BRONZE AXE (YÜEH)

Less heavy and more slender than the previous types, with the *nei* placed symmetrically, and without shoulder-slits. The slightly curved cutting edge is, in relation to the blade, noticeably broader than in the foregoing types. The lateral margins are slightly thinner than the blade and are set off from it by a ledge. The motif of a coiled dragon here appears in relief and openwork. The scales on the body differ in that the double arcs are replaced by curved lines. The décor on the neck resembles that of no. 7, but there is no broad frame nor a splint-hole here. The fairly weak blade is slightly warped. Near the lower left corner there is apparently a break which has been repaired with the help of some powdered patina. On the whole, the patina is bright emerald-green and is covered by darker crusts and some reddish brown spots; a heavier concretion covers the left shoulder. Shang or Chou I.                                    Pl. VI.

Length 178 mm; weight 275 gr.

Two kindred specimens of more thickset proportions and with asymmetrically placed shafting-plates were published in Umehara's *Anyang Treasures* (Pl. 23: 1-2; 1 = *Shina Kodō Seika,* VII, 94), a variant without detached margin, in *Ch'ih An Ts'ang Chin* (2: 38).

In Stockholm, two fine, heavily corroded axes both having the same inscription certainly are Shang pieces. One, in the Museum of Far Eastern Antiquities, is approximately the same size as ours; the second, in the collection of the King of Sweden, is larger (Karlgren, "Some Weapons and Tools," nos. 51, 52).

A sixth example is reproduced in C. T. Loo's catalogue, *An Exhibition of Ancient Chinese Ritual Bronzes* (Pl. 33: 13).

## (*9*) BRONZE AXE WITH TUBULAR SOCKET

This uncommon and very solid type combines the heavy square neck (*nei*) of the shoulder-axes with an elliptical tubular socket which extends beyond the base of the slender blade. An animal mask in strong relief occupies the upper half of the blade, overlapping the tube with its horns. The square butt is adorned by a crosslike quatrefoil with a whorl-circle in the center and spirals filling the gussets (the whorl-circle on the one side has five indentations, that on the other side four). The shaft-tube is nearly elliptical in section (18: 29 mm). Slightly scarred cutting edge. Smooth bright emerald-green patina with reddish brown and brown-violet patches and dark green coatings. Shang or Chou I.                                   Pl. VII.

Length 185 mm; weight 550 gr.; length of socket 85 mm.

No comparable specimens have become known so far. Still, one may refer to an interesting axe in the Rutherston Collection, in which a *t'ao-t'ieh* blade is combined with shaft-hole and rectangular *nei;* that axe, on the other hand, the most impressive feature of which is the human head on top of the socket, lacks the characteristic of the socket extending over the blade (*Shina Kodō Seika,* VII, 97 = Sirén, *History of Early Chinese Art,* I, Pl. 58). Considering the relative scarcity of socketed types among early Chinese bronze axes in general, one may draw attention to that group of primitive small axes represented by nos. 16, 17, 18, 19 of this Catalogue.

The quatrefoil on the *nei* recalls the ornamentation of a *tsun* in the Sumitomo Collection (*Senoku Seishō,* I, 24) that is attributed to the Shang dynasty by Jung Keng (*Shang Chou I Ch'i T'ung K'ao,* I, 395; II, Pl. 271, no. 516). Instead of the whorl-circle it has an eye in the center, as is the case in a related ornament called "square with crescents" by Karlgren ("Yin and Chou in Chinese Bronzes," p. 98; Pls. 17: A 269, 22: A 110, 24: A 226).

## (*10*) HEAVY BRONZE AXE WITH ASYMMETRICAL CUTTING EDGE

Stout broad blade, growing slightly broader toward the asymmetrically curved edge, with slits at the shoulders, and asymmetrically placed perforated *nei.* Decoration: on a broad zone stretching over the upper part of the blade, two heraldically twined dragons in high relief, with their heads turned back to each other, and with scales cut into their bodies; beneath them, a pair of smaller, snakelike animals with diaper-pattern flanks a semicircle with two fangs — the motif of the jaws free of any organic connection. Below that zone, there is a band of five ornamented triangles in flat relief pointing toward the edge. A *t'ao-t'ieh* in *cloisons* occupies the end of the shafting-device, framed by a notched border on three sides. The ornaments strike the eye by an unusually neat, sharp-edged make. The patina on the neck has a grayish tone; on the blade and decorated parts it comprises whitish green, copper-red, and emerald-green shades with thin dark green crusts between. Shang.          Pl. VIII.

Length 205 mm; weight 830 gr.

As to its ornamentation, this specimen again is unique. Supplementing my remarks on the scale pattern of the coiled dragon of the axe no. 7, I may refer here to the very same motif in the representation of snakes on two Shang tripods (Jung Keng, *Shang Chou I Ch'i T'ung K'ao,* Figs. 20 and 27; *Yeh Chung P'ien Yü,* I, *shang* 9; II, *shang* 7) as well as on a square *ting* in the Trautmann Collection which is certainly not later than the beginnings of Chou (G. Ecke, *Sammlung Trautmann,* no. 7).

## (*11*) BRONZE AXE (*YÜEH*)

With a long *nei* in symmetrical position and wide slits in the shoulders of the blade which energetically broadens toward its gently rounded edge. Both cutting and lateral edges are marked by a ridge running along the contour. A big and elegantly drawn *t'ao-t'ieh* decorates and strengthens the blade; a smaller one of a variant design appears in a sunken square on the heavy tang (again the contrast of relief- and *cloison*-technique as alluded to under no. 7 above). Grayish patina with thin crusts of oxide in more or less dark shades; the neck has preserved a brown-bronze tone. Shang or Chou I.
                                                                    Pl. IX.

Length 178 mm; weight 660 gr.

In spite of its rich decoration — which once more is quite singular — this robust and heavy piece must not necessarily be considered as a mere ceremonial weapon as is sometimes suggested in similar cases. It is a full-fledged weapon.

## (*12*) BRONZE AXE (*YÜEH*)

Similar to but considerably lighter than no. 11. On the tang appears an animal mask disfigured by corrosion; on the blade, three embossed whorl-circles and a row of hanging triangles with engraved ornaments. The piece seemingly has been repaired and its color heightened by means of some lacquer patina. Probably Chou I.
                                                                    Pl. IX.

Length 193 mm; weight 296 gr.

Variants of this type are in the following collections:
(1) Museum of Far Eastern Antiquities, Stockholm (Harada and Komai, *Shina Koki Zukō,* I, Pl. 4: 3 = Karlgren, "Some Weapons and Tools," no. 40); flat design; strongly widening edge; no lashing-slits in the shoulders. Regarded as Anyang find. (2) *Yen K'u Chi Chin* (*hsia*: 2); similar to the first; attributed to the beginnings of the Chou dynasty — rightly, I believe. Weight: 390 grams. (3) *Ch'ih An Ts'ang Chin* (1: 34 = Fig. 25 above). Similar to the first; counted as a Shang piece. Weight: 500 grams. (4) Sumitomo Collection (*Senoku Seishō,* III: 135 = Karlgren, "Some Weapons and Tools," no. 38). In his *Explanatory Notes,* Hamada defined this axe as a dance-axe, which is a doubtful hypothesis in view of the heavy weight of 600 grams. The decoration consists of circles of round bosses instead of whorl-circles, resembling therein the following large axe (no. 13) of the Jannings Collection. (5) L. Clarke Collection (Karlgren, "Some Weapons," no. 39). Almost symmetrical; slotted shoulders; décor in thin raised lines; three comparatively small bosses.

## (*13*) LARGE BRONZE AXE

In the form of the *yüeh,* with asymmetrical, slanting cutting edge. On both sides of the short and heavy tang are slits for the lashings. The lateral margins in openwork decoration are slightly thinner than the blade itself. On the blade, running along the base, there is a broad band in low relief occupied by three rings or circular walls rising 5 mm above the surface, each of which encloses seven concentrically arranged small round pillars with flat tops. Between these rings two *t'ao-t'ieh* masks are incised, whereas a dragon fills the narrow outer space on either side. In bold relief again, their tips pointing toward the cutting edge, three lancets with median crest, flanked by two half-lancets, are suspended at the lower border of the zone with the rings. Animal heads with scaly horns and ornamental fillings of the tips are incised in these lancets. The lowermost part of the blade is set off by a low ridge running parallel to the gently curved cutting edge, which displays some slight scars.

Apart from several glossy spots, the axe is coated by a dark emerald-green verdigris. Parts freed from it appear in a bright greenish gray interspersed by patches of dark yellow-bronze and some ochreous concretions.

The thickness at the neck is about 4.5 mm; at the zone with circles, about 9 mm; in the middle of the blade, about 7 mm; leaving aside all the decorative reliefs, the body diminishes in thickness steadily from the base to the edge.

Allegedly found at Ssu-p'an-mo 四盤磨 near Anyang. Probably Late Shang.                                                                 Pl. X.

Height 345 mm; width 370 mm; distance between shoulders 275 mm; height of the neck 45 mm; weight 5800 gr. (Fig. 71).

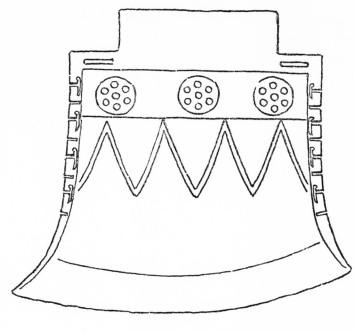

Fig. 71: *Large axe of the Jannings Collection, no. 13 (1/4).*

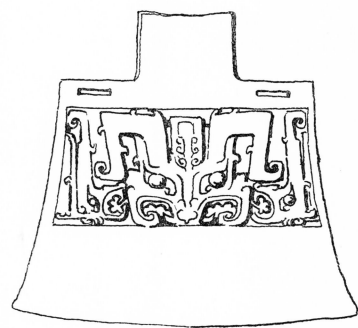

Fig. 72A: *Large axe of the Lochow Collection, Cologne (1/4).*

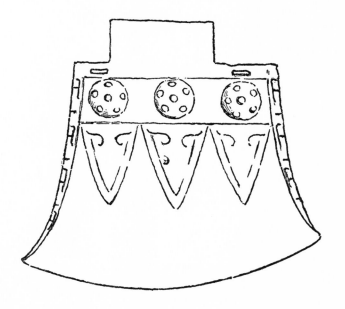

Fig. 72B: *Large axe of the David-Weill Collection, Paris (1/4).*

This tremendously heavy axe with its significant device of the slanting edge cannot have been handled as a weapon. It may have been used for killing sacrificial animals, or, perhaps, it served the crueler purpose of executing prisoners or other unlucky ones whose lives a bloody rite demanded. The object itself speaks thereon in its own unequivocal language.

There is a slightly smaller variant in the David-Weill Collection, Paris (Burlington House Exhibition 1935-36, Cat. no. 197; *Commemorative Catalogue,* Pl. 18), a diagram of which is given here together with that of the axe. For the Paris specimen (height 301 mm; width 320 mm) attention should be called to its narrower and asymmetrically placed neck-plate as well as to its relatively shorter cutting edge. Instead of the openwork, there are grooves only, and relief ornamentation is limited to three circular buckles set with six knobs near the base, the rest of the decoration being in intaglio.

A considerably smaller, strongly corroded axe in the Hellström Collection, Mölndal (Sweden), should also be mentioned here with regard to its comparable form, proportion, and decoration, although it does not contribute much to the chronological question; *Yeh Chung P'ien Yü,* I, *hsia:* 10 b (= Karlgren, "Some Weapons and Tools," no. 56); cp. the Introduction, chapter I, Axes, Group B III (1).

Another smaller and slenderer specimen in the Sumitomo Collection (*Senoku Seishō,* III: 135), which offers an exact parallel especially in the decorative scheme of three circular bosses, has been referred to above (no. 12). This piece bears a pictograph of undeniable Shang style, for which reason it was selected by Karlgren as an example of the Shang bronze decoration ("Yin and Chou in Chinese Bronzes," Pl. 28: A 187). The Sumitomo axe, because of the unification and concinnity of its décor, appears to be of a somewhat later date than the large axe discussed here.

None of the foregoing examples, however, quite matches an imposing axe in the Lochow Collection, Cologne (Fig. 72A). It is a piece which in dimensions and weight slightly exceeds the Jannings specimen (width 378 mm; weight 5850 gr.), and it is distinguished by a symmetrical blade, the upper half of which is occupied by a *t'ao-t'ieh* in a magnificent openwork design.

## (*14*) BRONZE AXE WITH SEMICIRCULAR CUTTING EDGE

Evenly convex blade with a wide, somewhat irregularly rounded hole in the center. Quadrangular — nearly square — lashing-slits in the shoulders and in the tang, which as in a shouldered stone celt projects from the blade without a ridge or step. The semicircular edge springs forth with a rounded salient. It is sharpened but not faceted. An opaque apple-green patina, with brown patches on one side, deprives the piece of its metallic character. This solid and handy weapon measures about 6 mm in thickness around the hole. Probably Shang.                                                                    Pl. XI.

Length 138 mm; width 95 mm; weight 280 gr.

The type, which as far as I know is unique at the present moment, may at first sight appear to be no more primitive than the decorated specimens nos. 4-12. However, there are several features in it which are not found in other axes and, therefore, cannot have been derived from them: (1) the round edge; (2) the absence of a ridge separating blade and tang; (3) form and position of the slits; (4) the wide round opening in the blade — which, however, is not too rare in other types (cp. Introduction, Ch. I, Axes, Group B I, Fig. 20). But it is the coincidence of all these factors which constitutes the peculiarity of the specimen, a peculiarity eventually enhanced by (5) a blade that has the gentle convexity of a fine stone celt. Now, these factors have parallels — not to say their origins — in stone and jade axes of the late Neolithic and the early Bronze ages (see the discussion of the piece in ch. I, Axes, Sundry Types, Fig. 28). Some examples, which cannot claim to constitute a typological series, may help to elucidate this.

Fig. 73: *Stone celt (ca. 1/3).*

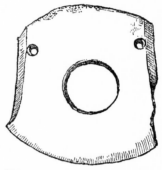

Fig. 74: *Greenstone axe (1/3).*

The shouldered stone celt (Fig. 73) from Sui-tung 綏東 (Jehol) with its unfinished perforation begun on both sides may represent a forerunner of the type (Fig. 75) in this collection; it is in the Port Arthur Museum (*Ryojun Hakubutsukan Zuroku,* Pl. 3:7; cf. I. Yawata, *Contributions to the Prehistoric Archaeology of Southern Jehol,* Fig. 9, right). It should be added here that the shouldered stone axe as such, though without perforation, also occurs farther south in Manchuria, and in Shansi and Honan (Yawata, in "Kōko-gaku Zasshi," XXVI/11, 1936: 696, Fig. 7; C. W. Bishop, *Antiquity,* Dec. 1933, Pl. 3:5; *Select Specimens of Antiquities,* Pt. V, Pl. 9; J. G. Andersson, "Researches into the Prehistory of the Chinese," Pl. 24:2).

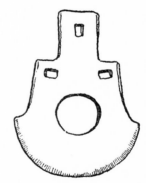

Fig. 75: *Bronze axe (1/3).*

Fig. 74 shows a greenstone axe of unknown origin (possibly from North Honan). With regard to the large perforation, the trim of the edge — splayed like that of a metal tool — and particularly the two smaller holes in the upper corners, this axe, in spite of all the differences that remain, has much in common with the bronze specimen, Fig. 75. The phenomenon of the wide bore-hole in the middle of the blade also recurs in the bronze types, Figs. 75, 76. These large perforations are not rarely seen in early stone axes (cf. Una Pope-Hennessy, *Early Chinese Jades,* Pl. 24; S. C. Nott, *Chinese Jade,* Pl. 12-right; author's collection; not published).

Fig. 75 is a diagram of the axe no. 14, to which another bronze piece of slightly larger dimensions but dissimilar silhouette may be added, Fig. 76 (Collection: Fujii, Yūrinkan, Kyoto, after S. Ume-

Fig. 76: *Bronze axe (3/10).*

hara's *Anyang Treasures,* Pl. 19:1), a piece most closely resembling that in Fig. 20 above. Apropos of the Fujii specimen, Umehara, too, suggests a possible connection with stone hatchets of an earlier stage (*ibid.,* p. 34). Comparable material was brought together by the same author in his "Note on Bronze Tools and Weapons."

The bronze types adduced here are discussed in the Introduction, Axes, under Group B I and Sundry Types.

The superior, fine shape of the small axe-head no. 14 will be recognized at once when compared with the following type.

### (*15*) AXE WITH ROUNDED CUTTING EDGE

Remotely akin to the foregoing specimen, this type shows an additional element which often occurs in the dagger-axes (*ko, k'uei*): a support for the shaft, formed by flanges standing out at acute angles on both sides of the base. The tang, which is put symmetrically, has a notched lower corner as have some *ko* types. Furthermore, quite exceptionally, it has an ogival opening pointing to the butt. The blade, stout and somewhat shapeless, has a wide round hole near the base. The slightly scarred cutting edge was sharpened. Rough, beautiful patina of whitish green with glossy patches in black-green. Numerous pustules of oxide on the reverse side. Chou I(?). Pl. XI.

Length 190 mm; weight 490 gr.

The small supports recur in the *k'uei* no. 46 and the *ko* no. 72, the notched tang, in the two *ko* nos. 58, 59. A similar axe without supports for the shaft is reproduced in *Chou Chin Wen Ts'un,* 6/2:116.

### (*16*) SLENDER BATTLE-AXE

With tubular socket. The body of the axe like a solid wedge tangentially meets an oval strong-walled shaft-tube, clasping it with two rounded ribs. The shorter upper and the longer lower parts of the socket likewise are girt by one rib and two ribs, respectively. From the neck protrudes a small hammer with rounded head. A band with two rows of knobs divided and framed by fillets, with two lozenges interspaced, runs across socket and blade to a round hole, enclosed by a ring set with knobs, in the middle of the blade; thence a thin midrib extends toward the edge. Beautiful glossy blackish patina of metallic luster, with patches of bright turquoise color and emerald-green crusts. Shang — Chou I (?).                    Pl. XII.

Length 162 mm; width of socket 25:16 mm; weight 542 gr.

There are, to my knowledge, no more than six other specimens of this rare type with its attractive tectonic decoration; they are in the following collections:

1) Murray, London (Koop, *Early Chinese Bronzes,* Pl. 69 B) — with fluted socket;

2) Lu Mou-te, Peking ("Chung Kuo Shang Ku T'ung Ping K'ao," Fig. 6 = Umehara, "Note on Bronze Tools," Pl. 4:1) — likewise with fluted socket;

3) Eumorfopoulos, London (Yetts, *Eumorfopoulos Collection Catalogue*, Pl. 69: A 145) = Fig. 6 above;

4) Museum of Far Eastern Antiquities, Stockholm (O. Janse, "Quelques antiquités d'un caractère Hallstattien," Pl. 3: 1) — with blind perforation;

5) Museum of Far Eastern Antiquities, Stockholm (J. G. Andersson, "Hunting Magic," Pl. 10: 5);

6) Yü Hsing-wu, Peking (*Shuang Chien I Chi Chin, hsia* 47) — without the round hole in the blade but retaining the ornament of the ring with knobs, like 4 above; plain socket.

As to the question of the origin and chronological place of these axes as well as of the following ones (nos. 17, 18, 19), the reader is referred to the Introduction (ch. I, Type A IV). Among the Shang weapons with their sumptuous and fantastic animal ornaments they seem like strangers.

## (*17*) SLENDER SHAFT-HOLE AXE

Wedge-shaped blade on a long socket of oval section. The socket tapers slightly toward the top; near the lower rim it slightly bulges. Opposite the blade there is a small hammer (or stud). The wall of the socket, with an average thickness of 1-1.5 mm — the neck being somewhat stronger — shows breaks near both apertures. Blunt, scarred edge; traces of use on the faces. A smooth dark green patina — preserved only at several points on the socket — seems to have once covered the whole piece; by re-using or scouring it, the patina has been rubbed off so that the yellow bronze lies bare at the exposed parts. No decoration. Chou I (?)                    Pl. XII.

Length 107 mm; height of socket 71 mm; weight 220 gr.

Rare type; related to the heavier and larger battle-axe no. 16, but of a more primitive character.

Closely similar to an axe from Hsün-hsien (North Honan) of Chou I age in the Freer Gallery (*Freer Catalogue*, Pl. 49: 34.13), discussed in the Introduction, chapter I (Fig. 7).

To what extent a quite inadequately reproduced specimen of the Lu Mou-te Collection, Peking ("Chung Kuo Shang Ku T'ung Ping K'ao," Fig. 7), which can be judged only from the silhouette, actually belongs here, cannot be decided without a better reproduction. The socket of that axe has a slightly longer upper part and a loop near the lower aperture.

## (*18*) SHAFT-HOLE AXE

With broad and fairly strong blade on a tubular socket of flat-oval section (diameter 25: 15 mm; thickness of the wall ca. 1.5 mm). Instead of the stud (as in nos. 16, 17), a nearly square plate proceeds from the neck here. Only a round boss adorns the faces of the axe, while the lower part of the socket is girt by three thin ribs. The edge is struck blunt, and under the smooth, deep green patina heavy scratches run across the faces. Crude casting from a valve mold. Chou I (?).                    Pl. XII.

Length 133 mm; height of socket 82 mm; weight 240 gr.

This type cannot directly be linked with the foregoing specimens. Nevertheless, for the shaft-tube with butt in the form of a small rectangular plate, several examples are cited here. Two of them, said to have come from North-China, were published by O. Janse ("Un groupe de bronzes anciens," p. 114). Another one with a dagger-like blade, acquired by O. Karlbeck at Yü-lin-fu in Shensi, was first described by Andersson ("Hunting Magic," Pl. 10: 3). Finally, attention may be drawn to a highly peculiar axe from the so-called Tomb of the Elephant, the extremely long socket of which likewise is provided with such a butt-plate flanked by two knobs or, rather, spikes (Royal Ontario Museum; cf. W. C. White, in the *Illus. London News,* April 20, 1935, p. 640), recalling socketed battle-axes with three spikes as found in Assur and Luristan (see Introduction, ch. I, Figs. 1 C and 29).

### (*19*) BRONZE AXE (*YÜEH*)

Broad blade with a round perforation off the base which is provided with two shafting-slits and a low ridge between them, a stop-ridge for the shaft. Toward the rounded edge which was sharpened, the blade markedly widens. The tang is not quite symmetrically placed, and its axis deviates from that of the blade. The tang has a round hole in the middle and a cast sunken character above that hole. From the butt to the edge the tool gradually diminishes in thickness. Apart from some rough greenish crusts, the axe shows dark brownish smooth faces. Shang.          No illustration is available.

Length 180 mm; weight c. 250 gr.

The glyph (Fig. 77) probably depicts the head of an animal with horns, led or grasped by a hand.

Fig. 77: *Inscription on the tang of the axe no. 19.*

### (*20*) SMALL SHAFT-HOLE AXE

With quadrangular blade and slightly curved edge. The socket — not higher than the blade itself — is of flat oval section and bears an angular small hammer. Three longitudinal ribs run over the blade, which has slightly raised margins. A thin wooden shaft is preserved in remnants. Dull, stained, apple-green patina with some earth-sinfew copper-red spots left blank. Chou (?).          Pl. XIII.

Length 105 mm; lower aperture of the shaft-hole 15: 10 mm; thickness of blade near the base ca. 3.5 mm; weight 133 gr.

Primitive casting from a valve mold. The "seams" are neither hammered nor rubbed smooth after casting. Apparently, there is nothing more primitive among the materials of this collection. The stud at the neck, which also occurs in technically more refined types, does not sensibly influence here the center of gravity; perhaps its origins are due to the exigencies of bronze casting, so that this protuberance was, *au fond,* nothing but a filling of the inlet channel in a clay or stone mold.

Three small axes of this type are contained in the Yūrinkan Collection, Kyoto (Umehara, *Anyang Treasures*, Pl. 18: 5-7), but they are dissimilar in that the socket is much shorter than the blade's height and thus has the shape not of a tube but rather of a ring. These shaft-rings are placed either in the middle of the blade or at the upper margin. Thin ridges cast crosswise (see Fig. 11 above) or at acute angles constitute another particular of these rings. The blades, however, have the same longitudinal ribs, sometimes in greater numbers. The ornamental crosses or angles are explained by Umehara as residues of the once functional lashing (*ibid.,* p. 34). As for the rest, he does not put forward any judgment about the pieces beyond the date "Anyang."

Two further pieces with shaft-rings, but devoid of any décor except longitudinal ribs, are in the Port Arthur Museum (*Ryojun Hakubutsukan Zuroku*, Pl. 9: 2, 3). The meager statements of the catalogue confine themselves to measurements and the dating "Chou."

The Museum of Far Eastern Antiquities owns three other examples of this type, all said to have been found at Anyang (Karlgren, "Some Weapons and Tools," nos. 28, 29, 30).

As to the typological position of this tool, one can gather some information from its simple structure, the artlessness of its shape, and its technical imperfections. In no respect could it rank with Shang pieces. Nor is it possible to explain it as only a technically inferior product or, perhaps, defective derivative of the Anyang stage, since all the formal prerequisites are lacking. This type seems to belong to a sphere quite different from that of the Shang weapons with their inextricable relations to the ritual bronzes of the Anyang stage. Thus, a date earlier than "Anyang" might be considered.

## (21) HEAVY SHAFT-HOLE AXE

Rectangular blade with strong round longitudinal ribs which also embrace the socket. The socket, flat-oval in section (aperture 28: 17 mm), is not at right angles with the blade but is in a slightly oblique position. The neck is provided with a thick trapezoidal butt-plate. Cast in a valve mold, ridges or "seams" at the shaft-hole rims having been ground smooth afterward. A poor-looking gray-green patina with some malachite patches covers the piece, with the exception of a few copper-red spots left blank. Chou (?).　　　　Pl. XIII.

Length 185 mm; height 63 mm; weight 540 gr.

Whether this hitherto unknown type, the date of which for want of any *point d'appui* must remain open, represents a weapon or a working-tool is hard to decide. Compared with the primitive small axe no. 20, it is a far more sophisticated tool. The flat oval socket, the butt-plate, and the rough casting are features, on the other hand, which apparently do not indicate a late date.

Perhaps this type should be connected with a group of small narrow-bladed axes with grooves and sockets extending beyond the base, mentioned in the Introduction (ch. I, Type A Va, Fig. 8; Type A

V b, Fig. 9). A related specimen in *Shan Chai Chi Chin Lu* (11:25) bears an inscription that might prove a Shang date, if its authenticity were unquestionable.

(*22*) SMALL PICKAXE

With a round, trihedral-pointed pick and a blade with vertical, slightly curved cutting edge. The shaft-hole is full oval in section (lower width 24:18 mm; upper width 22:17 mm). Smooth "streamlined" body with a dark lustrous bronze tone. Three incised characters on the blade. Chou IV (?).    Pl. XIII.

Length 144 mm; weight 186 gr.

Diverging in shape from the few Chinese picks published before (M. Loehr, "Chinesische Pickeläxte"), this specimen is not easily given its proper place. From Siberia, where the pickaxe abounds, there is no exact parallel. A sturdy iron pick with tetrahedral point and a rounded hammer from Gorodok (to the north of Minusinsk) lends itself to comparison (F. R. Martin, *L'Age du Bronze au Musée de Minoussinsk*, Pl. 8:13) without giving a hint as to the absolute date of the present object, which none the less typologically reveals itself as belonging to the Iron Age.

As to the authenticity of the engraved characters, a certain reserve might seem in place, not for their style or the nature of the patina, but for the fact that inscriptions exist which could well have served as patterns for the present one. They are to be seen on weapons (*ko, mao*, i.e., dagger-axes and spearheads) of late Chou time (cp. *Shuang Chien I Chi Chin*, hsia 28; *Fu Chai Chi Chin; Meng Wei Ts'ao T'ang Chi Chin*, chung 23; *San Tai Chi Chin Wen Ts'un*, 20:33), and mostly are read "*huang kung yu* 皇宮右." The reading "*kung*," however, seems incorrect; Ch'en Chieh-ch'i's interpretation of that graph as (a variant for) "*i* 邑" is more convincing (*Fu Chai Ts'ang Ku Mu*, vol. hsin-ssu, ch. 12, no. 7). Likewise, the reading "*huang*" for the first glyph may not be taken as absolutely reliable, although there is perhaps no better substitute reading; in *Cho I Chai I Ch'i K'ao Shih* (30:8 b), the first and second characters are considered as a place name — without phonetic equivalents being given.

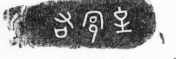

Fig. 78: *Inscription on the pick-axe no. 22.*

(*23*) ARROWHEADS

*a*) Arrowhead of bone with strong midrib and round tang, the lower end of which is broken off. Two barbed wings with drawn tips and sharpened edges. Length 57 mm. Probably Shang.    Pl. XLVI.

The same type occurs also in bronze (Umehara, *Anyang Treasures*, Pl. 13) as the commonest form of the arrowheads excavated at Yin-hsü (cf. Li Chi, *Preliminary Report on Excavations at Anyang*, II, p. 243).

*b*) Three two-winged arrowheads with strong rib and tapering stem. Rough gray-green patina. Lengths 60-65 mm. Shang (?)
Pl. XLVI.
Two comparable specimens in Umehara's *Anyang Treasures*, Pl. 14:4.

*c*) Trihedral tip with sunken faces between the edges. Round foot, pointed stem. Bright olive-colored patina. Length 103 mm. Chou III-IV.
Pl. XLVI.

*d*) Trihedral tip with slightly curved and protruding edges. Crusty green patina. Length 95 mm. Chou III-IV.    Pl. XLVI.

*e*) Short trihedral tip with long stem, similar to the foregoing types. Greenish gray patina with a malachite-colored crust at the stem. Length 136 mm. Chou III-IV.    Pl. XLVI.

*f*) Trihedral tip with slenderer head. Greenish crust at the head, blank stem. Length 147 mm. Chou III-IV.    Pl. XLVI.

*g*) Very slender point of same type as (*f*). Glossy gray patina at the head, rough green patina at the stem. Length 155 mm. Chou III-IV.
Pl. XLVI.

*h*) Trihedral point with exceedingly long stem. Rough green patina at the head; gray and bronze-colored at the stem. Length 169 mm. Chou III-IV.    Pl. XLVI.

*i*) Trihedral point of the foregoing type, with oxide-crusted stem. Length 170 mm. Chou III-IV.    Pl. XLVI.

*k*) Small trihedral head on a very long stem of triangular section, without a round foot below the point (as in nos. 23 c-i). Rough grayish green patina with bluish spots. Length 184 mm. Chou III-IV.
Pl. XLVI.

*l, m*) Two two-winged, barbed heads with strong midrib and short stem. Very sharp, neatly faceted edges. Patina of grayish olive tone. Length 62 mm. Chou IV.    Pl. XLVI.

*n*) Long two-winged arrowhead with strong midrib and short stem. Curved, long, slender-tipped wings, the faces of which meet in a crest at the upper part of the fairly broad point. Transversely ground sharp edges. Sunken fields between rib and wings. Thin grayish green crust of oxide on bronze-colored ground. Length 72 mm. Chou IV.    Pl. XLVI.

*o*) Broad two-winged tip with curved wings whose slenderly drawn-out barbs are propped against the stem which forms a crest in the upper part. As in the foregoing specimen (*n*), there are small sunken fields between the rib and wings, pleasingly designed with round arches. Long tapering stem. Dully glimmering bronze with a thin gray-green layer of verdigris. Length 94 mm. Chou IV.
Pl. XLVI.

These few specimens of arrowheads furnish a very incomplete view of the existing wealth of types. A more detailed treatment, therefore, of this important subject cannot be undertaken here, especially so since both chronologically serviceable material and special investigations are still lacking. Hence the vague dates for the specimens described above.

## (24) JADE SPEARHEAD IN BRONZE SOCKET

Leaf-shaped blade of greenish and grayish jade with a particular staining into an immaterial cool green caused by bronze oxide; well polished and provided with a crest which disappears toward the base. The blade is mounted on a bronze socket of oval section (17:10 mm), slightly tapering and crowned by a heart-shaped setting. This setting, a rhythmic variant of the outline of the blade, is adorned by a *t'ao-t'ieh,* the curvilinear design of which is artfully related to the whole. Another animal mask, likewise turned to the point, fills a zone near the lower edge of the socket, and instead of the curves of the upper one, horizontal lines dominate here, corresponding to the rim. On the long and narrow space above it, a triple row of acute-angled zigzags steeply moves up and down, formed — like the rest of the ornaments — by fine ridges. The heart-shaped haft is slightly damaged in its topmost parts. Two lateral loops attached above the lower animal mask may have served to fasten a pair of tassels or tail-hairs rather than lashings or thongs. Rough dark green patina with ultramarine patches and earthy concretions in the cavities of the ornaments. Allegedly found at Ssu-p'an-mo 四盤磨 to the west of Anyang. Shang.
Pl. XIV.

Length 182 mm; length of the blade, ca. 105 mm.

There are only a few specimens known of these beautiful jade spearheads, which — like bronze hafted *ko* (nos. 2, 3) and various emblematic weapons — can only have been used on ceremonial occasions and which obviously are too fragile for any practical purpose. The specimens are in the following collections:

1) Winthrop, Fogg Art Museum (Umehara, *Anyang Studies,* Pl. 38:2): socket without loops; turquoise inlay; dissimilar shape of blade.

2) Raphael, London (*ibid.,* Pl. 38:1; *Anyang Treasures,* Pl. 25:1; *Shina Kodō Seika,* VII, 91; Pelliot, *Jades archaïques,* Pl. 3:2; Karlgren, "Some Weapons," Pl. 3:18): socket without loops; turquoise inlay; similar blade with slightly narrower base.

3) Winthrop (?) (formerly Yamanaka, New York; Umehara, *Anyang Treasures,* Pl. 25:2; Huang Chün, *Ku Yü T'u Lu,* I:22b; Karlgren, "Some Weapons," Pl. 3:17): very slender socket without loops; turquoise inlay.

4) Unknown (*Ku Yü T'u Lu,* I:22a; Karlgren, *op. cit.,* Pl. 3:16): short slender socket without loops; seemingly without stone incrustation.

5) Unknown (*Yeh Chung P'ien Yü,* III, *hsia*: 14): two pieces, with lateral loops; seemingly not incrusted. The blade of one specimen has a perforation. Both appear to be smaller in size than the aforementioned pieces.

(25) BRONZE SPEARHEAD (*MAO*)

Relatively small blade that branches downward into two broad bands whose tapering ends form inward-bent volutes. The socket of pointed oval section widens to the lower edge (aperture 35:20), its upper part being embraced by the branching bands in relief. Two lateral flanges reaching from the outer edge of the volutes to the lower part of the socket increase longitudinal rigidity. Dull patina in lively colors such as sea-green, terra-cotta, sienna, and a lusterless dark green, with isolated emerald-green spots. Shang.    Pl. XIV.
Length 170 mm; weight 225 gr.

Uncommon type with regard to the almost elegant volute design as well as to the short lateral counterforts, which meet those volutes somewhat abruptly. There was a comparable spearhead in the collection of Tuan Fang (*T'ao Chai Chi Chin Lu*, 3:48). Distinguished by slightly curved flanges making a more fluid silhouette, that specimen lacks the attractive detail of the volutes, and its socket is four-cornered in section.

(26) SPEARHEAD (*MAO*)

Bronze, with a gray, hardly oxidized surface of metallic luster, some copper-red spots, and thin dark green crusts. The blade has a marked crest and is rhombic in section. It embraces a sunken field in the form of a pointed leaf, the base of which coincides with the top of the four-edged socket. The edges of the blade — by fusion with the lateral counterforts — are drawn down nearly to the rim of the socket. Angular openings at the ends take the places of loops. Only the tip of the blade is sharpened. The decoration consists in a *t'ao-t'ieh* looking toward the point, and acute-angled zigzags with ornamental filling. Shang — Chou I.    Pl. XV.
Length 260 mm; width of socket 26:33 mm; weight 385 gr.

Common type, whose typological classification is touched upon in the Introduction (ch. II, Spearheads, Figs. 36 E, 37). The particular tin-colored surface which betrays hardly any sign of decomposition is the result either of a special alloy or an additional metallurgical treatment after casting. A similar quality of bronze will be found in the dagger no. 85 and the partisan no. 106 below.

For allied pieces, see *Anyang Treasures* (Pl. 18:4 = Fig. 36 D); *Meng Wei Ts'ao T'ang* (*chung*: 22); *Ch'ih An Ts'ang Chin* (fol. 41); Karlgren, "Some Weapons" (Pl. 2:9-14).

(27) SPEARHEAD (*MAO*)

Slender blade with slightly hollowed faces that enclose a narrow sunken field the contour of which repeats that of the blade. The top of the shaft-tube penetrates into that field. A median crest stops near the concave edge of the socket, which is flat oval in section and only

15: 10 mm wide. No loops. Blackish, bright green, and gray-olive glossy patina with thin greenish layers. Probably Chou I.     Pl. XV.

Length 247 mm; weight 140 gr.

This extraordinary light piece probably belonged to a javelin with very thin shaft. The shape is not common. There is one specimen in the Yūrinkan Collection, Kyoto, which is comparable with regard to its proportions but lacks — apart from other details — the winglike tips (barbs) of the blade, characteristic in the present case (cp. Umehara, *Anyang Treasures,* Pl. 18: 1 = Fig. 40 B). A hollow or concave cut of the lower edge of the socket is encountered very often in Chan-kuo (Chou III-IV) spearheads. It would not be justified, however, to date the present piece that late on the basis of a single criterion.

## (28) SPEARHEAD (*MAO*)

Of slender shape and smooth outline. Socket and blade are no longer separable but fused into one another. Only a slightly curved recess accentuates the beginning of the blade. A strong, faceted midrib runs from here to the point where it becomes flush with the slanting facets of the remarkably sharp edges. The socket, with a lower width of 35:30 mm, shows a full, two-pointed oval section. A beautiful smooth patina in varying shades of grayish olive and apple-green with turquoise-blue films and some crusts covers the piece. Chou III-IV.     Pl. XVI.

Length 344 mm; weight 340 gr.

A round tube, the foot-mounting of the shaft belonging to this spearhead, appears as no. 78 below.

A few words pointing out the physiognomy and different expression of this particularly beautiful large specimen — more easily seen when compared with earlier forms — may be not out of place here. The tip, or the point, here starts as it were from the lowermost edge, quite in contrast to the foregoing type: the socket by a nimble widening takes in the entire length of the blade; the outline nowhere is interrupted, nor is the surface of this piece, which has as a characteristic that its parts are no longer discernible as such but have merged into one body. The archaic types, on the other hand, distinctly display their parts: socket and blade or wings, clearly separated in a simple structure. Not that the earlier forms, for that matter, were inferior or less useful weapons, but the way in which by contraction and unification a shape was developed that perfectly expresses the function gives this spearhead its particular physiognomy.

A similar specimen of this widespread type, likewise associated with a shoeing-tube, from Hsü-chou 徐州 (Anhui), was shown by C. T. Loo at Detroit in 1940 (J. M. Plumer, *An Exhibition of Ancient Chinese Ritual Bronzes,* no. 58, Pl. 33).

Fig. 79:
*Décor of the spearhead no. 29.*

#### (*29*) SPEARHEAD (*MAO*)

Of similar type, but lighter and shorter than the foregoing, and showing a slightly different mode of transition between blade and socket. The midrib, which here is flatter, starts from a point nearer the rim of the socket and is marked by a small animal-head. Decorated socket of pointed oval section. Slightly concave rim with some breaks. Dull patina of gray-olive with some dark blue-green patches. Chou IV.                                                                Pl. XVI.

Length 281 mm; lower width of socket 30: 22 mm; weight 210 gr.

The little animal-head — not very clear in the present case — also occurs on a spearhead with a nielloed diaper pattern in the David-Weill Collection, Paris (*Commemorative Catalogue*, Pl. 20: 175; O. Janse, "Le style du Houai et ses affinités," Pl. 53: 2).

An almost identical specimen is in the Sirén Collection ("Collection Osvald Sirén," *Ars Asiatica*, VII, Pl. 1: 5).

#### (*30*) SPEARHEAD (*MAO*)

With a very slender leaf-shaped blade and a round socket running through to the point. The rim of the socket (diameter 22 mm) is even. Near the lower margin is a meander zone; somewhat above are two curved loops with an animal mask between them. The edges are sharpened in fine facets and the point is of tetrahedral shape. On one side, there is a sunken pictograph, representing a bird — probably cast (Fig. 80). Thin dark green patina over a glossy blackish surface. Chou II-III.                                                            Pl. XVI.

Length 250 mm; weight 155 gr.

Apparently rare design, no counterparts having been published. The glyph as well as the debased *t'ao-t'ieh* ornament suggests the late Western or early Eastern Chou periods.

#### (*31*) SMALL SPEARHEAD

Pointed oval socket, narrow wings with two pointed projections and well-sharpened faceted edges. Thin cornered midrib. A splint-hole above the concave rim of the socket. Apple-green patina, feebly coated by layers in deep green and reddish tones. Chou IV (?).

Pl. XXXIV.

Length 118 mm; weight 65 gr.; socket width 21: 13 mm.

#### (*32*) HEAVY DRAGON-HEAD KNIFE

Large strong knife with curved and broadened back that runs into the more strongly bent handle. The handle is terminated by an animal-head, below which a small round loop is attached. Both sides of the handle are adorned by a row of rectangularly cut turquoise stones, prevalently bright greenish, framed by engraved serrated bands. A crest of blunt spikes on the back of the handle emphasizes its quasi-organic meaning — as an animal's neck or body. The head springs

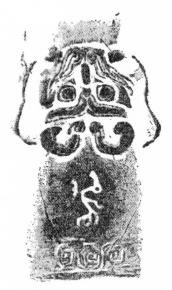

Fig. 80:
*Décor of the spearhead no. 30.*

Fig. 81: *Dragon-head of the knife no. 32.*

forth bulkily, and the open jaws with a high muzzle, baluster-shaped horns, ears that stand out, and protruding eyes set with little disks of turquoise give it a ferocious expression. The underside of the lower jaw is open. There is a break in the blade near the point. The patina shows a few brown-violet spots, notably at the grip and the head; as to the rest, it has a coarse, flaky, and crusty texture in an intense dull green. Shang.                                                                  Pl. XVII.

Length 310 mm; weight 390 gr.

Among the animal-head knives said to have come from Anyang, the present specimen is unique so far. With the incomparable ferocity and vigor of the heavy angular head and the splendor of its turquoise incrustation, this knife tells something about Shang art which the sacrificial vases do not. Some of the vases, on the other hand, do offer close parallels in their plastic animal-heads (e.g., *Shina Kodō-Seika,* I, 72; N. Palmgren, "Yinstil-Studien," Pl. 17, Fig. 35), particularly some *kuang* whose covers represent themselves as monsters with bared teeth and baluster-shaped horns (J. Trübner, *Yu und Kuang,* Pls. 46, 51; Jung Keng, *Shang Chou I Ch'i T'ung K'ao,* Pls. 351, 352, 354).

At first glance it may seem that such a knife has nothing in common with animal-head knives from the Steppe or from Siberia but the animal-head decoration, which however — like the stone incrustation — is here patently Chinese in character. Yet the unassuming pattern of serrated borders at the handle constitutes an element that also is found in the North, while for China, remarkably enough, it is apparently restricted to knives from Anyang (see also the knives nos. 33 and 40 below). Undeniably, one again faces here the problem of whether or not these knives should be traced back to Siberian sources, a problem which does not a priori exclude the possibility of an inverse course (cf. Introduction, ch. IV).

A detail that perhaps claims some typological importance is the ring-loop below the dragon's head, which here appears isolated from the head. Contrary to this, these loops are commonly attached to the throats of the animal-heads so that they fit in more organically. The position of the ring in this example looks a little unbalanced, as though it were not the ultimate solution (as, for instance, the attachment in the knife no. 33 below may be regarded).

### (*33*) LARGE HORSE-HEAD KNIFE

Slightly curved handle that broadens somewhat toward the guard. The blade continues the same curve for a third of its length, whereupon it recurves. Save below the guard, its faces are plain. The edge has lost its original roundness by repeated sharpening. A fine simply formed horse-head constitutes the hollow-cast pommel. It has a cleft underneath and contains a bronze nodule (as a rattle). The eye-sockets once were set with turquoise disks. The ears touch each other at the tips. A loop is attached to the throat. A longitudinal double serrated band, crossed by three fluted and serrated transverse zones, decorates the grip. Whitish green patinated bronze with deep green spots. Shang.                                      Pl. XVII.
Length 263 mm; weight 108 gr.

### (*34*) SMALL HORSE-HEAD KNIFE

Similar to the foregoing, but with continuously bent back and thoroughly hollowed blade. The handle has a simple decoration of three fluted bands running transversely. The pommel is shaped as a horse-head with slightly opened mouth, narrow slits of nostrils, and small turquoise disks as eyes. Patina: very bright whitish clouded sea green, some protoxide-red, and darker crusts. Handsome light piece. Shang.                                      Pl. XVII.
Length 200 mm; weight 55 gr.
The only parallel hitherto known is a piece of nearly the same size with a fragmentary blade that was in the possession of C. T. Loo (Salmony, *Sino-Siberian Art,* Pl. 36: 3).
Typologically and — with regard to their animal-heads — stylistically related knives, which till recently were *in toto* localized in the Ordos region (cf., for instance, Andersson, "Hunting Magic," Pl. 5: 2, fragment of a knife with an elk-head), have appeared in the Peking market designated "Anyang" (G. Ecke, "Über einige Messer aus Anyang"). Among these newcomers, a perfectly shaped specimen should be particularly mentioned here (*ibid.,* Pl. A: III) for the reason that it bears an elk's head whose noble realism and subdued vitality immediately recall the horse-heads of the two knives here published.
Furthermore, there is a formally not too widely different though certainly somewhat later horse-head on the large ceremonial knife no. 40 below, which must be dated not later than Chou I and therefore

furnishes an argument in favor of the early date proposed for the two knives nos. 33 and 34.

Another *point d'appui* is given by horse-head tools from a reliable Shang tomb inventory (Tomb of the Elephant, mentioned under no. 18 above; cp. the text under no. 40 below).

A gap between animal-heads of this kind and the dragon-head of the knife no. 32 above is obvious — and, at the same time, rather enigmatic. While the dragon-head is typically Shang, the horse-heads clearly can be placed alongside the more realistic creations of the Steppe and Siberia including such objects as the perhaps still pre-metallic bone sculptures from the Yenisei region (G. Borovka, *Scythian Art,* Pl. 68 A, B).

### (*35*) KNIFE WITH RAM'S HEAD

Large, strong knife with a broad but relatively thin blade, which is framed by a slightly arched back and a guard. The handle meets the blade in a blunt angle; pointed oval in section, it is slit open longitudinally on both sides, with a blackish clay core filling the upper and lower halves. A herringbone pattern in thin raised lines, cut by a transverse ridge with a serrated band, covers the faces of the handle. The ram's head — which presumably contains the core, too — with strong horns standing out freely, is realistically and purely plastically rendered. Patina: gray-green bright surface, partly blackishly oxidized glossy spots, and dull greenish concretions. Chou I (?)

Pl. XVIII.

Length 275 mm; weight 224 gr.

The type recurs in a variant with ring-handle (no. 38) which also shows the herringbone ornament. The handle with the (not rarely seen) long slit, crowned by a similar head, figures in one of the Anyang knives published by Ecke ("Über einige Messer aus Anyang," Pl. A: V); but the head of that specimen makes one also perceive how unusually realistic the treatment of the present head is: spontaneous, animated, and of a certain heaviness.

With reference only to their blades, three other knives with somewhat baroque elk-heads deserve mention here: (1) Andersson, "Hunting Magic," Pl. 5: 1; (2) V. Griessmaier, *Sammlung von der Heydt,* no. 87 = A. Salmony, *Sino-Siberian Art,* Pl. 36: 5; (3) Egami and Mizuno, *Inner Mongolia, Suiyüan Bronzes,* Corpus III, Knives: A 1. Griessmaier (*op. cit.*) points to Siberian parallels, i.e., the same type of knives belonging to the Karasuk stage.

### (*36*) KNIFE WITH ANIMAL-HEAD

Long knife, slightly arched. Blade and handle have the same profile, and the broad back starting from the pommel continuously tapers toward the point. The blade is set off by a narrow ridge. Extremely conventionalized, the animal's head is formed by bulbous faces with

round eyes, two obliquely placed longish loops as ears, and a small loop as muzzle. The edge apparently was not sharpened. Rough green-gray patina with earthy concretions. Chou I (?). Pl. XVIII.
Length 305 mm; weight 228 gr.

## (*37*) KNIFE WITH BIRD-HEAD

Light knife with recurved point. The back runs through to the knob, which consists in a ring with a beak springing forth from it — hence, a bird's head. The handle is short and very narrow. On the whole, the piece does not look like a knife for practical use. Crusty dull green and earthy patina. Chou I-II (?)    Pl. XVIII.
Length 215 mm; weight 82 gr.

## (*38*) KNIFE WITH RING-KNOB

With broad blade framed by the back and a transverse ridge as guard. The handle, of pointed oval section, and probably still holding the clay core, stands slantingly in relation to the blade, and broadens a little toward the joint. A herringbone pattern in thin fine raised lines between longitudinal fillets embellishes the handle, which is terminated by a broad, flat, oval ring. Thin, rough patina in dull gray-green and red-brown tones. On one side an oxidized strip of cloth of well-preserved texture has impressed itself on the surface, covering half the breadth of the blade and parts of the ring-knob; it is a fine fabric in simple weave. Chou I (?).    Pl. XIX.
Length 267 mm; weight 165 gr.
The blade is of similar structure as, only broader than, that of the knife with the ram's head (no. 35), which cannot be distant in time. Several variants of ring-handle knives form part of the Elephant-Tomb inventory and thus are proved to have existed in the Shang period (cf. W. C. White, in the *Illustrated London News*, April 20, 1935, p. 641). Among the knives from the Ordos and Suiyüan regions, which partly are of much later date, ring-knobs are a most common device (cf. Egami and Mizuno, *Inner Mongolia, Sui-yüan Bronzes,* Corpus III, Knives, notably A 2, J 53). In Central Siberia, ring-knob knives also occur at an early date, in the Karasuk period (cf. *ibid.,* p. 45).

## (*39*) KNIFE WITH RING-HANDLE

The radially grooved oval ring of this specimen is distinguished by three conical buttons protruding, at ninety-degree intervals, from the outer rim. The blade and the handle have one continuously arched back. The handle is set off by a transverse ridge extending beyond the edge and is decorated by a longitudinal cord pattern in low relief. Apple-green and turquoise-colored patina, glossier and tending to an olive tone at the handle, with rough concretions. Chou I-II.    Pl. XIX.
Length 277 mm; weight 170 gr.

Ring-knobs bearing similar buttons or cones again belong to the elements common to both China and Siberia. And again they exist as early as the Shang, datable by context (Tomb of the Elephant; W. C. White, *op. cit.*). Siberian specimens from the Minusinsk area are depicted in Martin's *L'Age du Bronze au Musée de Minoussinsk* (Pls. 11:6, 13:5). Two pieces in the Tokyo and Kyoto University collections acquired in Peking are attributed to the Suiyüan group by Egami and Mizuno (*Inner Mongolia*, Pt. II, Pl. 41:9, 10 — both provided with loops beneath the ring-knob). More closely related to the present specimen is a knife in the Sumitomo Collection (*Senoku Seishō*, III: 141), whose "pre-Han date" as adopted by K. Hamada has been recently revised by G. Ecke ("Über einige Messer aus Anyang," p. 153).

The early date of this type is corroborated by the Tomb of the Elephant find, but there are relevant objects of much later date which cannot be passed over in silence. I refer to bronze vessels from the North Chinese borderland, Siberia, and South-Russia, with handles studded with buttons quite similar to those on the ring-knobs of the knives in question. It would be difficult to assume that there was no connection at all between the knives and the vessels so adorned. (Cf. *Ryojun Hakubutsukan Zuroku*, Pl. 14:5 — vessel ascribed to the Han period, with an inscription that is not reproduced; S. Umehara, "A Study on Bronze Kettles Found in the Northern Part of China," Figs. 7, 8.)

### (40) CEREMONIAL KNIFE

With horse-head handle. Broad and heavy blade, which presumably never was sharpened, with broad back, concavely drawn edge, and upcurved point. The oval, solid handle is adorned by a transverse serrated band near the blade and by a herringbone design in longitudinal stripes, separated by a plain band in the middle. The handle is terminated by a plastic horse-head of severe design with protruding eyes, pointed flat ears, narrow forehead (continuing the back of the handle), and broad muzzle. A diaper chain in low relief runs on the evenly tapering back of the blade. Well-balanced and fluid shape. An incised character in the cross-cartouche (*ya-hsing*) appears on one side of the blade. Shang.                          Pl. XIX.

Length 445 mm; weight 700 gr.

The very particular form of a blade that broadens at the tip and ends in a steeply recurved point — seemingly unknown among Ordos types — is represented once more by a specimen from the Tomb of the Elephant dating from Shang times (White, *op. cit.*, Fig. 17), a tomb situated near Ssu-k'ung-ts'un 司空村 north of the Huan River, to the west of Anyang.

A horse-head knife and fittings with horse-heads also form part of that find (now in the Royal Ontario Museum in Toronto); they have been published by H. Kühn ("Chronologie der sino-sibirischen Bronzen," Pl. 57). These heads — one of them with trappings — diverge from the present one insofar as their eyes are round or set with turquoise disks (as is the case with nos. 33 and 34 above) but not plastically shaped.

The diaper chain on the back occurs on a knife dating from the Shang, according to Shang Ch'eng-tso (*Shih Erh Chia Chi Chin T'u Lu, Ch'i* 契, fol. 33). The Shang date as well as the sacrificial character of this knife type — further illustrated by nos. 41 and 42 — is also suggested by palaeographic testimony (cp. Chewon Kim, "Über eine Gruppe chinesischer Messer").

The glyph incised on the knife (Fig. 82) is not legible.

Fig. 82: *Inscription on the knife no. 40.*

### (*41*) CEREMONIAL KNIFE

With a row of six dragons placed on the back of the broad, thin, and warped blade. The handle, which is not set off but simply continues the back, is terminated by a wide ring. Judged by its structure, the tool cannot have served any practical purpose. Fairly homogeneously gray-green patina, with violently burst-open blisters on the blade. A break in the ring. Shang or Chou I.　　　Pl. XX.

Length 387 mm; weight 422 gr.

A comparable knife of probably somewhat later date, which formerly was in the possession of Yamanaka, shows a row of nine dragons on the back (Chewon Kim, *op. cit.,* Pl. 6:d).

### (*42*) CEREMONIAL KNIFE

The blade, resembling those of the two foregoing specimens, has a well-sharpened edge, and instead of an ordinary handle is provided only with a tang projecting at the back of the blade. Rough green and gray-green verdigris on a dark grayish ground. On one side a fine fabric, attached and preserved by bronze oxide, covers the blade. Shang or Chou I.　　　Pl. XX.

Length 350 mm; weight 372 gr.

There is one closely related specimen, likewise with short tang, from the Tomb of the Elephant (White, *op. cit.,* p. 641, Fig. 17). Another tanged knife, although its shape diverges in that the blade lacks the characteristic broadening and trimming upward of the tip, should be mentioned here because of a character it bears (*v. Shuang Chien I Chi Chin, hsia* 40). Precisely the same character is found on an oracle bone fragment (*Yin-hsü Shu Ch'i Hou Pien, hsia* 15 b center) and thus affords fairly reliable palaeographic evidence for the early date of these knife types.

Furthermore, decorated specimens of the same type exist which also cannot be dated later, as, for instance, in the O. Raphael Collection, London (*Commemorative Catalogue,* Pl. 20, no. 245 — erroneously called "halberd"), or in the K. Kurokawa Collection (Umehara, *Anyang Treasures,* Pl. 27:1).

Fig. 83: *Inscription on the k'uei no. 43.*

(*43*) DAGGER-AXE (*K'UEI*)

Strong triangular blade with marked median crest and symmetrically placed tang (*nei*) with a horizontal slit. Two vertical slits to facilitate lashing are in the shoulders of the blade. An irregularly rounded sharp-edged (probably cast) hole in the blade. A character in sunken lines appears on the butt. Beautiful patina in bright grayish and bluish green shades, with some blackish brown coating. Shang.

Pl. XXI.

Length 211 mm; weight 404 gr.

This piece came from a private collection in Peking and was published by the former owner (*Ch'ih An Ts'ang Chin*, 38). The text of that catalogue (excluding measurements) may be translated here:

> *K'uei* . . . with plain body, without ornaments. The hole in the center did not serve for fastening. On one side of the tang [*ping* 柄, which is incorrect for *nei* 內], there is a character whose meaning and pronunciation we do not know. This character, which has been found hitherto neither in oracle bone nor bronze inscriptions, probably belongs to that category which designates buildings and houses; it may be recorded here for further research. Reddish surface with kingfisher-blue and greenish colouring. Thick and heavy, of powerful simplicity; a Shang product.

As the author rightly thinks, the perforation of the blade was not done for practical use, no more than in the case of the perforated axes (cp. the remarks under no. 14 above).

As to the name of this type, *k'uei,* which is clearly different from the incomparably more numerous *ko,* the reader is referred to the Introduction (ch. III, Dagger-Axes).

The present shape seems to be rare. Three specimens, likewise undecorated, in the Lu Mou-te Collection, Peking, are reproduced in outline drawings in Umehara's "Note on Bronze Tools and Weapons" (Pl. 12: 1-3 = Fig. 44: 1, 5, 7); these specimens do not entirely resemble ours nor each other. Their proportions, on the other hand, are about the same, and they are designed symmetrically, with the *nei* in the axis of the blade. An elaborate variant with hooked projections at the shoulders, midrib, and slightly asymmetrical *nei* without a hole, was in Lo Chen-yü's collection (*Cheng Sung T'ang Chi Chin T'u, chung*: 54; *San Tai Chi Chin Wen Ts'un,* 19: 21 b); it suggests the *chi* 戟 types from Hsün-hsien (cp. *Hsün-hsien I Ch'i,* 28-30) and probably dates from the Chou I period.

(*44*) DAGGER-AXE (*K'UEI*)

Triangular blade strengthened by a kind of shield at the base, with broad rounded midrib, shafting-slits, and a round hole near the tip of the shield. The *nei* is placed above the axis; it is perforated, and decorated with a theriomorphic ornament in thin *cloisons* within a rectangular frame. Covered by a rough patina in green-brown, dull green and grayish shades. At one spot, the bare metal shows in a dark copper-tone. Heavy, stout piece. Probably Shang.     Pl. XXI.

Length 230 mm; weight 473 gr.

Specimens exactly corresponding to this type apparently do not exist. A related piece with somewhat slenderer blade and a bulbous boss adorned by a whorl-circle instead of the hole in the shield, found at Anyang, is contained in *Shuang Chien I Chi Chin T'u Lu* (*hsia:* 13 = Fig. 44: 11).

There are two further specimens with asymmetrically placed *nei*, which display extremely broad bases and correspondingly broad blades. One of these pieces has the shield-reinforcement less accentuated, while the second has none; neither has a midrib. The first one is a well-known *k'uei* with turquoise inlay in the Eumorfopoulos Collection (Yetts, *Eumorfopoulos Catalogue,* Pl. 69: A 147; Umehara, *Shina Kōdō Seika,* VII: 83; Koop, *Early Chinese Bronzes,* Pl. 67 B; Sirén, *History of Early Chinese Art,* I, Pl. 18 C; = Fig. 44: 8). The second one was published not long ago, with the remark that it had been unearthed at Anyang in 1939 (*Yen K'u Chi Chin T'u Lu, hsia:* 19 = Fig. 44: 4).

Finally, a *k'uei* in the David-Weill Collection with decorated tang and a midrib (Umehara, "Note on Bronze Tools and Weapons," Pl. 12: 4 = Fig. 44: 2) should be mentioned: it appears to represent a stage preceding the last-mentioned two examples.

## (45) DAGGER-AXE (K'UEI)

Slender triangular blade with midrib and shield-like reinforcement at the base, provided with lashing-slits of unequal length. The tang stands somewhat higher than, and slightly oblique to, the blade axis; it has a round perforation and is longitudinally grooved at the end. The shield is decorated with a kind of *t'ao-t'ieh* consisting only of eyes and horns. The horns, filled with spirals, are drawn down to the *canthus anterior* of the eyes, which, in consequence, are curiously wide-set. The whole ornament is designed in raised lines on spiral-pattern ground. The edges were not sharpened. Patina: pinkish brown copper tone with bright green dots and films of a darker green; rough emerald crusts in the grooves of the butt and on the *t'ao-t'ieh*. Shang or Chou I. Pl. XXI.

Length 250 mm; weight 412 gr.

The date results from comparison of the very peculiar design of the *t'ao-t'ieh* with similarly abstract variants on bronze vases; this suggests the end of the Shang or beginning of the Chou dynasties (see, for instance, a tripod in the Shiobara Collection, Tokyo; *Relics of Han and Pre-Han Dynasties,* Pl. 13 = *Hai Wai Chi Chin T'u Lu,* 4).

It is rather exceptional that this blade is not perforated, for in general the perforation can plainly be counted as one characteristic trait of this kind of dagger-axe. There is a counterpart — as far as the lack of the perforation is concerned — in the Lu Mou-te Collection, Peking (Umehara, "Note on Bronze Tools," Pl. 12: 1 = Fig. 44: 1).

(*46*) DAGGER-AXE (*K'UEI*)

With shaft-supports. The relatively short blade is strengthened by a broad midrib which starts from the perforated "shield." At the base of the blade small flanges stand out at acute angles, designed to engage the shaft and to supplement the usual lashings through the shoulder-slits. The "shield" is decorated with symmetrically arranged meander patterns, as is the tang which emerges from the middle of the base and slants slightly downward. There is no hole in the tang. Crusty patina in colors ranging from green to turquoise; the blade, where it has been freed of the crust, shows a cloudy whitish green with dark brown spots. Rather sturdy type. Shang or Chou I.      Pl. XXIII.

Length 222 mm; weight 270 gr.

Typologically significant is the appearance, here, of a merely decorative "shield" at the base. Evidently, it is a residue of the once structurally important reinforcement (as seen in nos. 44, 45; cp. also no. 49 below). This would seem to indicate a sensibly later date. But, a similar piece bears Shang glyphs (*San Tai Chi Chin Wen Ts'un,* 19:3 = Fig. 44:16), and a closely allied type — though without shaft-supports — in the Kishi Collection, Kyoto, is regarded as a Shang piece by Umehara (*Anyang Treasures,* Pl. 20:3 = Fig. 44:12); a third related specimen combines a Shang style *t'ao-t'ieh* on the "shield" with Shang glyphs on the *nei* (*San Tai Chi Chin Wen Ts'un,* 19:2 = *Anyang Treasures,* Pl. 20:2 = Fig. 44:14). This last specimen, by the way, shows the characteristic of the perforation of the blade much more pronounced than do the other variants, including no. 46, in which the round hole has almost disappeared. Another kindred example without shaft-supports, published as a Chou weapon by Umehara (*Shina Kodō Seika,* VII: 85), is in the British Museum.

It is the detail of the shaft-support that demands that a possibly later date be considered. Not very numerous, such halberds mostly belong to Chou times (as, for instance, no. 72 below). On the other hand, the flanges or wings then have, as a rule, a more elaborate shape than in the present case.

Whether the object just described can properly be counted among the *k'uei* types or not is a question which must be given thought. I call it a *k'uei* (not a *ko*) because the form of this weapon — as in the case of no. 45 above — has been derived from types for which the name *k'uei* has been adopted. In the "line of descent," the form approaches the *ko,* and Umehara indeed prefers — which is only reasonable in the presence of such difficulties of nomenclature — a more general, noncommittal term: "archaic *ko*" 古式戈 (cp. *Anyang Treasures*).

(*47*) JADE (*KO*) IN BRONZE HAFT

Blade of largely calcified, whitened jade which was once pale greenish gray in color; slightly corroded, coated by some earthy sinter. The blade was ground so as to give it a low median crest and faceted edges, while the base was adapted to the narrow socket of the bronze haft. This haft consists in a *t'ao-t'ieh* adorned shield, vertical lugs (to fasten the shaft), and a perforated shafting-plate (*nei*) with rounded butt. The butt, notched at the lower side, with sloping edges decorated by alternating dots and ribs, encloses a dragon ornament. The patina is smooth olive green at the shield, dull black-green at the part that was covered by the wooden shaft, and somewhat less dark at the butt. Shang.                                   Pl. XXII.

Length 262 mm; length of the jade blade 140 mm; thickness of the blade in the center ca. 6 mm.

The Louvre owns a similar dagger-axe with a beautiful dark jade blade in a comparably shaped and decorated haft (Sirén, *History of Early Chinese Art,* I, Pl. 18 B; *Ausstellung chinesischer Kunst,* Berlin, 1929, Cat. no. 52; Umehara, *Shina Kodō Seika,* VII: 90 b).

For the place in history of such ceremonial weapons — for all jade, marble, or stone dagger blades belong to that category, be they mounted in metal hafts or not — see Introduction, ch. III.

Further remarks on published specimens under no. 48 below.


## (*48*) JADE *KO* IN BRONZE HAFT

Regularly and finely worked blade of dark, warm brown-green feebly translucent jade. The median crest, gently bent down toward the point, runs between hollow-ground faces. The faceted edges end with curves where the blade tapers off toward the tip. Near the base is a conical perforation with a shallow counter-bore. Simple, plain bronze socket with vertical lugs of unequal length and a *nei* with splint-hole and rounded butt which descends. The descending butt is adorned with an animal ornament in raised lines: a large-eyed bird with turned-back head. Patina of the bronze haft: shiny, in olive-green, apple-green, gray, and reddish tones; dull bluish green in the cavities of the ornament. Shang.                         Pl. XXII.

Length 242 mm; length of the jade blade 126 mm.

This particularly elegant weapon exemplifies the consummate stone technique of the time. The introduction of bronze for all varieties of implements was in China not followed by a decay, but rather by a refinement of stoneworking. Metallic prototypes, as in the present case, had a stimulating influence in that they induced the craftsman to surpass rather than imitate them (wherein he was aided by the unrivaled beauty, but hampered by the fragility of his medium, jade). The shaping of the edges, the faceting in particular — also found in the relatively frequently occurring miniature jade blades of kindred type (e.g., *Ku Yü T'u Lu, First Pt.,* 1: 17, 18; Pelliot, *Jades archaïques,* Pl. viii) used as burial gifts — is only seen in jade objects, never in bronze blades of the same type and age. It should be added, however, that among those ceremonial or parade halberds there also occur more robust and heavier jade blades of comparatively archaic appearance, the bronze hafts of which sometimes are embellished with splendid turquoise incrustations.

Three of such stately weapons dating from Shang or early Chou times were on exhibition in 1936 at Burlington House (Cat. no. 207 — A. Hellström; no. 208 — O. Raphael; no. 209 — A. H. Pillsbury). Another six highly divergent specimens from the G. L. Winthrop Collection, Harvard, have been published by Umehara (*Anyang Studies,* Pls. xxxiii-xxxvi). A variant with broad short blade was displayed by C. T. Loo in 1940 at Detroit (J. M. Plumer, *An Exhibition of Ancient Chinese Ritual Bronzes,* Pl. 33: 12). Three quite unpretentious jade *ko* figure in Huang Chün's *Ku Yü T'u Lu, First Pt.,* 1: 20-21 a; the latter also appears in Pelliot's *Jades archaïques,* Pl. 3: 1, in Yetts's *Eumorfopoulos Collection Catalogue,* and in *Shina Kodō Seika,* VII: 90 a.

The ornament on the descending butt also occurs, in a slightly less complicated form, on a bronze *ko* in this collection (no. 61, below).

### (49) DAGGER-AXE (K'UEI)

Stout, heavy triangular blade with rounded point. Short vertical lugs at the base, which has no shafting-slits. The tang is quadrangular in shape, and has a round hole. A triangular elevation reinforces the blade at the base, inlaid with turquoise and depicting a heraldically addorsed pair of birds with long beaks and very long crests, their eyes set with oval *cabochons.* The end of the tang, too, is adorned by turquoise filling the sunken parts of a *t'ao-t'ieh* ornament in a rectangular frame. Patina: glossy blackish ground with some whitish green, coated to a large extent by thin gray-green layers of verdigris. Allegedly found in the vicinity of Anyang. Shang.        Pl. XXIII.

Length 228 mm; weight 450 gr.

This model diverges, it is true, from the *k'uei* types nos. 43-46 in that it has short lugs, i.e., elongations of the base as shafting-device instead of the usual slits; but since it corresponds to those types with regard to the form of the blade, the position of the tang, and the strengthening shield, I think it justifiable to assign it to the *k'uei.* Strictly speaking, it is a transitional model between the *k'uei* and the *ko,* and thus would require a typological category of its own — as does the following slenderer specimen (no. 50).

There are no counterparts known so far.

### (50) DAGGER-AXE (KO)

With symmetrically placed quadrangular tang, short vertical lugs elongating the base, and broad flat midrib. Decoration of the butt: a large sunken glyph *ts'e* 冊 between two dragons (Fig. 16); same configuration on the reverse side, with the glyph *shih* 史. Patina: brown and copper-colored surface with dirty-green crusts. Shang.        Pl. XXIV.

Length 232 mm; weight 340 gr.
Rare design.

Fig. 84: *Inscription and decoration of the ko no. 50.*

(*51*) DAGGER-AXE (*KO*)

With convex blade that rises strongly above the plane of the tang
(*nei*) and the lugs. Undecorated. Round hole in the *nei*. Bright
water-green and partly rust-colored patina with thin green coating.
Shang or Chou I.                                    Pl. XXIV.
    Length 217 mm; weight 295 gr.
    The *nei* is placed asymmetrically, somewhat below the upper edge
of the blade. The types hereafter described show the final, so to speak,
normalized form of the *ko* with the upper edges of blade and *nei*
brought onto the same level.

(*52*) DAGGER-AXE (*KO*)

With strongly convex blade, lugs, and rectangular *nei* with a hole;
the butt of the *nei* is grooved lengthwise. Bright sea-green patina with
protoxide red spots and dark encrustations. Shang.        Pl. XXIV.
    Length 242 mm; weight 425 gr.

(*53*) DAGGER-AXE (*KO*)

Very heavy specimen with broad-based blade, which is further reinforced by a convex shield only slightly smaller than the blade itself.
The *nei,* as thick as the lugs, is on a level with the upper edge of the
blade. It has a hole and is adorned with a whorl-circle between a pair
of pictograms signifying knives(?) in sunken relief. Rough, crusty,
speckled patina in lively emerald, olive, and blackish green. At some
places the process of oxidation has brought about a flaky structure.
Shang.                                              Pl. XXIV.
    Length 246 mm; weight 548 gr.(!).

Fig. 85:
*Decoration of the ko no. 53.*

    The whorl-circle ornament occurs rather often on Shang weapons;
it has already been noted twice in the present collection (nos. 4, 9,
12 above). It is possible that the sunken parts of the ornament originally were filled with paste or inlaid with stones, most probably turquoise. There are apparently no parallels to this remarkable specimen. With the sole exception of an extraordinarily large type (no.
63), it is by far the heaviest among the *ko* here published.

(*54*) DAGGER-AXE (*KO*)

With slender but sturdy convex blade, lugs, and rectangular neck-
plate, that has an unusually large round hole. The butt is decorated
with a *t'ao-t'ieh* in raised lines. Patina: blackish on the decorated
part, in varying green shades on the blade. Shang or Chou I.
                                                   Pl. XXV.
    Length 258 mm; weight 420 gr.
    What a hole of such a wide diameter was intended for is not clear.
A bolt of corresponding thickness would endanger the solidity of the
shaft, while a bolt of normal dimensions could hardly be securely attached. Yet the opening seems to be original.

Fig. 86:
*Decoration of the ko no. 54.*

**(55) DAGGER-AXE (KO)**

With strong blade that has a scarcely noticeable crest and low shaft-supporting ridges at the base, with lugs slightly bent back, and with rectangular tang. An animal mask set with turquoise adorns the butt, the stones being relatively large and ranging in color from sky blue to a yellowish green. Shiny gray-green ground with some dull violet, covered by darker gray-green crusts and blisters. Probably Shang.

Pl. XXV.

Length 250 mm; weight 425 gr.

**(56) DAGGER-AXE (KO)**

Similar to, but less heavy than, the foregoing piece. Decorated with a likewise similar *t'ao-t'ieh* without turquoise. Irregular splint-hole. Bluish gray glossy ground, coated by bright green encrustations and blisters. Shang or Chou I.    Pl. XXV.

Length 235 mm; weight 265 gr.

**(57) DAGGER-AXE (KO)**

Fig. 87:
*Inscription on the ko no. 57.*

With rectangular tang and lugs. The blade, with softly trimmed crest, rises a little above the plane of the tang and lugs; at the base it is adorned with an incised *t'ao-t'ieh* of advanced style in triangular shape. The butt of the *nei* shows a character framed by the cross-cartouche (*ya-hsing*) and enclosed by broad sunken lines on three sides. Round hole in the *nei*. Poor grayish and copper-colored patina with thin crusts. Chou I.    Pl. XXV.

Length 232 mm; weight 285 gr.

This *ko* previously formed part of a private collection in Peking, and was recently published (*Ch'ih An Ts'ang Chin*, 52) with the acceptable date "Western Chou." For the character a reading "*chao fu* 召夫" and a newer variant reading "罦" are given. The first interpretation is not admissible since it divides the glyph into two; the second reading is incorrect. According to the *Ku Chou P'ien* (39: 21) the glyph should be read "kuei 規." (The examples quoted there can be supplemented by the inscription on a bell of the *nao* type in Lo Chen-yü's *San Tai Chi Chin Wen Ts'un*, 18: 7 a.)

**(58) DAGGER-AXE (KO)**

With the butt rounded and notched at the lower corner, and slightly thinner at the part which when mounted was inserted into the cleft. The blade is faintly curved, has a crest, and rises above the plane of the lugs. Round hole in the *nei*. Ornamentation in sunken design filled with turquoise, representing an animal-head with a large turquoise boss as the eye on the left side, and a pictogram "house with double roof" on the right side. Patina: bright gray-green and whitish green ground with malachite coatings. Shang or Chou I.

Pl. XXVI.

Length 253 mm; weight 405 gr.

The ornament being somewhat hard to recognize in the reproduction, the reader may refer to Fig. 88, which clearly renders an almost identical design from the following piece.

The glyph "house with double roof" is represented in a similar form in *Ku Chou P'ien* (71 : 13 a .5, *s.v.*⟨glyph⟩ ) and *Chin Wen Pien* (*fu-lu, shang* 19 b. 5) among the unexplained characters.

## (59) DAGGER-AXE (KO)

Akin to the foregoing one, with a sunken ornament on the tang representing an animal's head with a claw beneath. The lower lug is broken off. Old excavation; blackish brown, with rough bright greenish coating on the blade. Chou I. Pl. XXVI.
Length 260 mm; weight 268 gr.

A group of allied specimens with variants of the animal-head is contained among the rubbings in *San Tai Chi Chin Wen Ts'un* (19: 15b-18a). In the present case one can establish that the hole in the tang is placed behind the shaft. Thus, the perforation has been used, not for a splint or bolt, but for laces, tassels, or streamers.

## (60) DAGGER-AXE (KO)

The blade has an unmarked crest, and the lower lug is longer than the upper one. The *nei* has a rounded drooping butt. Its ornament in thin *cloisons* is fully set with turquoise, the varying colors of which — presumably so chosen by the craftsman — give off a mosaical glitter. Smooth bluish gray oxidized surface on the one side; as to the rest, there is a rough patina in dull green and ultramarine blue. Traces of a fine tissue on the reverse side (not shown in the reproduction). Probably Shang. Pl. XXVI.
Length 254 mm; weight 255 gr.

The ornamental design, nearly absorbed in the glittering surface, is the same, on the whole, as that on the jade *ko* no. 48 and on the following specimen, no. 61.

## (61) DAGGER-AXE (KO)

With rounded down-curved butt, similar to, but somewhat larger and heavier than, the previous type. Small hole overgrown with oxide in the *nei*; a wider hole in the blade near the base. The border enclosing the ornament on the butt — an animal figure in sunken lines — is notched like the segmented flanges on Shang bronze vessels. The blade again shows a barely discernible crest. Smooth patina in cloudy green shades on the blade and the butt, rough and darker at the shaft section. Shang(?). Pl. XXVI.
Length 280 mm; weight 383 gr.

The axis of the lugs or, if considered as a unit, the vertical bar, device for shafting, does not stand at right angles to the blade, which

Fig. 88:
*Decoration of the ko no. 59.*

consequently, when hafted, slightly rises. The *rising blade* is a characteristic of the developed Chou types. It has not appeared among the specimens listed so far. They all show blades which have — the shaft taken as vertical — a horizontal position with the point, as a rule, lowered. Otherwise, the *ko* no. 61 is so closely related to archaic types that it cannot well be dated later than around the end of the Shang dynasty.

A detail claiming attention is the perforation of the blade, which suggests the jade *ko* no. 48 and the *k'uei* types nos. 43, 44, 46. This perforation seems to be a property of this type, for it occurs alike on two closely akin (and therefore not published) specimens in the Jannings Collection, as well as on a piece with similar decoration unearthed in 1929 from a Shang tomb near Hsiao-t'un (cf. *Prel. Report on Excavations at Anyang*, III : Li Chi, "Fu Shen Tsang," Grave 18.3, Pl. 7). The latter find, too, is evidence in favor of a Shang date for the present object.

### (62) DAGGER-AXE (KO)

Of unusual length, with rounded downward curved butt and a slender strong blade with smooth crest. The lugs are vertical and of unequal length. Rounded point. Hole at the shaft passage. The ornamentation, perhaps representing a dragon, is in relief on sunken ground; the cavities were probably once filled with a colored paste. Patina: cloudy, light and dark sea green and copper red, with thin layers of darker green. Near the point, on one side only, there is an impression of basketwork. Shang or Chou I.          Pl. XXVII.

Length 323 mm; weight 470 gr.

Counterparts of comparable length will not often be found. Nevertheless, there have existed even larger types as, for instance, a giant blade of ca. 410 mm length in the K'ai-feng Museum (rubbing published by Kuan Po-i, *Yin-hsü Ch'i Wu Ts'un Chen*, I, fol. 1).

### (63) LARGE KO WITH THE FIGURE OF A BIRD

Extraordinarily long blade with a sharp crest accentuated by a thin rib, and with faceted edges. The tang, somewhat thinner than the blade, without lugs or hole, is terminated by a large bird-figure in profile. The bird, when the *ko* was attached to a shaft, looks downward. Of late Shang style, the bird is sharply articulated by contour and incised lineament: a beast with mighty beak and tremendous claw, plume, and tail, with a large elliptical eye that alone stands out plastically. A greenish gray patina with brownish spots covers the surface. A crust of verdigris apparently has been scraped off, for there are numerous traces of scratching and grinding. End of Shang or Chou I.          Pl. XXVII.

Length 387 mm; weight 685 gr.

In the Museum of Far Eastern Antiquities at Stockholm is a variant which has shafting lugs and differs in some details of the bird-figure (reproduced in outline drawing by S. Umehara, "Note on Bronze Tools and Weapons," Pl. 12:13).

Provided with wings in slightly oblique position, and decorated with equally proportioned but less compact figures of birds is a group of three uniform *ko* with inscriptions, which came from Paoting (Honan) and was acquired by Lo Chen-yü (*Meng Wei Ts'ao T'ang Chi Chin T'u, chung* 1-3; also in *Chou Chin Wen Ts'un,* 6/1: 68, 69). Together with these three pieces a fragment of the same type is contained in *Hsiao Chiao Ching Ko Chin Wen T'a Pen* (10: 88 b sqq.). The inscriptions of all of these four specimens suggest their Shang date.

Another variant, without lugs or shafting-bar, in the Berlin Museum has a divergent form of the bird, which is placed transversely, more splendidly designed, and cast in relief. The blade, moreover, shows an additional ornamentation by a *t'ao-t'ieh* in thin raised lines (cf. Umehara, "Note," Pl. 11:5).

## *(64) KO* WITH ANIMAL ORNAMENT

As in the foregoing specimen, the tang is not perforated, and it is terminated by a fantastically shaped animal ornament. This ornament, which in some essential traits corresponds to the large bird (of the *ko* no. 63), would hardly be taken as an animal, were it not for the fact that it has an eye. The fairly acute-pointed blade is provided with a shafting-bar, short above, somewhat longer below. The patina is of light grayish and whitish green and copper red, overlaid by dark green concretions; the raised lines of the ornament show a glossy gray-green. Shang or Chou I.                Pl. XXVII.

Length 275 mm; weight 296 gr.

A related specimen with a somewhat less intricate ornament, said to have come from Anyang, is dated Shang by Yü Hsing-wu (*Shuang Chien I Chi Chin, hsia:* 15). Another one, that has a less blurred lineament and a median-crest blade, is in the Museum für Völkerkunde, Munich (Cat. no. 26-1-8). Together with a series of *ko* butts with turquoise incrustation, generally regarded as Anyang finds, it was published by Umehara (*Den Inkyo hakken no dōseihin ni tsuite*) when it was still in the possession of the late Mr. Wannieck. Whether the bizarre animal ornament was derived, as Umehara believed, exclusively from those splendidly decorated butts which show a kind of dragon design, remains questionable; for what they have in common with this bizarre ornament restricts itself to a pair of outward bent hooks above the eye. (Reproductions of the compared butts are also found in *Shina Kodō Seika,* VII: 87, and in Lo Chen-yü's *Yin-hsü Ku Ch'i Wu T'u Lu,* 12 a, where they are wrongly explained as handles of sacrificial vessels.) The features this queer ornament has in common with the bird types such as illustrated by no. 63, on the other hand, are structural ones, which have gained a distinctly organic meaning in the bird-figure. Possibly there were several prototypes which contributed to, and eventually coalesced into, this odd shape.

It is certainly clear that the *ko* type dealt with is connected with a species of thinly cast blades unfit for practical use, which probably were made as burial gifts. Such blades, with a strongly conventionalized and somewhat shapeless ornament reminiscent of the present one, had been acquired *in loco* by the Anyang excavators (cf. *Preliminary Report*, III: Li Chi, *Fu Shen Tsang*, Pl. 4). Two allied specimens are in the Archaeological Collection of the Kyoto University (Umehara, *Anyang Treasures*, p. 35, Fig. 15).

Two particularly large *ko* of the same design as no. 64 are contained in *Hsiao Chiao Ching Ko Chin Wen T'a Pen* (10:82); another two, of average size and divergent with regard to the ornament, are reproduced in Umehara's *Anyang Treasures*, Pl. 16: 4-5.

### (65) DAGGER-AXE WITH SHAFT-RING (*CH'Ü*)

Instead of a tang or shafting-plate that passes through a cleft in the wooden shaft, this type is provided with an oval shaft-ring which is narrower than the blade and is terminated by a squarish butt. It is a type which has a dagger-like pointed blade like the *ko,* but was hafted like an axe. The butt is decorated with glyphs in intaglio: "ear," flanked by two "knives"(?) (Fig. 89). Patina: whitish turquoise-colored at the butt; the other parts show a shiny and reddish surface with green, ochre-yellow and black-green coatings. The cavities of the ornaments are filled with a reddish brown substance. Shang.
Pl. XXVIII.

Length 230 mm; shaft-hole width 27: 20 mm; weight 415 gr.
"Dagger-axe": J. M. Menzies, in his foreword to J. M. Plumer's catalogue *An Exhibition of Ancient Chinese Ritual Bronzes,* objected to the designation "dagger-axe" without however proposing a more suitable one. He says: "The *ko* has sometimes been called a dagger-axe, but the *ko* is neither a dagger nor an axe" (*ibid.,* p. 8). The dagger-axe, of course, is neither dagger nor axe, but a combination of them, that is, a thrusting weapon with a shafting-device like that of an axe and mounted as an axe.

This ringed type, too, already existed in Shang times (cp. Li Chi, *Yin-hsü T'ung Ch'i Wu Chung,* pp. 82-84; Umehara, *Anyang Treasures,* p. 34). It further seems that this type, though more developed and sophisticated than the ordinary *ko* with flat tang, was not the historical successor of the latter, but was rather restricted to the Shang. For under the Chou the tanged types predominate by far, while *ko* with shaft-ring or shaft-tube (such as nos. 70 and 75 below) are rare exceptions.

As explained in the Introduction (ch. III, Dagger-Axes), the name *ch'ü* 瞿 is adopted here for the ringed type in order to distinguish it from the type with flat tang.

Whether the ornamental graph in the middle really has to be interpreted as "ear" is, of course, open to question, much as is the case with the definition "knives" of the framing pointed blades. If the reading proves to be correct, the whole apparently constitutes a primary form of the character *erh* 刵 "to cut the ears," with the knife rendered twice for reasons of symmetry. Cutting off the ears — trophies, brutally verifying the number of enemies slain in battle, or evidences of inflicted punishment — was practiced under the Chou (cp. *Shu Ching, K'ang Kao,* and the important inscription of the *Hsiao Yü Ting* 小盂鼎, *Liang Chou Chin Wen Tz'u Ta Hsi K'ao Shih,* fol. 35).

Fig. 89: *Decoration on the butt of the dagger-axe no. 65.*

(*66*) DAGGER-AXE WITH SHAFT-RING (*CH'Ü*)

Variant of the foregoing type, the blade being slightly asymmetrically curved downward. The neck-plate shows an animal mask with a lozenge placed between the horns. Glossy bright green patina with faint crusts. Shang. Pl. XXVIII.

Length 240 mm; width of the shaft-hole 32: 20 mm; weight 440 gr.

For curiosity's sake it may be mentioned here that the author of a well-known commentary to the *K'ao Kung Chi* of the *Chou Li,* Ch'eng Yao-t'ien (1725-1814) interpreted a similar ornamental mask thus: (the animal-head — not recognized as such — is the character) *yung* 用, and the lozenge stands for *k'ou* 口, the whole signifying Chou 周 and resembling a human face (cp. *K'ao Kung Ch'uang Wu Hsiao Chi,* ch. 2).

(*67*) DAGGER-AXE WITH SHAFT-RING (*CH'Ü*)

Akin to the last one, save that its blade has a more slender point and a more strongly marked median crest. On the butt there is a glyph cast in sunken design. Smooth light green-gray patina with darker concretions. Shang. Pl. XXVIII.

Length 240 mm; width of the shaft-hole 30: 20 mm; weight 285 gr.

The same type was excavated at Anyang (Li Chi, "Yin-hsü T'ung Chi Wu Chung," p. 83, Fig. 5). It also occurs — with the same inscription — in several collections: *Yen K'u Chi Chin T'u Lu, hsia,* fol. 15, no. 21; *Ch'ih An Ts'ang Chin,* fol. 47; *San Tai Chi Chin Wen Ts'un,* ch. 19: 20 b; J. M. Plumer, *An Exhibition of Ancient Chinese Ritual Bronzes,* Pl. xxxiii, no. 9.

Hypothetical readings of the character are *mao* 矛 (*Yen K'u*), *kan* 干, or *tzu* 子 (*Ch'ih An*), of which the latter two are unlikely. Plumer thinks it might be the symbol for a tribe or clan. I should like to add that the glyph somewhat resembles an early dagger type characterized by two small prongs above the base of the blade (e.g., H. Rivière and others, *Collection Osvald Sirén,* Pl. II, no. 10).

(*68*) DAGGER-AXE WITH SHAFT-RING (*CH'Ü*)

The crest of the blade is accentuated by a thin rib. The butt is furrowed longitudinally. Shiny greenish gray patina, thin coatings of darker green. Shang. Pl. XXVIII.

Length 255 mm; width of the shaft-hole 25 : 20 mm; weight 310 gr.

A similar specimen, allegedly unearthed at Anyang in 1939, is contained in *Yen K'u Chi Chin T'u Lu, hsia,* fol. 23, no. 33.

### (69) *KO* WITH SHAFT-RING AND VERTICAL EDGE

Crested blade, slenderer than those described so far. The lower cutting edge is drawn downward in a curve to form a vertical edge with correspondingly elongated base. Below the ring, which in relation to the blade is placed axially, there is a narrow lashing-slit in the base. The butt extending beyond the ring widens toward the end. It bears a sunken pictogram (Fig. 23). The patina leaves partly uncovered the grayish black, glossy metal, which elsewhere is coated by a dull gray-green oxide with darker shades and rust-colored spots between. Shang or Chou I. Pl. XXIX.

Length 230 mm; width of the shaft-hole 25 : 16 mm; weight 286 gr.

This fairly rare type holds a place between Shang forms and the common Chou *ko* with flat heel (*nei*) and descending edge (*hu*), as illustrated by the *ko* no. 74 below.

A counterpart without decoration in the Yūrinkan Collection, Kyoto, is dated Shang by Umehara (*Anyang Relics,* Pl. xv, 5).

A specimen with relatively short blade and rounded point, the vertical-edged part (*hu*) of which is prolonged — in the manner of Chou types — by a shafting-bar, allegedly excavated near Anyang in 1938, is given a slightly later date, *viz.,* Shang or Early Chou, by the owner, Liang Shang-ch'un (*Yen K'u Chi Chin T'u Lu, hsia,* fol. 34, no. 48).

The glyph engraved on both sides of the butt may be a variant of the character *i* 亦 (cf. *Ku Chou P'ien,* 39 : 24-25; *Chia Ku Wen Pien,* 10 : 13 b — 14 a), approaching the archaic forms of *ta* 大, *fu* 夫, and *t'ien* 天. An exact parallel seems not to exist, but an undeciphered glyph with two dots instead of the short strokes — presumably a variant — should not be overlooked (*Chin Wen Pien, fu-lu, shang,* 2b; also *San Tai Chi Chin Wen Ts'un,* ch. 2 : 27a).

Fig. 90:
*Inscription on the ko no. 69.*

### (70) *KO* WITH OPENWORK SOCKET

Crested blade with vertical edge (*hu*) combined with a long socket. The socket, which is oval in section, extends beyond the base above and below and is provided with a butt projecting opposite the horizontal blade. This socket is cast in openwork designed as grooved thongs wound in zigzags around the shaft. It is crowned by an oval ring jutting out to the rear and decorated with a grooved S-spiral; its lower rim is girt by horizontal ribs. The butt, which has an irregularly quadrangular silhouette, is slit horizontally, losing strength toward the outer edge. Smooth emerald-green patina, with the yellow-brown metal lying bare at some exposed spots, and with blackish green in the cavities and more inaccessible parts. Chou I-II (?). Pl. XXIX.

Length 171 mm; lower aperture of the socket 23:18 mm; weight 283 gr.

Stray type. The whole appearance, make, and decoration do not tally with the Chou bronze craft as represented by countless specimens, but rather suggest the world of Sino-Siberian bronzes, in which geometric ornaments, the S-spiral, openwork, and a cruder technique are frequently seen. (Cp. Egami and Mizuno, *Inner Mongolia*, Pt. II, p. 26, Fig. 16 F = Andersson, "Hunting Magic," Pl. 7:1 — hilt of a dagger with openwork zigzag; A. Salmony, *Sino-Siberian Art*, Pl. 40:1-2 — openwork scabbards.) The form of the blade, on the other hand, cannot well be separated from current Chinese types.

The long shaft-tube of certain Chan-kuo types (as, for instance, no. 75 below) has nothing whatsoever to do with the present structure.

There exists a likewise very rare type of axe or halberd with pointed blade and a vertically drawn edge — in this akin to the present *ko* — but with a small hammer or stud instead of a neck-plate. The rare type is represented by two examples in the collection of Liu T'i-chih (*Shan Chai Chi Chin Lu*, 11:26-28; *Hsiao Chiao Ching Ko*, 10:109), examples which can be linked with a distinct group of axes. They have some characteristic details in common with oval-bladed battle-axes (Introduction, ch. I, Axes): (1) the long socket; (2) the small projection at the neck; (3) the loop near the lower rim of the socket; (4) the decoration which consists of open angles filled with rings. (See text Figs. 3, 15 above.) On account of these parallels, a date as early as Shang-Chou I may be assumed with some probability for the two *ko*-axes in the Liu Collection.

A piece allied to the Liu *ko*-axes in the David-Weill Collection, Paris, bears a disk fitted with small rings in lieu of the projection on the neck of the socket (O. Janse, "L' Empire des Steppes et les relations entre l'Europe et l'Extrême-Orient dans l'antiquité," Pl. 5:13 = Fig. 15 B). The ornamentation consisting of angles open toward the blade is absent in this case, but the disk just mentioned reappears on the oval-bladed battle-axe in Stockholm (O. Janse, "Quelques antiquités chinoises d'un caractère Hallstattien," Pl. 3:3 = Fig. 3 A); there can be no doubt, therefore, that the David-Weill specimen also belongs to the group just described.

Finally, a tool *sui generis* in the von der Heydt Collection must be recalled here. It is a dagger-axe with a long blade and a roofed socket slightly bent back on top and fitted with a quadrangular neck-plate (V. Griessmaier, *Sammlung von der Heydt*, no. 80 = Fig. 16 B). A decoration of dots and rings in rows definitely connects this piece with the group of small socketed battle-axes which were dealt with under no. 16 above (cp. text Fig. 6 above). Thus, the close relationship of a socketed *ko* type with the Sino-Siberian complex is once more demonstrated.

The early date, seemingly a corollary from the associations pointed out above, cannot simply be transferred to stray type no. 70, for the horizontal slit in the butt is an innovation which, to my knowledge, only came into fashion in the period Chou I — when it superseded the round hole of the Shang types. Consequently, the present *ko*-axe may date from Chou I at the earliest. The décor, however, rather suggests a later date, say Chou II. For want of safe supports for comparison, the date proposed above remains hypothetical.

### (71) DAGGER-AXE (KO)

Slender, curved, slightly convex blade with shafting-bar in oblique position and accordingly rhombic heel, which is relatively long. A round perforation in the heel (*nei*); a small lashing-slit in the base on a level with the lower edge of the heel. The shafting-bar is thinner than the blade and is provided with narrow flanges. Cast of an alloy seemingly rich in tin. Glossy silver-gray surface with some verdigris and malachite coatings. Chou I or slightly later.    Pl. XXIX.

Length 245 mm; weight 270 gr.

Exactly corresponding analogies are missing, but the following *ko* (no. 72) resembles the present one in several respects.

A flanged bar or flanged lugs have not been encountered among the dagger-axes described thus far. The fully developed flanges apparently do not date back beyond the Chou (neither does the horizontal slit in the *nei*), although approximative solutions are likely to have preceded them, as stop-ridges or small supports actually did. *Ch'ih An Tsang Chin* (fol. 55) depicts a *ko* with a broader and more straightened blade which nonetheless is not entirely dissimilar to the present one; it is provided with a kind of flange and, bearing a Shang pictogram "knife and hand," it may well be of Shang date and thus represent a forerunner of the types with flanged bar. It also has the narrow slit at the base. The strikingly rigid, accurate, mechanical, jejune character of the present *ko,* on the other hand, is absent in that piece.

A specimen which is important for the chronological order of Early Chou types should — in spite of formal divergencies — still be mentioned. It is a *ko* with asymmetrical point, short *hu* (vertical edge) with a large slit, oblique bar with flanges, and quadrangular tang without perforation, inscribed "Ch'eng Chou 成周" (see text Fig. 45:8). Professor Jung Keng, the owner, assigned it to the beginnings of Chou (*Sung Chai Chi Chin T'u Lu,* fol. 32; text fol. 21). The inscription is included in *Cheng Sung T'ang Chi Ku I Wen* (*pu-i, chung*: 32b) together with a parallel (32a) from an unpublished *ko*.

### (72) DAGGER-AXE (KO)

Resembling the foregoing, but with a shorter heel notched at the lower corner. Oblique shafting-bar without flanges; instead, small shaft-supports appear on both sides of the base, which has one vertical slit. The blade is rather narrow, faintly convex, and its downward prolongation (the *hu*) is longer than that of the *ko* no. 71. Again it seems that a particular bronze alloy was used, producing a smooth, shiny, silvery black ground, which here is largely coated by a thin, rough patina of bluish green and brownish green tones. The shaft-supports, standing off at acute angles, are shaped like leaf-tips, with the edges coiled inward and forming plastic volutes. Chou I(?).

Pl. XXX.

Length 218 mm; weight 212 gr.

The structural detail of the shaft-supports already occurred in the axe no. 15 and the *k'uei* no. 46. Similarly formed, but not plastic, it will be seen once more in the partisan no. 106.

## (73) DAGGER-AXE (KO)

With a vertical extension (*hu*) of the lower edge and a very long thin blade with strengthened rim. A spiral pattern in fine raised lines fills the space within the rim and a smaller field on the butt of the *nei*. Along the shafting-bar, which stands obliquely, there are two vertical slits and, topmost, a round hole. Patina: dull, light gray-green; in the cavities of the ornaments almost exclusively brown; tip, rim, and heel coated by prevailingly green crusts. Break in the blade. Chou II(?).

Pl. XXX.

Length 302 mm; weight 300 gr.

Rare type which, on account of its fragility, must be regarded as a ceremonial weapon. The specimen formerly was in the collection of Li T'ai-fen, who published it under the designation "*chi* 戟" (*Ch'ih An Ts'ang Chin*, 63), without data other than "Chou."

## (74) DAGGER-AXE (KO)

With rising blade and a vertical extension (*hu*) of the lower edge, which recedes at a right angle. With exception of the *hu*, the blade (*yüan*) has sharp faceted edges. The base is flanged to facilitate shafting. The heel (*nei*) has a horizontal slit and a notch at the lower corner. The shafting-bar starts from the lower edge of the *nei* and extends beyond the *hu*. Four superposed lunular holes in the base of the blade: one above the *nei,* three below it. The partly bronze-colored, partly tin-colored surface is covered by a thin greenish gray patina and some earthy concretions. Chou II-III.     Pl. XXX.

Length 210 mm; weight 260 gr.

This specimen exemplifies the standardized, common Chou type, the classical *ko*. The forms are sharp-cornered, well balanced, and definite in appearance. It is not yet known when this type first issued. In view of the lack of reliably datable material, even an exhaustive investigation would not yield a satisfying answer to this question (cp. Introduction, ch. III, Dagger-Axes).

### (75) *KO* WITH SHAFT-TUBE

Blade and heel have roughly the same shape as those of the previous type, while the *hu* shows only two slits instead of the lunular holes. The *nei,* meeting the blade in the common way, penetrates a round bronze tube as long as the base of the blade, which it touches. The shafting-bar, cutting into the tube, extends beyond the lower aperture. The tube is crowned by a hollow-cast bird-figure fixed by a rivet. The bird turns back its head toward the point, and has its beak sunk in the plumage as if sleeping. A faint gleam here and there from under the cover of oxide reveals that the figure was gilded. The blade is coated by a layer of blue oxide over an apple-green ground, with some dull green and brownish patches between. The tube shows a patina in gray and green hues different from the rest. Chou III-IV.

Pl. XXXI.

Length 220 mm; diameter of the tube 22 mm; weight 340 gr.

Comparable specimens are not numerous. One is in the large collection of Liu T'i-chih (*Shan Chai Chi Chin Lu,* 10: 1). The tube is shorter there and juts out a little over the dorsal edge; it is surmounted by a bird sitting in the opposite direction, with the neck so bent back that the beak stands vertically. With regard to details, the reproduction, a drawing, obviously leaves much to be desired, as does that in *Hsiao Chiao Ching Ko,* 10: 1. In addition to the measurements given, the catalogue says only that the bird is plated with gold. But this laconic statement is followed by a thesis on the meaning of the word *pi* 柲 — commonly taken as the designation of the shaft through which the tang passes. With a display of quotations from the classics, Liu T'i-chih proposes that *pi* should be identified with the shaft-tube or ferrule as it here appears.

A second specimen with a tube of only half the length of the base — including the *hu* which is extraordinarily long — and a shafting-bar that starts from beneath the tube (a structure, in other words, that takes into account the presence of the ferrule) is contained in *Cheng Sung T'ang Chi Chin T'u Lu* (*chung:* 66). There is neither a plastic figure nor any other decoration. An inscription on the *nei* is illegible with the exception of the character "year," and thus unfortunately contributes nothing to the chronology of this category.

A third variant, still unpublished, appeared in the Peking art market some time ago. It possesses the elegantly shaped blade of the *ko with dented edge* (see no. 79 below), a correspondingly long, slender heel, and a round tapering tube which is a little longer than the base of the blade. The tube is surmounted by a bird in nearly the same attitude as that of our specimen: the head is raised; large spirals adorn the wings; the tail points to the blade, but, quite unrealistically, is formed like a long narrowly slit loop. A handle (or foot-mounting) belongs to that *ko,* which, though diverging in details, resembles the handle in the C. G. Seligman Collection, Oxford (cp. Andersson, "The Goldsmith in Ancient China," Pl. 9: 2).

There is a further example of a *ko* with bird-crowned tube in the A. Hellström Collection, Mölndal. W. P. Yetts gives an outline drawing of it in *The Cull Chinese Bronzes* (p. 98, Fig. 29). The blade is more slender, the narrow *nei* is sharpened, and the bird looks back toward the *nei* that likewise serves as a weapon. The tube, oval in section, is shorter than the *hu*.

At the same time, Professor Yetts points to an unpublished *ko* in the collection of H. M. Gustav Adolf, King of Sweden, that seemingly has lost the bronze tube (*ibid.*, p. 97).

Finally, splendid examples of *chi* 戟 have been brought to light during the 1942 excavations of Han dynasty tombs at Yang-kao-hsien 陽高縣 (Inner Mongolia), pieces that are provided with gold and silver inlaid, bird-crowned tubes of exquisite design, certainly not inferior in workmanship to anything of this kind previously known (Rostovtzeff's *Inlaid Bronzes of the Han Dynasty* being the representative work on kindred monuments). It is worthy of note that the birds again are so placed that the tails stretch toward the blade, and that they turn their heads back, looking toward the point of the blade. (Cp. C. Mizuno, "Kan kingin-saku seidō-ki.")

Apart from their practical purpose as a ferrule, these crowning birds also have, as Professor Yetts maintains, a magic meaning: "The hooked beak suggests a bird of prey, an eagle or hawk. If we seek the train of thought which prompted the choice of this kind of bird as a suitable ornament for a *ko* haft, we find it in the primitive and universal belief that like produces like. The eagle or hawk is proverbially keen-sighted and quick to strike its prey with deadly effect. Its figure on the haft is therefore not merely ornamental; it tends also to endow the weapon with qualities of the bird, so that the owner may slay his enemy with unerring aim. Here is an instance of sympathetic magic. . . ." (*The Cull Chinese Bronzes*, p. 95). Such conceptions (cp. also Li Chi, "Fu Shen Tsang," in *Prel. Report on Excavations at Anyang*, III, 469) perhaps had to do with the choice of the decorative elements. Albeit, some observations may be adduced which seem rather to contradict the idea of a magical function.

Birds: Does the representation of a sleeping bird — as in the present example — agree with Professor Yetts's interpretation? Three *ko*-axes, the blades of which immediately recall the sharp beak of a bird of prey (nos. 80, 81, 82 below), are decorated with plastic groups including bird-figures. These birds are shown as succumbing to tigers, or — if one hesitates to accept such an interpretation — as only one element among several, with the tiger dominating. If it was the bird which invested these weapons with magic power, such configurations would not be quite appropriate. The tigers, moreover, also appear as crowning figures on bells, showing that they have no special relation to the weapons, and that they did not function — as might otherwise be surmised — as magic agents replacing the birds.

Jaws: The motif of the open jaws (on the axes nos. 3, 4, 5, 6, 10 above), to which an underlying notion of similar kind would have to be assigned, likewise appears on sacrificial vases. It is not likely that the meaning of the same motif varies. On the vases, the meaning of the fanged jaws may be that they defend and protect the vase and what it holds; they cannot well signify to strike or bite as does an axe. It is the threatening appearance of the bare teeth and fangs, then, that applies equally well to both container and axe. Thus, the inference is that the motif was chosen to terrify the foe, be it a demon, a warrior, or a culprit. If so, the principle of sympathetic magic — to produce like with like — does not hold good for the jaws-motif. To return to the birds: the assumption of a magical significance is all the more questionable since the jaws, a prominent motif often found on much earlier weapons, cannot be regarded as evidence of magic practice.

A structural detail of the present *ko* type, the *shaft-tube,* which engages the topmost part of the shaft, should also be touched upon here. Yetts (*op. cit.,* p. 98) seems to hold that these tubes invariably are oval in cross section, with the narrower side turned toward the blade. However, the specimens here described (no. 75) or referred to (*Cheng Sung T'ang;* Peking art market) show that round tubes occur as well.

With due regard to all the diversities of structural and ornamental nature, it seems certain that none of the pieces in question is prior to the end of Chou III at the earliest; they rather date from the Chou IV and, like the Yang-kao-hsien finds, from Han times. Their scarcity on the one hand, and their lack of uniformity on the other, lead to the conclusion that this tool was neither common nor widespread.

Finally, there exists a group of *chi* 戟 (most simply defined as *ko* with an additional, spearhead-like vertical blade); these likewise were hafted by means of round tubes. I recall the iron blades with bronze tubes found in the necropolis of Lo-lang 樂浪 in Korea near Heijō, an emporium founded under Han Wu Ti (140-88 B.C.). The most ancient burials at Lo-lang date from around 100 B.C., and these *chi* would hardly be older than that; perhaps they are considerably later, for that small Chinese polity flourished for nearly half a millennium. At any rate it is certain that the weapons, if made in local workshops, are based on Chinese models, which in their turn could antedate the earliest burials there. Actually, a bronze *ko* with inscription dated the year corresponding to 222 B.C. has been found at Lo-lang (T. Sekino, S. Yatsui *et al., Rakurō-gun jidai no iseki,* text Figs. 201-2, p. 345 sq.; also *Shū Kan ihō,* Pl. 55 top). Thus, regarding the detail of the shaft-tube, there is no necessity to transfer the late Han date to finds from China proper, though one had better bear in mind the late occurrence of the types in question.

The specimens alluded to, fragments in part, are in the Fine Arts School in Tokyo and in the private collections Fukuda 富田, Nakanishi 中西, and Ikuda 多田 (Sekino, Yatsui, *ibid.,* text, pp. 353-56,

Figs. 210-16). Another iron *chi* was found in the lavishly equipped tomb no. 9, excavated by Sekino in 1916; among other things that tomb contained two dated lacquer trays imported from Ssechuan, the dates of both pieces corresponding to A.D. 8 (*ibid.*, pp. 97-105 on the trays, p. 87 sq. and Fig. 20 on the weapon; vol. I, Pl. 47: 331 = weapon; Pls. 58-60: nos. 417-23 = lacquer wares; one of the trays also in Umehara's *Shina Kan-dai kinen-mei shikki zusetsu*, Pl. 25). The tomb and the iron *chi* with a bronze tube thus probably date from soon after A.D. 8.

## (76) SHAFT-MOUNTING (*T'UN*)

Bronze, with a rough apple-green patina and patches of blue and brown oxides. The upper part of the object — often called a *ko* handle — is formed as a socket of oval section, with rivet-holes on both sides. The lower part is solid and polygonal in section; it is strongly attenuated toward the hooflike foot, which has a convex underside. Upper and lower parts are separated by a projecting zone. The wall of the socket is adorned with silver inlaid geometrical décor — volutes, compound diagonally (Fig. 91). A withered fragment of

Fig. 91: *Design of silver inlay no. 76.*

the wooden shaft as well as two small and short wooden bolts (that were driven into the shaft) are preserved. Furthermore, there remain undecayed traces of a crude tissue that was used to stuff the wooden stick tightly in the shoe. Chou IV.              Pl. XXXIV.

Height 99 mm; width of the socket 27: 18 mm; weight 150 gr.

Shaft-foot mountings appear to be a novelty of the Eastern Chou period or, more exactly, Chou III; there are as yet no examples of an earlier style. (A mounting such as no. 84 below is an outstanding exception in itself; it has nothing to do with the present type). A series of more splendidly adorned specimens is reproduced by Andersson ("The Goldsmith in Ancient China," Pls. 7-11); several examples widely differing among themselves are contained in W. C. White's *Tombs of Old Loyang* (Pl. 68). Their ornaments in general belong to that geometric style the pre-Han date of which was established by Andersson (*op. cit.*), while its evolutionary phases were, more recently, elucidated by Bachhofer ("Bronze Figures of the Late Chou Period," p. 323 ff.; *A Short History of Chinese Art*, p. 46 ff.).

For further comparison with the present specimen, I wish to refer in particular to a tripod with lid from Chin-ts'un 金村 near Loyang with extremely rich gold and silver incrustation that was in the possession of C. T. Loo (see Umehara, *Senkoku-shiki dōki no kenkyū*, Pl. 119; B. Karlgren, "New Studies," Pl. 59: 1).

It is generally assumed that mountings of this kind were designed for handles of halberds, dagger-axes, and the like; the shaft-hole sections decidedly point in that direction.

### (77) SHAFT-MOUNTING (*T'UN*)

In the shape of a tiger. The tiger bites into the lower rim of the socket, which slightly tapers and is almost oval in cross section. The joints of the animal — a solidly cast, magnificent, animated sculpture — are accentuated by volutes filled by fine spirals, and with nuclei set with turquoise buttons. The design of the skin consists in freely distributed, transversely hatched stripes. A chain of cowry shells is laid round the neck. The forelegs seize the lower rim of the socket, which is adorned with spirals. From under this rim come forth claws of a bird, grasping at the tiger's paws. With his hind legs, the tiger holds a smaller animal, which is lying under him, facing his body; the fragile, slender legs of the victim appear (in the side view) at the tiger's flanks and tail, the forelegs bent the hind ones straight. The skin of the small quadruped, apparently a deer, is characterized by fine short striae. Its head adjoins a *t'ao-t'ieh* mask that fills the space between the tiger's forelegs, elaborately designed and delicately executed. (The aforementioned bird claws may belong to that *t'ao-t'ieh*.) Near the opening of the socket, which has two narrow, longish rivet-holes, there is another cowry-string ornament. Smooth olive-green patina with some reddish brown and green concretions. Allegedly excavated in Hui-hsien 輝縣 (North Honan). Chou III-IV.    Pl. XXXIV.

Length 104 mm; width of socket 22:15 mm; weight 97 gr.

Animal sculptures decoratively applied to vessels, as handles, supports, or plastic adornment of covers, are often met in the Ch'un-ch'iu and Chan-kuo (Chou III-IV) periods. The artistic qualities of this piece, however, of an expressive and full-blooded realism within the limits of the style, and its perfect blending with the requirements of the tool, remain extraordinary.

Fig. 92: *The shaft-mounting no. 77.*

The cowry-motif as such, frequently used on collars of animals, also is a characteristic ornament of the Chou III-IV periods (cp. Jung Keng, *Shang Chou I Ch'i T'ung K'ao,* I, pp. 151-52); cowries on animals: Janse, "Le style du Houai" (Pl. 52:3, 55:2), Salmony, *Sino-Siberian Art* (Pls. 18:8, 31:1), also no. 82 below; cowries on

other objects, such as covers of tripods: Umehara, *Senkoku-shiki
dōki* (p. 38, Fig. 12: 1, Pl. 29); an axle-cap: *ibid.* (Pl. 110: 2). For
the questions of the distribution and meaning of the cowry as an amu-
let, charm, symbol, ornament, or money, the reader is referred to the
chapter "Aphrodite's Symbol" in J. G. Andersson's *Children of the
Yellow Earth,* and A. Salmony's paper, "The Kauri Shell in Chinese
Bronze Art."

The tiger-skin pattern recurs in a pair of tigers (?) forming the
handles of a bronze jug (*Senkoku-shiki dōki,* Pl. 78) and, particularly distinctly, on a *tsun* in animal shape dating from the Ch'un-
ch'iu period, according to Jung Keng (*Ku Kung,* vol. XV; *Shang
Chou I Ch'i T'ung K'ao,* Fig. 701).

## (*78*) FOOT-MOUNTING OF A SPEAR-SHAFT

Belonging to the spearhead no. 28. It has the form of a long, round
bronze tube tapering to the bottom, which has three radial notches.
Superb apple-green and bluish patina. Fragments of the withered
shaft have remained inside. Chou III-IV.               Pl. XXXIV.
    Length 154 mm; diameter of the aperture 25 mm.
    A similar shaft-shoe, with thickened mouth-rim and three-pointed
foot, likewise found associated with a spearhead, was on exhibition in
Detroit in 1940 (J. M. Plumer, *An Exhibition of Ancient Chinese
Ritual Bronzes,* Pl. 33: 58).

## (*79*) *KO* WITH DENTED EDGE

One of a pair, with long, slender, curved, rising blade and likewise long and slender heel. The blade has a median crest and well-
sharpened faceted edges. A fuller section of rhombic shape com-
pensates for the rigidity lost as a consequence of the slenderness of
the blade, which toward the tip slightly broadens. The downward
elongation of the edge (*hu*) has three pointed projections, likewise
sharpened. The narrow shafting-bar, jutting out below the *hu,* is
thinner than the base of the blade. The heel (*nei*), also slightly rising,
elegantly cornered and provided with a short horizontal slit, has
sharpened edges like the blade itself. Above the *nei* there is a small
slit; three longer ones below the *nei* are covered by bronze oxide.
Bright, opaque apple-green patina, with blue and bluish green concretions. Chou IV.                               Pl. XXXII.
    Length (both specimens) 312 mm; weight (a) 345, (b) 325 gr.
    This weapon is very different from the archaic *ko* types, which
were simpler, heavier, more robust, and more grave in character. As
a result of a more daring and free construction, an appearance more
impetuous, labile, acute, and swift was created. The angular relations of the whole contribute very much to that appearance. The stiff
rectangularity of the early types is avoided here. Because it rises and
has an acute-angled tip, the heel seems agile and "wagging." An impression of lability and nonrigidity even is produced by the broaden-

ing of the blade near the point. In all this, differences of style are implied, differences which suggest a section in the history of the Chinese mind.

As so often has to be admitted, it cannot yet be accurately stated when this type first appeared. During the Chan-kuo period, at any rate, it goes side by side with the common, though sometimes similarly slender *ko*, without entirely displacing broader and stouter forms.

Among the *ko* with dented lower edge the inscriptions of which furnish a vague but not to be overlooked chronological pointer, the following examples should be cited:

1) *Chou Chin Wen Ts'un*, 6/1: 26 b = *Hsiao Chiao Ching Ko*, 10: 39 b: *ko* of a Ch'en tzu X 陳子〇戈. Ch'en, a small state in East-Central Honan, ceased to exist in 479 B.C. This date can be regarded as a fairly reliable *terminus ante quem*. The rulers of that state had, according to tradition, the title of dukes, *kung*, but Chou inscriptions show so many authentic instances of titles at variance with historical records that one need not hesitate in identifying the Ch'en of the *ko* inscription with that in written history.

2) *Chou Chin Wen Ts'un*, 6/2 *pu-i*, *ko*, fol. 2a: *ko* with an inscription of six characters which recur in the same sequence in a longer inscription of another *ko* (see no. 3) of the same origin and date. It resembles the *ko* no. 79. The inscription states that it was the weapon of a king of Yen (郾=燕). Hence, a *terminus post* 323 B.C. would be given, for the prince of Yen assumed the royal title in that year (*Shih Chi*, ed. Ku Chieh-kang, I, p. 403; II, p. 204, *s.v.*, I Wang 易王 tenth year). The question again arises whether the Yen rulers had not unofficially claimed and used the royal title at an earlier date.

3) *T'ao Chai Chi Chin Hsü Lu*, 2: 21 = *Chou Chin Wen Ts'un*, 6/1: 8b: *ko* of a king of Yen, hence datable between 323 B.C. and 221 B.C., when Yen was extinguished. The name of that king has not been satisfactorily deciphered, but apparently can be identified with none of the Yen kings in the *Shih Chi*. The weapon itself is designated in that inscription by the character *k'uei* 戣, written 𢧵 (cp. the terminological remarks in the Introduction, ch. III, Dagger-Axes). This specimen diverges from no. 79 in that the blade has a broad, cornered midrib which, running between chamfers, ends in its middle, while the down-curved edge has only two spikes.

4) The type just described is seen once more in a fragment in the Lo Chen-yü Collection, bearing an inscription of King Hsi 喜王 of Yen, who reigned 254-221 B.C. (*Meng Wei Ts'ao T'ang Chi Chin T'u, chung:* 10).

5, 6) In the same collection there are another two *ko* of simpler structure, and with only one spike projecting at the point where the lower edge passes into the vertical one (*ibid., chung:* 11-12). They likewise bear the name of King Hsi of Yen and thus demonstrate that various types coexisted even within rather narrow regional boundaries.

7) *Yen K'u Chi Chin T'u Lu* (*hsia*, fol. 33, no. 46) reproduces a *ko* of a king of Yen similar to that mentioned under (4). The catalogue says that it was unearthed in 1937 at I-hsien 易縣 (Hopei), that is, in the environment of the ancient residence of the Yen princes. This *ko,* which shows what must have been the original length of the fragment (4), also dates from the years 323-221 B.C.

8) *Meng Wei Ts'ao T'ang, chung:* 4 = *Chou Chin Wen Ts'un,* 6/1 : 50 a: a *ko* which, merely on palaeographic grounds, can be ascribed to the late Chou time. It is worth mentioning because it combines with a *hu* of three spikes (as no. 79) a cornered midrib (as specimen 3 above). The build, on the other hand, is stouter and heavier than that of no. 79; it is probable that it antedates the latter.

The specimens listed above include only such material as has a direct bearing on the chronology. They all point to Chou IV, leaving open the possibility of a somewhat earlier development.

## (*80*) PICKAXE WITH PLASTIC DECORATION

Pointed blade with crest and sharply faceted edges on an oval socket. The socket is crowned by a plastic group of animals, jutting out widely to the rear. Bronze, with glossy blackish green patina.

The configuration shows a *tiger* or feline beast of prey turned toward the blade into which it bites, and grasping a bird of prey with its paws. The body of the beast, energetically bending and rearing, forms a mighty curve, rhythmically continued by the tail. A wing-volute connects the neck and the back. A smaller volute props the tail against the hind leg. Spiral patterns in fine lineament cover the body of the tiger, accentuating the joints. The *bird,* with the wings opened out and the claws stretched forward as if about to alight, is turned in the opposite direction. Its head and neck, craning, spring forth horizontally from the socket, which is covered on top by the bird-figure. Its wings expand to the median of the blade, their tips adjoining the feline's lower jaw. With the exception of the freely projecting head, which is sculptured in the round, the bird is executed in finely chased relief. The whole group is a highly artistic creation: the two animal bodies form structural parts of the weapon and at the same time are transformed into ornaments with beautiful rhythmic outlines.

The lower part of the socket is strengthened by two slightly convex zones. There is an irregularly formed rivet-hole between these zones on either side. The aperture of the socket has a width of ca. 20: 13 mm. Allegedly found in the region of Yü-lin-fu 榆林府 (Shensi). Chou III.                                                                      Pl. XXXIII.

Length 163 mm; weight 210 gr.

A counterpart of this excellently preserved state axe which, as a weapon, comes close to socketed *ko* types (as no. 70 above), is in the Stoclet Collection, Brussels (O. Kümmel, *Jörg Trübner zum Ge-*

*dächtnis,* Pl. 34). In some details it differs from our specimen: the blade is thicker and rhombic in section; the socket is shorter; the curve of the lower edge is almost symmetrically balanced by the bird's neck, which projects less abruptly than it does here; the chased ornaments, too, slightly diverge. But, on the whole, the pieces appear to be contemporaneous.

Kümmel characterized that weapon as follows: "Die prächtige Ausführung des 'Papageienschnabels,' wie die entsprechende Waffe bei uns hiess, steht praktischer Verwendbarkeit keinesfalls im Wege. Im Gegenteil gibt die Ausgleichung des Klingengewichts durch die plastische Gruppe der Waffe eher eine grössere Handlichkeit und Wirkung. Sie wird also schwerlich eine rein zeremoniale Bestimmung gehabt haben" (*ibid.*).

Another kindred specimen, in the David-Weill Collection, Paris, was published by O. Janse ("Le style du Houai et ses affinités," Pl. 51:4). The blade, again of divergent form, has broad edges that enclose a plait pattern running parallel to them. The animal group is ornamental to a lesser degree; it was not as completely subject to rhythmic, ornamental shaping as was the one above described. The tiger of the pickaxe no. 80 appears as a concinnate, somewhat abstract composition of curves rather than an animal sculpture, whereas that of the David-Weill axe is simpler, and in a way more natural. Instead of the winged volute at the neck, a cornered straight block occupies the same place in the David-Weill piece, which is evidently more primitive also with regard to this detail. The socket is in open-work and, as in the Stoclet specimen, rather short.

A further representative of the group is the following item, no. 81. The question of the typological sequence and the age of all of these pieces will be treated under no. 82.

### (*81*) PICKAXE WITH PLASTIC DECORATION

Strongly corroded bronze, covered, with the exception of a few spots, by an exuberant bright green patina. Stout short blade of rhombic section on an oval socket, which is slightly disfigured. Above the socket a plastic animal group, widely jutting out to the rear. A roll with oblique striae goes round the socket above the rim. There is no rivet-hole.

As in the foregoing axe, the upper half of the blade is engaged and continued by a feline beast cast in the round. It only roughly corresponds to the tiger on the axe no. 80, whereas the grouping and composition entirely do so. The lower half of the blade, in a curve that partly coincides with a bird's wings, meets the top of the socket. The upper part of the socket again is occupied by, or rather is identical with, the body of a large bird. Its head and neck freely project rearward. The patina makes it impossible to trace ornaments on the bellies of the two animals. Differing from the preceding one, the "tiger's" head markedly interrupts the silhouette, and the horizontal bridge behind the tiger's neck takes up the horizontal edge of the blade. Something like a goatee hangs down from the lower jaw of the beast. Here the bird's wing does not point upward, but is bent down to the lower edge of the blade. The design of the plumage likewise is different.

At both sides of the median crest, the blade is decorated with gold-foil spiral patterns; the gold apparently was hammered into undercut shallow fossae and then rubbed smooth. Allegedly found in the region of Hui-hsien (North Honan). Chou III.    Pl. XXXIII.

Length 152 mm; width of the socket 19 : 13 mm; weight 160 gr.

As regards the blade with the horizontal bridge at the tiger's neck, and the lowered circle of the tail, the present specimen approaches the Stoclet axe (mentioned under no. 80); this also holds true for the socket. The "goatee" is an element found alike in the David-Weill piece (*v.s.* no. 80), though the form is at variance with the present one.

The district of Hui-hsien (Wei-hui-fu 衞輝府), whence also the beautiful *ko* handle in tiger shape (no. 77 above) is said to have come, is an archaeologically known area. Time and again objects turn up in the Peking market which are said to have been excavated there and stylistically belong to the later Chou III or early Chou IV periods. Ku-wei-ts'un 固圍村, famous for the lacquered beams and archaic lacquer fragments found there, is situated in just that district. (For Hui-hsien finds, cp. O. Karlbeck, "A Honan Grave Find"; J. G. Andersson, "The Goldsmith in Ancient China," p. 18 ff.; Umehara, *Senkoku-shiki dōki,* p. 69 f. and Pl. 124; *Kokka* 500; *Shū Kan ihō,* Pls. 7, 8; W. P. Yetts, *The Cull Chinese Bronzes,* no. 12; M. Loehr, "Clay Figurines and Facsimiles," *Monumenta Serica,* XI, 1946.)

For the date, see remarks under no. 82 below.

*(82)* PICKAXE WITH PLASTIC DECORATION

Short strong blade with down-curved lower edge; the broad edges are set off sharply from the middle field, which is convex. Obtuse point; the edges are faceted but not sharpened. Oval socket, tapering toward the top and ending at the middle of the blade. Adjoining the upper part of the blade, projecting to the rear, and drawing down at the neck of the socket, there is an elaborate plastic configuration of intricately intertwined animals. The lower part of the socket is strengthened by two fillets and is pierced by squarish rivet-holes between them. A plaited ribbon girds the upper part. The rim is irregular and uneven, probably due to a break that would also account for the shortness of the socket. The surface — that of an old excavation — shows steel-gray and melon-green tones; it is coated by gray-green and dark green verdigris at the edges and on the animal group, and by some malachite concretion at the socket.

The animal group again consists of a quadruped with sharp-pointed claws and a bird, but here the bird holds a snake in its beak. The head of the beast cuts into the upper edge of the blade. A cowry collar lies around its neck, whence an S-shaped volute proceeds to the snakelike, meander-covered body. The shoulders are marked by double volutes. The foreleg enters the middle field of the blade, touching a round boss with a shallow cavity — setting, presumably, for a turquoise or malachite disk that has been lost; the elbow overlaps the plait pattern on the socket. The horizontal section of the body above the socket is hollow; it constitutes the roof of the socket. In softened right angles, bearing winged volutes, the beast's body winds back and, after branching off an upcurved projection, downward to the joint of the hind paw. This paw, again occupied by volutes, is groping upward and touches a broad band which overlaps the body; obliquely striated (as plumage often is), this band issues from the socket, but there its design resembles a snake's skin.

The bird is sitting, head downmost, on the back of the socket. The organic parts where the bird meets the body of the dragon-like quadruped just described are strangely indistinct. It is not impossible that such obscurity, or an appearance of transmutation, was brought about deliberately. It almost seems as if the dragon's body were transformed into or continued in that of the bird, mainly because the dragon's tail is nowhere discernible. On the other hand, the minutely chased feathers of the wings are quite clear, as are also the scaly feathers at the breast and neck of the bird, the head of which has large round bulbous eyes surrounded by a granulated ring.

The snake is seized by the bird behind the head, which is raised. It is gripped a second time by the beak of the bird near the coiled-up tail. Except for a smooth median stripe, the snake's body is finely granulated all over.

A hook connecting bird and socket in the height of the plaited band is treated as the plumage; so is a prop between the bird's neck and the lowermost part of the dragon: whether it represents the tip of the wings or another winged volute of the dragon is not clear.

On the middle field of the blade appears, on both sides, an incised inscription (Fig. 93). First quarter of the fifth century B.C.

Pl. XXXIII.

Length 150 mm; weight 268 gr.; width of socket 20: 15 mm.

The inscription of this weapon, the provenance of which unfortunately is not known, affords a fairly reliable clue for its absolute age. The inscription reads: *Han Wang Shih Ch'u tso wei yüan yung* 邗王是楚作爲元用 "Shih Ch'u, King of Han; made for supreme use."

*Han* is the name of a place which was walled in 486 B.C. by King Fu-ch'ai of Wu 吳王夫差 in order to make it a stronghold on the then newly constructed canal linking the Yangtse and Huai rivers (*Tso Chuan, Ai Kung,* 9th year; Legge, *Chinese Classics,* V, 818-19). That that city — the modern Yang-chou 揚州 in Kiangsu — belonged to the territory of Wu is attested by the *Shuo Wen* (VI, *hsia, s.v.* 邢). The reading *han* (instead of *kan*) is after Juan Yüan (*Tso Chuan Chiao K'an Chi; Shih San Ching Chu Su*, 58:9a).

*Wang,* "king," is the pretentious title of the lord and commander of Han, presumably a prince from the House of Wu, which was extinguished by Yüeh 越 in 473 B.C. (*Shih Chi,* 31; Chavannes, *Mém. hist.,* IV, p. 32).

*Shih Ch'u* must be the name of that petty sovereign. It sounds peculiar and foreign, but no other reading seems possible. The glyph *shih* 是 is clear, while *ch'u* 楚 deviates from its usual forms in Chou epigraphy. One might think of deciphering it as *mao* 楙, but there is no satisfactory parallel to support this reading either. (Cf. *Ku Chou P'ien,* 86:36 b ff. for 是; 86:37 b ff. for 楚.) The name is not recorded, and therefore has particular historical interest.

*Yüan yung* is a formula more often seen in Chou weapon inscriptions, and nearly always in connection with princely names. For instance:

1) . . . 作宮行元用; *ko* of a prince of Liang 梁 (*Ch'i Ku Shih,* 10:25 b f., with the interpretation 元用＝大用 "first use means grand use"; *Ferguson Catalogue,* p. 998).

2) . . . 作造公族元用 . . . ; *ko* of a prince of Ch'in 秦 (*Ch'i Ku Shih,* 10:28b; *Ferguson Catalogue,* p. 998).

3) . . . 作造公族元用 . . . ; spearhead of a prince of Ch'in with same inscription as (2). (*Cheng Sung T'ang Chi Ku I Wen,* 12:17 a; *Ferguson Catalogue,* p. 1019).

4) . . . 作元劍寶用之; sword of a duke of X (*Cheng Sung T'ang Chi Ku I Wen,* 12:19 a; *Ferguson Catalogue,* p. 1031).

5) . . . 爲用元劍; sword of a duke of X (*Cheng Sung T'ang Chi Ku I Wen,* 12:19 b; *Ferguson Catalogue,* pp. 1032-33).

6) . . . 自作其元用; sword of a king of Wu (*Liang Chou Chin Wen Tz'u Ta Hsi T'u Lu,* 155 a, *K'ao Shih,* 154 b; *Ferguson Catalogue,* pp. 1031-32). Kuo Mo-jo advocates the interpretation *yung* 用 ＝ *ch'i,* 器 "implement/tool," which, however, is contradicted by the examples (4) and (5), and struggles with the exhortative character of the present phrase.

7) . . . 作爲元用; sword in the Freer Gallery (*Cheng Sung T'ang Chi Ku I Wen,* 12:20; *Liang Chou Chin Wen Tz'u Ta Hsi T'u Lu,* 279, *K'ao Shih,* 240 a ff.; *Ferguson Catalogue,* p. 1034; O. Kümmel, *Jörg Trübner zum Gedächtnis,* Pl. 35, p. 70; *Freer Catalogue,* Pl. 50, no. 29.19).

Kümmel translated the passage thus: "Gefertigt zu gutem Gebrauch." Wenley's translation in the *Freer Gallery Catalogue* runs: "Made for righteous use." A counterpart of the Freer Gallery sword, with identical inscription, was among the objects of the Li-yü 李峪 (Shensi) find acquired by the Louvre (G. Salles, "Les Bronzes de Li-yu," Pl. 44 c). Kümmel's translation, apparently done without the help of the readings in Chinese epigraphical works, can be maintained for the passage in question, although "good" may have to be modified.

Fig. 93: *Inscription on the pickaxe no. 82.*

The examples show that *yung* 用 was also used as a verb "to use" (4, 5, 6). Thus, the corresponding noun "use" is valid in the other cases, and it is not necessary to replace it by *ch'i* 器, "implement." *Yüan* is more difficult. Twice it is used as an adjective with "sword" (4, 5); as for the rest, it is either adjective or adverb referring to "use"—"to use." A literal translation of "original" does not agree with the probable meaning of an adjective used with "sword," nor is it very convincing in connection with "use." Liu Hsin-yüan's interpretation would demand renderings such as "big sword" or "grand sword"— defensible, but unsatisfactory. However, *yüan* can be taken also in the sense of *shan* 善 "able, fit, good" (as repeatedly in *Kuo Yü, XIX: Wu Yü*), and further in the sense of "highest, supreme" (*Kuang Ya, Shih Ku, shang,* second series), which would well fit a princely weapon.

In the Cull Collection there is a vessel of the *hu* 壺 type with a décor of the same style as in the present pickaxe no. 82 (Yetts, *The Cull Chinese Bronzes,* no. 12; Jung Keng, *Shang Chou I Ch'i T'ung K'ao,* I, 442; II, Pl. 393, no. 743). The vessel bears an inscription that refers to a meeting of several feudal lords at Huang-ch'ih 黃池, and also names a king of Han. Possibly it is the same king of Han who owned axe no. 82. Unlike the axe with its short inscription, the Cull vase does not bear the king's name. It was possible, therefore, to surmise that the Han king mentioned in the vase inscription was identical with Fu-ch'ai, king of Wu, because he not only legally held the royal title, but also was overlord of Han. The probability of that identification, considered by Professor Yetts, dwindles, however, in consequence of the name Shih Ch'u inscribed on the axe.

The aforesaid meeting at Huang-ch'ih took place in 482 B.C. on invitation of King Fu-ch'ai (cf. Chavannes, *Mém. hist.,* IV, p. 30). Thus the Cull vase inscription — likewise incised and palaeographically closely related with that on the weapon — reaffirms both localization and age of this pickaxe, which must have been cast between 486 (construction of the canal; fortification of the city of Han) and 473 (end of the state of Wu). Even allowing for smaller shiftings, the fact remains that with this axe one gains an important chronological clue.

The question of the relative age of the three *ko*-axes, nos. 80, 81, 82, is still to be answered. It is not difficult to recognize as derivative the highly intricate configuration of specimen no. 82, in which beast and bird and snake are interwoven in the almost actionless ensemble of a kind of decorative openwork plaque. As to nos. 80 and 81, there is more simplicity. The group of animal and bird is thematically distinct; the figures do not coalesce; accessories such as plastic volutes, projections, and connecting pieces are sparingly used. The fact that these simpler formations do not comprise the theme of the complicated one (spatial relations; lineament; the snake) makes it evident that they were not developed by reduction or simplification of the latter. The decoration of axes nos. 80 and 81 is comparatively more primitive and thus older than that of no. 82. Hence, they will have to be assigned to the latter half or the last quarter of the sixth century B.C.

It must not be overlooked that the animal composition of the axe no. 82 has not directly been evolved from either no. 80 or 81. Rather the existence of interstages should be assumed. And in fact, there is at least one specimen to exemplify such an interstage: a second *ko*-axe in the David-Weill Collection (Janse, "Le Style du Houai et ses affinités," Pl. 51 : 3; *Shina Kodō Seika,* VII : 100 B; Sirén, *A History of Early Chinese Art,* I, Pl. XCV : B). Blade and socket are very similar to those of no. 82. Another resemblance is given in that the head and neck of the dragon-like beast fuse with the upper part of the blade. But for the rest, the animal group is shaped differently from all types adduced before. The beast forms a steep S-curve, and its hind legs rest upon the top of the socket; the bird-figure is here juxtaposed to the beast; it horizontally juts out far to the rear, clutching a snake in its beak. The threefold configuration of dragon, bird, and snake has here taken the place of the older one, the "combat between beast and bird," which has been abandoned, while the vertical arrangement of the bird-figure has not yet been perfected. The specimen thus evidently stands between such types as nos. 80 and 81 on the one hand, and 82 on the other. Janse also regarded it as stylistically earlier than the variant, cited above (under no. 80), in the same collection (Janse, *op. cit.,* p. 163). The absolute date of this *ko*-axe, therefore, will be "around 500 B.C."

Now, one can differentiate further within the earlier group of these state axes. The configuration of no. 80 — strongly ornamentalized and of studied rhythm — indubitably is later than those of no. 81 and the first David-Weill specimen (Janse, *op. cit.,* Pl. 51:4), both being less filed and a little more primitive.

For the sake of clarity, tentative dates are proposed hereunder for all the specimens described or referred to under nos. 80-82, the relative order of which is submitted without reservation:

| | | | |
|---|---|---|---|
| 1) | David-Weill I | =(Janse, *op. cit.,* Pl. 51:4) | Ca. 550-525 B.C. |
| 2) | Jannings I | =(no. 81) | Slightly later than 1 |
| 3) | Stoclet | =(Kümmel, *op. cit.*) | Ca. 525-500 B.C. |
| 4) | Jannings II | =(no. 80) | Ca. 525-500 B.C. |
| 5) | David-Weill II | =(Janse, *op. cit.,* Pl. 51:3) | Ca. 500 B.C. |
| 6) | Jannings III | =(no. 82) | Between 486 and 473 B.C. |

The order suggested above, though based only on the formal changes of the decoration, proves to be valid also with regard to the types themselves. The first four specimens have relatively long blades of varying profiles, with slightly broadened bases and, prevailingly, short sockets; the latter two have short blades of rhombic section, while the lower edges are elongated downward, necessitating correspondingly longer sockets.

### (83) POLE-TOP

Shaped as a horned animal-head on top of a round, slightly tapering socket. Identical on both sides, the faces are incised, quite unplastically, on the pattern of *t'ao-t'ieh* masks. Incisions at the steeply rising, pointed horns mark scales and, at their base, pairs of volutes symmetrically bent inward. Below the head is a set of telescoped triangles; the base of the outer one is broken up and rolled inward in spirals. The thickened zone at the rim bears a sunken glyph (Fig. 94). Beautiful light gray-green and turquoise-colored patina, thin enough to let the bronze color gleam through. Shang.   Pl. XLIV.

Height 133 mm; weight 183 gr.

Whether this object was a weapon or, what seems to be more likely, a pole-top or standard finial, is not known; nor is the name of the object known. A similar piece with plastic animal-head and shorter horns figures in *Yeh Chung P'ien Yü,* III (*hsia,* 20), where it is called *hsi-shou kan* 犧首干 "*kan* (shaped as) head of a sacrificial animal." The term *kan* is evidently chosen for the resemblance to the horns of the top part of the ancient character *kan;* but through having a cross as its lower part that character differs too widely in appearance to be taken as a drawing of the present type. *Kan,* moreover, means "shield," which does not tally either.

Another specimen, more slender and with long plain horns and no animal-head, is contained in *Shan Chai Chi Chin Lu* (10:54) under the designation *shuang-feng mao* 鋒矛 "double-pointed spearhead." This is a merely interpretive designation without any philological basis.

A third specimen of comparably archaic appearance, showing a head with ears and stout horns on a very short socket, said to have come from Anyang, is in the Hellström Collection, Mölndal ("The Exhibition, Stockholm"; *BMFEA,* 6, Pl. 5:3: "possibly the bronze point of a staff, in the shape of an ox's head").

Both designs, with animal-head and without, occur together among the Shang finds published by W. C. White (*Illus. London News,* April 20, 1935, Fig. 19, p. 641). There need be hardly any doubt, therefore, that all these specimens belong in the Shang period.

The pictogram which is encountered, though not frequently, on early weapons as well as offering vessels, has not hitherto been satisfactorily interpreted. Takada reads *lü* 旅 "troops," "500 men," taking the middle part — generally read *tan* 單 — as a shortened form of the character *tan* 犉, which again has to be regarded as a substitute (cp. *Ku Chou P'ien,* 27: 15-23; 27: 4 a ff.; 24: 39 b ff.). Takada's equation is not only somewhat forced but appears to be wrong, for the character *lü* 旅 is associated with the glyph in question in one early Chou inscription, where this glyph has the sense of a name (see *Shih Erh Chia Chi Chin T'u Lu,* II, *Ching* 鏡, fol. 2a). It is conclusive, therefore, that the glyph in Fig. 94 cannot be identified with *lü* 旅. No readings are offered in Jung Keng's *Chin Wen Pien* (*fu-lu, shang* 7a) or Nakashima's *Shoki Engen* (II, *shang* 1b).

Fig. 94: *Inscription on the pole-top no. 83.*

### (*84*) FOOT MOUNTING IN THE SHAPE OF A CLAW

Of whitish green oxidized bronze. Round socket, widening a little toward the aperture, with two holes. The claws are solidly cast, approximately four-cornered, and — whence their organic appearance — slightly thickened at the joints. The three long prongs are so placed that the points mark an isosceles triangle. A short, hooked clutch and a spur complete the picture of the claw of a bird of prey. A somewhat scoured sunken inscription is on the right side of the socket (Fig. 95). Probably Shang.                Pl. XXXIV.

Height 126 mm; diameter of socket 22 mm; weight 275 gr.

This hitherto unique heavy shaft-shoe type certainly did not belong to any common kind of weapon; but attached to a long shaft, even one carrying a banner or ensign, it would ensure fast hold in the ground. The form, on the other hand, recalls pictograms of axes with a three-pronged shaft-foot.

The character inscribed most probably reads *kung* 龏 (龔), as a variant form not hitherto traceable in epigraphy (cf. *Ku Chou P'ien,* 98: 34 b ff. for *lung* 龍; 57: 23 ff. for *kung* 龔).

Fig. 95: *Inscription on the foot-mounting no. 84.*

(85) BRONZE TANGED DAGGER

Double-edged, apparently not sharpened. Blade of rhombic section with tang and two rivet-holes in the tang. The heel of the blade is flanged and provided with a horizontal stop-ridge, a device for letting in and securing hold of the plates of the hilt, which have perished. Below the flanges, the blade broadens a little, then tapers off to the point. At the broad zone, identical on both sides, a human face in flat relief appears in a sunken field. Geometrically simplified, adapted to the blade outline, this face with its pointed ears and a narrowing chin, round-eyed, with strangely broad nose surrounded by a clumsy grooved contour, and with a vaguely cut mouth is — in spite of its primitively signlike inexpressiveness — not an artless product. It is the apprehension of the human face that is primitive, not the design as such. Below the face, the blade is decorated by double rows of scales, diminishing in size as they near the tip. In contrast to the dull verdigris at the heel, the blade itself shows a silvery hue with minor traces of oxidation; it looks as though it had been tinned. It was allegedly discovered at Hsün-hsien 濬縣 (North Honan). Chou I (?)      Pl. XXXV.

Length 217 mm; weight 155 gr.

This remarkable dagger type, which is not found in any collection previously published, can here by coincidence be presented in a variant (no. 86 below).

The dagger is by no means a current, let alone characteristic, weapon of the Early Chinese Bronze Age, nor did it later become so. Daggers hitherto known mostly originate from the northern regions where nomadic vestiges, derived from or traceable to Siberia, are common. The specimen here described, however, by virtue of the scale motif rather than by the unwarranted statement about its provenance, can safely be localized in China proper. (The motif was referred to under nos. 7 and 10 above).

A specimen such as the present one, typologically isolated and bearing an unusual décor, is not easily placed. For the most conspicuous stylistic element, the human face, is a rare subject in an art where images of animals and abstract ornaments reign, where, in other words, parallels are rare. Already in late Shang times quite realistic heads did exist (a pendant with plastic face found in Grave 1400 at Hou-chia-chuang; Umehara, "Hou-chia-chuang," I, p. 34, Fig. 6), which have counterparts from the Early Chou (a full-round bronze head from Hsün-hsien Hsin-ts'un, Grave 21; cp. Kuo Pao-chün, "Hsün-hsien Hsin-ts'un," Pl. 6: 3). One may add two small jade statuettes of a man with high headdress and a woman — the only Chinese parallel so far to the naked goddesses of Hither Asia and the Aegean — which perhaps date from Shang times (Winthrop Collection; Umehara, *ibid.*, II, Pl. 11). But in none of these examples has the simplification gone as far as with the face on the dagger. More closely related are the demon-face on the large bronze drum in

Fig. 96: *Ornamental head on the dagger no. 85.*

the Sumitomo Collection (*Senoku Seishō* III: 130), which is not later than Chou I, and a bronze plaque with human face in relief in the Museum of Far Eastern Antiquities at Stockholm (*London Exhibition Catalogue,* no. 193). Both display separation of constituent parts, the round eyes, the broad nose, the suppression of other details, peculiarities which are characteristic also for the face on the dagger no. 85. The *London Exhibition Catalogue* ascribed too late a date, I think, to the head in Stockholm (*viz.,* ca. 722-481 B.C.). The dagger, partly on account of the "scale" décor, and partly in consideration of the Sumitomo drum, cannot be dated later than Chou I.

The same date, by the way, was ascribed by Salmony to a jade statuette and a jade head also reminiscent of that on the dagger (A. Salmony, *Carved Jade,* Pls. 21:9, 20:6). "Shang or Early Chou," too, is the date considered for the extraordinary vessel with a cover shaped as a human face with horns in the Freer Gallery (*Freer Catalogue,* Pl. 13), a face strongly reminiscent of that on the dagger.

In connection with the question of age, I should like to point also to the coloring of the metal, its silvery surface. This silver tone is found in two other weapons in this collection, nos. 26 and 106, which belong to Chou I at the latest.

The following specimen of the same type (no. 86) gives the impression of being later; but, though somewhat divergent and less refined a product, it cannot for typological reason be separated from the present one. Apart from the kindred décor, it is the peculiar structure of the hilt that unites them and at the same time makes them appear strangers: the structure recalls Luristan dagger types from the late IInd millennium B.C. (cp. A. U. Pope, *A Survey of Persian Art,* Pls. 54 C, 55 A, B, the latter two pieces datable between 1123 and 1113 B.C., according to S. Langdon, *ibid.,* pp. 283-84).

## (*86*) BRONZE TANGED DAGGER

Similar to the foregoing, with softly crested blade and two loops at the base. The tang, which here is longer and perforated by three rivet-holes, likewise has short lateral flanges and a horizontal stop-ridge to frame the plates of the handle. Near the base of the blade again appears, on both sides, a human face in sunken lines, without framing contour. It differs from that on the first dagger by a less accurate make, and in some details such as rounded ears, a less broad nose, eyebrows, and long hair. Artificially heightened patina in light green tones, with crusts of a darker verdigris. Right across the face there is a break in the blade. Chou I-II(?). Pl. XXXV.

Length 252 mm; weight 185 gr.

Fig. 97: *Ornamental head on the dagger no. 86.*

## (*87*) SHORT SWORD

Bronze, with a gray-green dull patina; old excavation. The ogival blade of approximately rhombic section is strengthened by a median ridge, angular at the heel, more rounded toward the point. The tang

Fig. 98: *Ornaments on the sword no. 87.*

Fig. 99: *Ornaments on the sword no. 87.*

is solid and oval in section. Blunt, scarred edges that were once sharpened run almost parallel in the upper half, then, after a slight narrowing, converge. On both sides, near the base, there are somewhat shapeless sunken ornaments or signs: two figures with raised arms and two signs resembling spade-money on the one side; reptiles, seemingly, on the other. Chou IV(?). Pl. XXXV.

Length 330 mm; weight 230 gr.

The ornaments are utterly primitive. They are so devoid of the qualities usually found — rhythm, accuracy, clarity, symmetry — that one feels tempted to localize this sword outside of China proper. In Chinese weapons, decoration, lavish though it be, unvaryingly is subject to structure, shape, and articulation of the whole. Here it is not. The two figures (Fig. 98) neither correspond to each other, nor do they respect the given space. Instead of an orderly, organic, and well-balanced treatment, there is a tormenting obtuseness here. The same can be said about the ornaments on the obverse side (Fig. 99). It is a formal *niveau* incompatible with that generally found in Chinese weapons.

One perhaps might think of Southern provenance. There exists some tolerably comparable material from Indo-China: a spearhead with decorated blade, and a particular subtype of the Chinese *ko* from the Dong-son Period (Musée Louis Finot, Hanoi; see K. Shiratori *et al., Kodai Shina oyobi Indo,* pp. 258, 264).

However, short blades of this type, with solid tang (to be supplemented by a hilt or cord windings, and a pommel), were widespread in China proper, and were in use — apparently for a considerable time — alongside the more representative types with hilt cast in one piece with the blade.

So far, no excavation throws light on the beginnings of the various models. Only a few and late, i.e. Han time, tanged swords were unearthed by trained excavators in Southern Manchuria: one specimen from a grave washed bare by the Kuan-t'un-tzu River 官屯子河 near Mu-yang-ch'eng 牧羊城 below Mount Lao-t'ieh 老鐵山 on the Liaotung Peninsula (cp. "Mu-yang-ch'eng," *Archaeologia Orientalis,* II, Figs. 29, 30, Pls. 42, 43). Another two, from the vicinity of that grave, have faithful counterparts from China (*ibid.,* Fig. 31) and Korea (Sekino *et al., Rakurō-gun jidai no iseki,* II, Pl. 180: 841-44). These specimens have stout midribs and strongly curved edges, their heels being either slanting or rounded. They are of import only insofar as they prove the occurrence in China and the Chinese borderlands of short tanged swords around the beginning of the Han dynasty at the latest. It is a lower limit — near the time when iron blades began to be generally favored, and it says nothing about the advent of the bronze types.

In his "Notes sur quelques épées anciennes trouvées en Chine," O. Janse published a series of swords of this type originating from North- and Central-China, and kept in Swedish collections. In this first systematic investigation of Chinese swords from Bronze and

Early Iron ages — contributing much to a knowledge of typology and geographic distribution — swords with flat or rounded tang are grouped under category D. Within this category, Janse again differentiates:

D    I:   mostly long blades of rhombic section, without rib, the heel being rectangular;

D   II:   mostly short blades with rib and rounded or tectiform heel;

D III:   transitional types between D I and D II.

Accordingly, our specimen would fall under group D III, but there is no true counterpart among Janse's material, which hails from Honan, Shansi, and, more frequently, Anhui provinces. A further group,

D IV,   corresponds exactly to the next specimen, no. 88.

As to the date of his groups D I-III, Janse supposes that those types had arrived in both China and Europe or, more exactly, Western Europe, at about the same time. Cart burials from the fifth century B.C. in eastern France, he argues, the build and inventory of which reveal indubitably Scythian features, have tanged swords, and in China, tanged swords were found together with cart fittings which should be assigned to the fifth to third centuries B.C.; in China, too, Scythians or kindred tribes were to be regarded as having brought these swords ("Epées anciennes," pp. 97-99).

Janse does not specify the kind of Chinese cart fittings, or how they actually are associated with the swords. The opinion that it was the Scythians who had brought the sword to China was widely accepted until recently (cf. M. Loehr, "The Earliest Chinese Swords and the Akinakes"). Regarding the time, Janse justly goes far beyond Rostovtzeff, who held that the long sword was transmitted to China only by the Sarmatians, that is, from the third century B.C. onwards (M. Rostovtzeff, *Iranians and Greeks in South Russia,* pp. 129, 204). Janse's "fifth century," on the other hand, is of somewhat casual character: the Hsin-cheng Tomb   新鄭, Honan) cannot (with C. W. Bishop) be dated between 400 and 250 B.C. ("The Bronzes of Hsin-cheng Hsien"), for an inscribed bronze pan from that tomb mentions the name of Ying-tz'u 嬰次, prince of Cheng, who was put to death in 680 B.C. (Kuo Mo-jo, *Liang Chou Chin Wen Tz'u Ta Hsi K'ao Shih,* fol. 182 f.; Jung Keng, *Shang Chou I Ch'i T'ung K'ao,* pp. 370-71; see also the Introduction, ch. III, Dagger-Axes, note 45).

Thus, the bulk of the Hsin-cheng find — containing only a few weapons and not a single sword — most probably belongs to the time before 680 B.C. But that find neither serves to prove Chinese and European cart burials to be contemporary, nor to ascertain the age of any sword type. That tanged types (Janse D I-III) did exist as early as hilted ones or any other type whose age can be established for one reason or other, is a hypothesis, and that hypothesis is supported only by the fact that hilted swords of established higher age (than Han) have similar blade forms.

There are, however, some epigraphical testimonies, not taken into account by Janse, namely, short swords of the present category with pre-Han inscriptions. They are reproduced in Lo Chen-yü's *San Tai Chi Chin Wen Ts'un,* and may briefly be reviewed:

1) A specimen of category D III, with rectangular heel and strong midrib, bearing a late Chou inscription (20: 44a).

2) Four specimens of category D III or D I, apparently with convex blades and broad facets, all inscribed by King Hsi of Yen 郾王喜, who reigned 254-221 B.C.; cp. examples under no. 79 above (*op. cit.,* 20: 44 b-45 a).

3) One specimen of category D III or D I, similar to the foregoing types, with an inscription from the Ch'in period (?), and one specimen with broad-based tang — thus nearing category D-IV — with identical inscription (*op. cit.,* 20: 46 b).

These inscribed pieces remove any doubt as to whether the present type (no. 87) is of pre-Han age. Important is the fact that the blades of all of them are closely allied with earlier Chou types: slender, rather parallel-edged blades, in clear contrast to the blades generally shown by the aforesaid Han finds from Korea, South-Manchuria, and China: broad, with stout ridge, and of La Tène-like outline, vigorously curved or flamboyant.

Specimen no. 87 cannot safely be linked with any of the typological parallels presently known. This fact may be taken as a further argument that it originated outside the Chinese centers.

### (88) SHORT SWORD

The slender, leaf-shaped, scarred, two-edged blade is strengthened by a rounded midrib running through to the end of the tang. The tang widens gradually toward the butt of the blade. It has one rivet-hole at the margin, broken open at the outer rim. On either side of the blade, in the upper half, there are four small transverse ribs obliquely placed between median and right edge. Above the uppermost of these transverse ribs appear, also on both sides, a tiger-figure in flat relief and a sunken glyph; the tiger's head is turned toward the point, and lozenges mark the design of his skin (Fig. 100). On the heel of the blade, two further roughly scratched characters are recognizable. Covered by patina, they evidently are also of an early date, although presumably not original. Excavated long ago, the piece has a shiny dark green patina coated by some concretions. Found in Ssechuan. Chou III.                                                     Pl. XXXV.

Length 338 mm; weight 220 gr.

This sword formerly was in the collection of Professor Yü Hsing-wu, Peking, who published it in his *Shuang Chien I Chi Chin T'u Lu* (*hsia,* fol. 35) under the designation "Tiger Sword." His description runs as follows:

"The blade on both faces shows the figure of a tiger. The inscription has the character *p'ing* 平 on one side, the character *chü* 且 on

Fig. 100: *Décor of the sword no. 88.*

the other (of the median rib). One might take *Chü-p'ing* as a place name, but there is no such place in Ssechuan; in Yünnan only is there a Chü-p'ing-kuan 巨平關. Judged by its shape this piece belongs to a very early period, whereas the inscription, incised in thin strokes, may be ascribed to the late Chou time" (*ibid., hsia,* text fol. 8 a-b). The statement about the provenance from Ssechuan is given also.

Interesting and hardly questionable is the early date proposed. This vague "early" possibly can be made somewhat more exact by the style of the tiger figure. Compared with the tiger of the shaft-mounting no. 77 from about the beginning of Chou IV, the present figure is demonstrably earlier. It lacks features typical of the Chou IV style. At the same time it possesses a trait which facilitates dating: the claws nearly form a ring. Such claws frequently occur on animals and animal-shaped vases of the Chou II–III periods, after which they disappear. Suffice it to give two examples of animal-shaped vases: a tiger *tsun* in the Freer Gallery (*Shang Chou I Ch'i T'ung K'ao,* Pl. 372, no. 700), and a *tsun* in the form of a quadruped with bird-head (*ibid.,* no. 701 = *Ku Kung,* XV, mentioned under no. 77 above with regard to the design of the skin). Jung Keng dates both these pieces in the Ch'un-ch'iu period (*ibid.,* text p. 432), but a glance shows that the tiger *tsun* is older than the other one, which must be placed rather at the end of that period. In fact, Bachhofer proposed a date no later than toward 900 B.C. for the tiger vessels in the Freer Gallery (*Freer Catalogue,* Pls. 26-27) on account of the ornaments (*A Short History of Chinese Art,* p. 56; Fig. 47). The tiger's claws are nearly closed to a ring, the fabulous animal's are no longer so. The former still retains much of the rigid and angular lineament of the Early Chou style; the latter shows a fluent and spirited silhouette, and the body appears as an organism full of inner energy, characteristic of Early Chan-kuo animal sculpture, in clear contrast to the later creations of that epoch: enfeebled, gracefully dissolved forms of unrivaled movement. Now, the small tiger-figure on the sword fits in between these two examples so that it is difficult to say whether it is more akin to the first or the second one.

Comparable tiger-figures occur also in bronze inscriptions (e.g., *San Tai Chi Chin Wen Ts'un,* 7: 1a). They are of earlier style than the tiger on the sword, but already display the tendency toward ring-shaped claws while differing in posture and head-form. Two of the items belong to a *kuei* (*Heng Hsien Chi Chin Lu,* 23) which I think is not later than late Chou II or, to be more exact, probably not later than around 800 B.C. Thus, for the tiger on sword no. 88, which must be of more recent date, one arrives at a date between the eighth and seventh centuries, that is, roughly the same age as implied by comparison with the two *tsun* mentioned before. To date the sword in the seventh century at the latest seems therefore permissible.

The glyph at the side of the tiger is passed over in silence by Yü Hsing-wu. I did not succeed in finding a parallel. Palaeographically, it is so archaic that it favors an earlier date than the one just proposed.

If a simple question of date cannot be answered otherwise than by comparison with a variety of materials other than weapons, and only vaguely datable ones at that, the reason is in the present state of research. But the importance of the absolute chronology in just the case of the sword makes it necessary to be circumstantial. It is unavoidable, therefore, to proceed a little further in the discussion and inquire the *typological* place of sword no. 88.

The type agrees with Janse's category D IV ("Epées anciennes," pp. 73-74, 89, 100-101). Janse knew, as he said, of only five specimens of this type, all preserved at Stockholm. Save that three of them were acquired at Peking, nothing is known about their provenance. As to their date, Janse was mistaken. He assigned them to an age later than that of D I-III — assumed to exist "from the 5th c. at the latest" (cp. remarks under no. 87 above)—without more valid reasons than these: a dagger in its tang resembles swords of D IV type; that dagger has an ornament which "at first glance seems to go back to Chou times but nevertheless must belong in the Han time" (*ibid.,* p. 101). The conclusion was that the type D IV was in use under the Han, and consequently is later than D I-III types. The ornament of the dagger in question (*ibid.,* Pl. xi, 7) actually is, as Janse justly felt, an Early Chou ornament; but misled by an erroneous date set forth by E. A. Voretzsch (*Altchinesische Bronzen,* Fig. 64) he regarded the dagger as late, and the whole group D IV with it. It is easy to revise this today, but since no special investigation has been made in the meantime — except for my article "The Earliest Chinese Sword and the Akinakes"— it is advisable to have the terrain cleared. The date of the present type (with flat tang) thus is quite open and demands to be established anew.

Among the "D IV" specimens published by O. Janse, the aforementioned dagger (with curved blade of 215 mm length) and one blade bereft of its tang (of 260 mm length, with an inscription that unfortunately is not reproduced: *op. cit.,* Pl. xi, 6) prove to be less closely related to the rest. As to the remaining three specimens, none shares the particular feature here to be observed of the transverse oblique ribs. Typologically akin otherwise, they have something in common that in turn is absent in no. 88: a second rivet-hole at the end of the tang (*op. cit.,* Pl. xi, 5, 8; Pl. xx, 3). One of the three swords bears a décor in flat relief with sloping outlines: an arm with the hand stretched toward the tip of the blade, and the head of a serpent likewise pointing to the tip; the serpent-head occupies the midrib, being half-framed by the arm which crosses the blade, and by the hand which is at right angle to the arm. On the reverse side, an animal figure appears, of which "it is difficult to determine the species." This sword belongs to Dr. E. Hultmark, Stockholm (*op. cit.,* p. 130; details Pl. xx, 4, 5). It further is distinguished by a significant technological feature: "La lame est ornée des deux côtés de 'taches' d'argent." As to the small animal figure of indistinct species, I dare only say that it seems to be older than Chou IV; even so, the mere presence of that figure on a lancet-shaped tanged blade links it still more closely with specimen no. 88.

Now, there is a parallel to the Hultmark sword, reproduced as a rubbing in *Chou Chin Wen Ts'un* (6/2: 108), with the same weird motif of the arm and snake-head on one side and the animal on the other. The catalogue does not give any explanation. The reproduction, though not very clear, permits one to recognize the silhouette of that animal: it is more gracefully drawn than that of the Hultmark sword, nearing the style of the Chou IV period. It can be put beside the figure of a fighting animal on a sword with hollow grip in the Hellström Collection, Mölndal (Janse, "Epées anciennes," Pl. xx, 1; details Pl. xxi; drawing: Janse, "Le style du Houai," Pl. 57 bis, 3), a sword which, with regard to the form of the blade, seems to be somewhat later than both the Hultmark specimen and its *Chou Chin Wen Ts'un* parallel.

The motif "hand and serpent-head" is represented on two further swords formerly belonging to Liu Ao 劉鶚, whose name is inseparably connected with the discovery and deciphering of the Shang oracle bones. Unfortunately, the reproductions are confined to the ornaments, leaving one in the dark as to the sword types (*Hsiao Chiao Ching Ko Chin Wen T'a Pen,* 10: 94 a). There is some probability of their belonging to the same category as Janse's D IV, since the reproductions follow immediately upon a dagger-like short "sword with dragon ornament" (*ibid.,* 93 b) under the very same denomination. A clear drawing of this latter specimen, a dagger not exceeding 234 mm in length, is contained in *Shan Chai Chi Chin Lu* (11: 3 b): the blade resembles that of the dagger with the human face (no. 85 above), while the décor — similar to that of a *ko* in the Sirén Collection (*Collection Sirén,* Pl. iii, 16) — recalls that small curved dagger which induced Janse to ascribe a late date to his category D IV. Like the curved dagger, this also tanged blade of the Shan Chai Collection cannot be later than Chou I-II, a state of things which is highly important for the chronological assessment of the whole group in question.

To return to Liu Ao's swords: their ornaments also contribute a little for chronological order. One of them bears an indistinctly drawn glyph which does not lead far. The other one exhibits again an animal figure with clearly recognizable ring-claws, in the company of a pictogram archaic to such a degree that one should not date it later than Chou I. The *Hsiao Chiao Ching Ko* refrains from deciphering it.

Finally, a parallel in *Ch'iu Ku Ching She Chin Shih T'u* (2:1) should be adduced, which is there defined as a dagger from the Hsia dynasty, *Hsia pi-shou* 夏匕首. This piece, ca. 280 mm long, has a particular trait — the two holes in the tang are pierced through the midrib, contrary to the usual removal of the lower perforation toward the edge. Presumably, this removal was an innovation which saved labor by shortening the toilsome process of drilling, and at the same time left relatively intact the rigidity of the median rib. One might well infer from that detail the "Hsia dagger's" typological priority, but even so it seems unlikely that any difference in time worth mentioning will thus be gained. The reproduction of an ornament near the heel — the text of the *Ch'iu Ku Ching She* misleadingly speaks of an unknown character — looks rather unreliable. Yet the central part of the ornament unmistakably shows an eye of a design which was entirely obsolete after Chou I-II. Likewise untrustworthy, it seems, is the rendering in outline-drawing of what appear to be comma-shaped ornaments placed obliquely between median and edge; I suppose that these "commas" in fact are to represent small slanting ribs (as in sword no. 88), inadequately and deceptively reproduced. As to the age, I do not think it permissible to go further than to say that this specimen is not later, but may be somewhat earlier, than the various swords cited above, with the exception, of course, of the two daggers (in Stockholm — Janse, "Epées anciennes," Pl. 11:7, and in *Shan Chai Chi Chin Lu,* 11:3b).

Summing up the material examined so far, one obtains the following data concerning the typological and chronological place of the short sword no. 88:

1) Dagger, *Shan Chai Chi Chin Lu* (11:3b)　　Chou I-II
Lancet-shaped blade with tang, datable according to the ornament.
2) Dagger in Stockholm (Janse, "Epées anciennes," Pl. 11:7)　　Chou I-II
Curved blade with tang, Janse's category D IV; datable according to the ornament.
3) Dagger, *Ch'iu Ku Ching She* (2:1)　　Chou II
Lancet-shaped blade with rivet-holes in the middle of the tang; tentatively dated on the basis of a detail of the ornament.

4) Ornaments of a short sword (*Hsiao Chiao    Chou II-III
      Ching Ko,* 10:94)
   Sword probably of same type as 3, 6, 7, 8;
   dated on the basis of an inscribed character
   and an animal figure; ornament: "hand and
   serpent's head."

5) Ornaments of a short sword (*ibid.*)    . . . . . . . . . . .
   Ornament: "hand and serpent's head" com-
   bined with an undecipherable glyph; not
   datable in itself.

6) Short sword, *Chou Chin Wen Ts'un* (6:    Chou III
      108)
   Ornament: "hand and serpent's head" combined with an animal figure.

7) Short sword in the Hultmark Collection    Chou III
      (Janse, Pl. 20:3)
   Ornament: "hand and serpent's head" combined with an animal figure.

8) Short sword in the Jannings Collection    Chou III
      (Cat. no. 88 — present specimen)
   Dated according to ornamentation and an
   undecipherable character.

9) Short sword in Stockholm (Janse, Pl. 11:8)    . . . . . . . . . .
   Date dependent on 3, 6, 7, 8.

10) Short sword in Stockholm (Janse, Pl. 11:5)    . . . . . . . . . .
    Date dependent on 3, 6, 7, 8. To judge from
    the form of the blade, this sword is perhaps
    somewhat later than the preceding speci-
    mens.

On the basis of ornamentation and palaeographical criteria, one
quite unquestionably arrives at a date before the middle of the Ist
millennium for sword no. 88 and the allied types; at least, to be more
exact, one is taken back to the sixth century but more probably to the
seventh, by a reckoning still rather too cautious. For the existence of
the daggers (1, 2), which can hardly be placed later than the tenth
century, reveals how early these types as such did live and that there
is no need at all to lower the dates.

The same result is attained when one comes to examine this type
simply as a type, without paying attention to ornamental accessories.
Typologically, this form is unquestionably less developed, less ma-
ture than the sword with hollow handle (as no. 100) or the sword
with ringed handle, the Chou sword par excellence (as nos. 97, 98).
This light, short, dagger-like thrusting-blade with its somewhat
vague and evidently archaic, triangular outline claims a greater age
than the crested rhomboid blades of consummate form and finest
faceting possibly could. It is highly unlikely that it should be placed
later than Janse's categories D I-III. (There are analogies of other

Early Bronze Age cultures in which the triangular dagger with tang appears first, as, for instance, in the older dolmen-graves of the Talysh, in Kish during the late IVth millennium, and in Harappa. Cf. J. de Morgan, *La Préhistoire orientale,* III, 203; V. G. Childe, *The Most Ancient East,* pp. 179 f., 206 f.). The occurrence of blades with tang or tenon (such as no. 87) toward the end of the Chou and in early Han times is not relevant to the chronological issue.

Specimens with datable inscriptions bearing on the chronological side of the matter do exist. For instance: several pieces date from the end of the Chou IV period; *San Tai Chi Chin Wen Ts'un,* ch. 20: 39 a right, 43 a, 46 b left, 47 b. For bronze types from the beginning of the Han dynasty approximately, excavated at Lo-lang, see Sekino *et al., Rakurō-gun jidai no iseki,* text Figs. 205-8 — in lance hafting. The types A, B, C (Janse) are broadly represented around the commencement of Chou IV. But there are inscribed pieces which even take one back to the late Chou III period, e.g., a hollow-handle sword attributed by Kuo Mo-jo to King Chu-fan of Wu 吳王諸樊 (*Liang Chou Chin Wen Tz'u Ta Hsi, K'ao Shih,* fol. *yu* 154b; *Ferguson Catalogue,* pp. 1031-32), who reigned 560-548 (Chavannes, *Mém. hist.,* IV, p. 6); another sword of the same type inscribed with the name of Chu-fan's youngest brother, known as the *Wu Chi-tzu chih tzu chien* 吳季子之子劍 (*Chou Chin Wen Ts'un,* 6/2: 94; *Ferguson Catalogue,* p. 1031; see the discussion under Cat. no. 93 below), datable somewhere between ca. 540-520 B.C. Chi-tzu is a name of Prince Chi-cha 季札 (Chavannes, *Mém. hist.,* IV, p. 6 ff., 21), who must have attained his majority about 560, because at that time it was insinuated to him that he succeed to the throne at the expense of Chu-fan, an offer he for moral reasons rejected. Since swords of typologically more developed design are traceable around and before 500 B.C., toward the end of Chou III, it becomes necessary to push back in the seventh century or farther (the absolute figures only mark the lower limit) the primitive tanged type no. 88.

What ornaments and typology demonstrate is corroborated, to a certain extent, also by literary tradition, which grants an early date to the sword. For literary dates and terminological questions see Introduction, ch. V, Swords.

## (*89*) DAGGER-KNIFE

With double-edged blade that is slightly curved. The handle is slit open lengthwise and crowned by a rattle. The rattle, of globular form and with four meridional openings, has a round boss with small cavity on top (that may have been set with a turquoise cabochon); it contains a small bronze ball. The handle, in the fashion of the "Sino-Siberian" knives, is hollow; it bears the simplest geometrical pattern: incised crossed lines. With two small triangles at both sides of the slightly prominent median crest, the decoration encroaches on the blade. The blade springs forth on the concave side, while being flattened on the convex side to form a small rest (*ricasso*) for the thumb. The verdigris is thicker at the rattle than at the other parts, which are largely covered by a malachite crust interspersed with reddish brown, brown-violet, and bright sea-green spots. Shang(?).    Pl. XXXVI.

Length 313 mm; weight 290 gr.

Types of daggers and knives with a rattle are not frequently seen. The following examples are published:

1) Knife, with slit handle that has two transverse junctions, the pointed blade meeting the handle at blunt angle. Port Arthur Museum (*Ryojun Hakubutsukan Zuroku,* Pl. 11:5; there dated "about Han").

2) Knife, with flat solid handle and small loop beneath the rattle; similar to specimen no. 39 with regard to the base of the blade and the cord pattern on the handle. Provenance: Anyang, 1939 (*Yen K'u Chi Chin, hsia,* fol. 49, no. 63; dated "Shang").

3) Dagger, with triangular blade and deep incisions at both sides of base; round handle decorated with angles ("Collection Sirén," *Ars Asiatica,* VII, Pl. 2:10; "influence scythe").

4) Dagger, of the foregoing type, the handle being decorated with slanting bands (Egami and Mizuno, *Inner Mongolia,* Pt. II, *Corpus II,* "Daggers": A 1; formerly in the possession of Yamanaka, Peking; "between 500-100 B.C.").

5) Dagger, with stout midrib and horizontal wings above the heel of the blade; solid handle, undecorated; a loop; the rattle covered by a flat disk (Andersson, "Hunting Magic," Pl. 5:3, "bought in Peking").

6) Dagger, with cap-pommel on a hollow handle open at one side; incisions at the heel — less deep than in 3, 4 — which is decorated with triangles as in specimen no. 89. Provenance: Monok, to the southwest of Minusinsk (G. v. Merhart, *Bronzezeit am Jenissei,* p. 59, Fig. 34). The décor is of Krasnoyarskian origin, and the dagger itself belongs to a group with handles terminated by pommels, rings, or rattles (*ibid.,* p. 55 ff.).

The ring-pommel variant of the Monok dagger type with its notched heel belongs to the inventory of that Siberian Early Bronze Age stage which is called Karasuk culture by S. A. Teploukhov, who dated it around 1000 B.C. (see above, under nos. 35, 38; for the Karasuk inventory, A. Salmony, *Sino-Siberian Art,* Pl. 3; cp. ch. VI, note 7 above). In the case of the present dagger, the Siberian touch is evident; its approximate contemporaneousness with Karasuk cannot well be questioned. Since the date of the piece is likely to be as early as Shang (see no. 2 of the above examples), the possibility arises that Karasuk was correspondingly early. The problem is more amply treated in the Introduction, ch. VI, Siberia in the Early Bronze Age.

Knives with jingles or rattles used in sacrificial rites are mentioned several times in the classics, under the designation *luan-tao* 鸞刀

(*Shih Ching,* Ode 210; Legge, *Chin. Class.,* IV, p. 376. *Li Chi,* 10: 25, 11:23, 24:18, 25:6; ed. Couvreur, I, pp. 561, 602; II, pp. 286, 326. *Kung-yang Chuan, Hsüan,* 12; *Chu Su,* ch. 16:4a). *Luan* in present form means "phoenix," but also — as a variant for 鑾 — "jingle," "bell," "bells of horse trappings." With reference to the passage in the *Book of Songs,* the commentator Mao Heng 毛享 says that *luan* 鑾 is a jingle, *ling* 鈴 (*Mao Shih Chu Su,* ch. 13/2: 13 a; cf. Karlgren's *Grammata Serica,* no. 178 f-h). There is no doubt, therefore, that this type should be identified with the *luan-tao* of the books. When K. Hamada laid claim on that name for a knife in the Sumitomo Collection (*Senoku Seishō,* 140), he was doubly mistaken: the headpiece of that knife is not the head of any bird but a conventionalized head of an elk, or an animal with antlers or horns at any rate, so that there is no possible relation to *luan* in either interpretation.

The *Shih Ching* passage, quoted in Legge's translation, runs:

> We sacrifice (first) with pure spirits,
> And then follow with a red bull;
> Offering them to our Ancestors.
> (Our lord) holds the knife with tinkling bells,
> to lay open the hair of the victim,
> And takes its flesh and fat.

Herein, the *luan-tao* presents itself as a sacerdotal tool, as it does in the *Li Chi;* it hence should fittingly be classed among ceremonial tools rather than weapons (as the knives nos. 40-42 above). But the use of this kind of knife in the ancestral cult of the Chou does not exclude the possibility that it had been a real weapon or an object of daily use in a remoter period or in other environments, such as that of a nomadic folk. The literary testimonies, moreover, evidencing the rise of this type to a ritual tool are considerably antedated by the actual specimen.

### (*90*) DAGGER

With triangle blade of rhombic section. The guard is broad, flat, roof-shaped, but with rounded outer contour. The hilt consists of a pair of round vertical bars with a thin wall between them save in the upper part, where the wall is broken. It is surmounted by a transverse hollow pommel approximately elliptical in outline, with an oval aperture at either side. Blade and hilt are cast in one piece. A light gray-green patina with rust-brown spots and some areas of lustrous deep green malachite covers it. Chou III(?).     Pl. XXXVI.
Length 245 mm.

I do not know of any specimen closely analogous to this dagger, which allegedly came from Suiyüan. For future dating, a comparison with a decorated piece of similar proportions from the C. T. Loo Collections will perhaps prove useful; Rostovtzeff, who published that decorated dagger, considered it a pre-Han type (*The*

*Animal Style in South Russia and China,* Pl. 23:3, text p. 77). The Loo dagger exhibits the same form of the guard in combination with a comparable hilt which, however, has an ornamental filling of four pony- or onager-heads superposed between the bars; the blade, in contrast to the present specimen, has a thick midrib. Pommel and guard, furthermore, are decorated with meander patterns.

Daggers provided with true tectiform guards are more frequent; see, for instance, Egami and Mizuno, *Inner Mongolia,* Pt. II, Pl. 39:1, a specimen with comparable hilt, which is only broader and not broken open.

Diverging more sensibly, but noteworthy because of the fact that it belongs to a closed find, is a dagger of 256 mm in length from the Luan-p'ing 灤平 grave described by T. J. Arne, who believed it to date from the second half of the fourth century B.C. ("Die Funde von Luan P'ing und Hsüan Hua," Pl. 1:1). Blade, guard, and horizontally perforated pommel are reminiscent of the dagger here published, whereas the flat-oval grip, a rare form, has nothing to do with it.

It must not be overlooked that Minusinsk is not poor with regard to allied forms. According to a remark of Merhart's, it would seem that daggers showing the vertical composition of the hilt dissolved into two bars were altogether later, or at least not older, than the family of the "gryphon-head daggers" with vertically grooved handles. At present, however, nothing definite as to the absolute date is purported by the Minusinsk material.

## (*91*) DAGGER WITH ANTENNAE-HILT

Slender blade without pronounced crest continuously running into the narrower flat handle, which has two longitudinal grooves. In the place of the guard, there appear two conventionalized "bird-heads" with large round eyes and short beaks. The pommel has the form of a flat bow the ends of which are bent over into volutes or "antennae." Prevailingly whitish green, the patina also shows iron-rust colored patches, and bluish green encrustations of choppy surface. Chou III(?).                                    Pl. XXXVI.

Length 245 mm.

Well-known Ordos type. Comparable specimens are described in Andersson's "Hunting Magic" (Pl. 6:1, 2) and in Egami and Mizuno, *Inner Mongolia,* Pt. II (Pl. 40:4; *Corpus II,* "Daggers": D 17-19); they come from the Ordos region and North-China.

A variant or a forerunner may be the pommel with two bird-heads that are facing each other (as, for instance, Salmony, *Sino-Siberian Art,* Pl. 39:2). Salmony, placing these pieces as late as about the middle of the Ist millennium A.D., remarks: "As in that region [Minusinsk], the arc ends with two facing eagle-heads. At times these are replaced with simple antennae in nearly every region to which this type has spread. The guard formed of two eagle-heads, back to back [as in the present case], is rare" (*ibid.,* p. 89).

In Minusinsk, the "gryphon-head dagger," as Merhart calls the type, apparently belongs to the Later Bronze Age or the time of the "Kurgans with collective burials," without however actually being recorded among those grave finds, as Merhart explicitly adds (*Bronzezeit am Jenissei*, pp. 123, 146). It was with the help of miniature daggers of identical type, cast as burial gifts, that their age was thus defined. The blades of the "gryphon-head daggers" are described by the same author as follows: (They have) *"fast ausnahmslos eine kräftige, oft zur Leiste ausgebildete, gelegentlich, bei Spätformen, durch Rinnen begleitete oder mehrfache Mittelrippe"* (p. 147); the leaf-shape is not found: *"Der breite Blattansatz führt immer zum Allgemeinumriss eines langgeschenkelten Dreiecks"* (p. 146).

Consequently, the Ordos specimens, as far as the shape of their blades is concerned, do not tally with the Minusinsk blades. Neither broad triangle blades nor strong ribs are found; invariably they are slender rhomboid blades, and a faceted one ("Hunting Magic," Pl. 6: 2) can certainly not be explained without reference to technical analogies among Chinese swords of the Chou III-IV periods. The look of Siberian "gryphon-head" dagger-blades is well illustrated in Borovka's *Scythian Art* (Pl. 40 A-C): three Early Iron Age specimens of bronze, bronze with iron hilt, and iron, very heavy and accurate in shape; any direct relation to the Sino-Mongolian variants seems quite unlikely.

Like Salmony, v. Merhart thinks of a close relationship between hilts with bird-heads and those with antennae (*op. cit.*, p. 164), and the aforementioned dagger (Salmony, *op. cit.*, Pl. 39: 2) shows that this is justified. There is a piece which apparently can serve as a proof for the pretended priority of the bird-heads, reproduced together with an antennae-dagger by H. Kühn (*Die vorgeschichtliche Kunst Deutschlands*, Pl. 412: 1.2); it looks as if that piece represented the traditional stage between bird-heads and volutes.

The important fact of a connection with the "gryphon-head" daggers may explain why one has to delve in the finical subject of the bird-head fashioned apex. The bird-head motif appears in European art during the earlier La Tène, about 400-300 B.C., among various ornamental intruders from the East, that is, South-Russia, Scythia, Caucasia (C. Schuchhardt, *Vorgeschichte von Deutschland*, p. 216). H. Kühn, without unduly belittling the leading role of Italic and Etruscan elements within La Tène, goes as far as to include — together with the Scythians — Siberia and China. He says: "Later, notably since 350 B.C., another element was received in the East [of Europe], which melted with the Etruscan influences: it is the Scythian element which originates from the Siberian world. Earlier that eastern world met the Hallstatt art; now, after 400, it encounters the La Tène art. Again the predominant ornamental principle of the Sino-Siberian group is taken over: the bird-head. In Siberian art, the bird-head is the very motif" (*op. cit.*, p. 132).

Viewed historically, this latter remark undeniably overrates the importance of the bird-head, for it plays no role in early Siberian art. What here matters is the phenomenon of the Eurasiatic spread of this motif during the earlier La Tène — roughly parallel with Chou IV. The question remains to be solved how the chronology of Minusinsk will be harmonized with the fact that this motif is traceable in fourth-century Europe, for Merhart's observations tend to show that the bird-head dagger "arrived" in Minusinsk — near the pre-supposed center of its origin — only toward the end of the Ananino epoch, not before the third century B.C. (*Bronzezeit am Jenissei,* pp. 122, 146, 180). This is evidently too late.

Another problem connected with the bird-heads may be touched upon here. Merhart says that the "gryphon-head" in the form of a bird-head with ears first appeared in the Minusinsk Bronze culture, but that this fanciful combination would be looked for in vain in the (then already past) full Bronze Age, or among "Old-Scythian" forms (*ibid.,* pp. 146-47). To this I wish to remark that those "gryphon-heads" or, as Salmony calls them, "eagle-heads," are not bird-heads at all, although they look like bird-heads. Three exemplary "bird-head" pommels in Borovka's *Scythian Art* (Pl. 40), assigned to the earlier East Siberian Iron Age, show this:

A) animal-heads with ears and beaks, resembling birds;
B) animal-heads, withered;
C) animal-heads, with almond-shaped eyes — not round ones as a bird's — ears, and a beaklike mouth (seemingly with a cere).

With the first specimen (A) one may further compare "bird-heads" superposed in double rows on Ordos dagger hilts (as Salmony, *op. cit.,* Pl. 39: 1, or Andersson, "Hunting Magic," Pl. 8: 2): a pair of the bird-heads exactly corresponds to what appears to be a tiger's head in double profile view on the Siberian hilt! Stripped of their strong plastic *modelé* and superficially viewed upon outline and prominent linear elements, the tiger-heads became so conventional-ized and degenerate as to resemble bird-heads. The iron dagger (C) is adorned with heads that are but a variant of the head of the big animal on a famous gold plaque from Verkhne-Udinsk (Borovka, *op. cit.,* Pl. 49 A): the ends of the big animal's antlers again have the "bird-head," but in fact each of those bird-heads is a reduced replica of the main head. This is still more clearly revealed by a wooden relief from Katanda (Altai) with the same motif in a cruder but perhaps somewhat earlier form (*ibid.,* Pl. 61 = Fig. 101): the heads terminating the branches differ from the head of the animal itself only in that they are smaller and have no antlers of their own. Sup-posing that a branch were isolated, it would indeed represent the "bird-head" of the Siberian pommels. Thus, the ears of the "gryphon-heads" from Minusinsk are easily explained.

In this connection, Borovka's interpretation of a Scythian iron *akinakes* with "bird-head" antennae from the Dnieper is quite en-

Fig. 101: *Elk-head with "bird-head" antler ends.*

Detail of a carved wood relief from Katanda. After Borovka.

lightening: "The outlines are those of an elk's head, but the long slit for the mouth and the cere below the eyes are traits belonging to the bird's head. It is a combination of two originally distinct motives" (*ibid.,* p. 49, Pl. 10 A). So, a certain ambiguity there may well induce the onlooker to see nothing but a bird's head. This ambiguity was also noted in Andersson's descriptions of animal-head plaques from the North-Chinese borderland ("Hunting Magic," Pl. 27: 4-8, text p. 271). An example of his (such as *ibid.,* Fig. 6) discloses — without prejudice to existing differences — a relationship not only with the Katanda elk-head (Fig. 101), but also with Scythian analogies from Kuban and Dnieper, where the birdlike appearance is particularly strongly pronounced (e.g., Borovka, *op. cit.,* Pl. 8). It is beyond my scope to deal with the problem of that ambiguity. Suffice it to state that a tendency of the Hunnic (?) sculptor to transform into a kind of beak the muzzle of the elk, horse, ass, or ram, can be observed in rather early and realistic figures as, for instance, in a wild ass which Andersson described thus: ". . . we see the movable head-part of a kulan (*Equus hemionus*). . . . But in this case the equine type has been strangely blended with another element. The neck and the ears are those of a wild ass, but the muzzle of that animal has been replaced by the curved beak of a bird of prey" ("Hunting Magic," p. 294; Pl. 30: 1). How far intention, symbolism, or simply mannerism have been at work here is a question apart which need not occupy us further. It is the complexity of the motif as well as the questionableness of the term "bird-head," generally, which should be considered in connection with the guard and antennae of the present dagger.

## (*92*) BRONZE DAGGER

With robust blade strengthened by a midrib. Apparently it often was resharpened and has thus become short. The handle, which is hollow, displays a rich ornamentation in alternating meander patterns executed in *cloisons* of about 1 mm in height. The cavities so created possibly were meant to contain — as the small rings certainly were — fillings of bits of precious stones or some vitreous substance. A thin ring-loop is attached in the middle of the hilt which has no guard. Smooth surface of brownish and brown greenish; at the more exposed parts, the pure bronze appears, while the cavities contain gray-green verdigris. Chou III-IV.                    Pl. XXXVI.

Length 195 mm; weight 180 gr.

Comparable specimens are in the collections v. d. Heydt (V. Griessmaier, no. 138 = Salmony, *Sino-Siberian Art,* Pl. 39:6) and David-Weill (O. Janse, "Le style du Houai," Pl. 53:1). The Heydt dagger, the blade of which has preserved the original length, has its hilt beautifully set with turquoise and covered with the intricate lacery of the Huai style décor. Moreover, it is provided with a short and rather broad guard. The David-Weill specimen is distinguished by an openwork handle and a blade that widens toward the base so as to form narrow shoulders; three thin ribs start from the base, which gradually sink in the surface before reaching the lower half of the blade.

Another specimen in Baron v. d. Heydt's collection (Griessmaier, no. 137) is connected with this group. The blade in this case is considerably longer, rhomboid, and asymmetrically pointed. The hilt is decorated with a strange figural motif, compared by Griessmaier with the handle (?) in shape of a monstrous being in the collection of H. M. Gustav Adolf, King of Sweden, and probably dates from the beginning of Chou III (*The Exhibition, Stockholm,* Pl. 25). The aforementioned dagger with turquoise inlay (v. d. Heydt) still reminds one of the demon's head, whereas there is not the slightest trace of it in the Jannings dagger.

## (*93*) SHORT BRONZE SWORD

With grayish brown patina. The blade is flat and has broad faceted edges; a cross section would show a narrow long hexagon. The upper part of the blade is slightly wider than the lower one, there being a contraction in the last third of its length. The base is covered by a comparatively thin rhombic plate which does not spring forth at the sides, and is just broad enough to serve again as a base for the handle. The handle is hollow and widens somewhat toward the end, which is fashioned into a broad flat ring. Seemingly, the handle was stuffed with a piece of wood that has decayed. A round button in the shape of an eight-petaled flower of 18 mm in diameter is set in the aperture; the substance, of dark green color and faint translucency, appears to be glass. In contrast to the perfectly ground facets, the middle tract of the blade has a rough, grained, crackled surface, or skin, as it were, perhaps resulting from some special treatment. Chou III-IV.

Pl. XXXVII.

Length 432 mm; blade length 342 mm; weight 428 gr.

This type, Janse's category B, "épées pourvues de poignée à douille" ("Epées anciennes," pp. 72, 85, 95 ff.) gives the impression of being more primitive than the following ones (nos. 94, 95). It should be admitted, however, that there is no proof as yet for the greater antiquity of the hollow-handle types as opposed to the swords with solid handle. There are no closed finds nor epigraphical dates to serve as a base. But one may refer once more to the hollow-handle swords from the ancient Wu mentioned above (under no. 88), the inscriptions of which, granting their genuineness and correct interpretation, lead back into the middle and later sixth century B.C.:

1) *Wu Chi-tzu chih tzu chien* 吳季子之子劍 (*Chou Chin Wen Ts'un,* 6/2:94: *Ferguson Catalogue,* p. 1031; Jung Keng, in *Yenching Hsüeh Pao,* XVI, 198), datable around 540-520 (see above, no. 88). For this investigation it does not matter whether there is a possible mistake of one or two decades. The question whether this object is reliable at all weighs much more heavily. It is perplexing that the rubbing in *Chou Chin Wen Ts'un* — let alone the coarse woodcuts in *Chi Ku Chai* or *Chin Shih So* — is not identical with that in *Hsiao Chiao Ching Ko* (10:99 b). The latter shows the highly elegant script in the elongated and somewhat manneristic ductus from early Chan-kuo times, whereas that of the *Chou Chin Wen Ts'un,* though identical in style and arrangement, appears inanimate and inferior, and moreover diverges in several details. The blade, too, is not the same. *Chou Chin Wen Ts'un* contains a rubbing of the whole of the piece including the hilt; *Hsiao Chiao Ching Ko* only exhibits the part inscribed. Is the *Chou Chin Wen Ts'un* inscription a fake? Suspicion seems not unfounded, the more so since one has to do with a sword of particular attractiveness for a historically well-read Chinese collector: a sword with an inscription published by Juan Yüan in his *Chi Ku Chai* (1804) not without telling what he knew about the tremendous sum paid for it in the seventeenth century, and pointing out at some length the antiquary and literary interest of the inscription (*op. cit.,* 8:20). The *Chin Shih So* (1822) reproduces in woodcut the inscribed part together with the hilt which, judging from the coarse silhouette, appears to be a round tube (*Chin So,* 2:16). In Fang Chün-i's *Cho I Chai I Ch'i K'ao Shih* (29:9 b-10; concluded in 1894) the inscription is copied from a rubbing in the author's possession. Dissimilar to both the older reproductions (from 1804 and 1822) and to that in *Chou Chin Wen Ts'un,* it essentially agrees with the elegant script in *Hsiao Chiao Ching Ko* (10:99 b), and its lesser fineness seems due to copying and lithographing. Fang Chün-i himself takes a critical stand toward the fact of divergencies in the *Chi Ku Chai* reproduction and adds that the authenticity or reliability of the latter had been doubted. His most striking argument is that according to tradition the inscription was executed in gold wire inlay, so that it was impossible to get a clear rubbing, if any; another argument is that the inscription was made without regard for the blade median.

To these objections he answers: the seventeenth-century owner of the sword, intending to have reproductions made of its inscription, would have ordered a facsimile carved in wood (for printing); as to the absence of a median (rib or crest), it has been noticed also among newly excavated swords, and, moreover, there is no actual overlapping of the median in that inscription; finally, pretended calligraphical weaknesses — as seen by others — are just those traits which deserve to be regarded as the aesthetically most praiseworthy ones. Fang's defense of the inscription (in the form accessible to him) is thoroughly objective and trustworthy. The corresponding form in *Hsiao Chiao Ching Ko* must then be genuine, that in *Chou Chin Wen Ts'un,* in consequence, false.

But how could Tsou An, the compiler of the *Chou Chin Wen Ts'un,* experienced in epigraphy, well knowing the sword-inscription of course, be deluded? Just because he knew it from literature, I think, and because a comparison with the renderings in *Chi Ku Chai, Chin Shih So,* and *Chün Ku Lu Chin Wen* (1895), upon which he could base himself, did not speak against the authenticity of his own *t'a-pen* — the *Cho I Chai* from 1894 having been imprinted only in 1935. Tsou An's *t'a-pen* bears a colophon from 1851. Why did he use that old squeeze for his book printed in 1916? Could he not have procured a new one or examined the original itself? Presumably not, because this sword, according to a note in *Cho I Chai,* had been lost. Thus, a rubbing from the supposed original made in the middle of the nineteenth century was something which Tsou An, with its historical importance in mind, understandably was not inclined to renounce. However, since a better variant of the inscription is contained in *Cho I Chai,* there must have existed, during the latter half of the nineteenth century, another original rubbing, which alone could be authentic. But, up to the publications of the good autography in *Cho I Chai* and the new *t'a-pen* in *Hsiao Chiao Ching Ko,* any suitable Chou sword provided with an inscription copied from the woodcut reproductions of 1804 and 1822 could pass for the rediscovered genuine sword. It is probable that Tsou An's *t'a-pen* from 1851 was made from a specimen of that kind.

To sum up, the inscription seems to be reliable. It is badly reproduced in *Chi Ku Chai* (1804), *Chin Shih So* (1822), and *Chün Ku Lu* (1895); the *Chou Chin Wen Ts'un* (1916) presents, to all appearances, a forgery derived from these bad reproductions; *Cho I Chai* (1894) has an autography based on a good squeeze; the *Hsiao Chiao Ching Ko* (1935) at last reproduces a good rubbing, perhaps taken from the genuine inscription — provided the sword still exists and the characters are in intaglio. But even though not unreservedly to be accepted, this rubbing, by virtue of the superior quality of the script type and because it cannot have been made up after the model of the fairly similar *Cho I Chai* autography printed in the same year, 1935, as the *Hsiao Chiao Ching Ko* itself, cannot well be discarded.

That the sword had a tubular handle is only vouched for by the cumbersome rendering in *Chin Shih So* and the objectionable representation in *Chou Chin Wen Ts'un*. Unless a mere caprice of the authors of the *Chin Shih So* is presupposed, one is justified in counting this specimen as a hollow-handle type.

To detach ourselves from the narrowness of the preceding paragraph, it may be added that the script style agrees with the date inferred from the name the inscription contains. There is no inner improbability, therefore, that would be opposed to our attempt to gain a chronological landmark with this sword.

2) *Wu Wang yüan chien* 吳王元劍 (*Chou Chin Wen Ts'un*, 6/2: 96 a; *Ferguson Catalogue*, pp. 1031-32; *San Tai Chi Chin Wen Ts'un*, 20: 46 a), a hollow-handle sword with midrib. It cannot be later, but well may be earlier, than 473 B.C., when Wu ceased to exist. Valued palaeographically, an earlier date is more likely. A Wu ruler named Yüan is not recorded. Kuo Mo-jo, taking *yüan* as a name, is inclined to identify "King Yüan of Wu" with Chu-fan 諸樊, who reigned 560-548 (*Liang Chou, K'ao Shih*, fol. *yu*, 154 b; cp. Chavannes, *Mém. hist.*, IV, p. 6). The equation remains uncertain, the more so since *yüan* is not necessarily to be regarded as a name; as seen above (under no. 82), *yüan* may be an adjective qualifying *chien*, "sword."

To these two swords dating before the middle of the Ist millennium, another two can be added, which point to later dates.

3) *Kao-tu chien* 高都劍 from the Tuan Fang Collection (*T'ao Chai Chi Chin Lu*, 5: 29), a hollow-handle sword with flat blade (as no. 93) ascribed to the time of the Ch'in dynasty. More important is:

4) *Ch'u Wang Yin-chang chien* 楚王歙章劍 "Sword of King Yen-chang of Ch'u," originating from the princely tombs at Shou-hsien 壽縣 (Anhui), with long rhomboid blade, hollow handle, and cast inscription. Being scoured off and therefore undecipherable to a large extent, the inscription fortunately still yielded the name. *Chang* 章 was the personal name of King Hui 惠 (reigned 488-432; Chavannes, *Mém. hist.*, IV, p. 381 sq.), and the identification of Chang with Yen-chang seems to be generally accepted (cf. T'ang Lan, *Shou-hsien so ch'u T'ung Ch'i K'ao Lüeh* — with partly superseded readings; Liu Chieh, *Ch'u Ch'i T'u Shih*, fol. 9, text fol. 4 b; Shang Ch'eng-tso, *Shih Erh Chia Chi Chin T'u Lu*, ch. *Tsun Ku Chai*, fol. 28 b-29). As to the syllable *yin* in the king's name and its substitution by Hsiung 熊 in traditional history, see B. Karlgren, "Yin and Chou in Chinese Bronzes" (p. 59, C 33). With this sword of the Ch'u ruler who can boast of the longest reign recorded for his dynasty, one gains once more a chronological mark between 488 and 432 B.C. for the type with hollow handle but crested blade (as distinguished from the flat blade of no. 93).

The Swedish material published by Janse does not contribute to the chronology of the present type. Thus, one cannot now go further than saying that there are epigraphic dates from "around 500 B.C.," allowing for diverging blade forms — and that a specimen particularly similar to no. 93, the *Kao-tu* sword from the former Tuan Fang Collection, is regarded as a relic from the latter half of the third century B.C. Under these circumstances and unless new datable pieces should emerge, Janse's theory of the higher age of his category B (as compared with A, such as nos. 94-99 below), which I myself think is right, remains unsupported by epigraphic evidence. (See also the remarks under no. 97 below.)

The feature of the crackled surfaces was noted also by Janse ("Epées anciennes," nos. 12, 23, 31, 34, 38, 42).

### (*94*) SHORT SWORD

Light gray-green patinated bronze, with patches of darker green. Crested blade of rhombic section, with narrow-faceted edges, attenuating from the lower third. The guard, which only slightly exceeds the width of the blade, has rounded shoulders with a saddle between them. A round solid hilt girt by two ring-rolls and crowned by a disk with a shallow depression rises from the saddle. Hilt and blade are cast in one piece. Chou IV.                    Pl. XXXVII.

Length 445 mm; blade alone 350 mm; weight 452 gr.

The type corresponds to Janse's category A ("Epées pourvues de poignée à renflements annulaires"; cf. "Epées anciennes," pp. 71, 84, 95 sqq.). It is the classical type of the ancient Chinese sword, which was in use for about five centuries and is accordingly frequently represented.

### (*95*) SHORT SWORD

Smoothly greenish gray patinated bronze with light blue coatings. Same type as no. 94, somewhat heavier, and with slightly larger pommel. On the handle are clear impressions of plaited cords. Chou IV.
Pl. XXXVII.

Length 447 mm; blade alone 351 mm; weight 500 gr.

The patina resembles that of many Huai-style bronzes from the region of Shou-chou 壽州 (Anhui), which during the Chou time belonged to the territory of Ch'u 楚. Quite likely the sword has to be localized there.

Traces or actual remains of handle-lacings are no rarity. One finds them, for instance, on the following two pieces (nos. 96, 97). Apart from cord lacings among the Stockholm specimens examined by Janse, occur lacings of cloth as well as remnants of wooden covers ("Epées anciennes," p. 71).

### (*96*) SHORT SWORD

With solidly cast round handle girt by two ring-rolls and surmounted by a concave disk-pommel. The guard is of the same shape as exemplified in the preceding two pieces. The blade, approxi-

Fig. 102: *Inscription on the pommel of the sword no. 96.*

mately rhomboid, is distinguished by relatively broad facets, and by faces which, as a result of a slight protrusion of the crest, appear almost hollow. The lower part of the blade narrows at a point a little higher than usual. At the grip, there are traces of lacings. Four characters are incised on the surface of the pommel (Fig. 102). Bronze, of tin-colored metallic luster, with a thin layer of patina in green shades and malachite. Chou IV or later.        Pl. XXXVII.

Length 458 mm; blade alone 363 mm; weight 642 gr.

The characters, except for *kuan* 官 "office," are next to undecipherable, especially the one on the right side. Their order seemingly corresponds to that usually met with in coins: from top, from right. The most likely reading will be this: *chün i kao kuan* 君宜高官 "may you attain high office." *Kao* is conjecture, based on this character's wide use in such formulas during the Han time. Identically worded inscriptions occur on a belt-hook (*Erh Pai Lan T'ing Chai,* ch. 4) and on a mirror (Karlgren, "Early Chinese Mirror Inscriptions," no. 12; cp. p. 15). The second character, which at first glance looks like *an* 安, is read *i* 宜 with reference to the context and the parallels quoted.

As to the formal side of the inscription, script style as well as arrangement point to a Han date. In the Warring States period, the characters would probably have been placed radially, as an ornament subject to the round, and referring to the object rather than to the beholder. But the characters may have been engraved later; the sword itself is of late Chou type.

## (97) SWORD OF A KING OF YÜEH

With turquoise-incrusted guard and a handle with ring-rolls. The blade, of rhomboid shape and with faceted edges, narrows very slightly in the lower part. The guard, which engages the handle and at the same time reinforces the heel of the blade, is of the same shape as foregoing specimens. It is ornamented with a highly intricate linear design in thin cloisons holding tiny turquoise bits. On close examination, this design proves to be an inscription in "bird script" characters revealing the name of a king of Yüeh 越 (Fig. 103). Inlay-work, equally minutely executed, embellishes also the ring-rolls. There are remnants and impressions of lacings with a fine plaited cord of less than 1 mm in thickness. Immediately below the pommel is a residue of a thick wrapping that looks like fibers of wood impregnated with bronze oxide. The troughed face of the disk has a decoration of concentric rings on a ground finely roughened by radial striae. The handle appears to be solid. Thick green patina areas on a surface which at many parts has preserved its original color and luster. Chou IV: first half of fourth century B.C.

Pls. XXXVIII, XL.

Length 643 mm; blade alone 540 mm; weight ca. 995 gr.

In the course of describing sword no. 93 above, the very few epigraphic supports available for establishing the age of the hollow-handle types were adduced and examined, and it was found that at best they lead one back to the middle of the sixth century, or at any rate to the time "around 500 B.C."

It must not be overlooked that these dates, signalizing what is oldest in the datable material, are of fortuitous character. But they seem late. One should expect to find earlier dates, for the present type with solid ringed handle (Janse's category A), which typologically is the more developed one and thus should reasonably have its place after the simpler, hollow-handled types, apparently also existing about the same time. This is an inference based upon the style of décor, the inscriptions, and the patina of many swords of this type. Two circumstances, however, pointed out by Janse ("Epées anciennes," p. 95) speak, though not conclusively, in favor of category A's belonging to a later stage: first, A-swords seem to be more numerous than B-swords; second, the Han dynasty tombs at Lo-lang in Korea still furnished a few A-swords alongside single-edged iron blades, but no B-swords at all.

The datable material extant will now be perused. The earliest specimen, according to its inscription, is:

1) The *Kung Wu wang Fu-ch'ai chien* 攻吳王夫差劍, "the Sword of King Fu-ch'ai of Wu" (*Shuang Chien I Ku Ch'i Wu, shang*: 41). The inscription permits one to date this piece between 495 and 473 B.C., that is, from the ascension to the throne till the year of the suicide of that king and last ruler of Wu (Chavannes, *Mém. hist.*, IV, pp. 25-33). The turquoise-set décor of the guard is identical with that on the Li-yü sword (Louvre; see 4 below), but the blade is of the ordinary rhomboid type.

2) Then there are several swords the guards of which are ornamented with an elaborate, grotesque script embedded in turquoise bits, reading *Yüeh Wang* 戉王 and meaning 越王 "King of Yüeh." These swords, with dissimilarities that need not be given attention here, were certainly all cast before 333 B.C., when Yüeh ceased to exist (*ibid.*, IV, pp. 438-39). Although it is true that the *Bamboo Annals* have an entry concerning a "present" of 300 ships, 5,000,000 arrows, rhinoceros horns, and ivory tusks received from "the king of Yüeh" in 312 B.C. (Legge, *Chin. Classics*, III, *Proleg.*, p. 175; cf. H. Maspero, *La Chine antique*, pp. 399-400 n. 1), it is more likely that these weapons date from the glorious days of Yüeh, and the script style likewise tends to preclude a late date. The swords in question are in the following collections:

a) Musée Cernuschi, Paris
b) G. L. Winthrop Collection, Fogg Art Museum
c) Liu T'i-chih (Shan Chai), Lu-chiang (Anhui)
d) T'ao Tsu-kuang (*Chou Chin Wen Ts'un*, 6: 105)
e) Jung Keng (*Sung Chai Chi Chin Hsü Lu, hsia*, fol. 129; text fol. 19-20a), where the preceding specimens are listed. Also reproduced in *Shuang Chien I Chi Chin, hsia*, fol. 36)

3) Closely allied with those five pieces are two swords from Shou-chou (Anhui), also listed by Jung Keng apropos of (*e*) above but apparently unpublished, which on account of the wording of their guard inscriptions are *counterparts* of the Jannings specimen no. 97. (The one of the two swords perhaps is identical with no. 97.) Their inscriptions fortunately differ in that the one instead of *"Wang Yüeh"* 王鉞 has the inverse order *"Yüeh Wang"* 戉王 and the name of that country written with additional radical *i* 邑. Jung Keng, who from an analogous spearhead inscription (see below) recognized that *Yüeh* signifies Yüeh 越, the state, not a person so named, and who in two papers devoted to the bird script (*Niao Shu K'ao; Niao Shu K'ao Pu Cheng*) has specially dealt with this subject, proposed the following reading:

"Yüeh Wang Chu-chih Yü-tz'u 者(越)王著(諸)旨於賜" (*Sung Chai Chi Chin Hsü Lu, hsia,* text fol. 20 a).

Fig. 103: *The inscribed guard of the sword no. 97.*

After rubbings of the National Palace Museum, Peking.

The same name, which is not recorded in written history, also appears on a bell (*Po Ku T'u,* 22:7; *Liang Chou, K'ao Shih, pu-lu,* fol. 1) and on the spearhead just mentioned in the collection of Marquis Hosokawa (*Shū Kan ihō,* Pl. 54; *Niao Shu K'ao,* Fig. 10; *idem, Pu Cheng,* suppl. Fig. 10; *Liang Chou, K'ao Shih,* Pl. 2 b = Fig. 41 D). Diverging somewhat from Jung Keng's reading is that of Kuo Mo-jo (*Liang Chou, K'ao Shih, pu-lu:* 1-2):

"Yüeh Wang Chu-chao Yü-shih 戉(越)王者(諸)召於賜," whom Kuo identifies with Chu-chiu Yüeh-hua 諸咎粵滑, a short-lived and infamous Yüeh ruler. According to the *Bamboo Annals* (Legge, *Chin. Classics,* III, *Proleg.,* p. 170), this Chu-chiu, by way of parricide, came to reign for three months and then was murdered himself in 376 B.C. (Chavannes, *Mém. hist.,* IV, p. 433, n. 5). It thus would appear that the year 376 was a hard and fast date for specimen no. 97, which has that name inscribed on it. However, the sequence of the Yüeh rulers after Kou-chien 勾踐 (till 465 B.C.) as given in the *Bamboo Annals* is at variance with both *Shih Chi* and *Yüeh Chüeh Shu* (Kuo Mo-jo, *op. cit., pu-lu* 1 b), wherefore one should be content with saying that this sword in all probability dates from the first half of the fourth century B.C.

4) Two other swords deserve to be mentioned here as outstanding representatives of the present category, although they are not datable within narrow limits. They are the sword from the Li-yü hoard (Louvre) and a very similar one in the Freer Gallery (see Umehara, *Senkoku-shiki dōki,* Pl. 25, text Fig. 8, showing the hilts of both pieces in drawings and sections; G. Salles, *Les Bronzes de Li-yu;* O. Kümmel, *Jörg Trübner zum Gedächtnis,* Pl. 35; *Freer Gallery Catalogue,* Pl. 50). Among the Li-yü bronzes there is none which bears an inscription save that sword, and its inscription offers, as does the counterpart in Washington, no chronological hints beyond its palaeographic or stylistic nature. The earlier Li-yü bronzes have been dated as early as "latter half of the 7th century B.C." by Bachhofer (*Art Bull.,* XXIII, 4, p. 321), while the *Huang-ch'ih Hu* 黃池壺 with an inscription referring to an event of 482 B.C. (Yetts, *The Cull Chinese Bronzes,* no. 12; *Shang Chou I Ch'i T'ung K'ao,* Pls., Fig. 743; cp. notes under no. 82 above) still has close parallels among the later Li-yü pieces, where the shape of that vase, the interlacery of dragons, the *t'ao-t'ieh,* the plastic plaited bands, and the animal-handles all alike recur. One does not go far astray, therefore, in placing the corresponding Li-yü bronzes also around 482 B.C. The two swords in Paris and Washington obviously do not belong to the older material from Li-yü while, by comparison with the few allied swords datable so early, they agree well with a date around 482 or, to put it more generally, around the first half of the fifth century. The dates as proposed by Kuo Mo-jo and Umehara are less precise: "Warring States" (*Liang Chou, K'ao Shih,* 240 f.) and "sixth to third century" (*Shina Kodō Seika,* VII: 101).

The above examples show that the type with ringed handle existed at least in the first quarter of the fifth century (1 above), perfectly standardized in every regard. So this type by dead reckoning takes one back to about 500 B.C. Accordingly, the interval between it and the — epigraphically earliest — hollow-handle type seems all but negligible, and it becomes evident that both types were in use side by side for a considerable time.

Thus it might seem as if the solid-handled type (A) appeared on the stage unheralded, abruptly, and almost simultaneously with that characterized by the flat rhombus-plate and hollow hilt (B), without displacing the latter and seemingly without any genetic affiliation, as though they stemmed from different sources. That would be a matter of historical significance. However, inner likelihood is against the epigraphically supported circumstances: the dates are by far too few in number and moreover are, as was said already, fortuitous. And, finally, there are some intermediate forms which should perhaps be taken as *transitional types* between A and B swords. Though not conclusively proving that A was evolved from B, they facilitate or at least make conceivable a typological demonstration of a genetic affinity. The blade-forms, on the other hand, are essentially the same in both categories; with this fact in mind, a connection or continuity is given at any rate. The filiation of the two types, if verifiable, again would be a matter of no less historical interest than the alternative. It would mean that the classical Chinese sword (A) is an independent creation of the Middle Kingdom, perfected long before a Sarmatian model found its way to China (cp. Introduction, Swords). Janse is convinced that *"les épées B se sont transformées en épées du type A"* ("Epées anciennes," p. 97).

Specimens of transitional hilt types are remarkably scarce (Fig. 104). They show these features:

*a*) the simple rhombus-plate combined with a hollow handle with ring-rolls (Stockholm; Janse, *op. cit.*, Pl. 12: 1);

*b*) the simple rhombus-plate combined with a solid oval handle (Stockholm; Janse, *op. cit.*, Pl. 6: 2);

*c*) the simple rhombus-plate combined with a solid handle with ring-rolls (Stockholm; Janse, *op. cit.*, Pl. 6: 7);

*d*) a broad guard that strengthens the junction of blade and grip, which is solid and is provided with ring-rolls (Stockholm, Janse, *op. cit.*, Pl. 7: 6).

These various formations unquestionably betray a wavering and undecided stage of transition. They represent, I think, experiments which failed to be adopted generally, experiments on the way from the light hollow hilt on the thin rhombus-plate to the solid hilt on a massive guard. They do not yet disclose what the ultimate, standardized form was to be, nor do they impart a clear evolutionary trend. But on the whole they suggest a transformation with byways and detours. This transformation must have taken place before the first appearance of the A-type sword, that is, some time before 500 B.C.

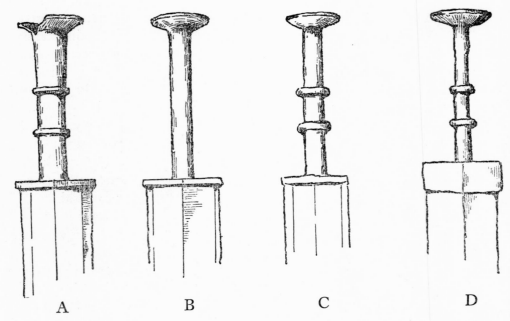

A          B          C          D

Fig. 104: *Four hilt types suggestive of affiliation between hollow-handle and solid ring-handle swords.*

If the thesis is tenable, the B-type swords datable around 500 B.C. (mentioned under no. 93 above) were tardy throughout, and their prime occurred perhaps a century or so farther back in time. It would be a chronological place which tallies with that of the still earlier archaic tanged sword (see no. 88 above).

### (*98*) BRONZE SWORD

Similar to the preceding specimen, with turquoise inlay at the guard. The décor of the guard appears to have been derived from the *t'ao-t'ieh* mask. Round, seemingly solid handle with two ring-rolls likewise set with minute turquoise particles. Concave disk-pommel with concentric rings on the upper face. Blade of rhombic cross section with faceted edges. The patina is of a fairly homogeneous brown-olive color, darkened in some places, with tinges of blue and bluish gray in thin coatings. At the hilt, the brown tone nears an iron-rust color. Chou IV.                    Pls. XXXVIII, XL.
    Length 605 mm; blade alone 495 mm; weight 930 gr.

### (*99*) BRONZE SWORD

Similar to the foregoing two specimens. The guard has sunken ornaments that perhaps were once incrusted with turquoise. Round solid handle with two ring-rolls and a small disk-pommel. On either side of the handle, "seams" that were not worked off indicate the position of the valves the sword was cast in. Beautiful whitish and bluish green patina in variegated nuances, leaving uncovered the glossy metal at some spots, which show a light green-gray hue. Chou IV.
                    Pls. XXXVIII, XL.
    Length 590 mm; blade alone 480 mm; weight 875 gr.
    The ornament with large round eyes appears, as in the case of the sword no. 98, only on one side of the guard, the reverse side showing a less intricate design.
    For comparison one may refer to a sword with a more simple eye-ornament on the guard, a typological outsider, in the Museum of Far Eastern Antiquities, Stockholm (Janse, "Epées anciennes," Pl. 10: 3). That specimen is noteworthy in that it has this shape of guard combined with a hollow handle, and so might be inserted in the small series of transitional types (Fig. 104).

### (*100*) BRONZE SWORD

With nearly round hollow handle topped by a flat-conical rim. A rhombus-plate serves as guard and base of the hilt. Blade with crest and faceted edges; rhombic in section, and unusually strongly narrowed in the lowermost third of its length. The extraordinary, beautiful patina of the blade looks like dark polished marble: shiny, blackish gray with a slight greenish hue. At the hilt the patina is dull and less dark. Chou III-IV.                    Pl. XXXVIII.

Length 550 mm; blade alone 453 mm; weight 690 gr.

For the date of the hollow-handle types, the reader is referred to the notes under no. 93 above.

The shiny black of the blade is indicative of a special metallurgical treatment it underwent.

### (*101*) BRONZE SWORD

With round solid handle surmounted by a disk that has a conical cavity ca. 35 mm deep. Below the rhombus-plate which engages the handle, there is a dragon-like bird-figure in high relief covering the width of the blade. It is a broad, crested blade with narrow facets and obtuse point, narrowing as usual in the lower third of the length. The surface shows a silvery metallic tone. By a special process (etching) an ornament has been laid over the whole surface of the blade: double lines crossing at the median and forming a continuous diaper pattern with short horizontal strokes drawn through each crossing. These lines contrast, dull against the glossy surface. The blade is twice broken through. It is partly coated by a gray-green crust of oxide turning into brighter green at the hilt. Chou III-IV.

Pl. XXXIX.

Length 455 mm; blade alone 365 mm; weight 680 gr.

The same technical treatment and the same pattern appear on a longer sword with ringed handle and heavy guard (Janse's type A) in the collection of Yü Hsing-wu, Peking (*Shuang Chien I Ku Ch'i Wu, shang*: 42, dated "Ch'un-ch'iu"), and on a related specimen in the Nezu Collection, Tokyo (Umehara, *Seizansō Seishō,* VI, no. 42, dated "Chan-kuo").

We find similar features on a spearhead in the David-Weill Collection, Paris (Fig. 41 E), which typologically is almost identical with the Marquis Hosokawa spearhead (Fig. 41 D) mentioned under no. 97 above. The diapers are more densely drawn there, while the short horizontal strokes seem to be absent (cp. O. Janse, "Le style du Houai," Pl. 53: 2; *Commemorative Catalogue,* Pl. 20: 175). The *London Catalogue* remarks: "With nielloed diaper pattern, Period of the Warring States," whereas Janse only states: "Double lignes de couleur foncée formant des rhombes" (*op. cit.,* p. 173).

It is worth remembering that etching of the metal by means of fruit acids was practiced about the same time also in the European La Tène, where even the diaper pattern itself was in fashion. Yet there is a difference there: the La Tène craftsman used iron instead of bronze. Strangely enough, the present sword shows another element which recurs in La Tène art and which was discussed above (under no. 91): the bird-head of the animal at the heel of the blade.

The occurrence in Dong-son (Tongking) of a sword with diaper pattern was observed by Janse (*op. cit.,* p. 174; cp. V. Goloubew,

"L'Age du Bronze dans le Tonkin et dans le Nord-Annam," Pl. 3: A-B).

### (*102*) LONG BRONZE RAPIER

Unusually long and very slender blade with faceted edges, gently hollowed on either side of the median crest. The blade is so long that — though of bronze — it is a little springy. Its width at the base is 30 mm (two-thirds only of the ordinary width), its thickness at the median, 6 mm; the relation between breadth and length is almost 1 : 25.

The guard, contrary to the common types, juts out considerably. It is sumptuously decorated with turquoise inlay in gold cloisons, with a pair of large bossed turquoise eyes on one side (as on the guards of the swords nos. 98 and 99). Extraordinarily long, too, is the hilt which could be wielded with both hands; the round, solid handle thickens somewhat toward the broad disk-pommel.

The pommel, on its troughed surface, is again set with turquoise bits held in place and symmetrically arranged by a golden quatrefoil with slender petals, and by thin gold walls in the shape of inward bound pointed leaves with rounded hooks running out into small spirals (Fig. 105). The middle part is slightly marred and so covered by the remains of an oxidized cloth that the original form of the ornament is no longer recognizable. The superb incrustation work was made with astoundingly regularly cut particles.

Gray-green and light grayish patina, partly covered by darker gray-green and by earthy concretions. On the shiny patina of the handle there are traces of a black-brown coating (lacquer ?) with narrow stripes of gold foil, pointing to an unusual treatment of the hilt. Alleged provenance: Shou-hsien 壽縣 (Anhui). Chou IV.
Pls. XXXIX, XL.

Length 936 mm; blade alone 733 mm; weight 745 gr.

Magnificent, hitherto singular type. The decoration, lightness, and length of this elegant rapier that would hardly stand a serious test suggest that it has to be regarded as a state-weapon. The extremely long hilt, in particular, is an outstanding feature (Pl. XL).

Fig. 105: *Ornament on the pommel of the rapier no. 102.*

As far as the gold ornament on the pommel (Fig. 105: the center is left blank because of the conditions described above) contributes something for the dating — mainly by comparison with the quatrefoil design on Chou and Han mirrors — it rather points to the end of the Chou IV period.

Among the Chinese bronze swords published so far, there is only one, to my knowledge, to exceed the present specimen in length. It is a tanged sword of somewhat dissimilar proportions, with both guard and pommel in jade, ca. 1105 mm in length, in the possession of C. T. Loo (Plumer, *An Exhibition of Ancient Chinese Bronzes*, no. 60, Pl. 37). Farther removed are two likewise tanged specimens with a length of 832 mm (Stockholm; Janse, "Epées anciennes," Pl. 15:4, Cat. no. 64) and 800 mm (British Museum; Koop, *Early Chinese Bronzes,* Pl. 64:B), respectively. Finally, an iron tanged sword remarkable for both the form and length of its blade of 976 mm may be adduced (Stockholm; Janse, *op. cit.,* Pl. 15:2, Cat. no. 71); it likewise points to a later rather than earlier date for the long blades.

### (*103*) IRON SWORD

With short tang and a narrow guard of bronze. The blade is rhombic in section and imperceptibly tapers from the 34 mm broad heel. The iron is thoroughly oxidized. Remnants of a wooden sheath soaked with rust cover part of the surface. The point is broken off. Han. Pl. XXXIX.

Length 578 mm; blade alone 503 mm; weight 540 gr.

Comparable specimens — iron blades with tang and with a bronze guard — are recorded as stray finds from Lo-lang in Korea; see Sekino, Yatsui *et al., Rakurō-gun jidai no iseki,* pp. 361-63; Figs. 226, 228, 229, 236). The fact that the bulk of the Lo-lang swords are made of iron has been observed by O. Janse, though with an underestimation of the ratio of the bronze types ("Epées anciennes," p. 93). As those Lo-lang finds, the present type probably dates from the Earlier Han dynasty.

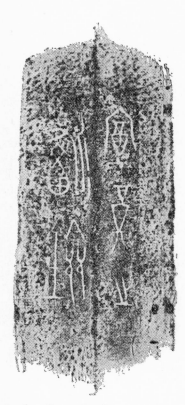

Fig. 106: *Inscription on the sword no. 104.*

### (*104*) SHORT TANGED SWORD

Bronze blade, slightly bent by pressure, with sharp crest, somewhat hollowed faces and narrow faceted edges. The narrowing in the lower third of the blade's length is strikingly pronounced. The tang, which is provided with a small rivet-hole, is approximately oval in section; it broadens a little toward the junction with the blade. The guard is lost, but the oxidation still shows its position. The blade bears an incised inscription comprising five characters (Fig. 106). Grayish and light green patina with protoxide-red and emerald-green coatings. Chou IV. Pl. XXXIX.

Length 385 mm; blade alone 300 mm; weight 325 gr.

The dating is based on the script type. The inscription reads: 盦奠 (? 富鄭) 之劃鐱(劍) *Yen Tien* (? *Fu Cheng*) *chih hua chien* "Thrusting(?) sword of Yen Tien (or Fu Cheng, according to the variants)." It must remain open whether the name has to be read as it stands; the two graphs may be loans for other characters. (For the deciphering of the first graph cp. *Ku Chou P'ien,* 76:44b; for the second, *ibid.,* 16:35 b.) The fourth glyph, *hua* or *huo,* according to *Shuo Wen* (IV *hsia,* head 137), means "a knife for stabbing, pricking, stitching, piercing, and so on, *chui tao* 錐刀." As an adjective to "sword" it seems to be unique, and tautological besides. What is more important is that the character *hua* 劃 apparently is met here for the first time in pre-Han epigraphy.

## (*105*) KNIFE-HALBERD

Of light gray-green and copper-red patinated bronze with green verdigris and some glossy grayish spots at the lower part. Broad and long, vertical, knifelike blade bent over on top and terminating in a backward hook. Along the back runs a narrow shafting-bar set off from the blade by low flanges and extending beyond the base of the blade. It is provided with two longish slits; a third may be hidden under the patina crust. The edge was sharpened. Near the base, there are two incised characters (Fig. 107). Shang. Pl. XLI.
Length 408 mm; weight 440 gr.

The two glyphs probably read *T'ien shih* 天豕, possibly *t'ai shih* 太豕 , "heaven-pig," or "great pig." They occur not rarely on Shang bronzes, but their significance is still unknown. Maybe they stand as symbol of a clan (cp. E. Erkes, "Das Schwein im alten China," p. 81 f.— where there is no reference, on the other hand, to this conspicuous epigraph).

Comparable specimens are in the Fujii Collection in Kyoto (Umehara, *Anyang Treasures,* Pl. 17: 1, 2), a decorated one in the G. L. Winthrop Collection (*ibid.,* 27: 1). Two variants of the same type — which is justly considered a Chinese peculiarity by Umehara — came into the Freer Gallery (*ibid.,* p. 37, Fig. 17; *Freer Catalogue,* Pls. 46, 47; *Tsun Ku Chai so chien Chi Chin T'u* 4: 41); they form part of a group of twelve weapons said to have been found at Hsün-hsien, and one of them bears the inscribed characters *K'ang Hou.* These data allow one to assign that weapon to the early days of the Chou dynasty: K'ang Hou was the first prince enfeoffed in Wei衛, the ancient territory corresponding to the region of the modern Northern Honan, and a younger brother of Wu Wang, founder of the Chou dynasty. (Cp. above, text Fig. 7, axe from Hsün-hsien, which also belongs to that group in the Freer Gallery.)

The ancient name of this type is not known. The type as such persisted down to the Manchus, and combat scenes on the Chinese stage in our day still give an idea how such a large slashing knife hafted to a moderately long shaft wielded with both arms was once handled.

Fig. 107: *Inscription on the knife-halberd no. 105.*

## (*106*) UNKNOWN PARTISAN TYPE

With point and two horizontal spikes. The point and the spikes — the upper one springing forth a little more than the lower one — are cut open and sharpened. The back is V-shaped. At the lower end it bears a long frontal loop, and rearward, somewhat higher up, there are two small heart-shaped wings as lateral shaft-supports. Through the openings of the horizontal spikes, lashings were laid and kept in place by low ridges. The bronze has a glossy silvery surface; it is largely coated by a thin gray-green patina. Alleged provenance: Hsün-hsien (Northern Honan). Chou I (?). Pl. XLI.
Length 280 mm; weight 540 gr.

Hitherto unique type. The heart-shaped shaft-supports recall the *ko* no. 72 which has a silvery blackish surface. The alloy used in the case of the present specimen appears to be the same as that of the spearhead no. 26 and of the dagger no. 85. These similarities in Early Chou pieces (in connection with the not verifiable localization in Hsün-hsien) favor the early date which is tentatively given here.

A Han time representation on an incised slab from a brick tomb shows a warrior with a partisan reminiscent of the present type: it has a point and two horizontal spikes and is mounted on a stick of a man's height. There is a difference, however, in that it is provided with a long and slender horizontal shafting-plate or tang (*nei*), such as *ko* and *chi* types used to have. (See Wang Chen-to, *Han Tai K'uang Chuan Chi Lu, hsia,* figures, no. 11.) The Han parallel therefore is irrelevant for the date of the specimen.

### (*107*) WEAPON FROM A WAR CHARIOT

In the form of two heavy dagger-axes (*ko*) combined with, and connected by, a blade with a sharpened wavy edge. The points of the *ko* are slightly downward. A shafting-bar with flanges standing out at right angles runs along the base, exceeding it in length. There are six slits for lashings cut in the blade: four of them fall to the portion with the wavy edge, two to the outer arms. At level with the *ko* are shafting-plates (*nei*) partly broken off and apparently also sharpened. Except the cutting-facets, the surface is coarse and unpolished. It would seem that this brownish gray patinated piece was excavated long ago. Chou III (?). Pl. XLII.

Length of the shafting-bar 612 mm.

Once more a unique type. Its size, weight, and unwieldiness argue that it was a weapon mounted on a chariot. The mode of mounting cannot, of course, satisfactorily be ascertained without further evidence. The asymmetrical *ko* tips suggest vertical attachment, whereas the wavy blade makes one think first of a horizontal position. Where on the chariot the piece was fastened also remains questionable. On the assumption that the chariots were to attack, a corresponding pole-projection so equipped would seem quite likely. For the purpose of warding off attackers charging or trying to board, attachment on the cart-box itself would be a plausible device. Apropos of the weapons belonging to the war chariot (*Chou Li, K'ao Kung Chi,* First Section), E. Biot gave an account of the following contrivance: "*La première espèce* [i.e., the *ko*] *est fixée obliquement, pour arrêter les ennemis qui voudraient monter sur les côtés du char. Les autres* [*shu* 殳, *ch'e-chi* 車戟, *chiu-mao* 酋矛, i.e., halberds and lances with long shafts] *sont maniées par les guerriers que porte le char*" (*Le Tcheou-Li,* II, p. 464, n. 3). It is not feasible to identify any of the chariot weapons of the *Chou Li* with the type here published. A kind of rigid pole-armament in form of a three-pronged lance allegedly in use during the Middle Chou period is mentioned without source by A. v. Pawlikowski-Cholewa, *Die Heere des Morgenlandes* (p. 37).

A similar texture of the surface, namely, polished facets and rough, crackled faces of the blade, was encountered in the sword no. 93 above.

### (*108*) LONG THRUSTING WEAPON (PIKE)

Flat blade tapering toward the tip, which is broken, with a round midrib forming a socket. Two semicircular loops above the aperture of the socket. Bronze, heavily coated with a crust of verdigris. Late Chou (?)                                                                                     Pl. XLII.
Length 750 mm; diameter of the socket 28 mm.

### (*109-110*) PAIR OF BRONZE AXES WITH IRON POINTS

Bronze shaft-hole axes with straight upper and curved lower edges, the faces widening toward the cutting edge. The shaft-holes, longish in section, still contain remnants of wooden shafts. Iron pikes are inserted in the upper openings of the socket stuffed, as it were, by the wood of the shafts, which were so hollowed as to engage the tapering tang of the iron blades. These blades completely fill the upper openings, their tips projecting a little from the lower aperture. The iron is thoroughly oxidized and brittle. Both axes have the same characters incised on the neck (Fig. 108). Bronze patina: stained gray-green and malachite, with strips of cloth impressions running aslant the surface of one of the axes. Chou III (?)          Pl. XLIII.
Length of the axe blades 136 mm; height of the neck 50 mm; width of the neck ca. 14 mm; length of the iron pikes 215-20 mm; weight of a single piece ca. 525 gr.

At first sight the iron blades will almost certainly be taken as handles. Yet their lancet shape and flatness, their position in relation to the axe bodies, and the remains of wood in connection with the decayed iron tangs tend to show that we are here confronted with a peculiar combination of axe and lance.

A comparable specimen found near Pyöng-yang in Korea shows that this rare type still existed in Han times and that it was then made of iron exclusively (cf. Umehara and Fujita, *Chōsen ko-bunka sōkan*, 2, p. 53, Fig. 72, Pl. 39: 72).

The glyph incised on both pieces has so far not safely been explained. The current readings are 𝑥 , thence *i* 擬 "evaluate/measure/calculate" (Takada, *Ku Chou P'ien*, 33: 3b, 55: 12b-14b) and 㨨 (?) (Kuo Mo-jo, *Chin Wen Ts'ung K'ao*, fol. 266 b; cp. *Hsieh Shih K'uan Chih*, 11: 8), or *i* 癸 as often occurring in combination with the cross-cartouche, *ya-hsing* (cp. R. S. Britton, *Fifty Shang Inscriptions*, p. 41 ff.), and most probably to be interpreted as a proper name in either of the readings.

It is curious that characters of such an archaic style should appear

Fig. 108:
*Glyphs on the axes 109-110.*

on an Iron Age tool. But suspicion arising from this fact is dissipated by an examination of the pieces themselves: the glyphs do not look as if they were forged. So, if incised soon after casting, the latest thinkable date should be around the beginnings of Chou III.

### (*III*) BRONZE MASK

Representing the head of a bovine *t'ao-t'ieh*. It consists of a convex bronze sheet of 1-1.5 mm thickness. The design is shallowly incised; the eyes bulge hemispherically, overlapping the incised contour; the nose is indicated in low relief. From the lips curved outward in a hook, horizontal fangs stand out, joining the middle part. The horns with soft crest are bent upward and strongly jut forth. Between horns and ears there are small openings which probably served for lashing. Near the tip of the horns the sheet is folded backward in angles so acute that the front view does not reveal this detail; the corners of these folded ends likewise have lashing slits. Chou I.    Pl. XLIV.

Width 235 mm; weight 300 gr.

A comparable specimen figures in *Tsun Ku Chai so chien Chi Chin T'u* (4:45), where it is defined as part or adornment of an armor; it bears the character *Wei* 衛 cast in relief on the reverse side. Wei, name of the fief given to K'ang Hou during the early reign of Ch'eng Wang, points to Hsün-hsien as the probable place of discovery (cp. remarks under no. 105 above). Actually, there has been found a round bronze plaque there, identically inscribed and regarded as a harness-plate (Sun Hai-po, *Hsün-hsien I Ch'i,* fol. 69; Kuo Pao-chün, *Hsün-hsien Hsin-ts'un,* p. 188, no. 6 — with discordant reading of that character). These circumstances leave hardly any doubt as to the Early Chou date of the mask, a date which is likewise advocated by its style.

Hsün-hsien further yielded two somewhat diverging bronze masks. One of them is distinguished by half-human features, while the other is equipped with horns or antlers. These objects, which are not suited to cover the face, are explained by Sun Hai-po as ventral harness-plates, *fu-k'ai* 腹鎧 (*op. cit.,* fol. 72-73). Such an explanation, not inconsistent in itself, would have the support of analogies from much later times as, for instance, apotropaic monstrous masks on the belly of armored *defensores fidei* of Buddhist iconography (e.g., Le Coq, *Bilderatlas,* Fig. 91: a Lokapāla in a fresco at Bäzäklik). Kuo Pao-chün, on the other hand, regards the Hsün-hsien masks as part of the paraphernalia of the *fang-hsiang* 方相, the shaman, magician, exorcist (*Hsün-hsien Hsin-ts'un,* p. 187, no. 4), and this view is shared by P. W. Meister in a paper summarizing the extant material ("Chinesische Bronzemasken," *O. Z.,* 1938, pp. 5-11). Since the exorcist, no matter what his accoutrements, has always had a warrior-like apparel (as befitted the armed opponent of evil spirits), the interpretation held by Kuo Pao-chün and Meister eventually agrees very well with the explanation of these masks as parts of a harness. The

nature of these masks, their demoniacal expression, their structural
side as well as their rather poor solidity undoubtedly justify taking
them as magic armor, such as a *fang-hsiang* could have worn. (On
the *fang-hsiang shih* 方相氏, see *Chou Li, Hsia Kuan;* tr. Biot, II,
p. 225; de Groot, *Religious System of China,* VI, p. 973 ff.; Laufer,
*Chinese Clay Figures,* Pt. I, p. 198 ff.) As an example of how such a
mask could have been worn on the belly, the reader is referred to the
reproduction of a Japanese Chung-k'uei doll in the Musée Guimet
contained in de Groot's work (VI, p. 1181, Fig. 18). But I do not insist on the validity of analogies so far-fetched. A mask like the present
one can well have been worn on the head or, as a phalera, on the chest.

### (*112*) BRONZE POLE-TOP

Thick-walled, strongly tapering socket of depressed oval section,
with rivet-holes in the broad sides and a large rectangular loop projecting from one of the narrow sides. On the upper rim of this socket
which is open on top, an ibex figure stands transversely to the
long axe. Showing a broad, summary *modelé,* this hollow cast ibex
presents itself best in profile view. Oxidation is scanty; a dull bronze
tone everywhere shows through a greenish tinge of verdigris. The
more exposed spots are scoured blank. Allegedly found in Suiyüan.
Chou II-III(?).                                             Pl. XLV.
    Height 138 mm.
Pole-tops with animal statuettes are frequently recorded among
Ordos finds. A peculiar parallel with a pair of ibexes leaning against
each other, a smooth, shiny, and seemingly finer casting, is in the
Hellström Collection, Mölndal (Andersson, "Selected Ordos
Bronzes," Pl. 15). A specimen in the possession of Messrs. Ton Ying
& Co., New York, shows a high-legged animal of slenderer build
with high rising horns propped against the neck (*ibid.,* Pl. 11). The
same type in a recrudescent variant, with the legs slit open as jingles,
is depicted in Salmony's *Sino-Siberian Art* (Pl. 6: 1).
Comparable crowning figures on sockets of varying shape, squarish
or round, occasionally represent stags, oftener wild asses (koulans)
with movable head; the boar and even the hedgehog make their appearance (Salmony, *op. cit.,* Pls. 5-8; Griessmaier, *Sammlung v. d.
Heydt,* nos. 96-98 — with references to further parallels in the corresponding text). Apart from these full figures, animal-heads, too,
were used as finials.
Whereas many of these things have their faithful and sometimes
almost identical counterparts in Siberia, and some of them have close
parallels even among the Scythian kurgan finds from the Pontus region (cp. Borovka's *Scythian Art*), it is not so with regard to China
proper. The Chinese forms are strangely foreign to them. The small
animal-head of pole-top no. 83, for instance, shows little plasticity,
but elegant lineament, ornamental, heraldic, solemn, abstract. The
same is partly valid for two eminent examples of Chinese pole-tops

with animal-heads in the possession of C. T. Loo and in the Freer Gallery (Umehara, *Shina Kodō Seika,* VI, p. 26), where plasticity grandly invigorates the linear conception; creations, by the way, the formal power and spiritedness of which make even the best Ordos sculptures, for all their natural warmth and charm, appear unsophisticated and simple. What here matters is that China has known pole-tops, but has shaped them quite differently from those of the Steppe.

As in the case of the mask no. 111 one has to ask again how far the present object has to do with weapons or military affairs. Salmony has summed up the various ways of using vertical finials thus: "The decorated poles probably served as a commander's insignia, as an army standard or for funeral ceremonies" (*Sino-Siberian Art,* p. 30). This judgment may justify the inclusion of this piece in a catalogue of weapons.

# BIBLIOGRAPHY

*Chinese Literature*    (Titles in alphabetic order)

An-yang Fa Chüeh Pao Kao 安陽發掘報告 (Preliminary Reports of Excavations at Anyang). Academia Sinica, Institute of History and Philology, I-III, Peking, 1929-31; IV, Shanghai, 1933. Chief ed.: Li Chi 李濟.

Cheng Chung Ku Ch'i T'u K'ao 鄭冢古器圖考 (12 chüan), Kuan Po-i 關百益. Kunming and Shanghai (Chung Hua Shu Chü 中華書局), 1940.

Cheng Sung T'ang Chi Chin T'u 貞松堂吉金圖 (3 chüan), Lo Chen-yü 羅振玉. Dairen, 1935.

Cheng Sung T'ang Chi Ku I Wen 貞松堂集古遺文 (16 chüan), Hsü Pien 續編 (3 ch.), Pu I 補遺 (3 ch.), Lo Chen-yü 羅振玉. Dairen, 1935.

Ch'eng Tzu Yai 城子崖. A Report of Excavations of the Protohistoric Site at Ch'eng-tzu-yai, Li-ch'eng Hsien, Shantung. Archaeologia Sinica, No. 1. Ed. by Li Chi 李濟, Liang Ssu-yung 梁思永, Tung Tso-pin 董作賓. Nanking: Academia Sinica, 1934.

Chi Ku Chai Chung Ting I Ch'i K'uan Chih 積古齋鐘鼎彝器款識 (10 ch.). Juan Yüan 阮元. 1804.

Ch'i Ku Shih Chi Chin Wen Shu 奇觚室吉金文述 (20 ch.), Liu Hsin-yüan 劉心源. Preface dated 1902.

Chia Ku Wen Pien 甲骨文編 (5 ts'e), Sun Hai-po 孫海波. Peking (Yenching University, Harvard-Yenching Institute), 1934.

Ch'ih An Ts'ang Chin 癡盦藏金 (1 ch.), Hsü Chi 續集 (1 ch.), Li T'ai-fen 李泰棻. Peking (National Normal College, Department of History, Archaeol. Institute), 1940-41.

Chin Shih So 金石索 (Chin So, 6 ch., Shih So, 6 ch.), Feng Yün-p'eng 馮雲鵬 and Feng Yün-yüan 馮雲鵷. Preface dated 1822; Introduction dated 1832.

Chin Wen Pien 金文編 (14 ch.), Fu Lu 附錄 (2 ch.), T'ung Chien 通檢 (1 ch.). Jung Keng 容庚. Peiping, 1925.

Chin Wen Ts'ung K'ao 金文叢考. Kuo Mo-jo 郭沫若. Tokyo (Bunkyūdō Shoten), 1932.

Ch'iu Ku Ching She Chin Shih T'u 求古精舍金石圖 (5 ch.), Ch'en Ching 陳經. 1813.

Cho I Chai I Ch'i K'ao Shih 綴遺齋彝器考釋 (30 ch.), Fang Chün-i 方濬益, 1894. Shanghai, 1935.

Chou Chin Wen Ts'un 周金文存 (6 ch.), Tsou An 鄒安. Shanghai, 1916.

Chu Shu Chi Nien 竹書紀年 (J. Legge, The Chinese Classics, III, Prolegomena, 105-83. Wang Kuo-wei, Ku Pen Chu Shu Chi Nien Chi Chiao 古本竹書紀年輯校 and Chin Pen Chu Shu Chi Nien Su Cheng 今本竹書紀年疏證, in

Hai-ning Wang Chung-k'o kung I Shu, Third Collection 海寧王忠慤公遺書, 1927).

Ch'u Ch'i T'u Shih 楚器圖釋. Liu Chieh 劉節. 1935.

Chün Ku Lu Chin Wen 攈古錄金文 (3 ch.), Wu Shih-fen 吳式芬. 1895.

Chung Kuo Shang Ku T'ung Ping K'ao 中國上古銅兵考, Lu Mou-te 陸懋德. Kuo Hsüeh Chi K'an, II, no. 2 (December 1929), 287-97.

Erh Pai Lan T'ing Chai Shou Ts'ang Chin Shih Chi 二百蘭亭齋收藏金石記 (4 ts'e). Wu Yün 吳雲, 1855.

Fu Chai Chi Chin Lu 簠齋吉金錄 (8 ch.) = the collection of Ch'en Chieh-ch'i 陳介祺. Teng Chi 鄧楫. 1918.

Fu Chai Ts'ang Ku Mu 簠齋藏古目. Ch'en Chieh-ch'i 陳介祺 (d. 1884). Wei-hsien 濰縣. 1925.

Fu Shen Tsang 俯身葬 ("Prone Burials"). Li Chi, in An-yang Fa Chüeh Pao Kao, III, 447-80.

Hai Wai Chi Chin T'u Lu 海外吉金圖錄 (3 ts'e), Jung Keng 容庚. Peking (K'ao-ku-hsüeh-shê), 1935.

Han Tai K'uang Chuan Chi Lu 漢代壙甎集錄 (2 ch.), Wang Chen-to 王振鐸. Peking-Yenching (K'ao-ku-hsüeh-shê), 1935.

Heng Hsien so chien so ts'ang Chi Chin Lu 恆軒所見所藏吉金錄 (2 ts'e). Wu Ta-ch'eng 吳大澂. 1885.

Hsi Ch'ing Ku Chien 西清古鑑 (40 ch.), Liang Shih-cheng 梁詩正 *et al.*; Palace Edition, 1755. (Hsi Ch'ing Hsü Chien, Chia Pien 西清續鑑甲編, 21 ch., 1909; I Pien 乙編, 20 ch., 1931; chief ed., Wang Chieh 王杰).

Hsi Chou Nien Tai K'ao 西周年代考. Ch'en Meng-chia 陳夢家. Chungking-Shanghai (Commercial Press), 1945.

Hsiao Chiao Ching Ko Chin Wen T'a Pen 小校經閣金文拓本 (18 ch.). Liu T'i-chih 劉體智. Shanghai, 1935.

"Hsieh Shih" Li Tai Chung Ting I Ch'i K'uan Chih Fa T'ieh 薛氏歷代鐘鼎彝器款識法帖. Hsieh Shang-kung 薛尙功, twelfth century. Re-edited by Juan Yüan 阮元, 1797.

Hsüeh T'ang so ts'ang Ku Ch'i Wu T'u 雪堂所藏古器物圖 (1 ch.), Lo Chen-yü 羅振玉. Title page dated 1923.

Hsün-hsien Hsin-ts'un Ku Ts'an Mu chih Ch'ing Li 濬縣辛村古殘墓之清理. Kuo Pao-chün 郭寶鈞, in T'ien Yeh K'ao Ku Pao Kao 田野考古報告, I (1936).

Hsün-hsien I Ch'i 濬縣彝器 (1 ch.), vol. sep. from Honan T'ung Chih, 河南通志 Wen Wu Chih 文物志; Sun Hai-po 孫海波. Peking, 1937.

K'ao Kung Ch'uang Wu Hsiao Chi 考工創物小記 (4 ch.), Ch'eng Yao-t'ien 程瑤田 (d. 1814). Huang Ch'ing Ching Chieh 皇清經解, 1829, ch. 536-539.

Ku Chou P'ien 古籀篇 (see T. Takada, Kochūhen).

Ku Kung 故宮 (45 ts'e). Peking: Publication of the National Palace Museum.

Ku Yü T'u Lu, Ch'u Chi 古玉圖錄, 初集 (4 ch.), Huang Chün 黃濬. Peking, 1939.

Li Shih yü K'ao Ku 歷史與考古, No. I. Mukden (National Museum), 1946.

Liang Chou Chin Wen Tz'u Ta Hsi T'u Lu 西周金文辭大系圖錄 (5 ts'e), K'ao Shih 考釋 (3 ts'e), Kuo Mo-jo 郭沫若. Tokyo (Bunkyūdō Shoten), 1935.

Meng Wei Ts'ao T'ang Chi Chin T'u 夢郼草堂吉金圖 (3 ch.), Hsü Pien 續編 (1 ch.). Lo Chen-yü 羅振玉. 1917-18.

Po Ku T'u Lu 博古圖錄 (30 ch.), compiled by order of Emperor Hui Tsung 徽宗 (r. 1101-25), by Wang Fu 王黼 *et al.*

San Tai Chi Chin Wen Ts'un 三代吉金文存 (20 ch.), Lo Chen-yü 羅振玉. Dairen, 1936.

Shan Chai Chi Chin Lu 善齋吉金錄 (28 ts'e), Liu T'i-chih 劉體智. Shanghai, 1934.

Shang Chou I Ch'i T'ung K'ao 商周彝器通考 (2 vols.), Jung Keng 容庚. Yenching Journ. Chinese Studies, Monogr. Ser. No. 17. Peking-Yenching, 1941.

Shih Erh Chia Chi Chin T'u Lu 十二家吉金圖錄 (2 ts'e), Shang Ch'eng-tso 商承祚. Nanking (University of Nanking), 1935.

Shou-hsien so ch'u T'ung Ch'i K'ao Lüeh 壽縣所出銅器考略, T'ang Lan 唐蘭, in Kuo Hsüeh Chi K'an, Vol. IV, No. 1 (1934).

Shu Ch'i Yüan Yüan 書契淵源 (see T. Nakashima, Shokei Engen).

Shuang Chien I Chi Chin T'u Lu 雙劍誃吉金圖錄 (2 ch.), Yü Hsing-wu 于省吾. Peking (Lai-hsün-ko), 1934.

Shuang Chien I Ku Ch'i Wu T'u Lu 雙劍誃古器物圖錄 (2 ch.), Yü Hsing-wu 于省吾. Peking, 1940.

Shuo Wen Chieh Tzu 說文解字 (30 ch.), Hsü Shen 許慎. Ca. 100 A.D.

Shuo Wen Ku Chou Pu 說文古籀補 (4 ch.), Wu Ta-ch'eng 吳大澂. 1883.

Sung Chai Chi Chin Hsü Lu 頌齋吉金續錄 (2 ch.), Jung Keng 容庚. Peking, 1938.

Sung Chai Chi Chin T'u Lu 頌齋吉金圖錄 (1 ch.), Jung Keng 容庚. Peking, 1936.

T'ao Chai Chi Chin Hsü Lu 陶齋吉金續錄 (2 ch.), Tuan Fang 端方. Nanking, 1909.

T'ao Chai Chi Chin Lu 陶齋吉金錄 (8 ch.), Tuan Fang 端方. Nanking, 1908.

Tsun Ku Chai Ku Ping Ching T'a Pen 尊古齋古兵精拓本 Huang Chün 黃濬. Peking (Rubbings of Selected Early Weapons; only a few copies exist).

Tsun Ku Chai so chien Chi Chin T'u 尊古齋所見吉金圖 (4 ch.). Huang Chün. Peking, 1936.

Yeh Chung P'ien Yü 鄴中片羽 I (2 ch.), II (2 ch.), III (2 ch.), Huang Chün 黃濬. Peking, 1935, 1937, 1942.

Yen K'u Chi Chin T'u Lu 嚴窟吉金圖錄 (2 ch.), Liang Shang-ch'un 梁上椿. Peking, 1944.

Yin-hsü Ch'i Wu Ts'un Chen 殷虛器物存眞 I (1 ch.), Kuan Po-i 關百益. Kaifeng (Honan Museum), 1930.

Yin-hsü Ku Ch'i Wu T'u Lu 殷虛古器物圖錄 (1 ch.), Lo Chen-yü 羅振玉, *in* I Shu Ts'ung Pien 藝術叢編. Shanghai, 1916.

Yin-hsü tsui chin chih chung-yao fa-hsien, fu lun Hsiao-t'un ti-ts'eng 殷墟最近之重要發現,附論小屯地層 Shih Chang-ju 石璋如, in Chung-kuo K'ao-ku Hsüeh-pao (Chinese Journ. Archaeol.), II (1947).

Yin-hsü T'ung Ch'i Wu Chung chi ch'i hsiang kuan chih Wen T'i 殷虛銅器五種及其相關之問題. Li Chi 李濟, *in* Ts'ai Yüan-p'ei Anniv. Vol. 慶祝蔡元培先生六十五歲論文集I, 73-104. Peking, 1933.

## *Non-Chinese Literature*

Åberg, N.
   Das nordische Kulturgebiet in Mitteleuropa während der jüngeren Steinzeit. Uppsala-Leipzig, 1918.

Altman, V.
   Ancient Khorezmian Civilization. JAOS, LXVII, 2 (1947).

Andersson, J. G.
   An Early Chinese Culture. Bull. Geol. Soc. China, V (1923).
   Preliminary Report on Archaeological Research in Kansu. Mem. Geol. Soc. China, Ser. A, No. 5 (1925).
   Hunting Magic in the Animal Style. BMFEA, IV (1932).
   Selected Ordos Bronzes. BMFEA, V (1933).
   Children of the Yellow Earth. Studies in Prehistoric China. London, 1934.
   The Goldsmith in Ancient China. BMFEA, VII (1935).
   Researches into the Prehistory of the Chinese. BMFEA, XV (1943).
   The Site of Chu Chia Chai. BMFEA, XVII (1945).

Arik, R. O.
   Les Fouilles d'Alaca Höyük. Rapport préliminaire sur les travaux en 1935. Ankara, 1937.

Arne, T. J.
   Die Funde von Luan P'ing und Hsuan Hua. BMFEA, V (1933).

Aspelin, J. R.
  Antiquités du Nord Finno-Ougrien. Helsingfors, 1877-84.
Äyräpää (Europaeus), A.
  Uber die Streitaxtkulturen in Russland. ESA, VIII (1933).
Bachhofer, L.
  Bronze Figures of the Late Chou Period. Art Bull., XXIII (1941).
  The Evolution of Shang and Chou Bronzes. Art Bull., XXVI (1944).
  A Short History of Chinese Art. New York, 1946.
Bernshtam, A. N.
  Osnovnye etapy istorii kultury Semirechya i Tyanshanya. Sovetskaya Arkheol.,
    XI (1949).
Biot, E.
  Le Tcheou-Li, ou Rites des Tcheou. Paris, 1851.
Bishop, C. W.
  The Bronzes of Hsin-cheng Hsien. Smithsonian Report for 1926. Washington:
    Smithsonian Instit., 1927.
  The Rise of Civilization in China with Reference to Its Geographical Aspects.
    Geographical Rev., XXII (1932).
  The Neolithic Age in Northern China. Antiquity, VII, 28 (1933).
Borovka, G.
  Scythian Art. Trans. by V. G. Childe. Kai Khosru Monographs on Eastern
    Art. New York, 1928.
Britton, R. S.
  Fifty Shang Inscriptions. Princeton, 1940.
Burkitt, M. C.
  Our Early Ancestors. An Introductory Study of Mesolithic, Neolithic and
    Copper Age Cultures in Europe and Adjacent Regions. Cambridge, 1929.
Burn, A. R.
  Minoans, Philistines, and Greeks B.C. 1400-900. London, 1930.
Chantre, E.
  Recherches anthropologiques dans le Caucase. Paris-Lyon, 1885-87.
Chavannes, E.
  Les mémoires historiques de Se-ma Ts'ien, I-V. Paris, 1895-1905.
Childe, V. G.
  The Most Ancient East, the Oriental Prelude to European Prehistory. London,
    1928.
  The Bronze Age. Cambridge, 1930.
  Eurasian Shaft-hole Axes. ESA, IX (1934).
  The Dawn of European Civilization. 3rd ed.; London, 1939.
Cohn, W.
  Eine frühe Hellebardenklinge. OZ (1934), p. 252.
Creel, H. G.
  Studies in Early Chinese Culture. First Ser. Baltimore, 1937.
  The Birth of China—A Study of the Formative Period of Chinese Civilization.
    New York, 1937.
Dalton, O. M.
  The Treasure of the Oxus, 2d ed.; London, 1926.
Dawson, C.
  The Age of the Gods. A Study in the Origins of Culture in Prehistoric Europe
    and the Ancient East. London, 1928.
Déchelette, J.
  Manuel d'archéologie préhistorique celtique et gallo-romaine. Paris, 1908 ff.
Delaporte, L. J.
  Mesopotamia; the Babylonian and Assyrian Civilization. Tr. by V. G. Childe.
    London, 1925.
Dörpfeld, W.
  Troja und Ilion. Athens, 1902.

Dullo, E.
Die kaukasischen Äxte der Bronzezeit. PZ, XXVII (1936).
Dussaud, R.
Haches à douille de type asiatique. Syria, XI (1930).
Eberhard, W.
Lokalkulturen im Alten China, I: Die Lokalkulturen des Nordens und Westens.
T'P, XXXVII (1942), Suppl.
Ebert, M.
Reallexikon der Vorgeschichte. Berlin, 1924-29.
Ecke, G.
Frühe chinesische Bronzen aus der Sammlung O. Trautmann. Peking, 1939.
Uber einige Messer aus Anyang. Sinolog. Arbeiten, I (1943).
Egami, N. 江上波夫, and S. Mizuno 水野清一
Inner Mongolia and the Region of the Great Wall. Archaeologia Orientalis,
B Ser., Vol. I. Tokyo and Kyoto, 1935.
Egami, N., K. Komai 駒井和愛, and S. Gotō 後藤守一
Tōyō Kōkogaku 東洋考古學. Tokyo, 1939.
Erkes, E.
Das Schwein im alten China. Mon. Ser., VII (1942).
Ferguson, J. C.
Catalogue of the Recorded Bronzes of Successive Dynasties (Li Tai Chu Lu
Chi Chin Mu 歷代箸錄吉金目). Peking, 1939.
Gaul, J. H.
Observations on the Bronze Age in the Yenisei Valley, Siberia. Papers Peabody
Mus. Amer. Archaeol. and Ethnol., Harvard Univ., XX (1943).
Golomshtok, E.
Anthropological Activities in Soviet Russia. Amer. Anthropol., XXXV (1933).
Goloubew, V.
L'âge du bronze au Tonkin et dans le Nord-Annam. BEFEO, XXIX (1929).
Goodrich, L. C.
A Short History of the Chinese People. New York, 1943.
Graham, D. C.
A Preliminary Report of the Hanchow 漢州 Excavation. Journ. West China
Border Research Soc., VI (1934).
Granö, J. G.
Archäologische Beobachtungen von meinen Reisen in den nördlichen Grenzge-
genden Chinas. Journ. Soc. Finno-Ougr., XXVI (1909), XXVIII (1912).
Griessmaier, V.
Sammlung Baron Eduard von der Heydt Wien. Ordos-Bronzen, Bronzen aus
Luristan und dem Kaukasus, Werke chinesischer Kleinkunst. Wien, 1936.
Grivtsov-Grakov, O.
Une trouvaille d'objets de l'âge du bronze dans la région du haut Tobol. ESA,
IV (1929).
Groot, J. J. M. de
The Religious System of China, I-VI. Leyden, 1892-1910.
Grousset, R.
L'Empire des Steppes. Paris, 1939.
Hall, H. R.
The Civilization of Greece in the Bronze Age. The Rhind Lectures, 1923. Lon-
don, 1928.
Hamada, K. 濱田耕作
Senoku Seishō 泉屋清賞. The Collection of Old Bronzes of Baron Sumitomo.
Explanatory Notes Pt. 1—Bronze Vases, by K. Hamada; Pt. 2—Ancient
Mirrors, by Y. Harada, 1921.
Select Specimens of the Archaeological Collection in the Department of Literature,
Kyoto Imp. University. Add. Vol. Kyoto, 1935.

Hančar, F.
  Die Nadelformen des Kaukasusgebietes. ESA, VII (1932).
  Alaca Höyük, WBKKA, XII (1938).
  The Eurasian Animal Style and the Altai Complex. Artibus Asiae, XV (1952).
  Urgeschichte Kaukasiens, von den Anfängen seiner Besiedlung bis in die Zeit
    seiner frühen Metallurgie. Wien-Leipzig, 1937.
Harada, Y. 原田淑人, and K. Komai 駒井和愛
  Mu-Yang Ch'eng 牧羊城. Han and Pre-Han Sites at the Foot of Mount Lao-
    t'ieh, South Manchuria. Archaeologia Orientalis, Vol. II. Tokyo-Kyoto,
    1931.
  Shina Koki Zukō 支那古器圖考 (Chinese Antiquities. Pt. 1—Arms and Ar-
    mour). Tokyo, 1932.
Heikel, A.
  Antiquités de la Sibérie Occidentale, conservées dans les musées de Tomsk, de
    Tobolsk, de Tumen, d'Ekaterinebourg, de Moscou et d'Helsingfors. Mém.
    Soc. Finno-Ougrienne, VI (1894).
Heine-Geldern, R. v.
  Archaeological Traces of the Vedic Aryans. Journ. Indian Soc. Oriental Art,
    IV (1936).
  Das Tocharerproblem und die pontische Wanderung. *Saeculum,* II (1951).
Hirth, F.
  Bausteine zu einer Geschichte der chinesischen Literatur. T'P, VII (1896).
Janse, O.
  Notes sur quelques épées anciennes trouvées en Chine. BMFEA, II (1930).
  Quelques antiquités chinoises d'un caractère Hallstattien. BMFEA, II (1930).
  Un groupe de bronzes anciens propres à l'Extrême-Asie Méridionale. BMFEA,
    III (1931).
  Le style du Houai et ses affinités. Rev. arts asiatiques, VIII/3 (1934).
  L'empire des steppes et les relations entre l'Europe et L'Extrême-Orient dans
    l'antiquité. Rev. arts asiatiques, IX/1 (1935).
Jettmar, K.
  The Karasuk Culture and Its South-Eastern Affinities. BMFEA, 22 (1950).
  Archäologische Spuren von Indogermanen in Zentralasien. Paideuma, Mitteil. z.
    Kulturkunde, V (1952).
Jochelson, W.
  Archaeological Investigations in Kamchatka. Washington, 1928.
Kanazeki, T. 金關丈夫, S. Mizuno 水野清一, S. Miyake 三宅宗悦
  Yang-T'eou-Wa 羊頭窪. Fouille d'un site préhistorique dans la baie de Hatowan
    près de Rioziun en Mandchourie Méridionale. Archaeol. Orientalis, B Ser.,
    Vol. III. Tokyo, 1942.
Karlbeck, O.
  Ancient Chinese Bronze Weapons. China Journ. Sci. and Arts, Vol. III, 3 (1925).
  Notes on the Archaeology of China. BMFEA, II (1930).
  A Honan Grave Find. BMFEA, II (1930).
Karlgren, B.
  Early Chinese Mirror Inscriptions. BMFEA, VI (1934).
  Yin and Chou in Chinese Bronzes. BMFEA, VIII (1936).
  New Studies in Chinese Bronzes. BMFEA, IX (1937).
  Grammata Serica. Script and Phonetics in Chinese and Sino-Japanese. BMFEA,
    XII (1940).
  Some Weapons and Tools of the Yin Dynasty. BMFEA, XVII (1945).
Kim, Chewon
  Über eine Gruppe chinesischer Messer. OZ, XIV (1938).
Kiselev, S. V.
  Drevnyaya Istoriya Yuzhnoi Sibiri. Moscow, 1951.

Koop, A. J.
Early Chinese Bronzes. London, 1924.

Koşay, H. Z.
Türkiye Cümhuriyeti Maarif Vekaletince Yaptirilan Ahlatlibel Hafriyati. Türk
Tarih, Arkeol. ve Etnogr. Dergisi II. Istanbul, 1934. (Report on excavations at Ahlatlibel.)
Ausgrabungen von Alaca Höyük. Ein Vorbericht über die im Auftrage der
türkischen Geschichtskommission im Sommer 1936 durchgeführten Forschungen und Entdeckungen. Ankara, 1944.

Kühn, H.
Die vorgeschichtliche Kunst Deutschlands. Berlin, 1935.
Chronologie der Sino-Sibirischen Bronzen. IPEK, XII (1938).

Kümmel, O.
Jörg Trübner zum Gedächtnis. Ergebnisse seiner letzten chinesischen Reisen.
Berlin, 1930.

Laufer, B.
Jade. Chicago, 1912.
Chinese Clay Figures, Pt. I—Prolegomena on the History of Defensive Armor.
Chicago, 1914.

Le Coq, A. v.
Bilderatlas zur Kunst und Kulturgeschichte Mittelasiens. Berlin, 1925.

Legge, J.
The Chinese Classics. Vol. I, Oxford, 1893; Vol. II, Oxford, 1895; Vols. III-V,
Hongkong, 1865, 1871, 1872.

Licent, E.
Les collections néolithiques du Musée Hoangho Paiho de Tientsin. Tientsin, 1932.

Lochow, H. J. v.
Sammlung Lochow. Chinesische Bronzen, II. Herausgegeben vom Sammler.
Peking, 1944.

Loehr, M.
Beiträge zur Chronologie der älteren chinesischen Bronzen. OZ, XII (1936).
Chinesische Pickeläxte. Mon. Ser., IV (1939-40).
Neue Typen grauer Shang-Keramik. Sinolog. Arbeiten, I (1943).
The Earliest Chinese Sword and the Akinakes. Oriental Art, I (1948).
Ordos Daggers and Knives. New Material, Classification and Chronology. First
Part: Knives. Artibus Asiae, XII (1949); Second Part: Daggers. Ar-
tibus Asiae, XIV (1951).
Tools and Weapons from Anyang and Siberian Analogies. AJA, LIII (1949).

Martin, F. R.
L'age du bronze au Musée de Minoussinsk. Stockholm, 1893.

Márton, L. v.
Dolchstäbe aus Ungarn. PZ, XXII (1931).

Maspero, H.
La Chine antique. Paris, 1927.

Meister, P. W.
Chinesische Bronzemasken. OZ, XIV (1938).

Menghin, O.
Weltgeschichte der Steinzeit. Wien, 1931.

Menzies, J. M.
The Appreciation of Chinese Bronzes. *In* An Exhibition of Ancient Chinese
Ritual Bronzes (see J. M. Plumer).

Merhart, G. v.
Bronzezeit am Jenissei. Wien, 1926.
The Paleolithic Period in Siberia. Amer. Anthropol., XXV (1923).

Meyer, Ed.
  Geschichte des Altertums. I, 2. 5th ed.; Stuttgart-Berlin, 1926. II, 2d ed.; Stutt-
    gart-Berlin, 1928.
Minns, E. H.
  Scythians and Greeks. Cambridge, 1913.
  Small Bronzes from Northern Asia. Antiquaries Journ., X (1930).
  The Art of the Northern Nomads. Proc. British Acad., Vol. XXVIII (1942).
Mizuno, S. 水野清一
  Kan kingin-saku seidō-ki 漢金銀錯青銅器. Hōun, XXXII (1942). ("Han
    gold and silver inlaid bronze vessels.")
Morgan, M. J. de, *et al.*
  Délégation en Perse, Mémoires publ. sous la direction de M. J. de Morgan. VIII:
    Recherches archéologiques. Paris, 1905.
  L'humanité préhistorique. Paris.
  La préhistoire orientale. Ouvrage posthume publié par L. Germain. III, L'Asie
    Antérieure. Paris, 1927.
Myres, J. L.
  Who Were the Greeks? Sather Classical Lectures, Vol. VI. Berkeley, 1930.
Nagahiro, T. 長廣敏雄
  Taikō no kenkyū 帯鈎の研究 ("Die Agraffe und ihre Stellung in der altchi-
    nesischen Kunstgeschichte"). Kyoto, 1943.
Nagy, G.
  Skythai Leletek. Arch. Ertesitö (1913).
Nestor, J.
  Zum Stande der Vorgeschichtsforschung in Rumänien. Ber. Röm. Germ. Komm.,
    XXII (1932).
Nioradze, G.
  Der Verwahrfund von Kvemo-Sasirethi. ESA, VII (1932).
Nott, S. C.
  Chinese Jade. London, 1936.
Palmgren, N.
  Yinstil-Studien. Ein Satz von drei Bronzen aus der Sammlung Nezu. OZ,
    XII (1936).
Pawlikowski-Cholewa, A. v.
  Die Heere des Morgenlandes. Militärische Beiträge zur Geschichte des nahen
    und fernen Orients. Berlin, 1940.
Peake, H., and H. J. Fleure
  Priests and Kings. Oxford, 1927.
  The Steppe and the Sown. Oxford, 1928.
  The Way of the Sea. Oxford, 1929.
  The Horse and the Sword. Oxford, 1933.
Pelliot, P.
  Jades archaïques de Chine. Paris and Brussels, 1925.
  The Royal Tombs of Anyang. *In* Studies in Chinese Art and Some Indian In-
    fluences. London: The India Soc. (*s.a.*).
Petrie, W. M. Flinders
  Tools and Weapons. London, 1917.
Plumer, J. M.
  An Exhibition of Ancient Chinese Ritual Bronzes Loaned by C. T. Loo & Co.
    Detroit: Detroit Instit. Arts, 1940.
Pope, A. U. (ed.)
  A Survey of Persian Art. London and New York, 1938-39.
Pope, J. A.
  *In* Freer Gallery Catalogue (see Anonymous).

Pope-Hennessy, Una
  Early Chinese Jades. London, 1923.
Radloff, V.
  Aus Sibirien. Lose Blätter aus dem Tagebuche eines reisenden Linguisten.
      Leipzig, 1884.
  Sibirskiya drevnosti. MAR, III, V, XV, XXVII (1888, 1891, 1894, 1902).
Rau, P.
  Neue Funde aus Hockergräbern des Wolgadeutschen Gebiets. ESA, IV (1929).
Rivière, H., S. Elisséev, G. Munthe, and O. Sirén.
  Documents d'art chinois de la Collection Osvald Sirén. Ars Asiatica, VII (1925).
Rostovtzeff, M.
  Iranians and Greeks in South Russia. Oxford, 1922.
  Inlaid Bronzes of the Han Dynasty in the Collection of C. T. Loo. Paris and
      Brussels, 1927.
  The Animal Style in South Russia and China. Princeton Monographs in Art and
      Archaeology, XIV. Princeton, 1929.
Rykov, P.
  Die Chvalynsker Kultur der Bronzezeit an der Unteren Wolga. ESA, I (1927).
Salles, G.
  Les Bronzes de Li-yu. Rev. arts asiatiques, VIII, 3 (1934).
Salmony, A.
  Sino-Siberian Art in the Collection of C. T. Loo. Paris, 1933.
  Carved Jade of Ancient China. Berkeley, 1938.
  The Kauri Shell in Chinese Bronze Art. Parnassus, IV, 6 (1932).
Schaeffer, C. F. A.
  Stratigraphie comparée et chronologie de l'Asie Occidentale (IIIe et IIe millé-
      naires). Oxford and London, 1948.
Schmidt, V. A.
  Die Kurgane der Stanica Konstantinovskaja. ESA, IV (1929).
  *In* FUF, XVIII (on the Turbino finds).
Schuchhardt, C.
  Vorgeschichte von Deutschland. 2d ed.; München, 1935.
Sekino, T. 關野貞, S. Yatsui 谷井濟一, *et al.*
  Rakurō-gun jidai no iseki 樂浪郡時代の遺蹟 (Archaeological Researches on
      the Ancient Lolang-District. Special Report of the Service of Antiquities,
      Vol. IV. 1 vol. text, 2 vols. pls.). Government General of Chōsen, 1925,
      1927.
Seligman, C. G.
  Bird-Chariots and Socketed Celts in Europe and China. JRAI, L (1920).
Shiratori, K. 白鳥庫吉, *et al.*
  Tōyō Bunkashi Taikei 東洋文化史大系: Kodai Shina oyobi Indo 古代支那
      及びインド. Tokyo, 1939.
Sidorov, A.
  Tüllenaxt von Ustsysolsk. ESA, VI (1931), 173-74.
Sirén, O.
  A History of Early Chinese Art, I-IV. London, 1929.
Speleers, L.
  Nos nouveaux bronzes perses. Bull. Musées Royaux d'Art et d'Histoire, Brus-
      sels, III (1931), IV (1933).
Takada, T.
  Ku Chou P'ien (Kochuhen 古籀篇). Tokyo, 1925.
Tallgren, A. M.
  KBr NOR = Die Kupfer-und Bronzezeit in Nord-und Ostrussland. SMYA,
      XXV (1911).
  "Svärdstavar" från Ural och Sibirien. FM, XXII (1915).

Collection Tovostine des antiquités préhistoriques de Minoussinsk conservées chez le Dr. Karl Hedman à Vasa. Helsingfors, 1917.

Collection Zaoussaïlov au Musée Historique de Finlande, I. Helsingfors, 1916.

(re Seima) in FM, XXII (1915) and Rig. II-III (1919-20).

(re Turbino) in FUF, XX (1921).

Fatjanovokulturen i Centralryssland. FM, 1924.

L'Age du cuivre dans la Russie Centrale. SMYA, XXXII (1922).

La Pontide préscythique après l'introduction des métaux. ESA, II (1926).

Caucasian Monuments. The Kazbek Treasure. ESA, V (1930).

Inner Asiatic and Siberian Rock Pictures. ESA, VIII (1933).

The Arctic Bronze Age. ESA, XI (1937).

Studies of the Pontic Bronze Age. ESA, XI (1937).

Some North-Eurasian Sculptures. ESA, XII (1938).

Teilhard de Chardin, P., and Pei Wen-chung

Le Néolithique de la Chine. Peking, 1944.

Teploukhov, S. A.

Ancient Burials in the Minusinsk Region. Mat. po Etn., III, 2 (1927).

An Attempt to Classify the Ancient Metal Cultures of Minusinsk. Mat. po Etn., IV, 2 (1929).

Timperley, H. J.

The Awakening of China in Archaeology. Illus. London News, April 4, 1936.

Toll, N.

Bronzedolche der Sammlung Zichy. ESA, IV (1929).

Trübner, J.

Yu und Kuang. Leipzig, 1929.

Umehara, S. 梅原末治

Den Inkyo hakken no dōseihin ni tsuite 傳殷虛發見の銅製品に就て (On Some Bronze Objects Allegedly Hailing from Yin-hsü). Shigaku, VIII/4 (1929). *Also in* Shina Kōkogaku Ronkō, pp. 309-25.

Kita-Shina hakken no isshu no tōyōki to sono seishitsu 北支那發見の一種の銅容器と其の性質 (A Study on Bronze Kettles Found in the Northern Part of China). Tōhō Gakuhō, Kyoto, I (1931).

Shina kodai no tōriki ni tsuite 支那古代の銅利器に就て (Note on Bronze Tools and Weapons in China). Tōhō Gakuhō, Kyoto, II (1931). *Also in* Shina Kōkogaku Ronkō, pp. 15-74.

Inkyo shutsudo no ichi ko-sō 殷虛出土の一古琮. Kōkogaku Zasshi, XXII (1932). *Also in* Ronkō, pp. 326-34.

Shina Kodō Seika 支那古銅精華, I-VII. Osaka: Yamanaka & Co., 1933.

Senkoku-shiki dōki no kenkyū 戰國式銅器の研究 (Etude des bronzes des royaumes combattants). Kyoto, 1936.

Anyang Treasures = Kanan Anyō ihō 河南安陽遺寶 (Selected Ancient Treasures Found at An-yang, Yin Sites). Kyoto, 1940.

Anyang Studies = Kanan Anyō ibutsu no kenkyū 河南安陽遺物ノ研究. Kyoto, 1941.

Shina Kan-dai kinen-mei shikki zusetsu 支那漢代紀年銘漆器圖說. Kyoto, 1943.

Kanan Chōtoku-fu gai Kōka-sō kobo-gun no gaikan 河南彰德府外侯家莊古墓郡ノ概觀 I—Hōun XXIX (1942), II—Hōun XXX (1943), III—Hōun XXXI (1944). Abbr. "Hou-chia-chuang."

Seizansō Seishō 靑山莊清賞. Illustrated Catalogue of the Nezu Collection, IV, Chinese Bronzes. Tokyo, 1942.

Umehara, S., and Fujita, R.

Chōsen ko-bunka sōkan (Survey of Korea's Ancient Culture). Nara and Kyoto, 1948. Vol. 2.

Voretzsch, E. A.

Altchinesische Bronzen. Berlin, 1924.

Vernadsky, G.

　Ancient Russia. A History of Russia, I. 3d ed.; New Haven, 1946.

Weinberg, S. S.

　Aegean Chronology: Neolithic Period and Early Bronze Age. AJA, LI, 2 (1947).

Wenley, A. G.

　*In* Freer Gallery Catalogue (*see* Anonymous).

White, W. C.

　Tombs of Old-Loyang. Shanghai, 1934.

　The Tomb of the Elephant. Illus. London News, March 23, April 20, May 18, 1935.

Yawata, I. 八幡一郎

　Chōyō fukin no shin-sekki-jidai iseki 朝陽附近ノ新石器時代遺蹟 (Neolithic Finds from the Vicinity of Ch'ao-yang, Jehol). Kōkogaku Zasshi, XXVI (1936).

　Nekka-shō hokubu no senshi-jidai iseki to ibutsu 熱河省北部ノ先史時代遺跡及遺物 (Contribution to the Prehistoric Archaeology of Northern Jehol). Report of the First Scientific Expedition to Manchoukuo, Sec. VI, Pt. III, April 1940.

Yetts, W. P.

　The George Eumorfopoulos Collection Catalogue of the Chinese and Corean Bronzes, Sculpture, Jades, Jewellery and Miscellaneous Objects, I-III, London, 1929-32.

　Chinese Contact with Luristan Bronzes. Burlington Mag., LIX (1931).

　The Horse: A Factor in Early Chinese History. ESA, IX (1934).

　An Early Chou Bronze. Burlington Mag., LXX (1937).

　The Cull Chinese Bronzes. London: Univ. of London, Courtauld Institute of Art, 1939.

## *Anonymous*

British Museum, A Guide to the Antiquities of the Bronze Age. 2d ed.; 1920.

The Exhibition, Stockholm = The Exhibition of Early Chinese Bronzes. Arranged on the occasion of the 13th International Congress on the History of Art, Stockholm, September 1933. BMFEA, 6 (1934).

Freer Catalogue = Smithsonian Institution, Freer Gallery of Art, Oriental Studies No. 3: A Descriptive and Illustrative Catalogue of Chinese Bronzes Acquired During the Administration of John Ellerton Lodge; Compiled by the Staff of the Freer Gallery of Art. Washington, 1946.

London Exhibition Catalogue = Catalogue of the International Exhibition of Chinese Art, 1935-36. 3d ed.; London, 1936.

Ryojun Hakubutsukan Zuroku 旅順博物館圖錄 (Catalogue of the Port Arthur Museum). Compiled by the Kantō Office 關東局. Tokyo, 1943.

Shū Kan ihō 周漢遺寶 (Relics of Han and Pre-Han Dynasties; Catalogue of the Exhibition Held in May, 1932). The Imperial Household Museum. Tokyo, 1932.

Tōyō Rekishi Daijiten 東洋歴史大辭典

## *Abbreviations*

| | |
|---|---|
| AJA | American Journal of Archaeology. |
| BEFEO | Bulletin de l'Ecole Française d'Extrême-Orient, Hanoi. |
| BMFEA | Bulletin Museum of Far Eastern Antiquities, Stockholm. |
| ESA | Eurasia Septentrionalis Antiqua, Helsinki. |
| FM | Finskt Museum, Helsinki. |
| FUF | Finnisch-Ugrische Forschungen, Helsinki. |
| IPEK | Jahrbuch für Prähistorische und Etnographische Kunst. |

| | |
|---|---|
| JAOS | Journal of the American Oriental Society. |
| JRAI | Journal of the Royal Anthropological Society. |
| MAGW | Mitteilungen der anthropologischen Gesellschaft Wien. |
| MAR | Materialy po Arkheologii Rossii, St. Petersburg. |
| Mon. Ser. | Monumenta Serica, Peking. |
| OZ | Ostasiatische Zeitschrift, Berlin. |
| PZ | Prähistorische Zeitschrift, Berlin. |
| RLV | Reallexikon der Vorgeschichte (see M. Ebert). |
| SMYA | Suomen Muinaismuisto-Yhdistyksen Aikakauskirja = Finska Fornmin-nesföreningens Tidskrift, Helsinki. |
| T'P | T'oung Pao, Leyden. |
| WBKKA | Wiener Beiträge zur Kunst-und Kulturgeschichte Asiens. |
| ZRORAO | Zapiski Otdeleniya Russkoi i spavyanskoi arkheologii Imp. Russkago Arkheologicheskago Obzhchestva, St. Petersburg. |

# INDEX

boar, 211
Boaro, 111
boat-axe, 99
Boghazköi, 95
Bohlken (Berlin dealer), 54
bone knife, 65, —— tool, 102
Borodino (hoard), 42-43, 48, 87, 95-100, 106, 110
Borovka, G., 140, 190-92, 211
British Isles, 42, 48
British Museum, 29, 37, 146, 206
Britton, R. S., 209
Brussels Museum (Musées Royaux d'Art et d'His-
toire), 28-29, 37
Bulgaria, 100
bull's head, 102
Burchard, Dr. O., 19

Cambodia, 35
Caspian Sea, 32
catacomb-grave (Middle Kuban), 97, 99-100, 108,
111
cattle, 85, 101
Caucasia, 109, 190
Caucasus, 6, 29, 73-74, 85, 92, 97, 111
Chang, King of Ch'u (= Hui Wang), 64
chariot, 41, 208, —— burial, 179
Chavannes, E., 34, 171, 173, 186, 196, 199-200
Ch'en (state), 60, 64, 166
Ch'en Chieh-ch'i, 52, 61, 64, 132
Ch'en Meng-chia, 84
Cheng (state), 59, 179
Ch'eng Chou (city), 58-59, 158
Ch'eng Wang, Chou king, 34, 58, 210
Ch'eng Yao-t'ien, 56, 78, 155
Chi-cha, prince of Wu (= Chi-tzu), 186
Chi-tzu, prince of Wu (= Chi-cha), 80, 82, 186
Ch'i tao (knife money), 65
Chia Tzu, prince of Ts'ai, 59
Childe, V. G., 30, 95, 99, 186
Chin-ts'un (site), 163
Ch'in (state), 60, 171, 180, 196
Ching, Duke of Sung, 59, 63
*Chou Li,* 82, 155, 208, 211
Chu-chia-chai (site), 65
Chu-chiu Yüeh-hua, Yüeh ruler, 200
Chu-fan, King of Wu, 186, 196
*Chu Shu Chi Nien,* see *Bamboo Annals*
Ch'u (state), 59-60, 62, 64, 196-97
Ch'u Te-i (= Tch'ou Tö-yi), 9, 34
Chü-p'ing-kuan, 181
Ch'üan Jung (tribe), 58

Chuang, Duke of Lu, 80
Chuang, King of Ch'u, 62
Chuang Wang, Chou king, 62
*Chuangtse,* 82
Chuisk R., 106
*Ch'un Ch'iu,* 59, 63, 80
Chung-k'uei, 211
Clarke, L., Collection, 71
claw-shaped shaft-shoe, 175
cloth (impression on bronze), 141, 151, 197, 205,
209
Contenau, G., 94
contracted skeleton, 94
copper-lined pottery, 85
copper tools, 86, 94-95, 102, 109
corded ware, 94
Couvreur, S., 188
cowry shell (ornament), 121, 164-65, 170
crackle (in bronze surface), 193, 197, 209
Creel, H. G., 33-34
Cull Collection, 172-73

dance, 5, 11, —— axe, 4, 124
David-Weill Collection, 6, 13, 21, 33, 37, 46-49, 51,
118, 125-26, 137, 145, 157, 168-69, 173-74, 193,
204
deer, 164
Denmark, 38
Dnieper, 191-92
Dniester, 87, 96
Dörpfeld, W., 91, 98
dog, buried with man, 86
dog figure, 37
*Dolchstab,* 49
dolmen, 186
Don R., 111
Donets R., 99
Dong-son, 178, 204
dragon, 18-19, 21-22, 120-24, 143, 147-48, 152-53,
170, 173, 201, 204
dragon-head, 67, 137, 139-40
Dussaud, R., 27-28
Dzungaria, 83, 87

eagle-head, 189, 191
Ebert, M., 97
Ecbatana, 27, 37
Ecke, G., 67, 123, 139-40, 142
Egami, N., 34, 68, 75, 81, 92, 107, 140-42, 157, 187,
189
Egypt, 33, 84, 88

*Plates*

PLATE I

*No. I*

PLATE II

*No. 2*

*No. 3*

PLATE III

*No. 4*

PLATE IV

*No. 5*

PLATE V

*No. 6*

PLATE VI

No. 7

No. 8

PLATE VII

No. 9

PLATE VIII

*No. 10*

PLATE IX

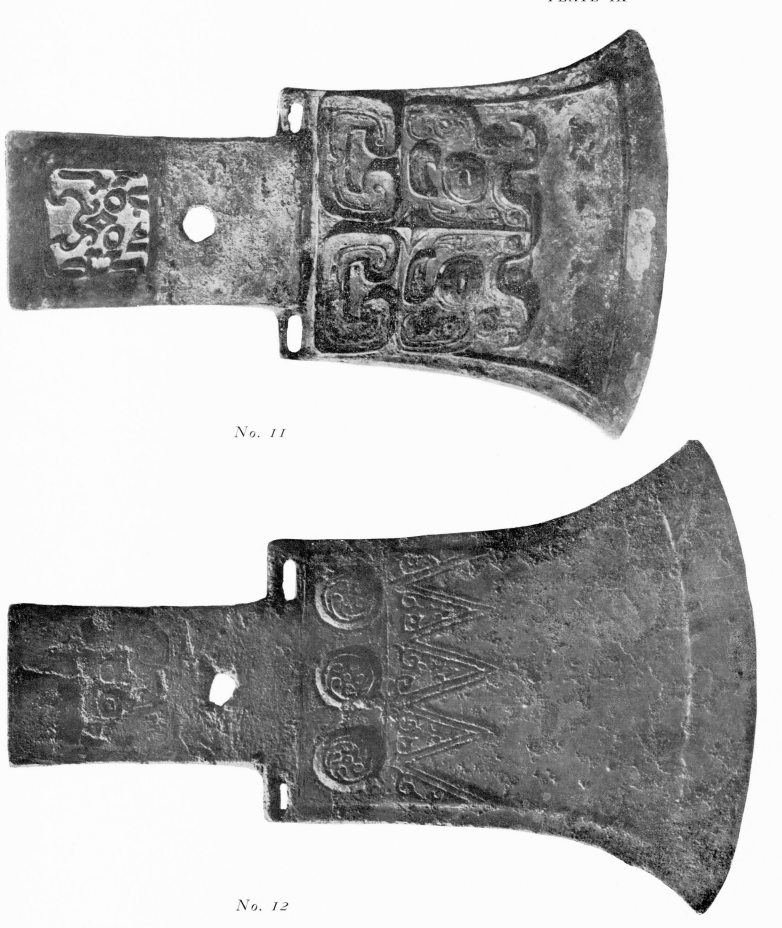

No. 11

No. 12

PLATE X

No. 13

PLATE XI

*No. 14*

*No. 15*

PLATE XII

No. 16

No. 17

No. 18

PLATE XIII

No. 20

No. 21

No. 22

PLATE XIV

No. 24                                    No. 25

PLATE XV

*No. 26*

*No. 27*

PLATE XVI

No. 28          No. 29          No. 30

PLATE XVII

No. 32                No. 33                No. 34

PLATE XVIII

No. 35           No. 36           No. 37

PLATE XIX

No. 38          No. 39          No. 40

PLATE XX

No. 41

No. 42

PLATE XXI

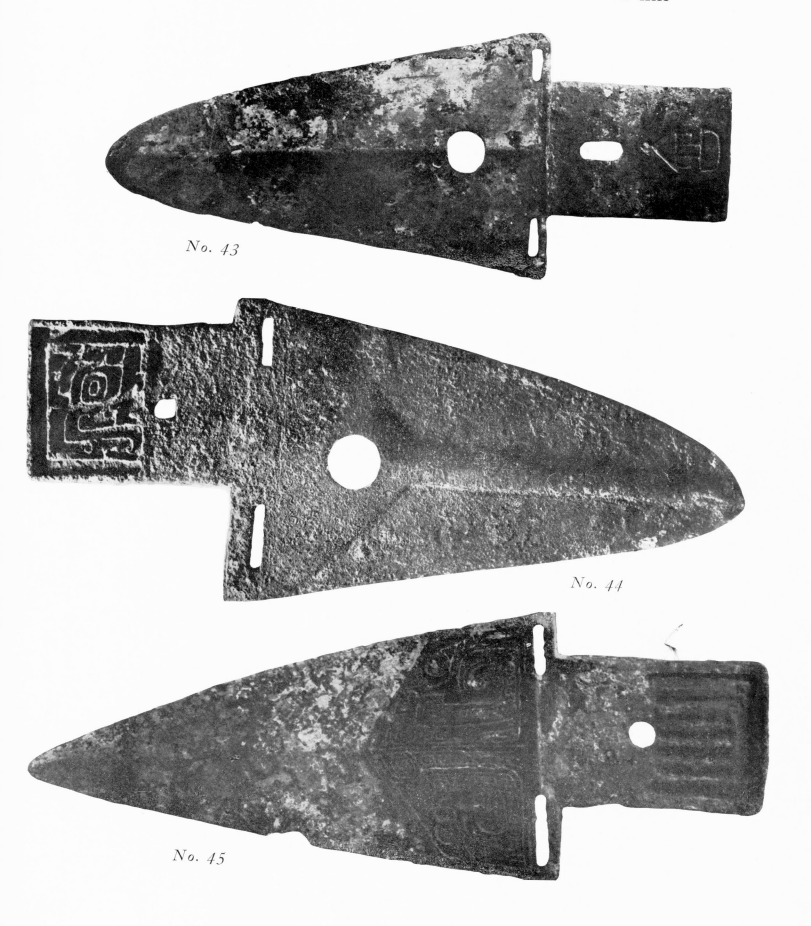

No. 43

No. 44

No. 45

PLATE XXII

No. 47

No. 48

PLATE XXIII

No. 46

No. 49

PLATE XXIV

No. 50

No. 51

No. 52

No. 53

PLATE XXV

No. 54

No. 55

No. 56

No. 57

PLATE XXVI

No. 58

No. 59

No. 60

No. 61

PLATE XXVII

No. 62  No. 63  No. 64

PLATE XXVIII

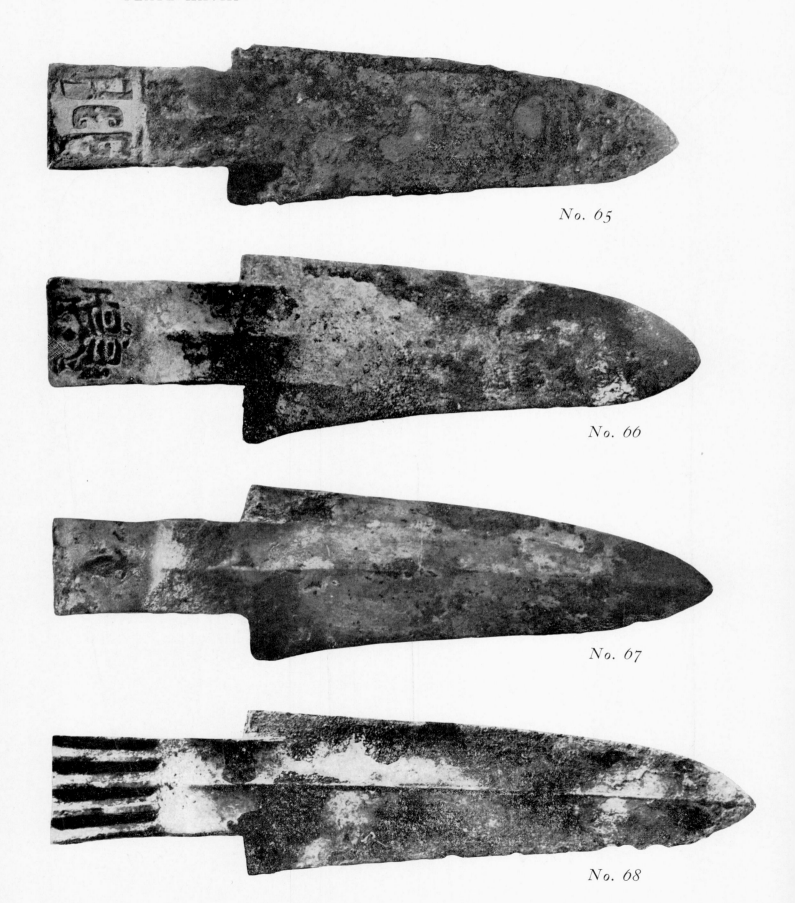

No. 65

No. 66

No. 67

No. 68

PLATE XXIX

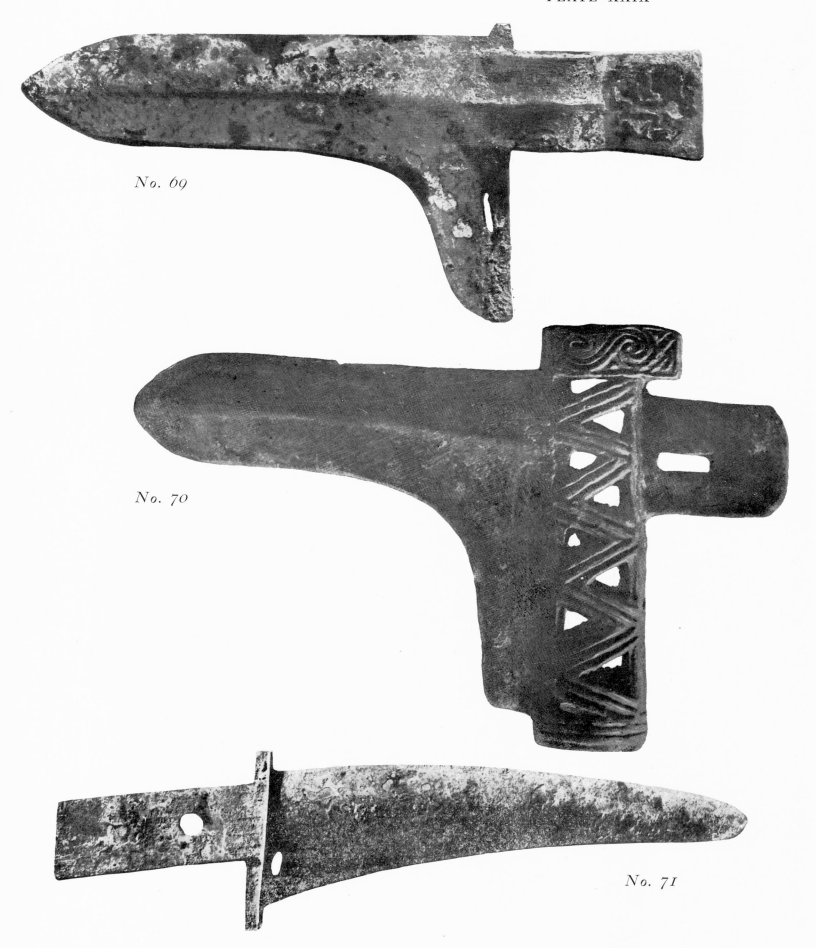

No. 69

No. 70

No. 71

PLATE XXX

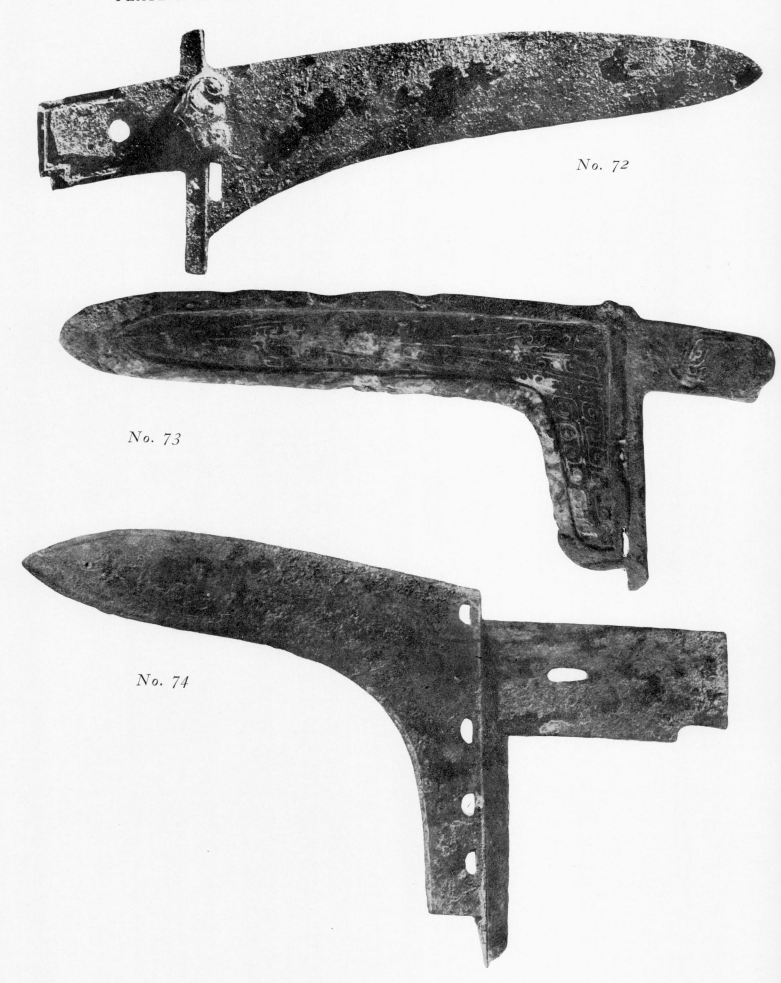

No. 72

No. 73

No. 74

PLATE XXXI

No. 75

PLATE XXXII

No. 79

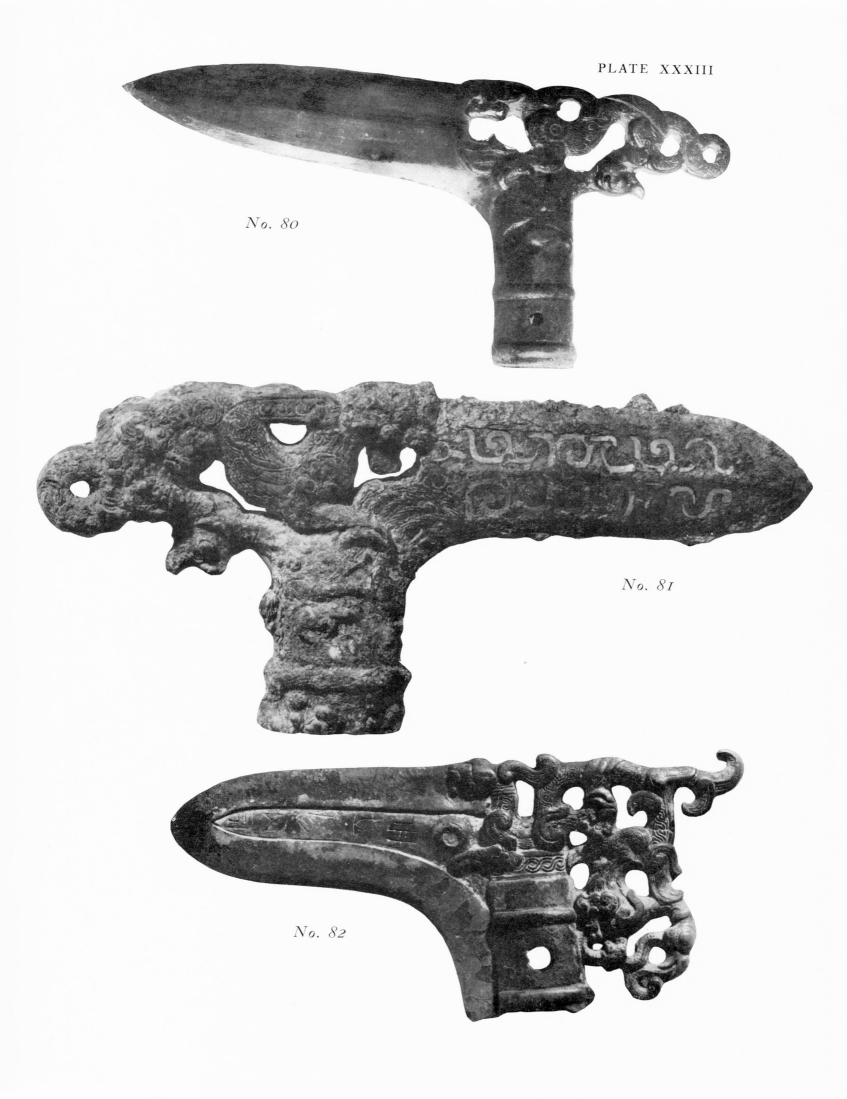

PLATE XXXIII

No. 80

No. 81

No. 82

PLATE XXXIV

No. 76          No. 31          No. 84

No. 78          No. 77

PLATE XXXV

No. 85          No. 86          No. 87    No. 88

PLATE XXXVI

No. 89          No. 90          No. 91          No. 92

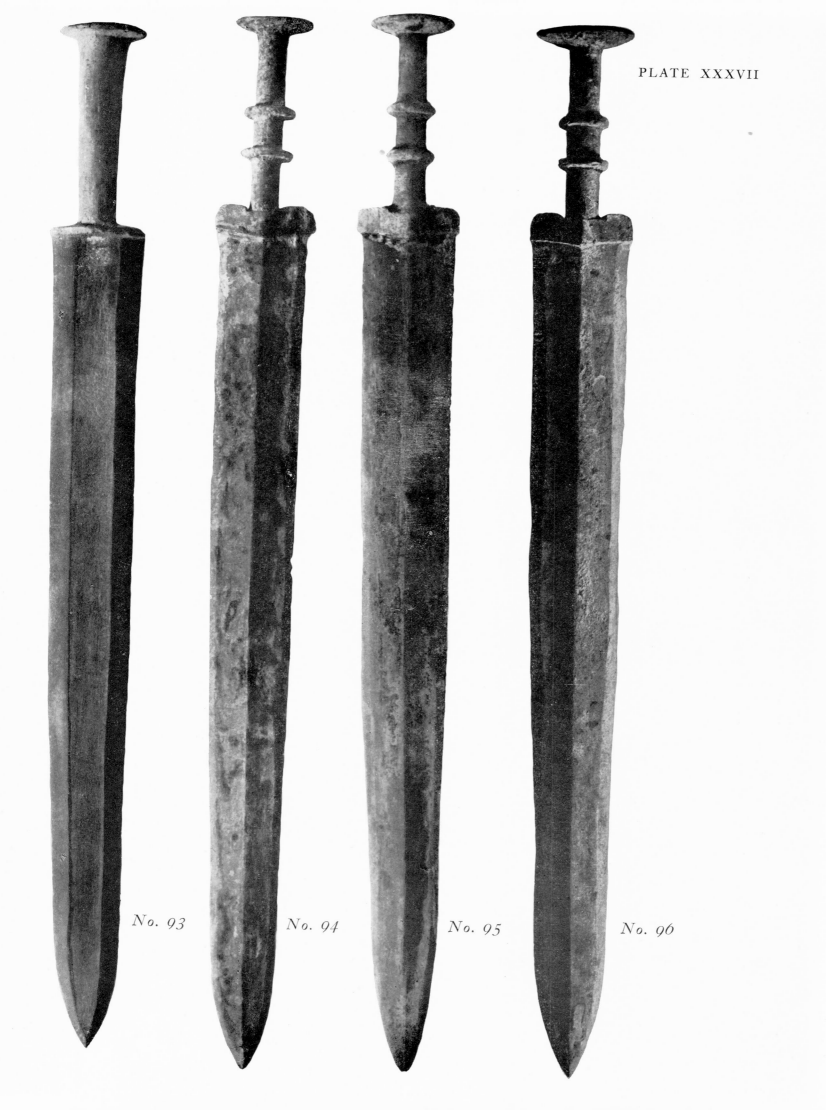

PLATE XXXVII

No. 93          No. 94          No. 95          No. 96

PLATE XXXVIII

No. 97        No. 98        No. 99        No. 100

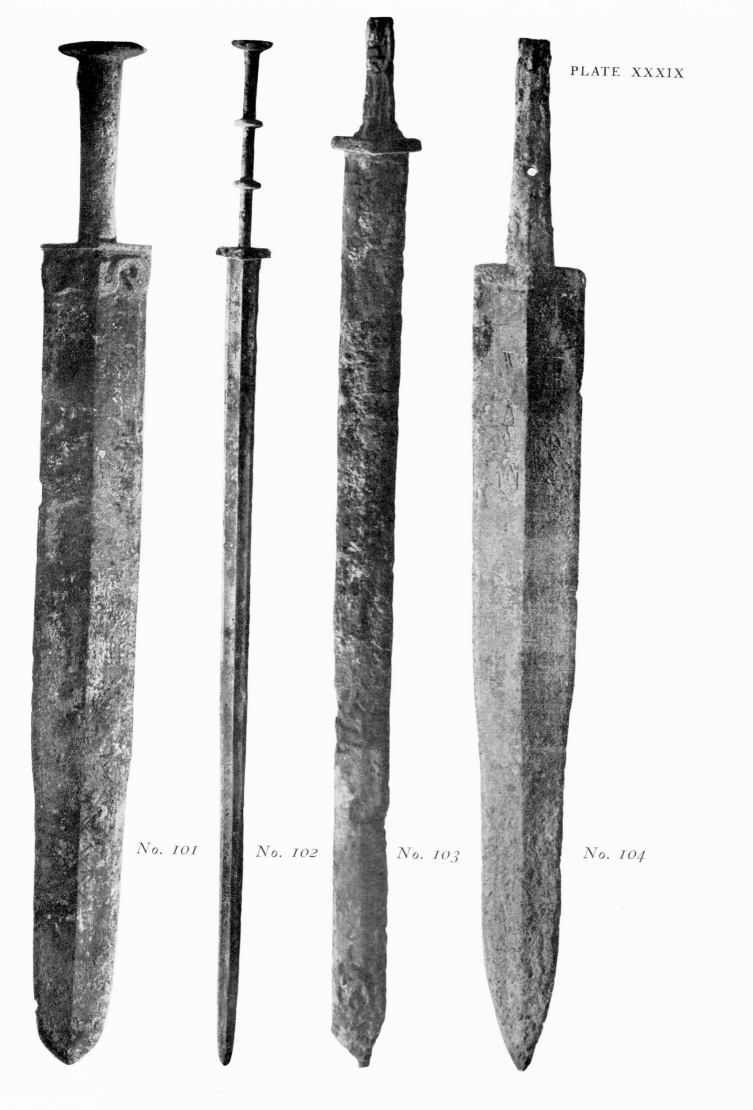

PLATE XXXIX

No. 101          No. 102          No. 103          No. 104

PLATE XL

No. 102 (Knob)

No. 98 (Detail)

No. 99 (Detail)

No. 97 (Detail)

No. 102 (Detail)

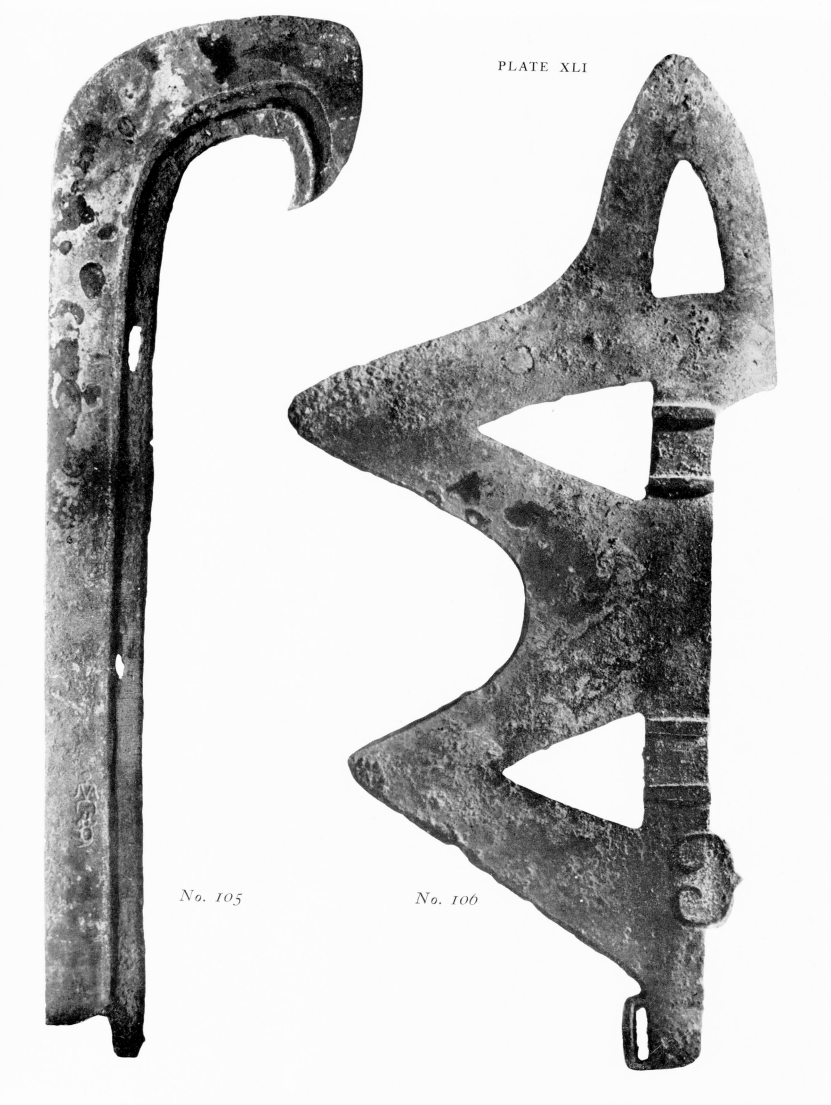

PLATE XLI

No. 105                    No. 106

PLATE XLII

No. 107

No. 108

*No. 109*

PLATE XLIV

*No. 83*

*No. III*

PLATE XLV

*No. 112*

PLATE XLVI

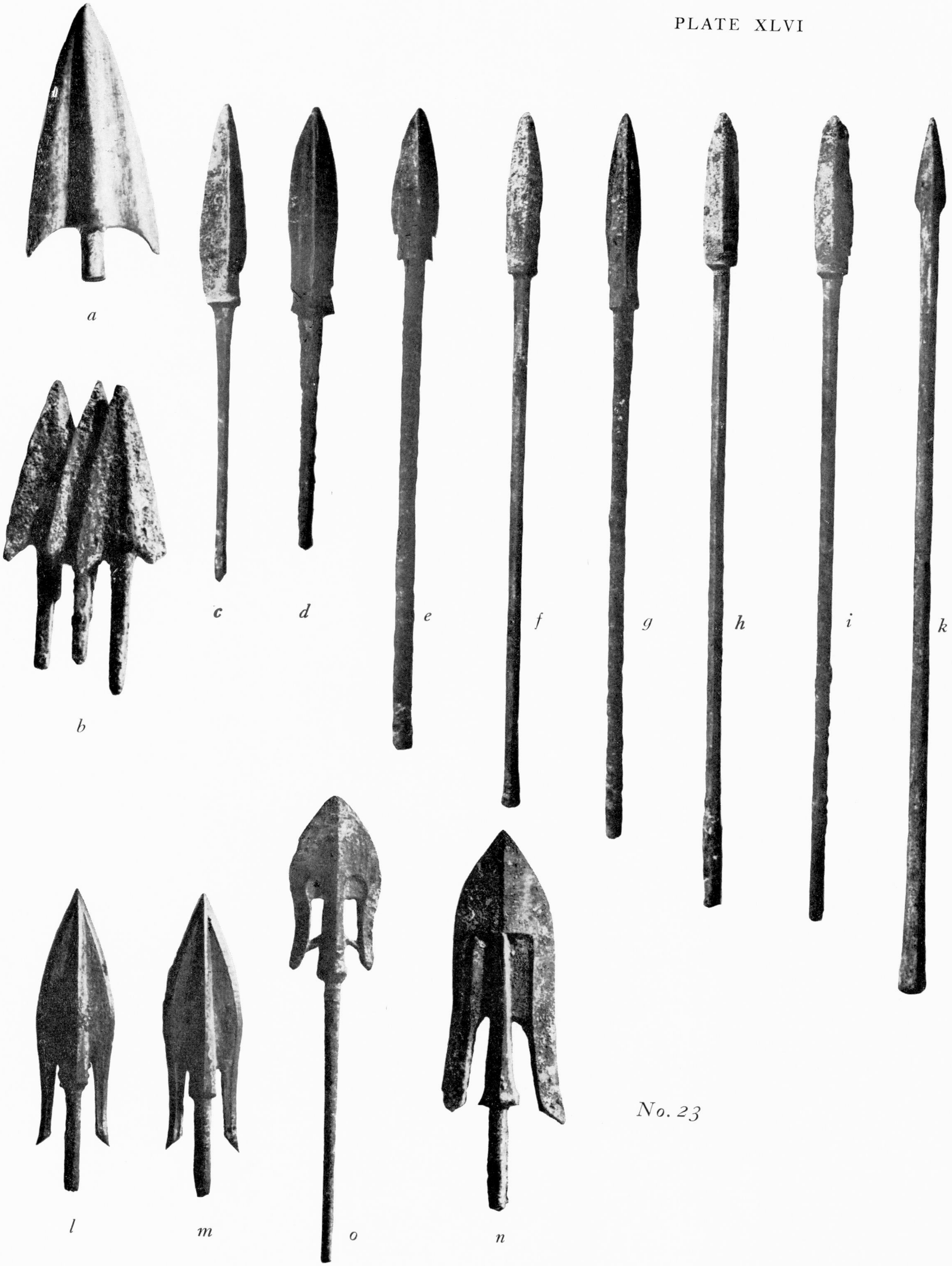

a

b

c

d

e

f

g

h

i

k

l

m

o

n

No. 23

The text of this book is Linotype Caslon, a refinement
of the original typeface developed about 1725 by
William Caslon from late seventeenth-century Dutch
types. The book was composed and printed by The Lord
Baltimore Press, Inc., and bound by The Albrecht
Company in Holliston's Library Buckram and Zanders'
Elephant Hide Cover. The paper is Strathmore Text
and Miamitint Gloss Enamel. The drawings in the
text and the archaic calligraphy of the Chinese title
are by the author; the subtitle in contemporary form is
by Elsie Lee. The book was designed by George Lenox.

M